Beyond the Q Impasse —
LUKE'S USE OF MATTHEW

Beyond the Q Impasse —
LUKE'S USE OF MATTHEW

A Demonstration by the Research Team of the International Institute for Gospel Studies

PREFACE BY
WILLIAM R. FARMER

ALLAN J. MCNICOL, EDITOR, WITH
DAVID L. DUNGAN AND DAVID B. PEABODY

Trinity Press International
Valley Forge, Pennsylvania

Trinity Press International, P.O. Box 851, Valley Forge, PA 19482-0851

Trinity Press International is a division of the Morehouse Publishing Group

Library of Congress Cataloging-in-Publication Data

Beyond the Q impasse : Luke's use of Matthew : a demonstration by the research team of the International Institute for the Renewal of Gospel Studies / preface by William R. Farmer ; Allan J. McNicol, editor ; with David L. Dungan, and David B. Peabody.

p. cm.

Includes bibliographical references and index.

ISBN 1-56338-184-2 (pbk. : alk. paper)

1. Bible. N.T. Luke—Relation to Matthew. 2. Two source hypothesis (Synoptics criticism)—Controversial literature. 3. Q hypothesis (Synoptics criticism)—Controversial literature. 4. Griesbach hypothesis (Synoptics criticism) 5. Bible. N.T. Matthew—Relation to Luke. I. McNicol, Allan J. (Allan James), 1939- . II. Dungan, David L. III. Peabody, David Barrett. IV. International Institute for the Renewal of Gospel Studies.

BS2555.2.B488 1996
226.4'066—dc21 96-36858

Printed in the United States of America

96 97 98 99 00 01 02 10 9 8 7 6 5 4 3 2 1

We dedicate this book
to our friend and colleague
†J. G. FRANKLYN COLLISON
2 April 1937 — 2 January 1986

ABOUT THE AUTHORS

The research represented in this volume was carried out with the assistance of grants from the International Institute for the Renewal of Gospel Studies. The Institute is an international, ecumenical, research institute focused on all aspects of Gospel studies. It holds conferences, sponsors research, funds publications, and provides seed money to scholars preparing major grant applications. The research team of the Institute has been working together since the late 1970s doing research and publishing books and articles in support of the Two Gospel Hypothesis (see Select Bibliography in the Appendix for a list of Institute Fellows' publications).

This is a work of collaborative research. It was composed and repeatedly reviewed by all members of the research team. Allan McNicol, along with the special assistance of David Dungan and David Peabody, assumed the main editorial responsibilities. The members of the research team in alphabetical order are:

Lamar Cope — Th.D. Union Seminary '71, is professor of Religious Studies and chair of the Department of Religious Studies, Carroll College, Waukesha.

David Dungan — Th.D. Harvard Divinity School '67, is professor of early Christian history in the Religious Studies Department, University of Tennessee, Knoxville.

William Farmer — Th.D. Union Seminary '52, is professor of New Testament *emeritus*, Perkins School of Theology, Southern Methodist University, Dallas, and currently research scholar at the University of Dallas.

Allan McNicol — Ph.D. Vanderbilt University '74, is professor of New Testament, Institute for Christian Studies, Austin.

David Peabody — Ph.D. Southern Methodist University '83, is professor of Religious Studies and chair of the Department of Religion and Philosophy at Nebraska Wesleyan University, Lincoln.

Philip Shuler — Ph.D. McMaster University '75, is professor of religion at McMurry University, Abilene.

CONTENTS

LIST OF SYNOPSES

List of Synopses (continued)

PREFACE

It is a privilege to be asked to write this Preface. Although I had suspected for years that there were many different kinds of evidence that a close literary connection existed between Luke and Matthew, even I had no idea just how strikingly systematic it would finally turn out to be. I might add that my friend and colleague Dom Bernard Orchard identified and explained the evidence that he saw in his pioneering attempt, *Matthew, Luke and Mark* (Koinonia 1976).

Most Gospel research projects presuppose that the Gospels of Matthew and Luke were composed quite independently of one another. This idea, combined with a belief that both evangelists used Mark, leads scholars to assume that Matthew and Luke made use of a second source called "Q." In this way it is possible, so it is claimed, to explain passages common to the Gospels of Matthew and Luke, but not found in the Gospel of Mark. But this approach also makes it impossible to see the full contours of Luke's systematic use of Matthew.

How did the idea arise that Matthew and Luke were composed independently of one another? The Introduction to this Demonstration begins by answering this question. Step-by-step we trace the development of this German idea. After it became a fixed assumption, not only in German but also in English research, Canon B. H. Streeter of Oxford University could, in 1924, dogmatically reject the important work of the German scholar Eduard Simons. Simons' book, the title of which was, *Did the Third Evangelist Use Canonical Matthew?* (1880), presented compelling evidence that he did. He succeeded in convincing the influential German expert in Gospel research, Heinrich Julius Holtzmann, that, contrary to what Holtzmann had published earlier, Luke indeed knew and used Matthew. When confronted on this matter, Canon Streeter responded that the acceptance of this conclusion would destroy the need for "Q". If Luke knew Matthew, his use of Matthew would offer the simplest explanation for the "Q" material in his Gospel. By brushing aside this important contribution of German scholarship, Streeter and the English-speaking scholarship dependent on him are at least partly responsible for the dogmatic defense of the Two Source Hypothesis that has resulted in the present impasse in Gospel research.

For example, Robert Funk, in his recently published *Five Gospels* (Harper Collins 1994), stated that the priority of Mark and the existence of "Q" (the Two Source Hypothesis) were pillars on which the research of the Jesus Seminar rested. In support of this position, Funk cited the same arguments Streeter published in 1924. But every one of these arguments has been discredited in the course of subsequent discussion of the synoptic problem and are no longer used by knowledgeable proponents of the Two Source Hypothesis, e.g., Frans Neirynck and Christopher Tuckett. Such is the deplorable condition of some of the so-called scientific study of the Gospels in the United States today.

As far as Germany is concerned, the Two Source Hypothesis belongs to a tradition of critical biblical research that has functioned for over a century as a stabilizing point of contact with the outside world for German scholars. Indeed, it has been a source of some pride, since this Hypothesis was the collaborative result of the best of nineteenth century German biblical scholarship. But this is now changing. Some German scholars are distancing themselves from the problematic results of the Two Source Hypothesis, especially the direction that "Q" studies are taking in prominent circles in North America. There is increasing openness to other ways of looking at the whole matter.

I hope that there will be a judicious openness to the lines of investigation my colleagues and I have taken in this book. We have become convinced that it is time to abandon the Two Source Hypothesis. It has led generations of biblical scholars into a whole series of disastrous errors regarding the Gospels, historical Jesus research, the history of early Christianity, and the very tools we use in our study of the Gospels. We urge our readers to be open to a more promising route of enlightenment scholarship, one that was initially pointed out by the late eighteenth century English scholar Henry Owen and his younger contemporary, the German text-critic, J. J. Griesbach.

When Owen published his *Observations on the Four Gospels* in 1764, he explained how Mark had combined Matthew and Luke, and then added a few suggestions as to ways in which Luke might have revised Matthew when composing his Gospel. A few years later, J. J. Griesbach of Jena published his famous *Demonstration that Mark Was Written After Matthew and Luke* (Jena 1790). However, Griesbach never published a demonstration that Luke had used Matthew. Nor did Griesbach's students do so. To remedy this lacuna in the Owen-Griesbach approach we present this second Demonstration.

In a day when "Q" research is engaged in producing ever more dubious reconstructions of early Christianity, a demonstration that there never was a "Q" in the first place is long overdue. The reasons why it has taken until now to match and complete what Griesbach began over two centuries ago, for this "second shoe" to drop, as it were, are carefully laid out in the Introduction to this book. It is a fascinating story, well worth knowing. The reasons for being confident that "Q" never existed, except in the minds of its scholarly adherents, are painstakingly documented in a careful but lively manner in the analysis of the texts of Matthew and Luke in the main body of this book.

In 1984, thirty experts in Gospel research gathered in Jerusalem for an unprecedented, two-week symposium on the source question in Synoptic studies. One of the few conclusions unanimously approved by all of the participants at the conclusion of the conference was the principle that the single most compelling argument to support any source hypothesis would be a complete redaction-critical analysis of the texts of all three Gospels in terms of that hypothesis. This book is just such a pericope-by-pericope, redaction-critical analysis of the text of Luke on the Two Gospel Hypothesis.

It is an earnest of work yet to come. Within the not-too-distant future, the Research Team of the International Institute for Gospel Studies will publish a companion volume containing a pericope-by-pericope redactional analysis of the Gospel of Mark on the basis of the same Two Gospel Hypothesis. This study will go far beyond the pioneering work of

Henry Owen and J. J. Griesbach on Mark, primarily because we have tools, techniques, and resources not available to them. Ultimately there must be a similar compositional analysis of the Gospel of Matthew that does not assume any dependence upon Mark or "Q." It will be accompanied by a full-fledged synopsis, comprehensively facilitating an understanding of our theory.

We offer these studies for examination and critique. As far as *Luke's Use of Matthew* is concerned, we are aware that there are other ways to interpret the evidence we have discovered. We have no doubt missed important clues and foreclosed options beckoning for further investigation. But should it turn out that the main outlines of our proposals do stand up, then a sweeping reevaluation of basic assumptions undergirding contemporary Gospel research will have to take place, not excluding the critical instruments so many take for granted: the gospel synopsis and the critical text. It is hoped that there will also be the possibility for a more reliable reconstruction of the historical Jesus and a more credible account of Christian origins.

William R. Farmer

ACKNOWLEDGEMENTS

Early Period

The research contained in this volume has been in preparation since the early 1970's if not before. In many ways, the Griesbach Colloquium at Münster University (1976) was the catalyzing event bringing together a small group of scholars interested in exploring the Griesbach Hypothesis more fully. This group was led by W. R. Farmer and Dom Bernard Orchard. Over the next ten years, they organized a number of conferences and seminars that resulted in several ground-breaking publications. None of these would have been possible were it not for the annual funding raised by Dom Bernard, whose sources wish to remain anonymous. Frank Collison, to whom this volume is dedicated, was an active member of that group until his untimely death in 1986.

The process of exploration at that time was greatly assisted by the friendly support and critique of a number of our European colleagues: Karl Rengstorf, Peter Stuhlmacher, Otto Betz, Martin Hengel, Georg Strecker, Ulrich Luz, Henning Graf Reventlow, Bo Reicke, Birger Gerhardsson, Ulrich Luz, and Henry Wansbrough.

On the American scene, following the Jerusalem Symposium on the Gospels (1984), we undertook a series of "consultations" and "groups" under the aegis of the Society of Biblical Literature. Especially pertinent was a series of sessions held on Luke's use of Matthew at the national SBL meetings (1992–1995). Of the more than 150 scholars who attended these sessions, we would like to acknowledge the following for their helpful comments and criticisms in response to our reports: Darrell L. Bock, J. Bradley Chance, Paul T. Coke, Thomas Couric, H. Edward Everding, Charles W. Hedrick, John S. Kloppenborg, Adrian Leske, Edward J. McMahon II, Daryl D. Schmidt, Marion L. Soards, Dennis Tevis, Joseph B. Tyson, William O. Walker Jr., and Frank E. Wheeler. A special word of thanks is due to Gene Lovering for his skill and patience in preparing our reports for the *SBL Seminar Papers.*

Institutions

Over the many years that the Research Group has met and worked on various aspects of the Gospels, we have benefited from funding for research leave, clerical assistance, and grants toward new equipment and/or travel, from the following institutions: Carroll College (Waukesha, Wisconsin), the Institute for Christian Studies (Austin, Texas), McMurry University (Abilene, Texas), Nebraska Wesleyan University (Lincoln, Nebraska), Perkins School of Theology (Dallas, Texas), and the University of Tennessee, Knoxville. As part of our regular thrice-yearly schedule of meetings of the Research Team, we received the kind hospitality of Pepperdine University (Malibu, California), the Church Divinity School of the Pacific (Berkeley, California), Holy Trinity Seminary (Irving, Texas), Nashotah House (Nashotah, Wisconsin), and the Episcopal Theological Seminary of the Southwest (Austin, Texas).

Libraries

A number of libraries have provided members of the Research Team with generous assistance and library privileges. We wish to acknowledge in particular Page A. Thomas, librarian at the Bridwell Library, Perkins School of Theology, Southern Methodist University, and Maria Grossmann, former Director of the Andover Harvard Library, Harvard Divinity School.

Financial support

None of our work would have been possible based solely upon the budgets of our home institutions. We have been fortunate in receiving the encouragement and generous financial support of a number of private foundations and individuals. Among these, particularly to be mentioned on the American side are: the Redman Foundation (Dallas, Texas), the Presbytery of East Tennessee, and the Independent Presbyterian Church (Birmingham, Alabama). In addition, the International Institute for Renewal of Gospel Studies has from its inception had a faithful group of interested lay persons with whom we have discussed our aspirations, shared our problems, and celebrated our accomplishments. We have always treasured their warm support, anchoring our work in the living community of faith. These friends and governors of the Institute are (in Dallas, Texas): Jean Henry DeBusk, Marjory and Paul Vickery, Carrie Jane Loftus, Jean and Parker Wilson, Elizabeth and Franklin Peabody, Gayla and Charles Blanton; (in Abilene): Gerald and Maxine Cockrell; (and in Knoxville): Rev. W. Edmund Carver, Betsey and Condon S. Bush, and W. Baxter Lee, Harold Stone, and John Minchey.

Publishers

As our reports took on definite shape, we were fortunate to have Watson Mills, the former director, and his production manager, the indefatigable Edd Rowell, of the Mercer University Press (Macon, Georgia), bring them out in the series: New Gospel Studies. For this volume, we wish to extend our deep gratitude to Harold Rast, director of Trinity Press International, and his superb production manager, Laura Barrett, for all they have done to make this volume a reality.

Our wives and families

Finally, we express appreciation to our wives and families. Sandy Cope, Anne Dungan, Nell Farmer, Patricia McNicol, Martha Peabody, and Anita Shuler have all made more accommodations for the demands of our scholarship than we can mention. Their support and encouragement has been the mainstay of our lives and we are deeply grateful.

ABBREVIATIONS

Secondary literature will be cited in footnotes at the bottom of each page. A few authors whom we cite frequently, as well as the standard reference works, have been referred to in the text of the Compositional Analysis using the abbreviations listed down the left side of this page.

ABD = *The Anchor Bible Dictionary,* ed. David Noel Freedman *et al.*, 6 vols. New York: Doubleday 1992.

Bauer *Lexicon* = Walter Bauer, *A Greek-English Lexicon of the New Testament and Other Early Christian Literature*, transl. W. F. Arndt & F. W. Gingrich. 4th ed. Cambridge: University Press 1952.

Collison = Franklyn J. G. Collison, "Linguistic Usages in the Gospel of Luke." Unpublished dissertation, Southern Methodist University 1977. Available from University Microfilms International, Ann Arbor, Michigan.

Fitzmyer = Joseph Fitzmyer, *The Gospel According to Luke*. 2 vols. Anchor Bible Commentary #28. Garden City: Doubleday & Co. 1981, 1985.

Goulder = Michael Goulder, *Luke: A New Paradigm*. 2 vols. Sheffield: JSOT Press, 1989.

Liddell-Scott *Lexicon* = Henry George Liddell and Robert Scott, *A Greek-English Lexicon*. 9th edition by Henry Stuart Jones and R. McKenzie. Oxford: Clarendon Press 1940.

Marshall *Luke* = I. Howard Marshall, *The Gospel of Luke*. New International Greek Testament Commentary. Grand Rapids: Wm. B. Eerdmans 1978.

Metzger 1994 = Bruce M. Metzger, *A Textual Commentary on the Greek New Testament. A Companion Volume to the United Bible Societies' Greek New Testament (4th ed.).* 2nd ed. United Bible Societies 1994.

Tevis = Dennis Gordon Tevis, "An Analysis of Words and Phrases Characteristic of the Gospel of Matthew." Unpublished dissertation, Southern Methodist University 1983. Available from University Microfilms International, Ann Arbor, Michigan.

UBS = *The Greek New Testament*, 4th ed., prepared by the United Bible Societies editorial committee, 1993. The committee members for this edition were: Barbara Aland, Kurt Aland, Johannes Karavidopoulos, Carlo M. Martini, and Bruce Metzger.

INTRODUCTION

Our Historical Context

In recent years, advocates of the Two Gospel Hypothesis have been challenged by colleagues to take up a matter which had received only passing attention, namely, the origin of the Gospel according to Luke. For many years partisans of this hypothesis have deemed it to be more important methodologically to tackle the question of the relation of the Gospel of Mark to the other two Synoptic Gospels. To this end, considerable time has been spent amassing evidence to show that all of the arguments used to support Mark's priority are false, circular, or inconclusive.[1] There were also a few compositional analyses of Mark published to show that the Two Gospel Hypothesis can give a plausible account of Mark's composition.[2] A logical outcome of our efforts has been the conclusion that neither Matthew nor Luke was composed on the basis of Mark or Q.

Our results have aroused considerable interest.[3] But as our publications against the priority of Mark and the existence of Q have increased and multiplied, scholars began to ask, "Well, if Mark and Q were not the sources of the Gospel of Luke, how *was* Luke composed?" Occasionally, we would hear the words added, "And do not think for a moment that we will believe you if you state that Luke used Matthew! It is *inconceivable* that Luke was composed with the Gospel of Matthew as his main source!"[4]

The present Demonstration is a response to those challenges. We took as our task the limited goal of giving a plausible account of the composition of the Gospel of Luke on the assumption that his major source was Matthew. Why are we able to accomplish

---

[1] The two main publications to be mentioned here which summarize our basic critique are "The Two Gospel Hypothesis Position Paper" prepared by the Research Team responsible for this volume; see *The Interrelations of the Gospels; A Symposium Led by M.-E. Boismard, W. R. Farmer, F. Neirynck* BETL 45 (Leuven: Peeters, 1990) 125-159, ed. D. Dungan. See also the consensus statement of the Neo-Griesbachian School with all major bibliographical references in D. Dungan, "The Two Gospel Hypothesis," in *Anchor Bible Dictionary* (New York: Doubleday, 1992) 6:671-679.

[2] The two main publications in this respect are the recent publication by A. J. McNicol, *The Synoptic Eschatological Discourse* New Synoptic Studies #9 (Macon: Mercer University Press, 1996); and our brief overview of the whole Gospel of Mark; see W. R. Farmer, D. L. Dungan, A. J. McNicol, D. B. Peabody, and P. L. Shuler, "Narrative Outline of the Markan Composition according to the Two Gospel Hypothesis," *Seminar Papers; Society of Biblical Literature Annual Meeting 1990* (Scholars Press, 1990) 212-239.

[3] See most recently, Christopher M. Tuckett, *The Revival of the Griesbach Hypothesis; An Appraisal.* SNTSMS 44 (Cambridge: University Press, 1983).

[4] The word is W. G. Kümmel's; we will discuss this statement further below.

what is widely believed to be impossible? The answer will become evident from the examination of the historical context which explains why this is the *chairos* for a work of this scope.

Origins of the belief that the author of Luke had no knowledge of the Gospel of Matthew

The widely held view that the author of the Gospel of Luke made no direct use of the canonical Gospel of Matthew is the result of two historical trends that arose in the late eighteenth century and came to a climax toward the end of the nineteenth century. The first of these trends was the rise and then decline of the idea that the author of Luke had used canonical Matthew, as adherents of this view did not provide convincing answers to objections raised against it.

The second trend was less straightforward. In the course of the nineteenth century, a firm consensus emerged which thought that the authors of Matthew and Luke had made use of a writing very similar to canonical Mark when they compiled their Gospels. Within the scholarship based upon this consensus, the question whether the compiler of Luke made use of Matthew always came up secondarily, i.e., only concerning the shared matter in Matthew and Luke not already accounted for as having come into each from Mark. These passages of Luke—displaced from their living contexts and treated as if they all somehow came from a single source—were laid out on the table next to similar passages from Matthew and examined for clues as to the origins of this "lost source." Synopses created to illustrate the priority of Mark exacerbated this trend. In the lines that follow, we will document each of these trends, but to tell the story, we must go back to the beginnings of modern Gospel source criticism.

During the eighteenth century in Europe, one of the earliest theories to explain how the Gospels were "humanly written," as they put it at the time, was the notion that Mark had been composed by someone who combined material taken from Matthew and Luke.[5] As part of this theory, the same scholars said that Luke was a revision of Matthew intended for use in the Gentile mission.[6]

Originally offered as an aid toward a more historical interpretation of the Gospels,[7] the theory was used by the early nineteenth century German church historian Ferdinand Christian Baur to buttress his thesis on the dialectical stages of early

5 The most important names are, in England: Henry Owen, *Observations on the Four Gospels Tending Chiefly to Ascertain the Times of the Publication, and to Illustrate the Form and Manner of Their Composition.* (London: T. Payne, 1764); in Germany: J. J. Griesbach, *Commentatio qua Marci Evangelium totum e Mathaei et Lucae commentariis decerptum esse monstratur* (Jena: Goepferdt, 1789-1790) ET: "A Demonstration that Mark Was Written after Matthew and Luke," in *J. J. Griesbach, Synoptic and Text-Critical Studies 1776-1976,* ed. Bernard Orchard and Thomas R. W. Longstaff (Cambridge: University Press, 1978) 68-102.

6 See for example Owen, op. cit., 23-25.

7 See Owen, iii.

church history. Baur pointed to the Gospel of Matthew as evidence for the original stage of Jewish Christianity, which was opposed by the second stage, Pauline Gentile Christianity. These two conflicting tendencies were then reconciled, in his view, by harmonizing tendencies, typified by Luke-Acts. The Gospel of Mark appeared later, he believed, as parts of Christianity consolidated into ritual and dogma-oriented "early [Roman] Catholicism" (*Frühkatholicismus*).[8]

Other hypotheses of how the Gospels were "humanly written" were also proposed. One of the more popular was the idea that the canonical Gospels were not directly related to each other at all, but were dependent upon a semi-oral, semi-written collection of stories and sayings of Jesus, a kind of "Ur-Gospel." This conception, first proposed by Lessing in 1784,[9] was picked up by J. G. Eichhorn of Göttingen University in 1794 and turned into a complex hypothesis consisting of numerous sources that were then incorporated into the canonical Gospels.[10]

Later, Eichhorn's student Heinrich Ewald, who also taught at Göttingen, produced an even more complicated hypothesis that combined elements from a number of scholars' theories. Like Eichhorn, Ewald began with Lessing's hypothetical Ur-Gospel. He then added Schleiermacher's suggestion that there may have been one source that consisted solely of Jesus' teachings (Papias' *Logia*), Lachmann's idea that canonical Mark was the closest representative of the "Ur-Gospel," and Weisse's conjecture that Matthew was created by combining Mark plus the Logia source. Ewald's hypothesis, which also included the positing of even other sources, was dismissed as hopelessly complicated, but it is possible to perceive, already at this early stage, the embryonic outlines of the later Two-Source Hypothesis. Important for our discussion is the fact that, when Ewald got around to a discussion of the canonical Gospel of Luke, he said the author of this gospel made use of every one of the earlier hypothetical sources, including canonical Mark, *but not Matthew.*[11] Ewald's consensus hypothesis is clear evidence of the wall beginning to rise in scholars' minds between the Gospels of Luke and Matthew.

---

[8] Ferdinand Christian Baur, *Das Christenthum und die christliche Kirche der drei ersten Jahrhunderte* (Tübingen: Fues, 1853). For a similar view fifty years later, cf. Rudolf Sohm, *Wesen und Ursprung des Katholicismus* (Leipzig: Teubner, 1912). On the use of this hypothesis by the "Tübingen School," see B. Reicke, "Griesbach's Answer to the Synoptic Question," in Orchard and Longstaff, eds., *J. J. Griesbach,* 65f.

[9] "Neue Hypothese über die Evangelisten als bloss menschliche Geschichtsschreiber betrachtet," in *Theologischer Nachlass* (1784) 45-72. ET: *Lessing's Theological Writings.* Selections in translation with an introductory essay by Henry Chadwick (London: A. & C. Black, 1956) 45-72.

[10] "Über die drei ersten Evangelien," in his *Allgemeine Bibliothek der biblischen Literatur* (Leipzig: Weidmann, 1794) 5:759-996.

[11] "Ursprung und Wesen der Evangelien," in *Jahrbücher der biblischen Wissenschaft* (Göttingen) 1 (1848) 113-154; 2 (1849) 180-224; 3 (1854) 140-177.

By the middle of the nineteenth century, there were numerous solutions to the synoptic problem vying for acceptance in France, Germany, and England. However, the dominant Griesbach solution that Mark was written third, based upon Matthew and Luke, was rapidly losing ground. Partly this was because it was used by theological radicals like F. C. Baur and his notorious disciple David Friedrich Strauss. Equally important was the fact that scholars just could not believe the claim that the author of the Gospel of Mark, confronted, for example, by such treasures in Matthew as the Beatitudes and the Lord's Prayer, would leave them out of his Gospel. Nothing in their idea of the early church helped them understand why a writer would create a later Gospel that left out so much rich tradition as the birth stories in Matthew and Luke, or the Temptation accounts, and many other stories contained in both of Mark's alleged sources.

These objections were never satisfactorily answered by nineteenth century advocates of the Griesbach Hypothesis. Instead, the opposite idea gained favor, namely, that the shortest Gospel (Mark) had been written first. Its comparatively poor Greek, its lack of major dogmatic elements found in the other Gospels (such as an account of the virgin birth and possibly the resurrection), and its seeming eye-witness vivid descriptions of historical detail also helped convince many scholars during the heyday of Romanticism that it was indeed the earliest.

The idea that Luke was created by someone who had access to canonical Matthew faced even tougher opposition. Scholars wondered why there are so many stories and sayings of Jesus located in different places in the order of Luke's narrative as compared to Matthew's. (This is particularly noticeable with respect to Jesus' teachings.) Whereas Matthew presents Jesus' teachings by means of a series of lengthy speeches, e.g., the Sermon on the Mount (Mt 5–7), the Mission Discourse (Mt 10–11), the Parables Collection (Mt 13), etc., Luke's Gospel has what appears to be much smaller versions of these lengthy speeches, with the rest of the sayings located all over his narrative, mostly in the Central Section (Lk 10–19). If Luke indeed followed Matthew's lead, why did he dismember Matthew's stately and powerful structure just to relocate a considerable amount of Jesus' teachings and omit the rest? Finally, why are Luke's infancy stories and his accounts of the Last Supper, the Trial, Death, and the Resurrection so different from Matthew's accounts? If he *did* make use of Matthew as a source, he must have *abandoned* it when he came to key points in his own narrative—a strange way to act.

Proponents of Matthean priority did not provide convincing answers to these questions either. Instead, some of them publicly abandoned the claim that the author of Luke had relied primarily on canonical Matthew in creating his Gospel. Notably, the

University of Berlin New Testament scholars W. M. L. DeWette[12] and Friedrich Bleek[13] adopted the notion that both Luke and Matthew had made independent and differing use of a mass of earlier written and oral sources, a forerunner of the *Grundschrift* concept later put forward by Holtzmann.[14] Neither gave up the claim that Luke had *also* made use of canonical Matthew, but they did add their support to the emerging consensus that Luke was created independently of the Gospel of Matthew. Thus when Eduard Simons published, late in the century, a defense of the idea that Luke had indeed used canonical Matthew, it caused a brief flurry and was soon ignored.[15]

Holtzmann's synthesis

By 1860, German universities were caught up in the tremendous controversy provoked by David Friedrich Strauss's *The Life of Jesus Critically Examined* (1835), which had called into question the entire historical reliability of the Gospels.[16] Heinrich Julius Holtzmann joined the fray while still a junior member of the theological faculty at Heidelberg. In 1863, he published *Die synoptischen Evangelien: Ihr Ursprung und geschichtlichen Character* (Leipzig: Engelmann), a meticulously argued vindication of the historical quality of the Gospels based upon a brilliant synthesis of contemporary Gospel scholarship.

What were the elements of Holtzmann's synthesis? First of all, he kept to Ewald's basic starting point, that the existing Gospels were not directly related to each other but all went back to a primitive *Grundschrift*. But he simplified Ewald's complex nine-

---

12 B. Reicke, "Griesbach's Answer to the Synoptic Question," in Orchard and Longstaff, *J. J. Griesbach,* 62, points out that one can account for DeWette's hybrid position from the influence of the Oral Hypothesis of Herder, DeWette's first teacher, and the direct utilization theory of Griesbach, his second teacher. For DeWette's discussion, see *Lehrbuch der historisch-kritischen Einleitung in die kanonischen Bücher des Neuen Testaments* (Berlin: G. Reimer, 1826); see 6th ed. 1860: "Erklärung des Verhältnisses zwischen Matthäus und Lucas," 168–184. ET: *An Historical-critical Introduction to the Canonical Books of the New Testament.* Trans. from the 5th, improved and enlarged edition by Frederick Frothingham (Boston: Crosby, Nichols, 1858); "Explanation of the Relation Between Matthew and Luke" 148–163.

13 *Einleitung in das Neue Testament* (Berlin: Reimer, 1862). ET: *An Introduction to the New Testament.* (Edinburgh: T. and T. Clark, 1869-70); see the discussion in W. R. Farmer, *The Synoptic Problem* (New York: Macmillan, 1964) 19f.

14 See comments by B. Reicke, "Griesbach's Answer" 62.

15 Eduard Simons, *Hat der dritte Evangelist den kanonischen Matthäus benützt?* (Bonn: Georgi, 1880). See Farmer, ibid., 40, 47n11; for the reaction in England, see Farmer 81.

16 See Henning Graf Reventlow, "Conditions and Presuppositions of Biblical Criticism in Germany in the Period of the Second Empire and Before: The Case of Heinrich Julius Holtzmann," in *Biblical Studies and the Shifting of Paradigms 1850-1914,* ed. Henning Graf Reventlow and William Farmer (Sheffield: Sheffield Academic Press, 1995) 274–276; further H.-H. Stoldt, *History and Criticism of the Marcan Hypothesis*, trans. Donald Niewyk (Macon: Mercer University Press, and Edinburgh: T & T Clark, 1980) 227f.

source hypothesis, dividing his *Grundschrift* into two primitive sources, a narrative source he called "Alpha" (which resembled Mark most closely and which later came to be known as *UrMarkus*), and a sayings source he labeled "Lambda" (which later became "Q"). Holtzmann agreed with the consensus that Matthew and Luke were not dependent on canonical Mark but on the lost original narrative source "Alpha." He also agreed with the growing opinion that Luke was not directly related to Matthew. Instead, he said that Matthew and Luke independently drew their sayings material from the hypothetical source "Lambda." At the conclusion was a brief chapter called "The Synoptic Gospels as Sources of History," with a paragraph on the "Picture of the Life of Jesus according to Source A," i.e., essentially the Gospel of Mark.[17]

Holtzmann's book was greeted as a masterpiece, not only because it seemed to proceed with such caution and deft mastery of the best of liberal Protestant Gospel scholarship, but also because it gave a solid answer to the doubts raised by Strauss about the historical Jesus.[18] However, there is more to this picture than meets the eye. The final chapter, giving a historical reconstruction of Jesus' life and character, harmonized perfectly with the economic and political aspirations of the new German *bourgeoisie,* and this part of the book received immediate acclaim.[19]

---

[17] Reventlow, "Conditions," 275f. For a helpful collection in English of some of the most important passages in Holtzmann's book, see Werner Georg Kümmel, *The New Testament; The History of the Investigation of Its Problems*, trans. S. Gilmour and H.C. Kee (Nashville: Abingdon Press, 1970) 152-155.

[18] It was not without critics, however. His senior contemporary Adolf Hilgenfeld wrote a scathing review; see David Peabody, "H. J. Holtzmann and His European Colleagues: Aspects of the Nineteenth Century European Discussion of Gospel Origins," in Reventlow and Farmer, ibid., 50–131, esp. 129. Equally significant, from our point of view, is the unpublished doctoral dissertation written in 1866 by Hajo Uden Meijboom of the University of Groningen, *Geschiedenis en critiek der Marcushypothese*, trans. and ed. John J. Kiwiet, *A History and Critique of the Origin of the Marcan Hypothesis 1835–1866*, New Gospel Studies #8 (Leuven: Peeters; Macon: Mercer University Press, 1992). Meijboom's dissertation contains a surprisingly sophisticated analysis of the key figures in contemporary French and German Gospel scholarship. He found many questionable elements in Holtzmann's work. Peabody concludes, "Meijboom's conclusions about the inadequacy of works by Wilke, Weisse, Ewald, B. Weiss, and Holtzmann in establishing the Markan Hypothesis have been confirmed in modern times by W. R. Farmer, H.-H. Stoldt, and, within a more limited perspective, by me" (Peabody, "Holtzmann," 60f.). As for Meijboom's valuable work, it hardly got beyond the Groningen library. David Peabody has examined Holtzmann's arguments and found evidence that he seriously misrepresented the research of Eduard Zeller on the use of linguistic characteristics to determine direction of dependence between two writings. Zeller had favored Griesbach's hypothesis, and Holtzmann, by misrepresenting Zeller's work, managed to reverse Zeller's conclusions to support Marcan priority, causing academic "slippage" of far-reaching consequences; see David B. Peabody, "Chapters in the History of the Linguistic Argument for Solving the Synoptic Problem," in *Jesus, the Gospels and the Church,* ed. E. P. Sanders (Macon: Mercer University Press, 1987) 61-67. It is not clear why Zeller did not protest (cf. Peabody, "Holtzmann," 126f.).

[19] See the excellent quotations about Jesus' character from Holtzmann's conclusion given in Kümmel, op. cit. above n.17. For a further discussion of Holtzmann's life-long pursuit of the values and aspirations of the new German middle class, see most recently Reventlow, "Conditions," in Reventlow and Farmer,

The consolidation of Holtzmann's synthesis

Holtzmann's scholarly prestige was considerably enhanced by his new position in Strasbourg. Some of the Protestant scholars whose works Holtzmann had chosen to synthesize in his *magnum opus* of 1863 also did well. In 1876, Bernhard Weiss was called from Kiel to be Professor at the University of Berlin. With Carl Heinrich von Weizsäcker replacing F. C. Baur at Tübingen, Holtzmann in Strasbourg and Bernhard Weiss in Berlin, the hypotheses based on the priority of Mark and a Sayings Source became dominant at these leading German universities, borne upon the academic shoulders of the carefully nuanced synthesis of Holtzmann.[20] The political unity of a Protestant dominated Germany was now matched by a corresponding unity of Germany's leading Protestant centers of (state supported) theological scholarship, both occurring under the watchful eyes of Bismarck. This was all the more necessary since Bismarck and the Protestant Churches in Germany were at that moment embroiled in a furious battle with the Vatican and German Roman Catholics (the *Kulturkampf*).[21] This defining moment of scholarly and political unanimity still resonates among liberal German Protestant New Testament scholars over one hundred years later.[22]

Holtzmann's work in particular attracted the attention of leading Protestant scholars in England, notably Cambridge-trained A. E. Abbott, and William Sanday, a don at Oxford. It would be a serious mistake to think that Holtzmann's results were simply taken over intact by these scholars. On the contrary, they became the springboard for extensive comparative study of the Gospels, particularly among the

---

ibid., 275-285. For an appraisal from his most gifted student, see Albert Schweitzer, *Von Reimarus zu Wrede; Eine Geschichte der Leben-Jesu-Forschung* (Tübingen, 1906; ET: *Quest of the Historical Jesus* (New York: Macmillan, 1948) 295: "The ideal life of Jesus at the close of the nineteenth century is the Life which Heinrich Julius Holtzmann did not write but which can be pieced together from his commentary on the Synoptics and his New Testament Theology."

20 For the genius of Holtzmann's solution, see Farmer, *Synoptic Problem* 44f.

21 For the best account of this particular period in German, state-controlled university life, see William R. Farmer, "State *Interesse* and Marcan Primacy: 1870-1914," in the volume edited by Reventlow and Farmer cited above, 15-49. Ironically, the best research on the history of the German universities has been done, not by German, but by English and American scholars; see the Select Bibliography in Farmer in ibid. 43-46.

22 This is W. G. Kümmel's paean to Holtzmann in his *The New Testament; The History of the Investigation of Its Problems,* trans. S. M. Gilmour and H. C. Kee (Nashville: Abingdon Press, 1970) 151: "Heinrich Julius Holtzmann...summed up all previous research [on the Gospels] in magnificent fashion (*in seinem die ganze bisherigen Forschung souverän zusammen-fassenden Werk*). He not only demonstrated most convincingly, by an appeal to the primitive character of its narrative style and diction, that Mark's Gospel was the source of the two other Synoptics, but also showed just as convincingly that we must assume a second source back of Matthew and Luke, one that consisted mainly of discourses... Holtzmann grounded the two source hypothesis so carefully that the study of Jesus henceforth could not again dispense with this firm base (*diesen Boden nicht mehr aufgeben konnte*)."

participants in the sixteen year, ongoing seminar on the synoptic problem at Oxford led by William Sanday (1894–1910). As their eventual publication *Studies in the Synoptic Problem* indicates, many alternative routes were explored.[23]

The main innovation brought about by the English scholars, primarily by Abbott and Burkitt, was to remove the carefully nuanced distinction between Holtzmann's Mark-like "Alpha" and the canonical Gospel of Mark. Instead, English-speaking Gospel source-criticism began to make a hard identification between canonical Mark and the primary gospel source used by Matthew and Luke.[24] Although not evident at the time, this step proved to have disastrous consequences for the hypothesis of Markan priority. Every German critic from Lachmann to Holtzmann, no matter how carefully they described the pre-canonical source in terms *resembling* canonical Mark, knew better than to take this final, fatal step.

When what must be considered as the final judgment of these Oxford and Cambridge scholars was finally published, namely, Canon Burnett Hillman Streeter's *The Four Gospels. A Study of Origins* (1924),[25] it is fair to say that the German Holtzmann had become the British Streeter.[26] Of course, Streeter's monumental work was supported by the extensive explorations published by F. C. Burkitt,[27] Sir John Hawkins,[28] A. E. Abbott,[29] and the impressive colored plates of W. G. Rushbrooke's *Synopticon*.[30] These works, more than any others, have succeeded in convincing generations of English-speaking scholars in Great Britain and North America that they should agree with their German colleagues and accept, as an "assured result of modern biblical science," the priority of Mark and Q.

Breaking free of the circular process

There were always a few scholars who fought against the tide and did not accept Holtzmann's synthesis. Among these could be numbered Adolf Hilgenfeld and Adolf

---

[23] *Studies in the Synoptic Problem By Members of the University of Oxford*, ed. W. Sanday (Oxford: Clarendon Press, 1911).

[24] See the discussion of this process in Farmer, *Synoptic Problem* 70f., 90f.

[25] Burnett Hillman Streeter, *The Four Gospels; A Study of Origins, Treating the Manuscript Tradition, Sources, Authorship, and Dates* (London: Macmillan & Co., 1924).

[26] The English scholars were thoroughly familiar with the whole spectrum of German research., cf. Sanday's comparative chart, published in Smith's *Dictionary of the Bible* (1893), of Holtzmann's hypothetical sources with those of Weizsäcker, Weisse, Wendt, and Beyschlag; cited in Farmer, *Synoptic Problem* 40n5.

[27] See especially F. C. Burkitt, *The Gospel History and Its Transmission* (Edinburgh: T & T Clark,1906).

[28] John Hawkins, *Horae Synopticae* (Oxford: Clarendon Press, 1899).

[29] See especially his influential *Encyclopedia Britannica* article, "Gospels," in *Ency. Brit.* 9th ed.; 10:789-843.

[30] W. G. Rushbrooke, *Synopticon; An Exposition of the Common Matter of the Synoptic Gospels* (London: Macmillan, 1880).

Schlatter. But they were a beleaguered minority and Schlatter's theological conservatism allowed many to dismiss him easily.

When the counterattack finally came, it did not emerge in Germany, but in English universities. It was directed at the weakest link in the chain of logic supporting the Markan Hypothesis in its English form: Streeter's claim that the argument from order of pericopes proved that canonical Mark was the primary narrative source of Matthew and Luke. In 1951, an English scholar, Basil Christopher Butler, published *The Originality of St. Matthew. A Critique of the Two Document Hypothesis* (Cambridge: University Press, 1951). In it he said that Streeter, Abbott, Burkitt, Wellhausen, and probably Hawkins had all fallen victim to "a schoolboyish error of elementary reasoning at the very base of the Two Document Hypothesis."[31] Whereas most Germans from Lachmann on down had been careful not to identify canonical Mark with the narrative source used by Matthew and Luke, these English scholars had done so, while still using Lachmann's arguments, which were valid only for a common lost source.[32]

Having refuted the main argument in Streeter's five arguments for the priority of Mark, Butler went on to demolish all of the rest as well, proving that they were either inconclusive or trapped in circular logic.[33] As for the argument from order of pericopes, Butler said it did no more than prove that Mark was some sort of "connecting-link...but not necessarily the source of more than one of them."[34] On this basis, Butler went on to argue in favor of what he took to be Augustine's view, that Mark was the abbreviator of Matthew, and that Luke was based on Matthew and Mark.

Fifteen years later, an American scholar, William R. Farmer, published *The Synoptic Problem. A Critical Analysis* (New York: Macmillan, 1964). In it Farmer went back to the beginning of the modern discussion of Gospel sources in the late eighteenth century, and documented the rise of one circular process after another, first in Germany and then in England. Along the way, Farmer cited case after case of errors in logic, questionable assumptions for which little or no evidence was given, and—most damning of all—repeated use of "non-scholarly factors" to enforce the scholarly consensus when all else failed. In his conclusion, Farmer broke with Butler's "Augustinian" hypothesis, presenting a schematic demonstration of the Owen-Griesbach theory that Mark had been compiled on the basis of Matthew and Luke. [35]

Apart from a few appreciative responses, the reactions to Farmer's book tended to

---

31 Butler, *Originality* 63.

32 See "the Lachmann Fallacy" in Butler, ibid., 62-71; esp. 65-67.

33 Loc. cit.

34 Ibid. 65.

35 See Farmer, *Synoptic Problem* 199-233.

fall across a narrow spectrum from stunned silence to outrage and even derision. There were widespread feelings of disgust; it was as if someone had "fouled the nest" of Gospel scholarship.

Nevertheless, after the shock subsided, a veritable flood of articles began to appear on every conceivable issue with respect to the Synoptic Problem. A lively, three-sided debate emerged.[36] A small but steady stream of studies began to re-open the question as to whether Luke had used Matthew.[37]

In the pages of the Introduction that remain, the outline of the most important evidence in support of the view that Luke used Matthew without access to Mark will be presented briefly. The full discussion of the texts belongs to the main part of the book, the Compositional Analysis of the Gospel of Luke.

The way out of the Q impasse

By way of conclusion, let us rehearse the usual reasons given by scholars today for assuming that Luke could *not* have used canonical Matthew. It will become immediately obvious how skewed the entire discussion is, as long as the theory of Markan priority is allowed to remain the fixed star guiding the discussion. Let us begin with Canon Streeter's famous statement in 1924 that it would take a "crank" to dismember Matthew and then make sure *not* to locate Jesus' sayings at the same point *in Mark's outline* where Matthew had put them.[38] Similar reasoning based on the same presupposition can be seen in the list proving that Luke did not know Matthew given by Werner Georg Kümmel, an influential historian of modern New Testament research:

1. "What could possibly have motivated Lk...to shatter Mt's sermon on the mount, placing part of it in his sermon on the plain, dividing up other parts among various chapters of his Gospel, and letting the rest drop out of sight?"
2. "How could anyone explain the fact that not once does Lk place material that

[36] A classic debate between advocates of the reigning Two Source Hypothesis, the Two Gospel Hypothesis (neo-Griesbach), and Multi-Stage Hypothesis (representative of considerable French scholarship) took place in Jerusalem in 1984; see *The Interrelations of the Gospels,* ed. D. Dungan. For an even-handed presentation of the key arguments between the Two Source Hypothesis and the Two Gospel Hypothesis, see especially A. J. Bellinzoni, Jr., with Joseph B. Tyson and William O. Walker, *The Two Source Hypothesis. A Critical Appraisal* (Macon: Mercer University Press, 1985).

[37] Besides those works produced by those within the Two Gospel Hypothesis orbit, especially notable are the two volumes of Michael Goulder, *Luke: A New Paradigm* (Sheffield: JSOT Press, 1989). See also Robert Gundry, "Matthean Foreign Bodies in Agreements of Luke with Matthew against Mark: Evidence that Luke used Matthew," in vol. 2 of *The Four Gospels* 1992, eds. F. Van Segbroeck et al., BETL 100 (Leuven: Leuven University Press/Peeters, 1992) 1467-1495. And finally Eric Franklin, *Luke, Interpreter of Paul: Critic of Matthew* JSNTSS 92 (Sheffield: JSOT Press, 1993).

[38] Streeter, ibid. 183.

he has in common with Mt at the same point in the Markan framework [apart from two early passages]?"

3. "Mt and Lk alternate in offering the original form of the material they have in common [i.e., where did Lk get it if he was dependent upon Mt?]."

These arguments were sufficient, declared Kümmel, with typical German understatement, to make the concept of Luke's direct dependence upon Matthew "*completely inconceivable*."[39]

Given this kind of authoritative ultimatum, it is not surprising to see these reasons dutifully repeated in handbooks of New Testament introduction, histories of early Christianity, and Gospel commentaries, elsewhere in the world. A good example is Joseph Fitzmyer's *Anchor Bible Commentary on the Gospel According to Luke I–IX* (Garden City: Doubleday & Co., 1981). In a section entitled "Luke's Supposed Dependence on Matthew," Fitzmyer lists six reasons "why it is unlikely that Luke has depended on Matthew."[40]

1. Luke never reproduces "the typically Matthean additions within the Triple Tradition."
2. Luke occasionally has versions of material similar to Matthew but in a different form.
3. "Why would Luke have wanted to break up Matthew's sermons, especially the Sermon on the Mount, incorporating only part of it into his Sermon on the Plain and scattering the rest of it in an unconnected form in the loose context of the travel account?"
4. "Apart from [the preaching of John the Baptist and the Temptation], Luke never inserted the material [common with Matthew] in the same Marcan context as Matthew."
5. "Analysis of the [material shared with Matthew] reveals that it is sometimes Luke and sometimes Matthew who preserves...the more original setting of a given episode."
6. "If Luke depended on Matthew, why did he constantly omit Matthean material in episodes lacking Marcan parallels?"

Notice how the first reason focuses attention only on the Lukan material shared with Mark and Matthew. Notice how the third and sixth reasons assume the priority of Mark. This is understandable in Fitzmyer's context, because, *as had become*

---

[39] Werner Georg Kümmel, *Introduction to the New Testament*, transl. of the 17th German ed. by Howard Clark Kee (Nashville: Abingdon Press, 1975) 64. Cf. idem, *Einleitung in das Neue Testament*, 14te durchges. Aufl. (Heidelberg: Quelle & Meyer, 1965) 32, "Daß Lk. seine mit Mt. gemeinsamen Stoffe unmittelbar aus Mt. übernommen habe, ...ist völlig undenkbar."

[40] Joseph Fitzmyer, *The Gospel According to Luke I–IX*, Anchor Bible Commentary #28 (Garden City: Doubleday & Co., 1981), 73–75.

customary, he preceded this list with seven pages of carefully reasoned arguments proving that Mark was Luke's main source.[41]

Since we categorically reject this premise, for reasons summarized in our *Anchor Bible Dictionary* article, these three arguments become moot. The remainder of the list are not arguments; they are just requests for information.

#2 Why would Luke give something similar to Matthew 's version but different?

#3 Why would Luke dismember Matthew's great speeches and locate them throughout his narrative?

#5 Why would Luke sometimes preserve an earlier version of a saying also found in Matthew?

The difficulty is, by leading into these questions on the basis of a demonstration of the priority of Mark, the damage has already been done and the requests cannot be answered with a clear and unobstructed field of vision. As we have seen, the popular solution is to posit some sort of lost source back of the non-Markan passages in Matthew and Luke—and thus to open the door to the sea of subjectivity called the Q Hypothesis.

In this work, we intend to set forth a better way. *Working as an interdisciplinary team using impartial instruments, taking Mark completely out of the picture and dispensing with Q*, we will address the questions above, and many others besides. Why did Luke not use Matthew's birth and infancy stories? Why is the order of Luke's Jesus' Galilean ministry so different from Matthew's? Can we explain the "enigma" of the Central Section?[42] Why is Luke's account of the Last Supper so different? These and many similar questions we will do our best to answer. It will remain for others to say how successful we have been.

---

[41] Fitzmyer, ibid. 66-73.

[42] Craig Evans and James Sanders, *Luke and Scripture; The Function of Sacred Tradition in Luke-Acts* (Minneapolis: Fortress Press, 1993) 108f., echo the view of many when they write: "The central section of Luke's Gospel has been an enigma of [New} Testament scholarship. Until Canon Streeter's *Four Gospels* this section was variously called the travel document, the Peraean section, the Samaritan document, and so on. Since Streeter it has almost universally been designated by the term 'central section.' Even so, little headway has been made into probing its significance, the reason that Luke arranged his material in this way, and the ideas he wished to convey in doing so."

Luke's Use of Matthew

As the preceding historical review of the scholarly discussion of the origins of the Gospels has shown, a major stumbling block for the view that the author of the Gospel of Luke used the canonical Gospel of Matthew was that the narrative order of Luke was vastly different from that of Matthew. If Luke used Matthew as a source, would he rearrange Matthew's narrative order in such a radical fashion? Advocates of the Griesbach Hypothesis had great difficulty in giving a convincing answer to this objection. Furthermore, the dominance of the theory of the priority of Mark and the universal acceptance of biased three-column synopses designed to illustrate that theory were additional precipitating factors hindering comprehensive comparisons between Luke and Matthew.

Our first task was to compare the entire text of Luke with the entire text of Matthew, as if Mark did not exist.[1] Without the Markan pericope divisions intruding into our examination of Luke's narrative flow, we immediately felt ourselves freed up to attend to what Luke was doing. We made pericope divisions in Luke's narrative unlike the standard divisions in our critical texts or synopses. These in turn led us to see many other parallels in the text of Matthew, not displayed in existing synopses. Although we normally worked with two-column synopses, sometimes we had to create charts with four, five, even eight columns, to display adequately the parallels we were seeing between Matthew and Luke.[2] This liberation from the blinders of three-column synopses was a critical step in opening our minds to Luke's use of Matthew.[3]

As we worked, we focused on one basic question: how can we account for the order,

---

[1] We quickly realized that the present critical text of Luke was itself a minefield through which we had to pick our way with extreme caution. We found Bruce Metzger's companion volume recording the UBS committee's reasoning very helpful in reaching our own conclusions; see *A Textual Commentary on the Greek New Testament; A Companion Volume to the United Bible Societies' Greek New Testament (3d ed.),* (London & New York: United Bible Societies, 1971); 2d ed. 1994.

[2] Ironically, we found it difficult to use the synopsis by our Institute colleague Dom Bernard Orchard, *A Synopsis of the Four Gospels in a New Translation; Arranged According to the Two-Gospel Hypothesis and edited by John Bernard Orchard* (Macon: Mercer University Press, 1982); cf. the same synopsis using the Greek text published by T&T Clark in 1983. In our view, Orchard's decision to bring Luke's Sermon on the Plain into sequential parallel order with Matthew's Sermon on the Mount was a foundational mistake.

[3] Creating new synoptic charts was easier since we could try out a particular arrangement on our computers, test it for accuracy and completeness, and then incorporate it into our discussions. As we grew in our understanding of the Lukan compositional techniques, we would go back and refine our synopses. At the same time, we could use modern computer-search programs to help us identify important grammatical constructions. All of this took much longer before computers became available for this kind of work.

content, and inter-relationship of the stories in Luke's narrative if canonical Matthew was indeed the main source utilized by the author of Luke? We tried to look at Matthew the way the Hellenistic Greek author of Luke-Acts might have, assuming he had set himself the task of creating a revision of the Gospel of Matthew for use among Christian Churches which gained their original impetus under the Pauline mission.

Overview of Luke's use of Matthew

The following is a general description of the way Luke utilized his major source Matthew. In Lk 1–2, Luke selected some elements of Mt 1–2 and combined them with non-Matthean traditions to create his Birth and Infancy Section. In Lk 3–9, Luke began following closely both the order and the content of Matthew, from Mt 3, the preaching of John the Baptist, down to Mt 18, a speech of Jesus dealing with intra-community discipline. However, Luke did not simplistically adopt the order of Matthew's pericopes from Mt 3 to 18. Rather, he created his narrative by moving forward through Matthew to a certain point and then—still following his own narrative agenda—*went back* to an earlier part of Matthew and proceeded to work his way forward in Matthew again. He repeated this procedure a number of times until he used most of the material in Matthew down to Mt 18 (a speech of Jesus dealing with community discipline). Here Luke stopped his method of successive utilization of Matthew's stories and sayings in order to create a lengthy teaching section loosely set against the backdrop of Jesus traveling toward Jerusalem (Lk 10:1-19:27). Known as the Lukan Travel Narrative, the method Luke followed here was to weave together sayings taken from the major speeches of Jesus in Matthew, mostly in the order in which the sayings occur within each speech in Matthew, around a number of themes appropriate for Christians in the Hellenistic world.

Finally, toward the end of the Travel Narrative at Lk 18:15, Luke returns to the narrative order of Matthew's Gospel. At this point, Luke mostly keeps in step with Matthew's narrative order until just before the end, when he branches off to create a smooth transition into the Acts narrative.

Thus we have described three distinctly different ways in which Luke has largely followed Matthew's order.

If this general description is accurate, it means that the author of the Gospel of Luke was a Hellenistic Christian writer who made systematic, intelligible, and respectful use of his most important source, the Gospel of Matthew, as well as other traditions. In the introductory section on "Luke's Compositional Techniques,"[4] we will elaborate more fully on some of the methods Luke adopted to shape and give excitement and forward momentum to his narrative.

---

[4] See below 29-33.

We are now prepared to give a brief synopsis of Luke's compositional concerns in each part of his narrative so that we can better understand how he used his major source, Matthew. We preface our account with this all-important rule: Luke's revision of Matthew was guided by a number of considerations which we will identify and explain in due course, but the most important of all was his determination to write a narrative that was "accurate," i.e., presented in what he considered to be an appropriate *chronological* order for a literary work.

Luke's use of Matthew in Lk 1–2

Luke prepared the first two chapters to show Jesus Christ's birth occurring among a poor family. It took place within a context of omens, signs, and other related divine activity which indicated that it had universal implications. Luke kept comparable birth and infancy stories that appear in the same order as they do in Matthew (cf. Mt 1:18–24/Lk 1:26–38 and Mt 1:25, 2:1–23/Lk 2:1–40). But it was not appropriate in Hellenistic biographies to begin as Matthew did with a lengthy genealogy and omit the customary preface. Moreover, Luke wished to make far more understandable than Matthew had done what Jesus' relationship was to John the Baptist. Luke picked up the theme of contrast/comparison between John and Jesus which also is implicit in later passages, such as Mt 3:1ff.; 11:2–19; 17:10ff., etc., heightened it, and used it as a dominant Lukan motif in rewriting the birth accounts of John and Jesus in Lk 1–2 and then continued it later on as well. Again, the royal/dynastic themes in Mt 1–2, although utilized by Luke, needed to be supplemented with other themes such as poverty, divine sonship, and universal savior traditions available to him. Finally, he felt it appropriate to provide a glimpse of Jesus' precocious wisdom as a youth. This is the material we have placed in Part 1 (Lk 1:1–2:52).

Luke's use of Matthew in Lk 3–9

At this point, Luke has arrived at Matthew's account of the preaching of John the Baptist (Mt 3:1), and he began following Matthew's order systematically. We have created a chart that shows how Luke used Matthew between Mt 3:1/Lk 3:1 and Mt 18:5/Lk 9:46ff. [see chart on next two pages]. Matthew's pericopes (these are our own divisions and the titles used—in abbreviated form—are also ours) are numbered in the first, left-hand column. The next five columns contain Lukan pericopes (again, these are our pericope divisions and our titles). If one takes a ruler and moves it downward comparing the order of pericopes in each Lukan column, most of them will be found to be in the same order as in Matthew's column. We have numbered the pericopes in Matthew's column to facilitate this comparison with the Lukan columns. It soon becomes apparent that Luke's procedure was to get what material he needed for each

Luke parallels Matthew's order of pericopes

Matthew's Basic Order (Mt 3:1-18:5)	Lk 3:1-4:44 Luke column 1	Lk 5:1-6:19 Luke column 2
1. John the Baptist 3:1-12	1. John the Baptist 3:1-18	
	[31. John Bap. in prison 3:19-20]	
2. Baptism of Jesus 3:13-17	2. Baptism of Jesus 3:21-22	
(Jesus' genealogy Mt 1:1-16)	[*Jesus' genealogy 3:23-38]	
3. Temptation 4:1-11	3. Temptation 4:1-13	
4. Preach in Galilee 4:12-17	4. Fame summary 4:14-16a	4. Fame summary 4:42-44 [sic]
5. Calls 4 disciples 4:18-22		* Calls 3 disciples 5:1-11
6. Begins preaching tour 4:23-25		
7. Sermon on mount 5:1-7:29	* Sermon in Nazareth, goes to Capernaum 4:16b-32	
8. Heals leper 8:1-4		8. Heals leper 5:12-14
		*Fame summary 5:15-16
	*Healing in synagogue 4:33-36	
	* Fame summary 4:37	
9. Heals centurion's son 8:5-13		
10. Peter's mother-in-law and many healed 8:14-17	10. Simon's mother-in-law and many healed 4:38-41	
11. Types of disciples 8:18-22		
12. Stills the storm 8:23-27		
13. Heals demoniac 8:28-34		
14. Heals paralytic 9:1-8		14. Heals paralytic 5:17-26
15. Call of Levi, etc. 9:9-17		15. Call of Levi, etc. 5:27-39
16. Women healed 9:18-26		
17. ~~Heals blind 9:27-31~~		
18. Heals dumb man 9:32-34		
19. Mission of Twelve 9:35-11:1	19. Begins tour 4:42-44	
20. J. B. & Jesus 11:2-19		
21. Woe to cities 11:20-24		
22. Jesus prays 11:25-30		
23. Works on Sabbath 12:1-8		23. Works on Sabbath 6:1-5
24. Heals on Sabbath 12:9-14		24. Heals on Sabbath 6:6-11
		[19. Jesus Calls 12 6:12-16]
25. Heals crowd 12:15-21		25. Heals crowd 6:17-19
26. Beelzebub acc. 12:22-45		
27. True relatives 12:46-50		
28. Parables of Kingdom 13:1-53		
29. Rejected in Naz. 13:54-58		
30. Herod about Jesus 14:1-2		
31. Death of John 14:3-12		
32. Feeds 5000 14:13-21		
33. ~~Walk on water 14:22-23~~		
34. ~~Various 14:24-16:12~~		
35. Peter confesses 16:13-23		
36. True disciples 16:24-28		
37. Transfiguration 17:1-13		
38. Heals boy 17:14-21		
39. Predicts death 17:22-23		
40. ~~Temple tax 17:24-27~~		
41. Who greatest? 18:1-5		

↔ *The beginning of Matthew's Community Regulations Section*

in successive segments of his narrative, Lk 3:1–10:22.

*The numbers in the columns are keyed to Matthew's Basic Order (on left). Each Lukan column contains a series of units parallel to Mt's Basic Order. There are some transpositions of Matthean units, however, indicated by [ ]. * indicates a unit only in Luke. Underlined items = main speeches in Mt. Units crossed out in Mt column = not used by Luke.*

Lk 6:20-8:21
Luke column 3

6. Heals crowd 6:17-19 [sic]
7. Sermon on plain 6:20-7:1a

9. Centurion's servant 7:1-10
 *Jesus heals widow's son 7:11-15

 * Fame summary 7:16-17
20. John the Baptist & Jesus 7:18-35
 *Woman anoints 7:36-50
 *Women disciples 8:1-3

28. Parable of the Sower 8:4-15
 * Example of the lamp 8:16-18
[27. True relatives 8:19-21]

is parallel to the beginning of Luke's ↔ Central Teaching Section

Lk 8:22-9:56
Luke column 4

12. Stills the storm 8:22-25
13. Heals demoniac 8:26-39

16. Women Healed 8:40-56

19. Mission of Twelve 12 9:1-6

30. Herod about Jesus 9:7-9

32. Feeds 5000 9:10-17

35. Peter confesses faith 9:18-22
36. True disciples 9:23-27
37. Transfiguration 9:28-36
38. Heals boy 9:37-43a
39. Predicts death 9:43b-45

41. Who greatest? 9:46-48
 * Faults of Twelve 9:49-56

Lk 9:57ff.
Luke column 5

11. Faults of would-be disc. 9:57-62

19. Mission of 72 10:1-12

21. Woe to cities 10:13-16
 * Return of 72 10:17-20
22. Jesus prays 10:21-22

(From this point down to Lk 19:27, Luke combined materials taken from Mt's speeches and unused narratives with nonMatthean tradition to create a lengthy series of teaching scenes for the guidance and instruction of the Christian churches in the international mission area.

This series of edifying vignettes concludes with Jesus' arrival at Jerusalem, Lk 19:28. At that point, Luke resumes following Matthew's Basic Order.)

part of his narrative, *going back* in Matthew's order when necessary to get something else, but, having gone back, moving forward again from that point in Matthew, selecting other material he wanted to utilize *in Matthew's order*, pulling new stories into his narrative that he had not yet used. By following this process of successive, cyclically progressive, orderly utilizations, guided by his narrative agenda, Luke eventually used most of the material between Mt 3:1 and 18:5.

To repeat: the series of Lukan columns shows that the order of pericopes in the Gospel of Luke 3:1–10:22 parallels the order of pericopes within the Gospel of Matthew (Mt 3:1–18:5) *within* successive divisions of Luke's narrative. This chart provides evidence in support of the hypothesis that Luke methodically created his narrative out of material drawn from Matthew.

What is not self-evident from this chart is *why* Luke selected the Matthean pericopes that he did, *when* he did. Here the task is to identify correctly what were the main narrative concerns that guided Luke as he sifted through the many collections of stories and sayings in Matthew, causing him to choose *this* story, then skip two or three pericopes to *that* story, then go back and pick up *those* sayings, and so on. In other words, why did Luke go down through Matthew to a certain point, then go back and repeat the process again, and then again, and again, each time utilizing stories in Matthew's sequence?

Many different explanations can and will be given for this series of sequential parallels between Matthew's order, chs 3–18, and Luke's order, chs 3–9. We offer the following general explanations only by way of introduction, leaving the reader to verify our claims by examining our detailed compositional analysis in the body of the book.

First of all, in Part Two, Lk 3:1–4:16a of Luke's narrative, beginning with the baptism, Luke wants to emphasize the role of the Holy Spirit in Jesus' baptism, not that of John (whom Luke keeps firmly subordinated to Jesus throughout), so that Jesus' sonship will clearly be affirmed as divine in origin and the Voice from Heaven can fittingly announce it as such. The second part ends with Jesus emerging triumphant from the wilderness after the first testing of his divine sonship.

In Part Three, Lk 4:16b–7:15, in good Hellenistic fashion, Luke depicted Jesus beginning his public activity in his home town. There Jesus gives a *brief* public speech, explaining who he is and what he intends to do, gracefully outlining the main themes of his public ministry. Into this scene Luke introduced material from a later point in Matthew to add the motif of bitter opposition against Jesus by his townspeople. Then Luke portrayed Jesus on his first tour or preaching journey, from Capernaum and back. During this journey, Luke made sure Jesus called all twelve of his disciples, so that his first, definitive speech to those who would be his followers would be given to all of his Apostles, not just three of them (as in Matthew). Moreover, Jesus' "Sermon on the Plain" is briefer, focusing mainly on God's preferential option for the poor and disenfranchised of the world, on non-retaliation as the appropriate response to evil, and on action as the appropriate response to the Word of God. As noted above, this Part concludes with Jesus' return to Capernaum.

In Part Four, Lk 7:16–9:36, Luke built toward the glorious climax of Jesus' Galilean ministry. He began with a transitional pericope describing the results of Jesus' visit to the village of Nain, where, after he healed the deceased son of a widow, the crowd exclaims, "A great prophet has arisen in Israel!" John the Baptist hears of Jesus' fame and sends a deputation with the question, "Are you really he who is to come?" Jesus gives an oblique answer to John, and so in this way the question of Jesus' real identity begins to come up. It is repeated throughout this Part until a definitive answer is given at the end by a Voice from Heaven: "This is My Son!" (Lk 9:35).

Following this glorious scene, clearly intended to be the climax of Luke's account of Jesus' Galilee ministry, Luke created an elaborate transitional unit (Lk 9:37-62) leading into the next major part of his narrative: the Son of God slowly traveling toward Jerusalem and martyrdom. To emphasize its character as a "suture" holding Parts Four and Five together, we have located the first half of this transitional unit in Part Four and the second half in Part Five.

Luke's use of Matthew in Lk 10–19:27

At this point, Luke has finished his re-ordering of the narrative sequence from Mt 3:1 through 17. Mt 18, a speech of Jesus commonly called the Community Regulations, is the point at which Luke stopped following Matthew's narrative order in successive divisions of his narrative and created a large parenetic section of his own, based on materials from all of Jesus' speeches in Matthew—again frequently in Matthew's order—plus some non-Matthean traditions of his own. It begins with a highly symbolic account, the Mission of the 72 Other Disciples (Lk 10:1–16), followed by Jesus' blessings on them when they return. (See Chart C in the Appendix for evidence of Luke's orderly use of Matthew in creating the Travel Narrative.)

After this comes a series of teaching scenes as Jesus journeys toward Jerusalem. These include God's blessing on those who spread the Word of God, God's faithfulness to answer the prayers of those who love him, the importance of avoiding the false beliefs of "this evil generation," warnings against hypocritical religious authorities, not being overwhelmed by the cares of this world, who will be saved, doing the Word of God, warnings against spiritual pride, and another teaching on prayer. Toward the end of this Part, at Lk 18:15, Luke resumed following the narrative order of Matthew into the events of Passion Week.

Luke's use of Matthew in Lk 19:28–24:9

From this point on to the end, Luke followed the general sequence of pericopes in Matthew fairly closely, although he revised each unit internally. We have divided this into two Parts. Our Part Six, Lk 19:28–21:38, opens with Christ's triumphal entry into Jerusalem (cf. Mt 20) and extends through Jesus' apocalyptic predictions (Mt. 24). However, Luke nuanced his version so as to remove particularistic Jewish elements from it, as well as much of its apocalyptic character. For instance, the eschatological predictions of doom on the Temple in Matthew were historicized by Luke through the addition of specific details from the actual destruction of Jerusalem in 70 C.E. by the Romans. His Hellenistic readers would certainly have known of that momentous conflict and would have concluded that Jesus' predictions had already come true.

Our Part Seven, Lk 22:1–24:53, contains Luke's carefully revised version of Matthew's Last Supper to give—in proper Hellenistic fashion at their last meal together—Jesus' final instructions and predictions to all of his Twelve Apostles, especially Peter. Luke elaborated Matthew's account of the detention and trial of Jesus (Mt 26, 27) so that Jesus had no less than three hearings before the appropriate Roman and Roman-supported authorities. In each case it was declared that Jesus was not guilty of any crime. In this way, Luke emphasized, even more strongly than Matthew had done that the true instigators behind Jesus' execution were some of Jerusalem's religious leaders.

Next, Luke thoroughly revised Matthew's account of the crucifixion (Mt 27), substituting for Jesus' cry of dereliction in Mt 27:46 a dialogue between the robbers and Jesus in which Jesus was shown to be serenely in control of the situation. Luke depicted Jesus dying with a pious prayer that God receive his spirit, in contrast to Matthew's final wordless scream (Mt 27:50). Following the burial and news of the empty tomb, Luke diverged from Matthew so that Christ's resurrection appearances took place in Jerusalem (not Galilee as in Mt 28) so that the narrative could continue straight on into the first chapter of Acts, where Jesus would be finally taken up into heaven.

For a summary of Luke's *sequential* use of Matthew, see the chart on the next page.

Summary of Luke's Sequential Use of Matthew

In composing Lk 1–2: Luke adopted elements from but not the order of Mt 1–2 while creating the first Part of his Gospel in a way appropriate for his narrative agenda.

In composing Lk 3:1–9:50: Luke began a *cyclic progression* through Matthew, moving forward and going back again, selecting Matthean units and combining them with materials of his own to create his chronologically-oriented narrative. In this way, Luke repeatedly moved forward through Matthew until he had used most of the narrative units in Mt 3–18:5, in what we have named Parts Two through Four.

In composing Lk 9:51–19:27: Luke depicts Jesus giving a series of teachings loosely based on a "Journey toward Jerusalem" motif, comprised of
(a) some of the remaining narrative units in Matthew—which he used in Matthew's general order—plus sayings omitted from units used previously,
(b) sayings from all of Matthew's sayings collections—which Luke interspersed throughout Lk 10–19 mostly in the same order these sayings occur within Matthew's speeches (i.e., but not necessarily in the general order of the speeches as they occur in Matthew), and
(c) non-Matthean traditions worked into the scenes where he thought it to be appropriate.
This Travel Narrative we have named Part Five.

In composing Lk 19:28–24:53: Luke followed the basic narrative order of Mt 19–28, considerably revising the content of each narrative unit. We have divided this material into Parts Six and Seven. Toward the end of Part Seven (Lk 24:13), Luke stopped following Matthew and, using non-Matthean tradition, composed a conclusion to his Gospel that anticipated the initial chapters of Acts.

❄ ❄ ❄

Linguistic, Rather than Sequential, Evidence that Luke used Matthew

It is one thing to compare two Gospels and notice striking macro-structural sequential parallels which seem to indicate that the author of a Gospel made use of an earlier Gospel. It is another thing to descend to the micro-structural level of linguistic phenomena and observe equally striking parallels in identical phrases and precisely similar turns of speech. When this occurs, three possibilities immediately present themselves: either A copied B, or B copied A, or both copied an earlier document. How should one decide among these three possibilities? When there is no hard evidence as to the date of writing or direction of dependence for either Matthew or Luke, how should cases of close *verbal* parallelism be assessed?

Examples of Matthean summary phraseology occurring in the text of Luke

One way to deal with this situation is to look for a special class of verbal parallelism, what might be called narrative summaries which function to close off one part of the narrative and lead into the next. The Gospel of Matthew has a number of such narrative summaries that are universally acknowledged as having come from the hand of the final compiler of the Gospel, not from a source.

Sermon on the Mount: And when Jesus had finished these sayings, the crowds were astonished at his teaching... (Mt. 7:28)

Mission Instructions: And when Jesus had finished instructing his twelve disciples, he went on from there to teach and preach...(Mt. 11:1)

Parables: And when Jesus had finished these parables, he went away from there and coming to his own country he taught them... (Mt. 13:53)

Community Regulations: And when Jesus had finished these sayings, he went away from Galilee and entered the region of Judea... (Mt. 19:1)

Eschatological Predictions: And when Jesus had finished all these sayings, he said to his disciples, "You know that after two days..." (Mt. 26:1)

Matters become interesting when fragments of such narrative summaries typical of Gospel A also appear in Gospel B, where they are not typical. Matters become even more interesting when such verbal parallels *do not occur anywhere else* in Gospel B *except where A and B are in sequential narrative parallel* (the phenomenon discussed above). When *that* combination of literary phenomena occurs, we have a rare "one-way indicator" that B has copied, not a common source, but A itself.[5]

The process of finding and identifying an author's typical narrative summary phraseology, when one has no idea what is source material and what is from the hand of the final author, is fraught with difficulty. In our work on the Gospels of Matthew and Luke, we have been fortunate to have the results of the research of Dennis Tevis, who succeeded in establishing the existence of a number of typical Matthean expressions, using an impartial method that did not rely upon any source hypothesis.[6]

Let us briefly examine two examples. Taking the famous summary passage mentioned above, we find:

---

[5] For a discussion of the history of this type of literary evidence, see especially David Peabody, "Chapters in the History of the Linguistic Argument for Solving the Synoptic Problem: The Nineteenth Century in Context," in *Jesus, the Gospels, and the Church,* ed. E. P. Sanders (Macon: Mercer University Press, 1987) 47–68. Eduard Zeller was the first to outline an accurate method using this type of evidence for solving the synoptic problem. See "Studien zur neutestamentlichen Theologie. 4 Vergleichende Übersicht über den Wörtervorrath der neutestamentlichen Schriftsteller," *Theologische Jahrbücher* 2 (1843) 443-543, esp. 443-477, 491-498, and 525-539. William R. Farmer outlined this type of argument in "Redaction Criticism and the Synoptic Problem," in *Society of Biblical Literature One Hundred Seventh Annual Meeting Seminar Papers---28-31 October 1971 Regency Hyatt House - Atlanta, Ga.*, 2 volumes (Society of Biblical Literature, 1971) 1:239-250, esp. 246-247 on the import for the Synoptic Problem of recurrent words and phrases that may *not* be capable of being identified as characteristics of the hand of the final redactor of a Gospel.

[6] See Dennis Gordon Tevis, "An Analysis of Words and Phrases Characteristic of the Gospel of Matthew," unpubl. diss. Perkins School of Theology, 1982. It can be purchased through University Microfilm International, Ann Arbor, Michigan.

Mt 7:28–29 And when Jesus finished these sayings, the crowds were astonished at his teaching, for he taught them as one who had authority...

Compare:

Lk 4:31–32 he was teaching them on the sabbath and they were astonished at his teaching, for his word was with authority.

Luke 7:1 After he had ended all his sayings in the hearing of the people, he entered Capernaum.

Mt 7:28–29 was created by the author of the Gospel of Matthew as the conclusion to Jesus' first great teaching discourse (the Sermon on the Mount). The presence of precisely this Matthean summary phraseology *both* at the conclusion of Jesus' first public discourse in Capernaum (Lk 4:31f.) *and* at the conclusion of *Luke's version* of Matthew's Sermon on the Mount (Lk 6:20–49), where Luke is clearly in sequential parallel with Matthew's order, is plausible evidence for Luke's direct dependence on the Gospel of Matthew (see our discussion below, p. 103).

Another example of this kind of thing can be found in the text of Lk 4:14–16. Because it is too complex to discuss in detail here, we just note the following:

(a) This is Luke's introduction to Jesus' first public sermon. Just as Mt 4:12–13 and 4:23–24 are Matthew's introduction to Jesus' first public sermon in his Gospel, so Lk 4:14–16 is in sequential parallel with Matthew's order *and* we find Matthean *summary phraseology* occurring here in the parallel text of Luke.

(b) This passage also contains echoes of other Matthean *summary phraseology* about the "report of Jesus' fame spreading throughout all the district" (cf. Mt 9:26, 31). In short, Lk 4:14–16 is a pastiche of Matthean *summary passages* occurring in parallel narrative contexts (see our discussion below, pp. 80-83).

None of this kind of phraseology is considered by anyone to come originally from a pre-Matthean source like the hypothetical Q. It contains certain phrases not found anywhere in Luke except those passages that are close contextual parallels with Matthew. As such, they offer evidence of Luke's direct use of Matthew.

Examples of Matthean grammatical constructions in the text of Luke

Another type of "one way indicator" that Luke is directly dependent upon the Gospel of Matthew is when we encounter characteristic Matthean grammatical constructions in the text of Luke, where the two are in close sequential, narrative parallel.

One example of this kind of phenomenon is the appearance of the genitive absolute followed by the word "behold" (ἰδού) in Luke. This grammatical construction is, according to Tevis, a unique literary characteristic of Matthew. It occurs eleven times in several different contexts throughout Matthew's Gospel (Mt 1:20; 2:1, 13, 19; 9:10, 18, 32; 12:46; 17:5; 26:47; 28:11). The only other place it occurs in all of the Gospels is in the Lukan parallel in the story of the arrest of Jesus.

Mt 26:47 Καὶ ἔτι αὐτοῦ λαλοῦντος ἰδοὺ Ἰούδας;

Lk 22:47 Ἔτι αὐτοῦ λαλοῦντος ἰδοὺ ὄχλος;

This appears to be strong evidence that Luke has taken over this Matthean construction directly from Matthew.[7]

Let us consider one more example from this second category. The verb προσέρχομαι followed by the dative occurs twenty-five times in Matthew. Except for three parallel passages in Mark and Luke (one of them in this example), it occurs nowhere else in the New Testament. It is found throughout Matthew, in places which unmistakably come from the author of the Gospel of Matthew. There is just one occurrence of this construction in the Gospel of Luke, precisely where Luke is in narrative sequential parallel and is identical to the language of Matthew for nine consecutive words.

Mt 27:58 οὗτος προσελθὼν τῷ Πιλάτῳ ᾐτήσατο τὸ σῶμα τοῦ Ἰησοῦ.

Lk 23:52 οὗτος προσελθὼν τῷ Πιλάτῳ ᾐτήσατο τὸ σῶμα τοῦ Ἰησοῦ

Again, we regard this as strong evidence that Luke copied directly from Matthew.[8]

An example of a favorite Matthean word occurring in the text of Luke

A third type of "one-way indicator"—although not as convincing as the foregoing for a number of reasons—involves the appearance of favorite *words* of Matthew in passages that are in close sequential parallel. One example is found in Luke 7:23 and 17:2, where the word σκανδαλίζειν "to stumble, cause to sin" occurs. This word occurs sixteen times in various contexts in Matthew but only twice in Luke, both in passages that are closely parallel to the Matthean order of narration. Again, this is evidence that Luke got this word from Matthew.

Conclusion

In a cumulative sense, the evidence of Luke's cyclic, sequential parallelism with the Gospel of Matthew, combined with the presence of verbal parallelism involving characteristic Matthean summaries, grammatical structures, and favorite terms in Luke's text, constitute a powerful argument for Luke's use of Matthew. Detailed presentation of these kinds of evidence will be found in the Compositional Analysis.

---

7 See Tevis, Display 41. In fact, Mt 9:10 should also be included.

8 See Tevis, Display 20.

Luke's Use of Non-Matthean Tradition

In the previous section we have outlined a case for Luke's use of Matthew. The presentation of arguments in favor of this hypothesis constitutes the central focus of this research project. However, as early as Luke's preface (Lk 1:1-4) there are indications that Luke used other source material in his composition.

Starting with Lk 1:1, the author indicates an awareness that a number of predecessors had taken up the task of giving a narrative account of the recent events surrounding the life and impact of Jesus of Nazareth. In Lk 1:3, the author asserts that he is now prepared to engage in writing his own account, having researched everything about these matters very closely from the beginning (ἄνωθεν).

Perhaps in contrast with these earlier narratives, Luke expresses a concern to arrange his composition καθεξῆς (which we interpret "in appropriate chronological order"). This claim would seem to suggest that these earlier accounts were not "orderly" in some way.

At any rate, Lk 1:1-4 reveals that Luke was aware of other narrative accounts of the Jesus-event, had researched them, and now was engaged in writing his own more trustworthy account. On the Two Gospel Hypothesis, we can account for Luke's use of one of these earlier narratives. It was the Gospel of Matthew. But since Luke writes of other narrative accounts in the plural, it is clear that he knew of one or more additional narratives besides Matthew. Thus, we have a right to expect that here and there, in addition to Matthew, Luke will be making use of other source material. For simplicity's sake we refer to all such source material as "non-Matthean tradition," without any effort in this study to determine whether there were more than one additional narrative account and, if so, how many such additional sources there may have been. When working with the text of Luke, the only further distinction we make, after having identified where Luke has used Matthew, is to determine when Luke is composing *de novo* and when Luke is copying another source. When non-Matthean tradition is marked by Lukan characteristics, we are led to consider that Luke may have composed that literary unit or that, if he used tradition, he considerably reworked it. When no Lukan characteristics are present and especially when non-Lukan characteristics are present, we conclude that Luke has copied non-Matthean tradition.

In sum, when we were unable to explain material in Luke either by Luke's use of Matthew or by clear evidence of Luke's own creative literary activity, only then were we prepared to posit that Luke used non-Matthean tradition.

In this book, we make no claims with respect to the precise form, structure, or history of this non-Matthean tradition aside from the textual evidence (Lk 1:1-4) that the author was aware of a number of narrative accounts of Jesus' activities. In addition to Matthew, Luke may well have had access to, and used, oral tradition or, in some cases (viz., the Passion Account), both oral tradition and written accounts. However, as said above, we make no attempt in this book to sort out the number or nature of these various sources.

Although Luke used Matthew in most instances, we found that Luke, with some degree of consistency, also used non-Matthean tradition throughout much of his narrative. Several instances where we found Luke using non-Matthean tradition will serve as examples of our position. First, there is a category where Luke has incorporated non-Matthean tradition into his narrative that has no parallel in Matthew and, lacking any substantial amounts of Lukan linguistic characteristics, could hardly be considered Lukan composition. The account of the Magnificat (Lk 1:46-55) and the Walk to Emmaus (Lk 24:13-35) are cases in point. Other examples would be several of the parables (viz., Lk 15:11-32; 16:1-8, 19-31).

A second category includes instances where Luke, although he has a parallel tradition in Matthew, chooses to follow the non-Matthean tradition. We have determined that we have an example within this category only after we have satisfied ourselves that there is an absence of both Matthean and Lukan linguistic characteristics in Luke. Generally, we have found only a few occurrences of this category. Examples would be "The Catch of Fish and the Call of Three Disciples" (Lk 5:1-11, cf. Mt 4:18-22, the "Call of Four Disciples") and "The Sinful Woman Who Washes Jesus Feet" (Lk 7:36-50, cf. "The Woman Who Anoints Jesus," Mt 26:6-13).

A third category would include instances where Luke has both a Matthean and a non-Matthean tradition and decides to conflate them. A possible example of this category would be the Parable of the Vineyard and the Tenants (Lk 20:9-18, cf. Mt 21:33-46).

Finally, there is a fourth category, exemplified primarily within the Passion Narrative, where Luke may have used both written and oral non-Matthean tradition alongside of Matthean tradition. These are cases that are difficult to sort out. We are open to the possibility that something like this may have happened in Luke's account of the Last Supper (Lk 22:14-23) and/or within the Trial Narrative (Lk 23:1-25).

Procedurally, at the beginning of our detailed notes to each pericope, under *General observations,* we include a statement of our conclusions about source-critical questions. However, as noted above, we are intentionally circumspect about identifying the specific nature of non-Matthean tradition when we identify it there as one of Luke's sources. A possible exception to this rule is that we note in several places that there are close verbal agreements between Luke and the Gospel of John or the Letters of Paul. In these cases, we draw attention to some of the linguistic evidence, but do not arrive at firm conclusions about the nature of the relationship between the text of Luke and the texts of these other early Christian authors. We would emphasize again that the major focus of this book is on Luke's use of Matthew. The whole matter of Luke's use of non-Matthean tradition, in order to be addressed adequately, would need to be the subject of another volume.

Is the nonMatthean tradition our "Q"?

The answer to this question is a categorical "No." This question would not even arise if it were not for a certain ambiguity in the current use of the designation "Q." The designation "Q" is today used in two different ways. The primary use of the term "Q" is to designate a hypothetical source written in Greek, which if we had it would help explain the agreements and disagreements between the texts of Matthew and Luke in passages where there is no parallel in Mark. This is a functional definition of "Q" based on the Two Source Hypothesis. It is the sense in which the International "Q" Project is understood to use the term. However, some Gospel scholars expand this hypothetical document to include sayings of Jesus not covered by this definition of "Q." This has led to the use of the term "Q" in a secondary sense, namely to refer to the "sayings tradition of Jesus" in a broad sense.

Few if any scholars would question that there was an extensive body of early Jesus tradition available to the evangelists, both oral and written, from which they could draw sayings of Jesus as they composed their Gospels. If this body of early sayings tradition is thought of as "Q," then, of course, it is legitimate to think of the non-Matthean sayings tradition in Luke as a very important part of "Q." Very important, for example, because it would include Lukan parables of Jesus like "the Good Samaritan" and "the Lost Son" in "Q."

But strictly speaking, if we use "Q" in its primary and classical sense, these parables are not included in "Q," because they do not belong to that tradition that is found in both Matthew and Luke but not in Mark. The hypothetical "Q" document being reconstructed by the International "Q" Seminar is a written document that is primarily derived from passages common to Matthew and Luke but not found in Mark. In this classical sense of the term, the Non-Matthean tradition in Luke has nothing to do with "Q."

With this point in mind, we can rephrase the problem in this way: "Is the nonMatthean tradition in Luke the same kind of hypothetical source as is "Q"? If it is, then does this not diminish the advantage that comes from being able to understand the Gospels without any need for an unknown source called "Q"? Are the authors of this book not in essentially the same predicament as the "Q" advocates, namely, in order to explain the Gospels, are they not hypothecating an unknown source used by Luke, which they are designating as 'nonMatthean tradition?'"

These questions deserve a careful answer. In crafting an answer we begin by making a distinction between hypothetical sources that are required by the data because there is no other way to explain the data, and hypothetical sources which are not required by the data because they can be equally well explained in other ways.

The source (or sources) designated by us by the general term "nonMatthean tradition" is (are) indeed hypothetical, since it (they) like "Q" does (do) not in fact exist. But such a hypothetical source (or sources) is required by the data, because there is no other known way to explain the data. What is the data that requires us to hypothecate a source (or sources)? We will use a particular saying of Jesus to answer this question. The text of the parable of "the Lost Son" in Luke is marked by linguistic usage that departs from the known linguistic usage of Luke. The simplest explanation for these non-Lukan characteristics is to hypothesize the existence of a source written in Greek from which Luke carefully copied this parable. To date there has been no other known way to explain this data. This source, then, is indeed a hypothetical one, because it does not in fact exist. However it is a hypothetical source required by the data.

Quite the opposite is true in the case of all "Q" sayings. "Q" sayings in Luke are typically characterized by being marked by *Lukan* linguistic characteristics. These Lukan linguistic characteristics are best explained as coming from Luke, not from any hypothetical source. Verbal agreements between Luke and Matthew in the so called "Q" material can be explained by Luke's use of Matthew. There is no need, therefore, to hypothecate the existence of "Q" to explain this data. All the data can be equally well explained by Luke's use of Matthew. Some of the data can be better explained in this way. For example, there are cases where the verbatim agreement between Luke and Matthew includes linguistic usages that are characteristic of Matthew. This kind of data is best explained on a hypothesis that acknowledges Luke's *direct* use of Matthew, rather than his copying some hypothetical source also copied by Matthew.

With this explanation in mind it is clear that the Two Gospel Hypothesis in comparison to the Two Source Hypothesis enjoys the advantage of not having to hypothecate the existence of a major unknown source called "Q." As for the unknown source or sources that we must hypothecate to explain the data that indicates that Luke copied material from the source (or sources), which we have designated as nonMatthean tradition, this data is there to be explained on any theory. This data does not weigh for or against any particular solution to the Synoptic Problem.

Some of Luke's Compositional Techniques Emerging from Our Study of Luke's Redaction of Matthew

Before describing what we found to be some of Luke's favorite compositional devices or techniques, a word of warning is in order. Our suggestions in this area are based on direct study of the Gospel of Luke when it is compared directly to the Gospel of Matthew. That is to say, we frequently found it to be the case that all current synoptic displays were more of a hindrance to our understanding than a help. Therefore, do not expect to verify our claims in this section by using any of the currently available synopses. The best way is to compare the text of Luke with the text of Matthew.

Second, it will be noted by those familiar with the discussion of Luke's compositional methods that what we suggest here will not sound like what is usually said about Lukan style and use of sources (typically Mark and Q). Our conclusions will sound surprising when compared to the traditional opinions of Two Source Lukan specialists, such as H. J. Cadbury.[1] Given our radically different source assumptions, these differences in results are to be expected.

With these preliminary clarifications in place, we are now ready to identify what we have found to be some of Luke's favorite compositional techniques.

As with any good Hellenistic author, Luke used a number of compositional devices which occur with such a degree of frequency that they may be considered characteristics of the author. The list below is not exhaustive. It is compiled from observations of Luke's compositional procedure garnered during our work sessions on Luke. It brings to the forefront some observations that have not been highlighted in earlier discussions on Lukan style.

To begin with, as we sought to understand Luke as a composer and communicator, we found it helpful to think of three meaning referents in terms of which Luke composed his narrative.

1. Luke's understanding of Matthew's narrative

Given our hypothesis, we were very aware of ways in which Luke seemed to interpret the text of Matthew. In this connection, we attempted to compare his understanding against our own (Two Gospel) understanding. We found what

---

1 See H. J. Cadbury, *The Style and Literary Method of Luke* (Cambridge: Harvard University Press, 1926). While Cadbury's work is time-honored and still useful, Frank Collison published a searching critique of Cadbury's and others' analyses of Lukan style, finding some of them misleading and others inaccurate. See "Linguistic Usages in the Gospel of Luke," in *New Synoptic Studies; The Cambridge Gospel Conference and Beyond,* ed. W. R. Farmer (Macon: Mercer University Press, 1983) 245-260.

seemed to be numerous cases where he rephrased the text of Matthew to produce a very different meaning. We found many places where he seems to have considered Matthew's narrative flow deficient and in need of supplement. For example, in our compositional analysis of Luke where Luke is parallel to Mt 4:12–13, we conclude that Luke considered Matthew's curt explanation of Jesus' itinerary as inadequate chronologically and narratively. As a result, Luke supplemented Matthew's account considerably with a series of additional explanations as to why Jesus left Nazareth and went to Capernaum.

2. *Luke's own narrative flow*

We assume that Luke as an author was generally aware of the many intricate connections and resonances he built into different parts of his own narrative. This included quite sophisticated work toward a gradual characterization of the disciples, carefully prepared lead-in and denouement around significant events such as the Transfiguration, and so on. We found it necessary to pay continual attention to Acts in this regard, since many of the key resonances and themes continue to remain active there as well.

3. *Luke's intended audience*

Not least important, Luke wrote with an eye constantly upon his intended audience, which we took to be congregations in the wider ecumenical mission, including the area(s) of Paul's missionary. Naturally, we could not ascertain the impact of Luke's narrative as such, but occasionally we observed Luke making a connection between sayings or events in Matthew in a way that seemed to us to have little to do with Matthew's presumed intended meaning, a connection which also crashed into his own narrative flow, as it were, but which seemed to us to make sense at the "intended audience level."

We do not mean these aspects to be mutually exclusive. Indeed, part of the interpretive task is to accurately assess the interplay and tension between all three levels simultaneously.

As with any good Hellenistic author, Luke employed a number of compositional devices. Some occur with such a degree of frequency that they may be considered characteristics of Luke himself.

Luke creates a smoothly flowing, well-proportioned narrative

As we attempted to understand Luke's complex utilization of his major source, Matthew, as he created his beautiful parallel Gospel account for the Christian congregations in the wider ecumenical mission, we often found ourselves confronted by an unexpected difficulty. We would find ourselves unable to decide where Luke meant for his narrative units to begin or end. Examination of synopses and critical texts revealed a wide variety of opinions. This difficulty applied especially to the large groupings of units we have named "parts" (as in parts in a book). In some cases, we could see how some pericopes should be grouped with the previous part, but we could also make a case for including them in the next part.

After several years of struggling with this problem, we eventually decided that the author of the Third Gospel *had intentionally concealed his transitions* from one part to another by creating overlapping, interlocking back-references and forward-anticipations, so that one part flowed smoothly into the next. We will mention numerous cases of this phenomenon throughout our compositional analysis, but the most notorious examples are the transition to Luke's central parenetic section (chs. 10–19), the entry into Jerusalem (or, where does the "journey to Jerusalem" actually finish?), and the conclusion to the Gospel (where the narrative actually goes right on into the first chapter of Acts).

If this indeed was a major concern of Luke, then one can understand why Matthew's large collections of unconnected teachings followed by equally large conglomerations of anecdotes may have been a major reason for Luke to seriously rework the Gospel of Matthew (as we can see from the chart of Luke's use of Matthew above; pp. 16-17).

After we had completed our compositional analysis of Luke one of our group discovered in an article by Jacques Dupont a reference to a passage in Lucian of Samosata which prescribed for the writing of history precisely the technique we had so frequently encountered in the Gospel of Luke.[2] Lucian's remarks are significant enough to quote in full.[3]

By way of introduction, we may note that, in the body of his speech Lucian insisted that the history should be truthful,[4] rhetorically skillful,[5] and written not just for the

---

2 See Jacques Dupont, "La question du plan des Actes des Apôtres à lumière d'un texte de Lucien de Samosate," in *Novum Testamentum* 21 (1979) 220-231.

3 The translation is ours. For another English translation, see Lucian of Samosata, "How to Write History," in *The Works of Lucian,* trans. K. Kilburn, Loeb Series (Harvard: University Press 1958) 6:66-67.

4 "How to Write History": the history should be truthful and not mere panegyric (ἐνγκώμιον) 7; the historian must be honest and accustomed to fearless expression (παρρησία) 41; he pays close attention to the facts (should be an eye-witness) 47; has a mind like a mirror—clear, bright, and accurate 50; if a myth (μύθος) comes along, tell it but in such a way the reader can decide for himself whether it is true or not 60; "everywhere (the reader should find) truthfulness" (ἀληθεῖα ἐπὶ πᾶσι) 61.

5 "How to Write History": the narrative is well-proportioned and flows smoothly 6; it is rhetorically skillful 34; words are put together gracefully 46; the facts have happened—it is up to the historian to present them clearly and articulately 50; "when a man has heard him he thinks afterward he is actually seeing what is being described" 51; "quickness (i.e., brevity) is useful in everything, especially if there is no end of things to describe...indeed a great deal should be omitted" (τάχος ἐπὶ πᾶσι χρήσιμον, καὶ μάλιστα εἰ μὴ ἀπορία τῶν λεκτέων εἴη...μᾶλλον δὲ καὶ παραλειπτέον πολλά.) 56; first the speeches should be appropriate for the person's character and occasion, then let the historian be as eloquent as he can 58.

present but for all future ages.[6] Near his conclusion, he turns to the question of proper proportion in the narrative, and explains how to make the narrative flow smoothly and gracefully. We underline key words in Greek and in our translation since many are important technical terms in genre discussions of the Gospels. The numbers in < > are keyed to our explanatory glosses following the quotation.

> . . . μετὰ δὲ προοίμιον, ἀνάλογον τοῖς πράγμασιν ἢ μηκυνόενον ἢ βραχυνόμενον, εὐαφὴς τε καὶ εὐάγωγος ἔστω ἡ ἐπὶ τὴν διήγησιν μετάβασις. ἅπαν γὰρ ἀτεχνῶς τὸ λοιπὸν σῶμα τῆς ἱστορίας διήγησις μαρκά ἐστιν. ὥστε ταῖς τῆς διηγήσεως ἀρεταῖς κατακεκοσμήσθω, λείως τε καὶ ὁμαλῶς προϊοῦσα καὶ αὑτὴ ὁμοίως ὥστε μὴ προὔχειν μηδὲ κοιλαίνεσθαι· ἔπειτα τὸ σαφὲς ἐπανθείτω, τῇ τε λέξει, ὡς ἔφην, μεμηχανημένον καὶ τῇ συμπεριπλοκῇ τῶν πραγμάτων. ἀπόλυτα γὰρ καὶ ἐντελῆ πάντα ποιήσει, καὶ τὸ πρῶτον ἐξεργασάμενος ἐπάξει τὸ δεύτερον ἐχόμενον αὐτοῦ καὶ ἁλύσεως τρόπον συνηρμοσμένον ὡς μὴ διακεκόφθαι μηδὲ διηγήσεις πολλὰς εἶναι ἀλλήλαις παρακειμάνας, ἀλλ' ἀεὶ τῷ πρώτῳ τὸ δεύτερον μὴ γειτνιᾶν μόνον, ἀλλὰ καὶ κοινωνεὶν καὶ ἀνακεκρᾶσθαι κατὰ τὰ ἄκρα.

> ...After the preface, long or short in proportion to its subject matter, let the transition to the narrative be gentle and easy. For all the body of the history is simply a long narrative. So let it be adorned with the virtues proper to (such a) narrative, i.e., progressing smoothly, evenly and consistently, free from things jutting out and gaps <1>. Then let the clarity (of the subject matter) show plainly<2>, achieved, as I have said, both by means of the text and by means of the interweaving <3> of the things (recounted). For he will make everything distinct <4> and complete <5>, and when finished with the first topic he will introduce the second, fastened to it and linked with it like a chain, to avoid breaks and a multiplicity of disjointed narratives. <6> No, the first and second topics must always not merely be neighbors but share and mix the edges (of the units) together. <7>

Comments:

<1> Things out of proportion to the rest of the narrative, like speeches that are too long or anecdotes that go on and on, losing the reader's interest. Also avoid sudden unexplained jumps or gaps between units, such as placing unrelated sayings next to each other with no explanation how one leads to the next.

<2> Or, appear on the surface; from ἐπανθέω. This has to do with the general intelligibility of a unit. Each story must be transparently understandable if it is to inspire or instruct the reader/hearer.

<3> From πλεγματεύομαι "to be intertwined or plaited" (of hair and wicker-work);

[6] "How to Write History": the author must have real political understanding and can communicate a real lesson 34; he should write not just to please his audience but for all posterity 61, 63.

cf. Liddell-Scott, *s.v.*, who translate συμπεριπλοκνῆ "interconnexion." It resembles the Greek term ἁρμονία *harmonia*, a term from carpentry referring to the method of creating strong, overlapping joints by shaping the edges of two planks so that they will fit above and below each other, then driving pegs through the overlapped portion (in boat building); in medicine, a *suture*.

<4> From ἀπόλυτος "loosed, free, unconditional, unconstrained." Kilburn's "distinct" is an excellent translation.

<5> From ἐντελής "full, complete"; of meals—the *last* course. "Distinct and complete" refer to a sense of satisfying completeness for each vignette.

<6> Or: "not be disjointed, with many narratives laid end to end." From παράκειμαι "to place beside," i.e., place things in sequence with no transitions.

<7> κατὰ τὰ ἄκρα "edges." The meaning here is similar to ἄκρα in the sense of the "ends" of mathematical lines or geometric figures (cf. Liddell-Scott, *s.v.* ἄκρα 6. "end or extremity"). Lucian says the author should blend and intermingle the beginnings and endings of units, causing them to *overlap*.

In sum, Lucian recommends that each story or vignette in the narrative should stand out with clarity and distinctness, like a series of cameo scenes. Each scene should contain hints of the previous scene and anticipations of the next, so that they all interlock and overlap. In this way the narrative will flow smoothly from one thing to the next, the way history does (as Lucian understood it). Of course, there are many differences between Lucian's preferred subject matter (which was how to write about war) and the Gospel of Luke, but the latter is a good example of a composition that can result from following Lucian's standards of Hellenistic historiography, rhetorical skill, and compositional gracefulness.

Luke uses journeys to organize his material and structure his narrative

It has long been recognized that the picture of Paul's missionary activity in Acts, with the three decisive journeys, is an idealized account that is difficult to square with Paul's own biographical statements in his letters. It has not been as clearly realized that Luke's portrait of Jesus in the Gospel also involves a number of idealized journeys and tours.

Luke has structured Jesus' Galilean ministry into a series of trips or journeys. The first starts from Capernaum at Lk 4:31 and ends back in Capernaum at Lk 7:1. A second series of journeys begins at Lk 7:11 with Jesus going to Nain, where a number of events take place. At Lk 8:1 Luke wrote, "Soon afterwards he went on through the cities and villages [of Galilee] preaching and bringing the good news of the Kingdom of God." This extended journey was Luke's framework for describing the most important events of the latter part of Jesus' Galilean ministry. Then Jesus sets his face to go to

Jerusalem (Lk 9:51). This journey takes up ten chapters (Lk 9:51 to 19:27) and is the framework for an extended series of didactic anecdotes and vignettes. After the events leading up to Jesus' trials, execution and resurrection, two associates of the Twelve walk to Emmaus and back to Jerusalem, bringing the Gospel to a close.

Besides Jesus' journeys are a number of trips and tours involving other people: Jesus' parents go from Nazareth to Bethlehem and back (Lk 2:1–40), Mary goes to visit Elizabeth and returns home (Lk 1:39–56), Jesus and his family go to Jerusalem when he was twelve (Lk 2:41–52). The Twelve disciples have their own missionary trip (Lk 9:1–10), as do the Seventy-two (Lk 10:1–17).

The journey motif was one of Luke's main structural devices to organize his source materials chronologically, to provide the feeling that this was the way things actually happened, and to lend the narrative an air of excitement and unpredictability. It invoked the familiar portrait of the wandering philosopher, "on the road," dispensing wisdom and healing as he fearlessly advanced towards his martyr's death.

Promise and fulfillment

As a Hellenistic historian keenly aware that the events he narrated took place within a grand design, Luke frequently highlighted his narrative account with echoes and allusions to the source of that design: scripture. This was a literary as well as a theological strategy. In contrast to Matthew, Luke preferred not to use the compositional formula of a direct citation from Scripture preceded by a fulfillment formulation. Instead, Luke anchored the story of Jesus within a wider historical context: Jesus was the one who would bring to fulfillment the hopes of Israel (cf. Lk 1:32–33; 2:11–14; 2:29–31). These hopes, embedded in the scriptures (especially the prophets), spoke of a Messiah who would come to his own, be rejected, and ultimately be vindicated. Luke compositionally structured his account of the narrative of Jesus' life within this schema. In the birth narratives he articulated not only the hope of the glory of the Messiah but also prepared the reader for the fact that he would suffer (Lk 2:34–35). Then, throughout his ministry, Jesus announced that as Son of Man he would suffer (Lk 9:22, 44; 17:25; 18:31–33; 22:22). And, finally, after he had suffered and been vindicated, Luke had the risen Jesus explain that this had to take place in keeping with the purpose and intent of scripture (Lk 24:25–27; 44–46). This strategy of explaining the life of Jesus in light of the overarching story of scripture was Luke's alternative to Matthew's prophecy-fulfillment pattern.

Male and female pairs

There is evidence that Luke adopted a literary strategy where he would place an account highlighting the role of a female with a similar account involving a male. This pairing may have served the literary purpose of underscoring the theological point made at this particular juncture in the narrative. Thus, the idea that Jesus was the true antitype of Elijah and Elisha was highlighted by the pairing of the account of the healing of the *centurion's* servant (Elijah) and the *widow* of Nain's son (Elisha) in Lk 7:1–17. This pairing does not occur in Mt. Other examples of pairing of female and male are found in Lk 15:3–10 (man with the lost sheep/woman with the lost coin); Lk 13:18–23 (man sowing the mustard seed/woman using leaven); Lk 10:29–42 (Good Samaritan/Mary and Martha); Lk 17:34–35 (two men sleeping/two women at a mill); and in a separated context, Lk 13:10–17 and 14:1–6 (healing of the crippled *woman* and the *man* with dropsy).

Lukan anticipations

Another of the literary devices used by Luke to maintain coherence within his narrative was the use of anticipations. This device is well known by students of Acts where quite frequently a figure will be introduced into the narrative through playing a small, almost intrusive role in a pericope only to appear somewhat later as a major character (viz., Saul at Acts 7:58; 8:1–3 and 9:1f.; Stephen at Acts 6:5 and 8:5; John Mark at Acts 12:12,25). A similar literary usage is evident in the Gospel of Luke (viz., Herod Antipater and Pilate at Lk 3:1 and Lk 23:6–25; Simon at Lk 4:38 and 5:1–11).

Conclusion

These are only a few instances of the very rich and nuanced compositional methods we have noted that Luke used to tie together his narrative account of Jesus' life. Present research on Luke's literary strategies in comparison with other Hellenistic authors reveals that he was able to use a wide range of rhetorical techniques to accomplish his literary purposes.

Major Themes in Luke
Emerging from Our Study of Luke's Redaction of Matthew

When an author incorporates another work into his own composition, he does so with his own purposes in mind. In his prologue, Luke states that he is writing a narrative derived from his own research. He has sources he is no doubt incorporating into his text. An examination of the manner in which Luke utilizes at least one of his primary literary sources, Matthew, enables one to see the way Luke has incorporated, refined, and developed his themes within his narrative creation. Here are some examples of the theological and ecclesiastical themes which emerge from our study of Luke's use of Matthew that appear to be important features which define the author's work.

Activity of the Holy Spirit

Clearly, Luke understands the role of the Holy Spirit to have been crucial to the overall story of the unfolding of God's plan of salvation. In both the Matthean and Lukan birth narratives, for example, Mary's pregnancy is attributed to the Holy Spirit, but the way this information is conveyed reflects a distinctively Lukan treatment. Luke presents a more Hellenistic and less passive description in Lk 1:35: "the Holy Spirit will come upon you and the power of the Most High will stretch out over you." Here Luke goes beyond Matthew in his description of the active presence of the Holy Spirit.[1] Whereas both accounts record Jesus having been led into the wilderness for temptation (Mt 4:1, Lk 4:1), Luke assures his audience of Jesus' readiness for temptation by adding that Jesus is "full of the Holy Spirit." For Luke, it is the bodily form of the Holy Spirit that descends upon Jesus immediately following his baptism (Lk 3:22, καταβῆναι τὸ πνεῦμα τὸ ἅγιον σωματικῷ).[2]

Of the remaining references in Matthew to the Holy Spirit, one is associated with blasphemy (Mt 12:32) while two are associated with baptism (Mt 3:11; 28:19). Luke, on the other hand, continues the active presence of the Holy Spirit. Luke's characters are "filled," "empowered by," have the Holy Spirit "come upon" them; they are to "rejoice in," to be "instructed by," or to "receive" the Holy Spirit.[3] Through his use of the

1 Compare Mt 1:18, "Mary will be found to be pregnant by the Holy Spirit" (cf. Mt 1:20).

2 Cf. Mt 3:16, [τὸ] πνεῦμα [τοῦ] θεοῦ καταβαῖνον.

3 Elizabeth and Zechariah are "filled" with the Holy Spirit (Lk 1:41; 1:67), Jesus is in the "power of the Spirit" (Lk 4:14), and has the Spirit "upon him" at his inaugural sermon (Lk 4:18). Luke uses Mt 11:25 in his account of the return of the seventy-two, and adds an appropriate response to the successful mission as Jesus rejoices "in the Holy Spirit" (ἠγαλλιάσατο τῷ πνεύματι τῷ ἁγίῳ, Lk 10:21). In Luke 11:13, Luke identifies πνεῦμα ἅγιον as the gift the Father gives to those who ask (not ἀγαθὰ as it is in Mt 7:11b). And, instead of the "Spirit of the Father" telling the disciples what they will say (in Mt's account of the sending of the twelve, Mt 10:20), those who witness to Christ will be taught "the things

Matthean material, Luke reveals his understanding of the Holy Spirit as playing a much more direct and active role in God's plan of redemption. This dynamic activity continues in Acts where the Spirit empowers the early Christian community in word and deed.[4]

Jerusalem and the Temple

Jerusalem and the Temple play a heightened role in Luke's narrative, a role not underscored in Matthew's Gospel. Outside of the Passion Narrative, there is only passing interest in Jerusalem and the Temple in Matthew. For Luke, by contrast, special attention to both appears as early as in the birth and early childhood narratives (Lk 1:9, 21, 22; 2:27, 37, 46). Here, faithful attention to Temple requirements according to Jewish law is portrayed. It is the location of the Temple to which Jesus' parents travel to observe proper Temple rites (Lk 2:22-39, 41-51; esp. 27 and 39). With Matthew, Luke presents the Temple as the locus of Jesus' activity when he reaches Jerusalem (Lk 19:45, 47; 20:1; 21:37; 22:52); however, unlike Matthew, it is also for Luke the initial gathering place for Jesus' followers after his death (Lk 24:53; Acts 2:46).

Luke locates Jerusalem as the scene of prophecies regarding Israel's future. Zechariah, Simeon, and Anna all reside in Jerusalem and are in the Temple as the soteriological events and prophecies begin to break forth (Lk 1:5-21; 2:25, 38). Anna speaks of the hope of the "redemption of Israel" (Lk 2:38) which Jesus later said was drawing near with the coming of the Son of Man (Lk 21:28, unique to Lk). In Jerusalem, Zechariah speaks of the Lord who has "visited and redeemed his people."[5] These are not Matthean themes. Simeon is at last ready to die since he has *seen* the Lord's salvation, which is a "light for revelation to the gentiles and for glory to thy people Israel" (Lk 2:32). "Light" used in this manner is not found in Matthew.[6] It is also in Jerusalem that the joy over the news of salvation is first recounted (Lk 1:14, 44, 58; 2:10).[7]

The theme of Jerusalem and the Temple is further enhanced by Luke's narrative structure. The Lukan birth narrative begins with Zechariah in the Jerusalem Temple (Lk 1:5-23), and concludes when Joseph and Mary present Jesus in the Temple to Simeon and Anna, thereby framing the John/Jesus infancy narratives (Lk 1:5-2:38). Jesus' visit to the Temple at age twelve (Lk 2:41-50) is a decisive event marking off the infancy/youth account from Luke's presentation of the activities of the adult Jesus.

---

it is necessary to say" (Lk 12:12).

4 E.g., Acts 2:4; 4:8, 31; 6:3, 5; 7:55; 8:15, 17; etc.

5 This occurs at the birth of his son, John (Lk 1:68), a theme reiterated elsewhere in Lk 7:16 (related to Jesus) and Acts 15:14 (in connection with the conversion of Cornelius).

6 Acts 26:23 identifies the suffering and resurrection as a "light both to the people and to the Gentiles."

7 Cf. also Lk 6:23; 10:20; 15:6, 9; 19:37; Acts 2:47; 5:41; 10:46.

Luke rearranges the Temptation account so that it ends with Satan taunting Jesus as he stands on the Temple pinnacle in Jerusalem (Mt 3:1-12//Lk 3:1-9).

Matthew's description of Jesus' final trip to Jerusalem becomes, in Luke, the destination of Luke's elaborately developed Travel Narrative in which Jesus resolutely journeys toward his suffering and death (Mt 20:17; 21:1; Lk 9:51, 53; 13:22, 33, 34; 17:11; 18:31; 19:11, 28). By the time Jesus reaches Jerusalem, over half of Luke's total narrative to that point has been devoted to creating a sense of anticipation of what will happen upon Jesus' arrival. This Hellenistic compositional technique, as employed by Luke, is very different from Matthew's version of the same event. With Matthew's version, Luke understands Jerusalem as the setting for Jesus' arrest, trial, crucifixion, and resurrection (Lk 22:47-24:12; Acts 10:39). Luke, however, goes further. It is a city inhabited by sinners (Lk 13:4; not in Matthew), which presents at least partial explanation for its eventual destruction (Mt 24:1-2; Lk 21:20, 24). Again, in contrast with Matthew, Luke portrays Jerusalem as the first to whom repentance and the forgiveness of sins will be preached (Lk 23:48-49; 24:47; Acts 1:2, 2:5-28; 4:16; 5:16, 28; 6:7; 10:39; unique to Luke).

Luke clearly treats Jerusalem and the Temple as playing a theologically dynamic role, in contrast to Matthew, who tends to view it as a geographical location where Jesus cleansed the Temple and eventually died. In Luke Jesus is raised in Jerusalem and stays there until the Ascension; in Matthew, Jesus appears to the disciples far from Jerusalem, in Galilee, where he ascends into heaven. Luke goes far beyond Matthew in utilizing Jerusalem and the Temple to focus on the theological tasks of his two-volume work as a whole. Yet, as significant as Jerusalem and the Temple are at the beginning of Luke's work, in the whole of his Gospel, and at the beginning of the second volume, by the time one reaches the second half of Acts, Luke intentionally shifts the focus of events away from Jerusalem and the Temple. Partly this is because Luke, as well as his audience, is well aware of the recent military siege and fiery destruction of Jerusalem by the Roman legions. Partly this is also because of the emergence and success of the ecumenical mission led by the Apostles Paul and Peter, under the guidance of the Holy Spirit.

John and Jesus in Comparison

One of the more striking set of themes developed by Luke in comparison with Matthew is the comparative portrayal of the persons of John and Jesus. In Matthew, the portrayal of John began with his ministry in Mt 3, moving to the baptism of Jesus at the conclusion of that same chapter, and climaxed in Mt 11 with Jesus' encomium to John. No doubt, Matthew's readers would make comparisons, but for Matthew Jesus was so far superior as to preclude any real comparison. Luke, on the other hand, composed an effective parallel structure involving John and Jesus so that the reader could not avoid a comparison of the two. Luke forced the issue by an elaborate series of comparisons which emphasized the superiority of Jesus as the central figure of Divine Revelation, while, at the same time, he provided the reader with a strong visual case for the continuity of the two ministries in the sense that both had a divine origin. Each comparison concluded with a focus on Jesus as the central character (Lk 1:39-45; 2:41-51). While the comparison structure is most evident in Lk 1-2, comparisons are not limited to these two chapters. They surface again and again.[8] In these latter passages, the issue is over Jesus and John as "prophet." Here, Lk 7:1-35 is instructive. John's disciples come to ask Jesus who he is in the context of the crowd's acclamation: "A great prophet has arisen among us!" and "God has visited his people." Following this, John's disciples ask Jesus John's question (it is repeated twice for emphasis). The point of the comparison implied in this and what follows in the Lukan text is that John is *a* prophet, but Jesus is *the* prophet through whom "God has visited his people."

To be sure, Matthew's portrayal did confront his readers with the importance of John the Baptist in relation to Jesus, but at places it might have seemed (to Christians out in the wider ecumenical mission) to go too far. For example, it is possible to read Matthew in such a way that Jesus is at first a disciple of John. Moreover, in Matthew, there is a calculated equating of John the Baptist and Elijah, something Luke wished to avoid (cf. Mt 11:14; 17:10-11). In any case, we regard many of Luke's carefully conceived comparisons between John and Jesus as remedial for these perceived ambiguities in the Gospel of Matthew.

Jesus' Role in the Divine Plan

Although the concept is certainly latent throughout the Gospel of Matthew, Luke's narrative is characterized by repeated explicit references to the over-arching divine plan of salvation that governs all of the characters and activities. This should not surprise us. The practice of describing events as coming about as the result of divine providence is a well-known Hellenistic rhetorical device, found in biographies, histories, and novels (romances).[9] Luke's main term in this respect is "plan or counsel" (βουλή), a term that does not appear anywhere in Matthew. Some of the key passages in which the concept of God's will or purpose are present include Lk 7:30; 23:51; Acts 2:23; 4:28; 5:38; and 20:27.

God's plan of salvation manifested itself above all in Luke's portrayal of Jesus.[10] The series of comparisons between John the prophet sent by God and Jesus concluded

[8] Lk 5:33; 7:11-35; 9:7-9; 11:1; 16:16; 20:1-80.

[9] On this subject, see most recently John T. Squires, *The Plan of God in Luke–Acts* SNTSMS 76 (Cambridge: University Press, 1993).

[10] Luke's presentation of Jesus as a "light to the nations" has been noted above; as has the portrayal of God's visitation of his people through him.

with John the forerunner of Jesus and thereby his subordinate. Indeed, John is not shown to be the one who baptized Jesus, the Holy Spirit is. Next, Jesus is depicted as, guided by the Holy Spirit, going out into the wilderness to combat Satan. After successfully undergoing this test, Jesus is again "guided by the Holy Spirit," when he inaugurates his public ministry. Eventually, "to fulfill the plan of God," Luke depicted Jesus turning toward Jerusalem, where he would suffer, die and on the third day, be raised from the dead.[11] The whole "plan of God" in the Gospel of Luke comes to a climax when God raised his "Son" so that redemption and forgiveness may be extended to Israel and then to the nations. Luke portrayed the *risen* Jesus explaining "God's plan" to Cleopas and his friend in the Emmaus story. Thus, the entirety of Luke's Gospel (and Acts) reflects his understanding of God's plan of salvation.

Eschatological Reversals

Very important for Luke is the theme of "eschatological reversal." It makes its first appearance in the *Magnificat* (Lk 1:51-53). Here we learn that God will "scatter the proud," "put down the mighty from their thrones," "exalt those of low degree," "fill the hungry with good things," and send the "rich away empty." Precisely the same themes are announced by Jesus in his inaugural sermon in Nazareth (Lk 4:18-19).[12] In Luke's version of Matthew's Sermon on the Mount, as well as a number of later places, the same themes are heard: the lowly will be uplifted, the sick will be healed, the poor will be exalted, the blind will see, and the lame will walk.[13]

Matthew also contains the concept of eschatological reversal, but Luke's treatment is strikingly different. For Matthew, the reversals will occur at a later time; e.g., in the day of Judgment (cf. Mt 5:1-11; 24–25). Luke, on the other hand, pictures these reversals *both now and* in the eschatological end time.[14] Luke's Jesus provides tangible evidence *in the present* of the eschatological reversal, in his scenes of Jesus' healing and in the scenes where Jesus associates with or eats with sinners (including stories describing great banquets which themselves contain the theme of eschatological reversal). This major theme in Luke comes to full fruition in the table fellowship of the ecumenical Christian community in Acts.[15]

---

[11] Cf. Lk 9:21-27, 43b-45, 51-56; 12:50-13:35; 17:24-25; 18:31-33.

[12] Jesus announces that Isaiah's prophecy is fulfilled in him that day, to proclaim "good news to the poor," "release to the captives," "recovery of sight to the blind," and the freeing of "those who are oppressed."

[13] Cf. Lk 7:22; 9:24; 13:30; 14:11; 18:9-14; 21:1-5.

[14] Two classic examples: Matthew's beatitude, "Blessed are the poor in spirit, for theirs is the kingdom of heaven" in Luke becomes "Blessed are <u>you</u> poor, for <u>yours</u> <u>is</u> the kingdom of God" (Mt 5:3; Lk 6:20): Matthew's "Blessed are those who hunger and thirst for righteousness, for they shall be satisfied" becomes in Luke "Blessed are <u>you</u> that hunger <u>now</u>, for you shall be satisfied (Mt 5:6; Lk 6:21a).

[15] One sees more clearly the ecclesiastical nature and meaning of Luke's use of eating as Jesus celebrates the Passover meal with his disciples, makes himself known to the disciples through the

Conclusion

To be sure, the examples of Lukan themes that Luke has utilized and developed through his use of Matthew are, at this stage, just that — examples. Only the tip of the iceberg may be seen and there is a definite need for much more research than can be attempted in the present book. Two conclusions, however, are worthy of note. First, many of the themes that Luke intends to stress are set forth clearly at the beginning of his Gospel (Lk 1-2). From that point onwards, they are consistently developed. They reappear in the scene of Jesus' baptism, the Temptation, the inaugural address, the first sermon to disciples, and so on throughout the Gospel. They continue on in Luke's depiction of the activities of the disciples in Acts. This means that a careful study of Lk 1-2 is crucial for an understanding of Luke's entire two-part narrative. Thus considered, we may better understand why Luke would feel impelled to revise Matthew' s first two chapters. Second, it is equally clear that Luke is an author quite at home in a Hellenistic environment, and the use of his sources demonstrates beautifully how an author of the first century could make use of a source for the benefit of his own literary purposes.

"words of institution" in the Emmaus story, and is later celebrated in the Eucharist table fellowship practiced by the church in Acts (Lk 22:7-30; 24:30-31, 43; Acts 2:42, 46; 10:9-16, 28; 11:1-18; 27:33-38).

Key to the Component Parts of Our Compositional Analysis of Luke

Our compositional analysis is based upon certain broad divisions of the first "book" containing the Gospel of Luke. These large divisions we have named Parts, within some of which are Sections. Each Section contains two or more pericopes. Each pericope contains a narrative summary followed by a compositional analysis. When necessary, we have provided Synopses and Excurses.

Parts

We consider Parts to be major divisions of Luke's two "books." In the first third of the Gospel, each Part is focused on one or two major events. Part Five is the Travel Narrative containing a series of edifying scenes. Parts Six and Seven divide Luke's Passion Narrative. We have divided the Gospel of Luke into seven Parts. Each Part begins with a brief Overview explaining what it is we think that connects all of the sections and pericopes in it.

Sections

At times, we have found it necessary to divide larger Parts into smaller Sections, made up of two or more pericopes. In Parts One through Four and Five through Seven, we precede each Section with a brief introduction setting forth our reasons for seeing the pericopes in question as belonging to this Section. In Part Five, the Travel Narrative, Luke's compositional and source-critical operations are more complex. In this Part we have placed an Overview at the beginning of each Section followed by Source-critical Observations.

Pericopes

Each pericope is composed of five elements:

The number of the pericope (these are our numbers).

The title of the pericope (again, these are our formulations).

Matthean parallel(s) to Luke's pericope.

On the left side of the line under the pericope title are the Matthean parallels that we will discuss within the Compositional Analysis for that pericope. References in parentheses are to units in Matthew that are not in Matthew's order. Parallels that are in their original order and also are in Luke's sequence are followed by a ===>. Lukan doublets are indicated in parentheses on the right side of the same line.

Narrative paraphrase

Directly under the line containing the Gospel references is a paragraph in san-serif type that is an interpretive paraphrase of the contents of the pericope. It has three purposes.

First, it recalls the contents of the pericope for the reader without necessarily relying on any particular English translation.

Second, our pericopes are often divided in ways that do not conform to any text currently in use. Our divisions are based upon our source-critical and compositional analyses. The narrative paraphrase that precedes them is a way to elicit the dramatic coherence of our (usually larger) pericopes.

Third, by rehearsing each pericope in a lively way, it is hoped that the reader will experience on the affective level the skill contained in Luke's composition of each account. (For an idea of Luke's goals and methods, see the discussion of "How to Write History" above, p. 32.)

These narrative summary paragraphs are set up in a different typeface so that the reader can move easily from one pericope to the next, to get a better impression of the dramatic flow *across* a number of Luke's scenes.

Compositional analysis

General observations. Each compositional analysis begins with General Observations of a source-critical nature. This paragraph first identifies where Luke is with respect to Matthew's general order of pericopes; whether he is following Matthew's order closely or loosely. Next it gives an overview of the main changes Luke has made in the Matthean source at this point. This discussion prepares the way for the detailed consideration of verses, which comes next.

Verse-by-verse observations. The body of the compositional analysis is comprised of verse-by-verse annotations introduced by the chapter and verse number in **bold text.** If there are further annotations *within* a discussion of a specific verse (or group of verses), these are set off by a •. In our analyses, we have adopted the following conventions: "Luke" and "Matthew" mean the *author* or final composer of each Gospel, while "Lk" and "Mt" refer to the *text*. The possessive forms are not as felicitous: "Mt's" and "Lk's"; they likewise refer to the *text*. The adjective "Matthean" ("Mthean" was unthinkable) when used by us, also refers to the *text*.

Synopses

We have provided synopses to clarify our compositional analyses where necessary. We considered collecting all of our synopses together and putting them in one place in the Appendix, but decided against it. Even the larger ones interrupt the flow of our discussion, they are critical to have *in situ* where the reader can look at them while reading our annotations. The main *raison d'être* of each synopsis is that no currently available synopsis enables the reader to quickly see the evidence we discuss in our source-critical arguments.

Excursus

Occasionally, we have inserted extended clarifications or Excursus in our compositional analysis that explain important features transcending or falling within Sections, or that elaborate upon Lukan themes or basic concepts.

Interwoven transitional units

We discovered that Luke carefully wove together the endings and beginnings of his stories, to create overlapping, interlocking pericopes and sections. In this way, he made the transitions from one part of his narrative to the next smooth and graceful (cf. the instructions of Lucian of Samosata, "How to Write History," above p. 32). We have identified these interwoven, transitional units as such, and—even though they themselves are unified narrative scenes or a series of scenes—we have usually split them in half, so that each half of a transitional unit falls within the Parts or Sections they weave together.

COMPOSITIONAL ANALYSIS OF THE GOSPEL OF LUKE

ACCORDING TO THE

TWO GOSPEL HYPOTHESIS

PART ONE LK 1:1–2:52

JOHN THE BAPTIST AND JESUS OF NAZARETH

Overview

Our attempt is to understand the compositional development of Lk 1:1-2:52 presupposing the Two Gospel Hypothesis, namely, that Luke has Matthew before him when he undertakes his writing. Even though Luke 1-2 cannot be placed in parallel with Matthew 1-2 pericope by pericope, the differences in the introductory sections of these two Gospels do not necessarily preclude contact one with another. From the standpoint of genre criticism, an author need not duplicate a source in order to be influenced by it, especially in the preliminary sections of his narrative.

Parallels Between Matthew 1-2 and Luke 1-2

Matthew	Luke
1. Mary and Joseph will serve as parents for Jesus (1:16, 18-20, 24; 2:11, 13, 19)	1. Mary and Joseph will serve as parents for Jesus (1:27-56; 2:4-5, 16, 19, 34)
2. Joseph is betrothed to Mary (1:18)	2. Joseph is betrothed to Mary (1:27; 2:5; cf. 1:35)
3. Virginity of Mary (1:18, 23)	3. Virginity of Mary (1:27, 34)
4. Conception by Holy Spirit (1:18, 20)	4. Conception by Holy Spirit (1:35)
5. Jesus' family is from the line of David (1:1, 6, 17, 20)	5. Jesus' family is from the line of David (1:27, 32, 69; 2:4, 11)
6. Angelic annunciation (1:20)	6. Angelic annunciation (1:30)
7. Child's name given (1:21)	7. Child's name given (1:13, 31; 2:21)
8. Jesus as Savior (1:21)	8. Jesus as Savior (2:11)
9. Child visited (2:11)	9. Child visited (2:16)
10. Visitors worship (2:2, 11)	10. Visitors worship (cf. 2:20)
11. Jesus is born in Bethlehem (2:1, 5, 6)	11. Jesus is born in Bethlehem (2:4, 15)
12. Herod is King (2:1)	12. Herod is King (1:5)
13. There is "great joy" (2:10)	13. There is "great joy" (1:14; 2:10)
14. Use of "righteous" (1:19)	14. Use of "righteous" (1:6; 2:25)
15. "Fear" (1:20; 2:22)	15. "Fear" (1:12, 13, 29-30, 65; 2:9)
16. Abraham (1:1-2, 17)	16. Abraham (1:55, 73)
17. Family's hometown is Nazareth (2:23)	17. Family's hometown is Nazareth (1:26; 2:4, 39, 51)
18. Genealogy (1:1-17)	18. Genealogy (cf. 3:23-38)

Although Luke's narrative account of Jesus' birth and infancy is vastly different from Matthew, the many parallels in the story-line of the first two chapters of both books listed on the previous page may be noted from the outset. Such a list is not offered as proof of our source hypothesis. However, the sheer number of these parallels invites further curiosity as to a possible literary connection. In the following general discussion, we will attempt to illuminate some of these connections.

The Composition of Luke's Birth Narrative

The Literary Setting of the Birth Narrative

In the opening Part of his account of the emergence of the Christian movement, Luke is concerned to provide an appropriate setting for his story. He anchors his story in the history of the people of God and intends to provide, in the setting, a context for certain major developments which will take place later in the story.

As with any other Hellenistic writer giving an account of the story of a particular people, Luke presumes that a pre-determined purpose (βουλή) has manifested itself in their history (cf. Lk 7:29; Acts 2:23; 4:28). Luke alludes to this by referring to "the matters which have been fulfilled among us" (Lk 1:1). This is developed further in the birth and infancy narratives which open with the announcement of an angel to a pious Zechariah. Zechariah's prayer has been heard, and he will shortly have a son (John) who will initiate the time of the fulfillment of God's purposes among his people (Lk 1:12-20). Subsequently, through the devices of visitations by angels, miraculous births, and inspired utterances, the divine purposes within the scriptures for the people of God begin to be brought to fulfillment (Lk 1:32-33, 54-55, 69-79; 2:11, 26, 29-32). In this way, Luke provides the setting for his story.

The Birth Narrative as the Ground for the Later Story

After the birth narrative, Luke's story will unfold through an account of how salvation will arrive through the restoration of Israel and the addition of the Gentiles to the people of God. Luke's procedure will be to highlight the roles of John the Baptist and Jesus as vehicles of this salvation.

Therefore, in alternating passages John the Baptist and Jesus are anointed to be the agents of the announcement of salvation (Lk 3:1-20; 4:14-41). In fulfillment of scripture, John's role was to create a prepared people through bringing them to repentance (Lk 1:16-17). Also, in fulfillment of scripture (Isa 61:1-2; 58:6), Jesus will inaugurate the new era through additional preaching and casting out demons (Lk 4:14-41). Ultimately, the goal of this ministry is for Jesus to occupy the throne of David (Lk 1:33; cf. Acts 2:29-35). Jesus calls disciples and presents the major themes of his kingship to them (Lk 5:1-6:49). John commissions his disciples for mission (Lk 7:18-34). Jesus commissions his disciples twice for mission (Lk 9:1-6; 10:1-16).

Upon the move of Jesus to Jerusalem (Lk 9:51-19:27) as Prophet-King, Jesus is rejected by the city's leaders, but vindicated through resurrection. In fulfillment of scripture, he is enthroned at the right hand of God (Lk 24:44-46, 50-51; Acts 2:29-35; 7:56). From heaven, Jesus bestows his Spirit upon the disciples; and in succession,

Israel is reconstituted, the Samaritans and Gentiles are incorporated into the people of God, and followers of the martyred John and crucified Jesus receive the Spirit (Lk 3:16; Acts 2:1-13, 39; 8:1-25; 10:44-48; 19:1-4). Thus the people of God await the re-appearance of Jesus (Acts 1:6-8; 3:20). This is the story for which Luke furnishes the setting. It highlights the impact of both John and Jesus from beginning to end.

Luke's Principle of Composition

Given the alternating focus on John and Jesus as the agents of the new age of salvation throughout the story, it is no surprise that this should be a central feature of the setting in Lk 1:5-2:52. Indeed, this is the central literary principle that informs the composition of this unit. There is the clearly delineated parallel account of the Annunciations of John and Jesus (Lk 1:5-38). Similarly there are the parallel accounts of the birth, circumcision, naming, and announcement of the future missions of John and Jesus (Lk 1:57-2:39). Indeed, the only other material, the visit of Mary to Elizabeth's house and Jesus to his Father's house, manifests a similar phenomenon of parallelism (Lk 1:39-56; 2:41-52).

The emphasis on Jesus, in the birth accounts, is understandable. However, Luke uses the phenomenon of parallelism to enhance the role of John within salvation history by describing his mission in relationship to the work of Jesus. This enhancement will flower later in the role of John as the one who prepares a repentant people (Lk 3:1-20); who is more than a prophet (Lk 7:26); and the one whose appearance marks off the old age from the new (Lk 16:16). Yet, at the same time, while Luke integrates the mission of John into the account of the new era, he clearly uses the birth account to portray Jesus as the central figure of his Gospel story. John is a prophet of the Most High (Lk 1:76): Jesus is the Son of the Most High (Lk 1:32). Jesus visits his Father's house (Lk 2:41-52): there is no similar development with John. John goes forth in the spirit and power of Elijah (Lk 1:17): Jesus will be taken up into heaven as Elijah (Lk 9:31, 51; 24:50-51). And, above all, Jesus is the Christ, and Elect Son of God (Lk 9:20, 35; 24:26, 46). Given this development of the story, the central emphasis on the alternating persons of John and Jesus, in the Lukan birth account, is effective and understandable.

The Use of Matthew in Lk 1:5-2:52

Luke appears to have had a major compositional goal to reflect the essence of Matthew's account of Jesus' birth in the setting of his story of Jesus' life. First, he stated that he researched earlier accounts from their beginning (παρηκολουθηκότι ἄνωθεν). On our hypothesis, we may infer that Luke had read the birth narrative of his major source, Matthew. This is also evident from a study of Luke's work. In keeping with Luke's stated intent to provide a well-ordered account, Luke furnished the essential data on Jesus' birth noted by Matthew (i.e., born to Mary as a virgin in Bethlehem, etc.; see chart above). Just as Luke would later re-order a considerable amount of Jesus' teaching found in various places in Matthew into his Travel Narrative, so he had no problem with re-ordering Matthew's birth account into a new arrangement. This included omission of some material Luke found in Matthew 1-2 and bringing in other material on the same themes to which Luke had access (see below).

Second, it is, nevertheless, remarkable how much of Matthew 1-2 is echoed in Luke amidst the discernible differences with Matthew. As in Matthew, Luke has a genealogy of Jesus (Lk 3:23-38/Mt 1:1-17). Just as in Matthew, Luke emphasizes the Davidic lineage, but stresses the parallel between Adam and Jesus (both sons of God by direct creation without precedents). Then Luke places his genealogy before the Temptation Narrative as a well-ordered introduction to the testing of God's Son (Lk 4:1-12). Luke 2:1-23 also echoes strongly Mt 1:25 and several places in Mt 2:1-23 in his birth account; indeed, Luke frames his account of Jesus' birth with echoes of Mt 1:25 (Lk 2:7, 21). In both Matthew and Luke, visitors come to see Jesus at his birth (Mt 2:1-12; Lk 2:8-20). In both cases they follow a celestial sign.[1] In Luke the shepherds follow the word of the angels while, in Matthew, the Magi follow a star. Instead of the rich, Luke has shepherds giving honor to Jesus because it befits his theme of Jesus coming to the humble and poor. Luke will eschew carefully throughout his Gospel any idea that Jesus' kingship will pose a direct threat to Rome, and thus Herod's slaughter of the innocents is understandably omitted. Finally, Matthew gives an account of Jesus' family's visit to Egypt and a return to Nazareth (Mt 2:13-23). Apart from a possible perception that such a lengthy trip would be implausible for a woman who had just given birth to a child, Luke does not have Jesus interact with Gentiles nor have them play a major role in his story in any significant sense until after the resurrection. This will come in Acts. According to Luke's account, Jesus is conceived in Nazareth. On the advent of her giving birth Mary goes to Bethlehem with Joseph to pay taxes. The child is born in Bethlehem and grows up in Nazareth in agreement with Matthew's account. Also, true to Matthew, Luke finishes his account with an emphasis on journeys. Luke has two journeys of Jesus' parents: both to Jerusalem (Lk 2:22-39; 2:41-51). Both of these journeys anticipate the later emphasis in the narrative on Jesus going to Jerusalem to claim his kingship (cf. Lk 19:11-40).

Although Luke uses his own compositional agenda in Lk 1:5-2:52 to provide the setting for his narrative, he also demonstrates great respect for the general content of Mt 1:1-2:23 within this section of his narrative.

Organizational "frames" in Part One and Luke's Gospel as a whole

It is important to note the way in which the Annunciation and birth stories have been framed by Luke. John's Annunciation begins with his father, Zechariah, in the temple (Lk 1:5-23). The final portion of Jesus' birth account also has Jesus and his family in the temple (Lk 2:22-40). Luke then added Jesus' visit to the temple at the age of twelve years (Lk 2:41-52). Thus, action in the temple frames the annunciations and the birth stories (Lk 1:5-2:39). It also frames Luke's Part One as a whole (1:5-2:52), which contains the only account of Jesus' youth preserved in the canonical gospels (Lk 2:41-52). Furthermore, Luke's Gospel ends with people in the temple praising God for the coming of the Messiah (Lk 24:53). Between these temple references, Luke has told how the Messiah promised in scripture has come and brought salvation to the people of God. Let us now go on to a detailed consideration of each pericope.

---

[1] John Drury, *Tradition and Design in Luke's Gospel* (London: Darton, Longman & Todd, 1976) 125.

¶ 1. The author's declaration
Lk 1:1-4

The account of Jesus' life begins with a carefully structured prologue. Like the prologues of contemporary Hellenistic-Jewish historical writers such as Philo and Josephus (especially the latter's *Contra Apionem* 1:1-4, 53, 55), this prologue also strongly accents the reliability of the narrative. It alludes to previous works on Jesus' life which were handed down to the time of the writer by reliable eyewitnesses and servants of the word (Lk 1:1-2). Coming to his own work, Luke claims that, having researched these sources, it became necessary for him to write an accurate account in the proper order of these things. The goal of such a work is to enable the reader to know with full assurance the validity of the things that came to pass (Lk 1:3-4).

General observations. Luke is the only canonical Evangelist to introduce his Gospel with a prologue. In form and function, Lk 1:1-4 is similar to other Hellenistic introductions to biographical narratives (e.g., in Philo, Josephus, Plutarch, Suetonius, and Diogenes Laertius).[2]

Matthew opened his account of Jesus with the word, βίβλος (Mt 1:1). Luke understood the literary custom of ancient authors stating their intentions for writing at the beginning of their "books." Accordingly, as with Matthew's βίβλος, Luke formulated a prologue in which he revealed his own intentions (having himself carefully examined the data) to write an account (admittedly not the first) which set forth in order a record of all that has taken place.

Luke was not specific about the particular genre he intended to employ. One notes the absence of genre designators such as "life," "history," "gospel"; or even references to the subject of the narrative (i.e., Jesus or the apostles). This lack of specificity may derive from the fact that this prologue sets the stage not only for the Gospel, but also for the Gospel's sequel, Acts. Luke has written one work in two volumes. Although Acts contains its own prologue, reference is clearly made in Acts 1:1 to the content of Luke's Gospel and, perhaps, to its prologue (τὸν μὲν πρῶτον λόγον). Luke's procedure is similar to that of Philo in his *Vita Mosis* written in two distinct parts (see also the prologue of Josephus, *Contra Apionem,* I, II).

• Grammatically, the prologue falls into two major divisions (Lk 1:1-2; 1:3-4). The major clauses of the two sub-divisions stand in a loose parallel relationship with each other. The reference to the many earlier writers in Lk 1:1 is balanced with a reference to the work of the author in Lk 1:3. And the attention given to the validity and sure transmission of the earlier works (Lk 1:2) is balanced with the claim that the present writer is producing a work to promote full assurance (Lk 1:4).

---

[2] We think this conclusion is generally valid, but see the recent investigation by L. Alexander, *The Preface to Luke's Gospel,* SNTSMS 78 (Cambridge: University Press, 1993).

Lk 1:1. The author speaks of many who have attempted (ἐπιχειρεῖν) to compile (ἀνατάξασθαι) a narrative account of things that have been accomplished among us. The use of ἐπιχειρεῖν can mean either that the author was reacting negatively to his sources (cf. Acts 9:29; 19:13 where the word has this connotation) or that these earlier narrative accounts were the basic models which the author (ἔδοξε κἀμοί) used as prototypes for his work. More than likely there is mild implied criticism of the earlier works. The contrast of καθεξῆς, "in proper sequence" (Lk 1:3), with ἀνατάξασθαι, "to compile" (Lk 1:1), underscores this point. If Luke's sources were somewhat divergent in narrative order (i.e., Matthew and other source material), Luke's careful attention to structure and order makes excellent sense. In contrast to the variant narrative orders of his sources Luke will provide an orderly account (καθεξῆς) to ensure full confidence (ἀσφάλειαν; Lk 1:4) about the truth of the coming of Jesus. This may imply that there was criticism already of Christian faith as being irrational because of the contradictions among the various accounts. Certainly, by the second century, this criticism had become widespread.

Lk 1:2. Luke's sources, despite their plurality and apparent diversity, are to be respected. They are based on the received testimony of "eye-witnesses and ministers" of the word. The use of αὐτόπτης "eye-witness" is a *hapax legomenon* for Luke. But the idea of the resurrection and the acts of God in early Christian history being verified by the testimony of personal witnesses is not unusual for Luke (cf. Acts 2:32; 13:31).

Lk 1:3. As we have noted, Luke claimed to have before him several diverse accounts of the things that happened in the founding of the Christian church. In Lk 1:3, Luke argues that he writes in suitable chronological sequence for a historical account (καθεξῆς) after having investigated these earlier works (παρηκολουθηκότι ἄνωθεν) accurately (ἀκριβῶς). There seems to be little doubt that Luke's use of καθεξῆς to refer to the proper chronological sequence is emphatic. Other appearances of this word in Acts (3:24; 11:4; 18:23) confirm this point. We are not suggesting that Luke claimed that the order of events he narrated in his work was the way they actually happened. Rather, his account is a plausible reconstruction, by a historian who has fully researched his sources, set forth in the manner typical of contemporary historical composition.[3] This would include such vehicles for a historical account as acknowledgment of divine purpose, accounts of amazing things happening at the births of the major protagonists, speeches, narration of journeys, banquet scenes, etc.

The main purpose of Luke's preface is to reassure his audience that the full truth of the scriptural promises (Lk 1:1) will be convincingly explained in his narrative. Luke is a composer, not a compiler who pieces together

[3] Cf. G. Sterling, *Historiography and Self-definition*; *Josephos, Luke-Acts and Apologetic Historiography*, Suppl.Nov.Test. 64 (Leiden: Brill, 1992) 344-346.

diverse accounts. In pursuing this literary and theological agenda, Luke found it necessary to make major changes in the literary order of his chief source Matthew (for a brief overview of Luke's use of Matthew, see above pp. 13–24). The Gospel of Matthew contains large blocks of Jesus' teachings and actions, arranged by subject not historical setting (resembling the Mishnah). Luke is concerned to develop a smooth, cohesive narrative in keeping with the established conventions of writing a historical account.[4]

Lk 1:4. The author brings the prologue to a conclusion with a reference to the λόγοι (cf. τοῦ λόγου in Lk 1:2) or "body of teaching" in which they have been instructed. In the face of doubts that may have emerged because of variations in earlier narratives, Luke's account is designed to set the record straight and provide full confidence (ἀσφάλεια) with respect to the truth of the matter. This use of ἀσφάλεια is a *hapax legomenon* for the Gospel of Luke, but the adjective ἀσφαλής occurs three times in Acts (Acts 21:34; 22:30; and 25:26). Authorial claims to narrative reliability are characteristic of Hellenistic prologues.[5]

EXCURSUS: REASONS FOR LUKE'S PARALLELIZATION OF JOHN AND JESUS

In this Part, Luke gave his account of the births of Jesus and John the Baptist in parallel fashion. In parallel order we find accounts of the Annunciation of John and Jesus and accounts of the births of John and Jesus. Between the Annunciation of John and the Annunciation of Jesus there is a small vignette on the visit of the mother of Jesus to the house of the mother of John. At the close of Part One, the child of Mary will visit "the house of his Father." It is probable that Luke had other traditions which he utilized as the basis of his composition in this Part. Luke's desire to reconcile Matthew's narrative with his nonMatthean tradition, along with his theological and literary concern to parallel the infancies of the major heroes of his narrative, John and Jesus, account for the main differences between Luke and Matthew at this point. Presuming that Luke did use some nonMatthean tradition for Lk 1-2, it appears that he rewrote this material substantially because it is suffused throughout with Lukan linguistic characteristics and constructions.[6]

---

[4] See the discussion of Lucian, *How to Write History*, in the Introduction, pp. 30-33.

[5] Cf. Josephus, *Contra Apionem*, 1.1.47-52; Philo, *Vita Mosis*, 1.4; and Plutarch, *Lycurgus*, 1.3; *Numa*, 1.4.

[6] Cf. J. A. Fitzmyer, *The Gospel According to Luke* (New York: Doubleday, 1981) 1:312; P. S. Minear, "Luke's Use of the Birth Stories," in *Studies in Luke-Acts*, ed. Leander Keck and J. Louis Martyn (Nashville: Abingdon, 1966) 113.

Diagram of Part One

The Annunciation of the Birth of John (Lk 1:5-25) — The Annunciation of the Birth of Jesus (Lk 1:26-38)

Mary Visits Elizabeth's House (Lk 1:39-56)

The Birth, Circumcision, and Disclosure of John's Mission (Lk 1:57-80) — The Birth, Circumcision, and Disclosure of Jesus' Mission (Lk 2:1-40)

Jesus Visits His Father's House (Lk 2:41-52)

Lk 1:57-80 and 2:1-40 have parallel concluding narrative statements (Lk 1:80; 2:40; cf. also Lk 2:52, following Jesus' visit to the temple). The childhood visit to the temple (Lk 2:41-52) in the last section of the chapter serves as a parallel to Mary's Visit to Elizabeth with its focus on Jesus and serves as a literary transition between the birth accounts and the adult ministries of Jesus and John.

The contents of this Part correspond to the rhetorical rules for an encomium; namely, that an author recount things that happen before, during, and after birth, if deemed appropriate.[7]

There are at least two motivating factors behind the structuring of Luke's narrative: (1) the clear delineation of the relationship between John and Jesus and (2) the identification of John and Jesus and their subsequent ministries with God's plan of salvation. Clearly underlying Lukan parallelism in this section is the rhetorical technique of comparison.[8] Similar comparisons in biographical introductions are found in Plutarch's *Lives*. Comparisons based upon similar character, deeds, and vocational accomplishments are especially evident in *Theseus* II.1-2, *Solon and Publicola* II.1, *Demosthenes* III.2-3, *Pericles* II, *Dion* I.1-2, and *Tiberius and Caius Gracchus* II. One notes especially the discussion in *Dion* I.1-2 where the parallels between Dion and Brutus are related to the teachings of Plato (the former having been a "disciple" of Plato). In *Demosthenes* III.2-3, the author notes of Demosthenes and Cicero that "it would seem that the Deity originally fashioned them on the same plan...," so similar are their lives. The parallel accounts of the Annunciations of John and Jesus and their birth narratives demonstrate Luke's focus on the harmony of the two ministries in concert with his presentation of the unfolding of God's plan of salvation. At the same time, the antiphonal progression of the narrative accents the decisiveness of God's action in Jesus, just as the section highlights the young boy's exceptional behavior in the temple, behavior that points forward to what will emerge in Jesus' ministry.

Let us now turn to a detailed examination of the pericopes.

---

[7] Cf. *Rhetorica ad Alexandrum* III-IV; *De Partitione Oratoria* XXI; and Quintilian, *Institutio oratoria* III.7.10-18).

[8] Cf. Aristotle, *Rhetorica*, I.9.20-25 and *Rhet. Alex.* 142a.25-30.

¶ 2. The annunciation of the birth of John
Lk 1:5-25

The author launches immediately into the account of the "things that have been accomplished among us." Luke locates the precise time when the narrated action commences as being the time of the particular political leader who was in control. It is the time of Herod the Great. John's aged parents (Zechariah and Elizabeth) are carefully identified as being of priestly origin and childless. While Zechariah is carrying out his priestly duties in the temple, the angel of the Lord (Gabriel) appears to him. Zechariah is deeply moved and troubled by the divine appearance. However, he is promised that his wife will bear a son and the name of the son will be John. Zechariah will be mute until his birth. The word of Gabriel begins to be fulfilled quickly. Zechariah emerges from the temple unable to speak a word and now back in his house he learns that Elizabeth has become pregnant. In the privacy of her home she reflected wonderingly.

General observations. In this account, Luke emphasized the continuity between John and Jesus. Both are of divine origin with John in concert with Jesus. This continuity is made evident in the parallel visitations by Gabriel to the father of John and mother of Jesus (Lk 1:19, 26). Miraculous divine activity is revealed in both birth accounts and in the angelic words in both stories.

There is no parallel in Matthew to this unit, but there are several echoes of the Matthean account of Jesus' birth (Mt 1:18-24). The angel appeared to the male informing him of the pregnancy of his betrothed under unusual circumstances (Mt 1:20; Lk 1:11, 13). The father of Jesus was told not to fear (Mt 1:20); Zechariah was told not to fear (Lk 1:13; cf. Lk 1:30; 2:10). Goulder (1:208) has also noted a faint echo of Mt 1:18 where Jesus is born ἐκ πνεύματος ἁγίου in Lk 1:15 where it is promised that John will carry out his mission in the power πνεύματος ἁγίου. The unit appears to be Lukan composition.

By far the most dominant factor in the composition of this unit is the theme that, as God has acted powerfully in the history of his people in the past, now He acts again with the Annunciation to Zechariah in the temple. The motif of the barrenness of OT mothers before a divine visit (Sarah, Rebekah, Rachel, the mother of Samson, and especially Hannah who prayed for a child at a temple at Shiloh) serves to prefigure this incident. Through the birth of a child under exceptional circumstances God has again begun to act.

Lk 1:5. Luke's opening phraseology, ἐγένετο + ἐν + a form of ἡμέρα, is characteristic of his composition (Lk 1:5, 59; 2:1; 6:12; 8:22; 17:26, 28; 20:1; Collison 239). The careful attention to the historical circumstances of the account is in keeping with the statement of authorial intention given in Lk 1:1-4.

Lk 1:6. As was Joseph (Mt 1:19), so John's parents are perceived as righteous (δίκαιοι). This terminology will be used for many of the pious throughout Lk (cf. Lk 23:50; Acts 10:22). The use of ἄμεμπτος with δίκαιος is found in I Thess 2:10. It is common Hellenistic terminology to describe a pious person (cf. Phil 2:15; 3:6).

Lk 1:9. Luke prepared for the visitation of Gabriel to Zechariah by stating that Zechariah was serving in the Temple, so the theme of the temple which is important for Luke is introduced at the outset.

Lk 1:10. The phrase πᾶς τὸ πλῆθος τοῦ λαοῦ (7 times in Luke-Acts) is a Lukan linguistic characteristic (Collison 174; Goulder 2:807) providing evidence that Luke has shaped this account.

Lk 1:13. εἶπεν δὲ πρός is the first use of πρός with a verb of saying. This is one of the most dominant characteristics of the text of Luke. It appears over 150 times in Luke-Acts and not at all in Matthew (Collison 9-10, 145).

Lk 1:14-17. The words for joy (χαρά and ἀγαλλίασις) are found throughout Luke-Acts as reactions to the coming of the new age. In these verses the role of John is stated in conscious imitation of language drawn from the LXX (cf. the use of ἐπιστρέφειν to describe John's role in bringing repentance in Lk 1:16-17).

Lk 1:17. The most interesting terminology for our purposes is John's description as one who will "make ready for the Lord a prepared people" (Lk 1:17). The language seems to echo both Mal 3:1 and Isa 40:3. For Luke, John is not Elijah returned. Rather, John is one who goes in the power *and spirit* of Elijah (cf. Lk 7:26-28) to gather the people for the coming of the Messiah.

Lk 1:19. The term εὐαγγελίζεσθαι is a linguistic characteristic of the author of Luke (Collison 51). This is further evidence that Luke has shaped this account.

Lk 1:22. The use of the periphrastic imperfect (ἦν διανεύων) is characteristic of the text of Luke (Collison 73).

¶ 3. The annunciation of the birth of Jesus

(Mt 1:18-24) **Lk 1:26-38**

In striking parallelism to the Annunciation to the aged Zechariah, the angel Gabriel makes a second appearance; this time it is to a virgin, Mary, who is betrothed to Joseph. The appearance is not in the temple, but at her lowly home in Nazareth. As with Zechariah, the presence of the angel deeply disturbs Mary. She is told to be calm. She learns that she is highly favored and that she will conceive and bear a son. Again, as with Zechariah, she is told the name to give her son and something of his future greatness. Jesus' future greatness, however, will far exceed that of John. Again, with the Annunciation to Zechariah, Mary is given a two-fold promise. She will conceive, even as a virgin, and she will find her aged kinswoman, Elizabeth, pregnant.

General observations. The essence of the Matthean account of the Annunciation (Mt 1:18-24) was taken over by Luke. Luke split Mt 1:18-25 by considerably expanding Mt 1:18-24 in Lk 1:26-38 and Mt 1:25 in Lk 2:1-20. Luke's use of Matthew here included Mary's betrothal to Joseph whose family lineage is from the house of David. There is the injunction by the angel not "to fear." In both Matthew and Luke we are told specifically that Mary is a virgin and will conceive through the power of the Holy Spirit. In both texts the parent is told to call the name of the son "Jesus." The major difference is that in Matthew the angel appeared to Joseph while in Luke the appearance was to the betrothed virgin Mary. The prominence of the father figure in the natural family is characteristic of the Christian-Jewish Gospel Matthew (cf. Mt 5:31). However, in Luke the central focus of the Annunciation was to highlight the virgin birth to a poor woman of humble estate. This is an early instance of what will become a major theme in Luke: the concern for the vindication of the poor (cf. Lk 1:51-52; 2:7, 8-18, 24; 4:18; 6:20; 16:19-31).

Lk 1:26. Analogous to Lk 1:5 Luke was careful to give the circumstances and location of the appearance of Gabriel. It is in the sixth month of Elizabeth's pregnancy and it takes place at Nazareth. This is Luke's literary reworking of the staid account of Mt 1:18, "The birth of Jesus Christ was this way."

Lk 1:27. In the two-fold reference to Mary as a virgin (παρθένος), Luke omitted Matthew's direct quotation from Isa 7:14 (Mt 1:22-23). Although he is definitely interested in the theme of prophecy and fulfillment, Luke will employ it narratively in his own manner, only occasionally taking over Matthew's extensive prophecy–fulfillment passages. However, Luke does echo the Matthean account of Jesus' genealogy by saying that Mary's betrothed (Joseph) was of the house of David (Mt 1:1-17). In Lk 1:32 Gabriel assures Mary that God will place Jesus on the throne of David. This is a major theme throughout the infancy account (Lk 1:69; 2:4; 2:11; cf. Lk 3:31). Be that as it may, for Luke, the true meaning of the promises of Scripture for the future glory of the occupant of David's throne are more universal, being ultimately fulfilled in the resurrection and ascension of Jesus (Acts 2:30; 13:34-37; 15:16) and the mission of the Church.

Lk 1:31. Luke's use of τίκτειν (Isa 7:14 LXX) echoes Matthew's use of Isa 7:14 (Mt 1:21-23). Luke also used συλλαμβάνειν. Four out of the seven Lukan usages of συλλαμβάνειν occur in the birth narratives (Lk 1:24; 1:31; 1:36; 2:21). Collison 65 considers that this is a probable linguistic usage of "other source-material" of Luke. In our judgment it is more likely to be Luke's own composition.

Lk 1:32. Jesus will be called μέγας ("great") as John was in Lk 1:15. Jesus is also called both a son of the highest (ὕψιστος Lk 1:35, 76) and a son of God. The term "the highest" is a divine title in the LXX (Gen 14:18; Num 24:16).

It occurs regularly in the Lukan birth narratives (Lk 1:32, 35, 76, 2:14). Among the Gentiles, it functioned as a general term for the deity.[9] This general acknowledgment of monotheism is typical of Luke. The two titles ("the highest" and "Son of God") are linked together in a fragmentary Qumran passage that anticipates the restoration of a Davidic ruler (4Q Ps Dan A^2 2:1). In Lk 1:76, John is called a prophet of the highest. Thus, Jesus functions as a son while John functions as a prophet before God. The primary focus on Jesus is protected.

Lk 1:35. John will be filled with the Spirit from his mother's womb (Lk 1:15). In an even greater act of power, Jesus will be conceived by the agency of the Spirit (Lk 1:35).

¶ 4. Mary visits Elizabeth's house
Lk 1:39-56

Mary comes to visit the house of Zechariah and Elizabeth. In a touching scene the expectant mothers, Mary and Elizabeth, visit with one another. When they meet, Elizabeth's baby leaps within her womb and she is filled with the "Holy Spirit." John's recognition of Jesus, even in the womb, is a fulfillment of Lk 1:15. Elizabeth praises Mary in elevated terms. But ignoring the compliment, Mary bursts forth in a song of praise to God highlighting the future accomplishments of the child she still carries in her womb.

General observations. This pericope falls into two parts: (1) the prose narrative of the visit of the two expectant mothers (Lk 1:39-45), and (2) the glorious *Magnificat,* or Song of Mary, on the future greatness of Mary's child (Lk 1:46-55). The latter is set in poetical form. The prose narrative is suffused with literary features characteristic of the text of Luke. It seems to be Lukan composition which sets the scene for the poem. Luke may have found the poem in source material other than Matthew. Normally, the fact that there is a sparse amount of terminology characteristic of the text of Luke in the *Magnificat* would lead to the conclusion that it comes from nonMatthean tradition. However, Luke could have composed it himself, by drawing together terminology from the Septuagint (e.g., Lk 19:42-44; 21:20-26). On balance, we are inclined to say that Luke used other tradition for the composition of Lk 1:47-55.[10]

Lk 1:39-41a. There is good evidence here for Lukan compositional activity. Ἀνθιστάναι is a Lukan linguistic characteristic (Collison 37). Pleonastic ἀνίστημι, used with another verb has been recognized as characteristic of

[9] Cf. A.D. Nock, *Essays on Religion and the Ancient World,* ed. Zeph Stewart (Cambridge: Harvard University Press, 1972) 1:425.

[10] Cf. R. Brown, *The Birth of the Messiah; A Commentary on the Infancy Narratives in Matthew and Luke* (New York: Doubleday, 1977) 350-355, 364, who suggests that the Magnificat came from a circle of Christian Jews.

the text of Luke since Hawkins.[11] Likewise, ἐν ταῖς ἡμέραις ταυταῖς (Goulder 2:804); πορεύεσθαι with εἰς (Collison 61); and πόλις (Goulder 2:807). There is terminology similar to Lk 1:40a in redactional passages at Lk 9:12, 51, 56, and 17:11; 22:39; 24:13. Finally in Lk 1:41a καὶ ἐγένετο ὡς (a characteristic of the text of Luke) is repeated in the infancy account in Lk 1:23 and 2:15 and thus is characteristic of the infancy account.

Lk 1:41b-45. This material is the Lukan analogue to the introduction of Elizabeth in Lk 1:23-25. In both instances the action takes place in Zechariah's house. However, in Lk 1:41-45 Mary is clearly the prominent figure who receives honor from God.

Lk 1:46-55. Mary's song may have a Lukan analogue in Elizabeth's song at Lk 1:25. Luke has taken Hannah as the prefigurement of Mary. After Hannah was given a child in 1 Sam 1, she burst forth in a song of praise in 1 Sam 2. It starts out "My heart exults in the Lord..." In 1 Sam 1:11 (1 Kgdms LXX), Hannah had prayed, ἐπιβλέψης ἐπὶ τὴν ταπείνωσιν τῆς δούλης σου, asking God to give her a son whom she would dedicate totally to the Lord. Mary, in Lk 1:48, praises God because ἐπέβλεψεν ἐπὶ τὴν ταιπείνωσιν τῆς δούλης αὐτοῦ.

• The focus of the *Magnificat* is upon God (Lk 1:46-47, 49) who has done (and will do) great things for His people. He has shown his strength by scattering the proud, putting down the mighty, and exalting the lowly (Lk 1:51-52). He has fed the hungry and helped his servant, Israel (Lk 1:53-54). God is said by Mary to be "my Savior" (Lk 1:47), and Mary affirms that He will do all of this through the child now being carried in her womb.

• Many have noted that the *Magnificat* seems to be a mosaic of Psalms and other OT texts. However, it is equally important to note the close correspondence between the *Magnificat* and Jesus' inaugural sermon in Nazareth (Lk 4:16b-30), a correspondence that finds further development in Luke's Sermon on the Plain (Lk 6:20-49) and the accounts of the Rich Man and Lazarus (Lk 16:19-31). For example, Lk 1:52-53 contains a reversal of circumstances similar to that found in Luke's record of Jesus' sermons. The "Mighty" will be put down from their thrones and those exalted will be the ones of "low degree" (Lk 1:52). The hungry will be filled and the rich will be sent away (Lk 1:53). This may be compared with "blessed are you poor, for yours is the kingdom of God" (Lk 6:20b) and contrasted with "woe to you that are rich, for you have received your consolation" (Lk 6:24). Or, "blessed are you that hunger now, for you shall be satisfied" (Lk 6:21) contrasted with "woe to you that are full now, for you will hunger" (Lk 6:25). That God will reverse the fortunes of the rich and the powerful who are associated with evil is the proclamation of Jesus that is signaled in the *Magnificat*.

---

[11] Cf. *Horae Synopticae; Contributions to the Study of the Synoptic Problem* (Oxford: Clarendon Press, 2d ed. 1909) 35-36.

To repeat, this introductory section of Luke's Gospel was clearly constructed so as to prefigure many of the most important features of Luke's adult portrait of Jesus. Out of this setting, given in the song of Jesus' mother, Luke will develop an account of the constant presence and work of God moving to accomplish His salvific purposes.

• There is a notable absence of Lukan linguistic characteristics in this poem. Even allowing for the fact that the author consciously appropriates terminology from the LXX, it would seem that the paucity of Lukan linguistic characteristics indicates that Luke has used a Christian-Jewish tradition at this point.

Lk 1:56. The last verse in the unit is Lukan composition. It simply states that Mary returned to her home (in Nazareth). Luke's use of ὑποστρέφειν εἰς is a characteristic linguistic expression of the author (Collison 67). Collison 146 lists the use of σύν here as a characteristic of Luke's other source-material. However, in the same entry he notes that σύν is a Lukan vocabulary item. We consider the use here to be part of Luke's composition of this verse.

¶ 5. The birth, circumcision, and disclosure of John's mission Lk 1:57-80

John's birth occurs with great joy. In keeping with covenantal obligations John is circumcised on the eighth day after birth and, in keeping with the earlier prophecy, his father regained the power of speech after his son was given the name of John. Upon the naming of John his father bursts forth in a song (the *Benedictus*) which discloses the Son's future role in Israel. God is praised because, in the coming of John, he is again visiting his people. His visitation is to bring fulfillment of the Abrahamic covenant through the deliverance of Israel from her enemies. It is disclosed that John initiates the deliverance through his gathering of a repentant people who will be ready to serve God through worship and thus receive salvation upon the advent of the Messiah.

General observations. As with the previous unit, this one is divided into two distinct divisions. First, there is the prose account of the attendant events surrounding the birth of John (Lk 1:57-66). The generous number of Lukan vocabulary items and linguistic expressions indicate that, in its present form, this is Lukan composition. Luke has provided the setting for the song. Second, there is Zechariah's song of praise. This functions as a disclosure of the impact of John's mission (Lk 1:67-79). This unit, like the *Magnificat*, has fewer Lukan linguistic characteristics. However, even though it could have functioned independently as a hymn in early Palestinian Christianity, when incorporated into the narrative, it carries theological freight that is totally resonant with Luke's theological agenda (see below at Lk 1:68).

While there are no parallels to the account of John's birth in synoptic traditions (other than the parallel Luke drew with Jesus' birth), there are striking parallels between the birth of Isaac and that of John. Both mothers, Sarah and Elizabeth, are in their advanced years and barren when they conceive. When their time was fulfilled to "bear," they give birth to a "son" (cf. Gen 21:1f. and Lk 1:57). In both instances, others "heard" and "rejoiced" with the respective mothers (cf. the use of forms of ἀκούειν and συγχαίρειν in Gen 21:6 [LXX] and Lk 1:58), and both sons are circumcised on the eighth day (Gen 21:4//Lk 1:59). Also, the giving of the names has divine origin (καὶ καλέσεις τὸ ὄνομα αὐτού... Gen 17:19 [LXX] and Lk 1:13; cf. also Gen 21:3 and Lk 1:60, 63).

Lk 1:57. The use of πιμπλάναι is characteristic of the text of Luke (Goulder 2:807). Collison 60, however, considers it highly probable it is characteristic of Luke's "other source-material". Its widespread and distinctive occurrence throughout Luke-Acts in various literary settings (22 times in Luke-Acts, twice in Matthew, and nowhere else in the NT) leads us to the conclusion that this term is characteristic of the author of Luke-Acts. Also, the use of χρόνος is a probable linguistic characteristic of the text of Luke (Collison 178).

Lk 1:58. The theme of joy (μεγαλύνειν / συγχαίρειν) at the coming of this event is an echo of Lk 1:14, 44, 47, 58 and continues throughout the book (cf. Lk 2:10; 6:23; 19:37; Acts 2:47; 5:41; 10:46). Outbursts of joy upon the fulfillment of eschatological promises is a major theme in Luke-Acts.

Lk 1:59-66. The use of καὶ ἐγένετο (Lk 1:59, 65) is a linguistic characteristic of Luke (Collison 42-43); and in Lk 1:59 it is followed, as in Lk 1:23, by a linguistic connection with a form of ἡμέρα. This seems to be evidence for Lukan compositional activity. The use of τίς + optative with ἄν is Lukan (Collison 209, 100-101). Also, παραχρῆμα is well distributed in Luke (Lk 4:39; 5:25; 8:44, 47, 55; 13:13; 18:43; 19:11; 22:60). Collison 154 regards it as a linguistic usage of Luke. There is considerable evidence of Lukan composition in these verses.

Lk 1:68. The use of ἐπισκέπτεσθαι to describe God's gracious visitation in bringing salvation to both Israel and the Gentiles is the first instance of a Lukan theological theme that emerges in full flower outside the infancy account (cf. Lk 1:68, 78; 7:16; Acts 15:14). The verbal reference to bringing redemption to God's people in Lk 1:68 is already an echo of the *Magnificat* (Lk 1:49, 51). The reference to the hope of redemption (λύτρωσις) with respect to Israel occurs again in Lk 2:38 and at the end of the Gospel. The era of redemption which starts with John will come first to Israel. That the leaders of Israel tragically will reject this salvation is a major theme throughout Luke-Acts.[12] Yet, the promise remains. Luke-Acts expects this redemption, inaugurated at the resurrection and ascension, to be fully

[12] R. C. Tannehill, *The Narrative Unity of Luke-Acts; A Literary Interpretation.* Vol. One: *The Gospel According to Luke* (Philadelphia: Fortress Press, 1986) 1:35-36.

completed in the future (Lk 21:24, 28; cf. Lk 24:21; Acts 1:6; 3:21).

Lk 1:69-72. Σωτηρία in Lk 1:69, 71 is a synonym for redemption in Lk 1:68. The salvation of Israel will entail the restoration of the house of David under the lordship of Jesus (cf. Lk 1:32-33, 71, 77; 2:11; Acts 7:25; 13:22-23; 15:16). This will be a major theme of Luke. As heard by a Gentile reader, the references to salvation would connote an unprecedented time of health and wholeness for the whole world.

Lk 1:70-75. This new era of the restoration of David's throne is also interpreted as a fulfillment of a promise to Abraham that God's people would be delivered in holiness and righteousness from their enemies (Gen 15:13f.; 17:4; 22:16-18; cf. Ps 106:10). Later this promissory text in Genesis (Gen 15:13f.) was interpreted in Acts as fulfilled in the worship of the early Christian community in Jerusalem made possible by the coming of Christ (Acts 7:5-7; cf. Acts 15:16). Luke already anticipates this with the phraseology λατρεύειν αὐτῷ in Lk 1:74.

Lk 1:76-77. John's mission is now synchronized with the events of this new age of salvation. Here John is said to be the prophet of the Most High (1:76). Earlier, Jesus was said to be the Son of the Most High (Lk 1:32; cf. Lk 8:28). The earlier message to Zechariah of "preparing the way" in Lk 1:17 is echoed again in Lk 1:76. The prophecy of Isa 40:3 in preparing a people of repentance by bringing to them a knowledge of salvation and forgiveness of sins is to be fulfilled in the mission of John (Lk 3:1-7; 7:26-27). The reference to ἄφεσις ἁμαρτιῶν is an important theme for Luke to describe the effect of the coming salvation (Lk 3:3; 24:47; Acts 2:38; 5:31; 10:43; 13:38; 26:18).

Lk 1:78-79. The *Benedictus* ends with a return to a description of the glory of the Messiah in this new age. He is described as the ἀνατολή ("The Rising Light" or "Dayspring") from on high. He will bring light to those who sit in darkness. Perhaps this reference to ἀνατολή indicates Lukan recognition of Matthew's account of the coming of the Magi (cf. ἀνατολή in Mt 2:2). In Jer 23:5; Zech 3:8, and 6:12 ἀνατολή is the Greek translation of the Hebrew word for "branch." The Hebrew *Vorlage* appears in a number of places in the Qumran materials as a reference to the restored ruler of the house of David (cf. 4Q Flor 1:11). Probably the idea here is that "The Dayspring from the house of David" will bring full light to the People of Israel by inaugurating a kingship which will bring healing and salvation. This connection between salvation and light is also made by Simeon (Lk 2:30-32). And as Tannehill notes, the light theme is also prominent in the commission of Paul (Acts 13:47; 26:17-18).[13] The reference to peace (Lk 1:79; 2:14; 10:5; 19:38, 42; 24:36; Acts 9:31; 10:36) is also characteristic Lukan terminology for the Messianic era.

[13] Ibid., 1:38.

Lk 1:80. The final summary statement on growth and maturing of the child, John, closes the unit. A similar summary statement, with parallel terminology about Jesus, rounds out the next unit in Lk 2:40.

¶ 6. The Birth, Circumcision, and Disclosure of Jesus' Mission

(Mt 1:25; 2:1-23) **Lk 2:1-40**

According to Luke it is the time of the census organized by Quirinius. Joseph and Mary, following the law of the land, go to the Davidic city of Bethlehem to pay taxes. Jesus is born in Bethlehem under circumstances of great poverty. Instead of a visit by the Magi bringing expensive gifts, as in Matthew, the newly born babe is visited by shepherds. As with the parents of John, Jesus' parents are pictured as humble and pious and deeply concerned to follow the demands of Torah. Mary's child is circumcised on the eighth day; in fulfillment of the prediction of the angel at the time of his conception he is given the name, "Jesus." Furthermore, in keeping with the law, the purification of Mary is accomplished and the presentation of her first-born (emphasized by Luke at his presentation at the temple) is accomplished. The latter provides the basis for two scenes of disclosure of Jesus' mission centering around the prophets Simeon and Anna. First, after Jesus is placed in the arms of the prophet Simeon, Simeon testifies that Jesus will be not only the Savior of Israel, but also the agent who will bring light to the Gentiles. More ominously, the first hint of non-acceptance of Jesus' message in Israel is also given. As the Matthean account ends with Jesus' parents going to Nazareth, likewise, having fulfilled the obligations of the law, Joseph and Mary return to Nazareth with their newly born son.

General observations. Parallels in the two Lukan birth narratives may be summarized in the following manner:

John	Jesus
a. Time arrived (Lk 1:57)	a. Time arrived (Lk 2:6)
b. Birth of a son (Lk 1:57)	b. Birth of a first-born son (Lk 2:7)
c. Zechariah speaks, blessing God (Lk 1:64)	c. Angel speaks/heavenly hosts speak (Lk 2:10-13)
d. Neighbors afraid (Lk 1:65)	d. Shepherds afraid (Lk 2:9)
e. Neighbors lay up in heart (Lk 1:66)	e. Mary ponders in heart (Lk 2:19)
f. Circumcised on eighth day (Lk 1:59)	f. Circumcised on eighth day; origin of name (Lk 2:21)
g. Zechariah filled with Holy Spirit (Lk 1:67)	g. Holy Spirit given to Simeon (Lk 2:25-27)
h. Praised in canticle of Zechariah (Lk 1:68-79)	h. Praised by Simeon and Anna (Lk 2:25-38)
i. Salvation for Israel (Lk 1:68-69)	i. Salvation given for all peoples (Lk 2:31-32)
j. Prepares & goes before the Lord (Lk 1:76)	j. Set for rise & fall of many in Israel (Lk 2:34f.)
k. Child grows, becomes strong (Lk 1:80)	k. Child grows, becomes strong and wise (Lk 2:40, 52)

By means of this set of comparisons one sees both how Luke has compositionally compared his characters in this section and the manner in which he moves the focus decisively from John toward Jesus. Luke has already echoed Mt 1:18-24 in the account of the Annunciation to Mary (Lk 1:39-56). Now Luke composes freely by using Mt 1:25 (echoing Mt 2:1-23) for the composition of this unit. Aside from the free utilization of the text of Matthew we can find no clear evidence that Luke used other traditions in the composition of this unit. Luke has not utilized Matthew's itinerary for the movement of Joseph and Mary in and out of Judea and, therefore, needs a reason for the journey of the family south to Judea.

Lk 2:1. Luke began the unit in a fashion very similar to the opening verse of his narrative story (Lk 1:5) by giving a record of the circumstances prevailing at the time of Jesus' birth. Only, on this occasion we are given the name of the world ruler (Caesar Augustus) rather than the name of a client ruler, Herod. Jesus is more significant than John and his birth will have implications for both Israel and the greater Roman world (cf. Lk 3:6). The verse is clearly compositional: post-positive δέ with ἐγένετο is a typical Lukan characteristic (cf. Lk 2:6; Collison 43); the use of ἡμέρα is a characteristic of the text of Luke (Goulder 2:804); also δόγμα Καίσαρος appears to be Lukan composition (cf. Acts 17:7).

Lk 2:2-5. The enrollment of Quirinius is the device used by Luke to get Joseph and Mary to the city of David. As with Matthew, the birth of Jesus in the city of David is a central feature of the narrative. The use of διὰ τό with the infinitive to express cause is a linguistic characteristic of Luke (Collison 126).

Lk 2:6-7. In the account of the bringing forth of a son (ἔτεκεν τὸν υἱόν) Luke used Mt 1:25a (ἔτεκεν υἱόν). Luke will use Mt 1:25b at the end of the account of the birth of Jesus (Lk 2:21). The reference to the first-born (πρωτότοκος) is a reminder that the right of succession to kingship usually goes to the first-born. There was earlier precedent for this taking place in the household of David (2 Chron 21:3). Luke strengthened a major theme that Jesus was born as heir to the Davidic throne without preserving the Matthean notion that Jesus was perceived to have been a threat to the local Roman-appointed monarch Herod. Indeed, Luke's statement that the child was placed in the manger underscores the point of his birth in powerlessness.

Luke 2:8-12. The reference to shepherds may also be connected with the OT prophecy of the Davidic king being born in Bethlehem and coming to secure and feed his flock (Micah 5:4, 8).

• For Luke, the poor shepherds were more suitable to welcome the savior than Gentiles who brought gifts of great wealth as in Matthew's account. Besides not wishing to have Gentiles skilled in astrology figure so prominently in the story of salvation at this point, the presence of shepherds is a more appropriate accent for the future direction of Jesus' ministry in Luke's Gospel.

• As with previous epiphanies in Luke 1, an angel appears (Lk 2:9). The command not "to fear" (Lk 2:10) also echoes the previous epiphanies (Lk 1:13, 30; cf. Mt 1:20).

• As noted earlier, the use of εὐαγγελίζεσθαι in Lk 2:10 is a favorite Lukan expression (Lk 3:18; 8:1; 16:16; Acts 5:42; 8:25, 40; 10:36; 11:20; 13:32; 14:15; 17:18). The term "great joy" (χαρὰν μεγάλην) expressed by the shepherds directly parallels the reaction of the Magi (Mt 2:10; cf. Goulder 1:247). This is slight evidence that Luke was aware of Matthew's account even though he did not follow it closely.

• The three-fold Christological expression of Jesus as "Savior, Christ, and Lord" in Lk 2:11 is striking. Luke has already used σωτήρ or its cognate, σωτηρία, to describe the anticipated coming redemption of Israel (Lk 1:47, 69, 71, 77). Now the babe in Bethlehem is to be the agent of this redemption. The combination of χριστὸς κύριος is somewhat unusual for Luke (see, however, Acts 2:36). The designation of Jesus as "Messiah - Lord" by the angel is a further statement of the child's appropriate right to become the heir to the Davidic throne. Again, Luke emphasized that this took place in the city of David. This is further affirmation that Jesus came from the line of David.

Lk 2:14. The word of the angelic host (*Gloria in Excelsis*) is strongly echoed at the scene of Jesus' entry into Jerusalem (Lk 19:38). These two texts highlight the element of tragedy explicated in the whole of the Gospel and Acts. The one designated to be Israel's future king and agent of her salvation (Lk 2:14) will be rejected by her leaders when he comes to claim that kingship (Lk 19:38-39). The use of δόξα is a statement of praise and honor for the absolute worth of Jesus (cf. Fitzmyer 1:410). It is an anticipation (cf. Lk 2:9) that Jesus will be the bearer of God's glory as it comes to bear expression later in his life (Lk 9:31; 24:26). Ἐιρήνη appears to be a linguistic characteristic of Luke (cf. Collison 172-173). The anticipation is that God's reign will be universal in heaven and on earth.

Lk 2:15-20. The visit of the shepherds is a major reversal of the visit of the Magi. Instead of exotic foreign men bearing gifts to the child in a house (Matthew), in Luke poor shepherds in Israel come without gifts to a child who was placed in an animal feeding trough. The emphasis on the humble circumstances of Jesus is a major theme of Luke (cf. Lk 4:18; 6:20; 7:22; 14:13, 21; 16:22; 18:22; 19:8; 21:3).

• As a Lukan composition, the passage has numerous Lukan linguistic usages. Especially noteworthy is the terminology in Lk 2:15 καὶ ἐγένετο ὡς (Collison 42, 121; cf. Lk 2:1, 6); βρέφος (Lk 2:16) to describe the child is characteristic of the text of Luke (Goulder 2:801); and ὑποστρέφειν in Lk 2:20 is a Lukan vocabulary item (Collison 67).

Lk 2:21. In Lk 2:21a (καὶ ἐκλήθη τὸ ὄνομα αὐτοῦ Ἰησοῦς) Luke clearly echoed Mt 1:25b (καὶ ἐκάλεσεν τὸ ὄνομα αὐτοῦ Ἰησοῦς). Luke has used Mt 1:25 as an *inclusio* around the birth account (Lk 2:7, 21). The rest of the verse appears to be mainly Lukan composition. Three characteristics of the text of Luke (πιμπλάναι, Collison 60, and Goulder 2:807; συλλαμβάνειν,

Collison 65; κοιλία Goulder, 2:805) appear in the same verse. The general thrust of the use of πιμπλάναi is to form an *inclusio* around the birth account which is highlighted by the visit of the shepherds (Lk 2:6, 21).

Lk 2:22-24. The thrust of this section of Luke's composition is to emphasize that Joseph and Mary were pious and devout persons who acted fully in keeping with the traditions of the faith of Israel. Note again the appearance of πιμπλάναι in Lk 2:22. With the use of κατά τὸ νόμον, another *inclusio* (Lk 2:22, 39) is created in this chapter. This *inclusio* sets apart and highlights the presentation of Jesus at the temple.

Lk 2:25-35. After John's birth and circumcision, his role in God's plan is disclosed by Zechariah in the *Benedictus* (Lk 1:67-79). Now, in parallel fashion, Jesus' future role is disclosed by the actions of the prophet Simeon.

• Simeon is described as a man δίκαιος and εὐλαβής (cf. Lk 1:6). This also anticipates Luke's description of another pious man, Joseph of Arimathea, who, at the end of the narrative in Lk 23:50-51 is described as ἀγαθὸς καὶ δίκαιος. Simeon awaited (προσδέχεσθαι) the consolation (i.e., vindication) of Israel. Likewise, Joseph of Arimathea awaited (προσδέχεσθαι) the kingdom of God (Lk 23:51). This deliberate structuring, utilization of phrases, and grammatical patterns occurring elsewhere in the Gospel indicate to us evidence of Luke's compositional techniques as a historian.

• χρηματίζειν is also found in Acts 10:22 in the sense of receiving revelation from God. It is used in a different sense in Acts 11:26. It can hardly be called a Lukan linguistic characteristic. Perhaps this is a Lukan echo of Mt 2:12, 22.

• The use of εὐλογεῖν τὸν θεόν in Lk 2:28 (cf. Lk 2:34) is possibly Lukan (Lk 1:64; 24:53; cf. Lk 1:68). Simeon, in anticipation of Jesus' future ministry praises God at the temple. At the end of the narrative, people praise God in the temple for the coming of the Messiah (Lk 24:53).

• It is difficult to say whether or not the *Nunc Dimittis* (Lk 2:29-32), along with the *Magnificat* and *Benedictus*, was in Luke's nonMatthean tradition. It has a moderate amount of Lukan linguistic terminology (τὸ ῥῆμα [Collison 176-77]; εἰρήνη [Collison 172-73]; σωτηρία [ten times in Luke-Acts and no occurrences in Mark or Matthew]; πᾶς/ἅπας ὁ λάος [sixteen times in Lk-Acts and listed by Goulder 2:807 as a characteristic of the text of Luke]). But these vocabulary items appear to be mainly a pastiche of phrases taken from Second Isaiah (LXX), that could have come from a source or have been composed by Luke himself. Most important is that in Lk 2:31, 32, we are given the first strong indication that Jesus' impact will not only bring to the people of God (Israel) salvation, but will incorporate the Gentiles in God's salvation as well (Lk 24:47; Acts 11:1, 18; 13:47 [where the light imagery of Isa 49:6 reemerges]; 28:28).

• Along with the good news of the arrival of the blessings of the Messianic era to both Israel and the Gentiles is the sober note to Mary that Jesus is set for "the fall...of many in Israel and as a sign provoking their opposition" (Lk 2:34). This is an anticipation of the major theme of the rejection of Jesus by the leaders of Israel (cf. Lk 13:33-35; 19:41-44; 21:20-24; 23:27-31; Acts 2:23; 3:13-15; 4:10-11; 13:27-29; 28:23-28). Indeed, this rejection, as a sword bringing to light the opposition to Jesus, would pierce the very heart of his mother (Lk 2:35). Perhaps this is the Lukan echo of Mt 2:13-18, the Massacre of the Innocents.

Lk 2:36-38. The introduction of Anna does not add much information to the disclosure of Jesus' future mission. Her pairing with Simeon is a feature of Lukan style where the action of a male and female are paired (e.g., the pairing of Zechariah and Elizabeth [also a minor role] in Lk 1:5-25; cf. 7:1-17; 15:3-10).

Lk 2:39. Luke has substituted a visit of the shepherds for the Matthean account of the visit of the Magi (Lk 2:8-20/Mt 2:1-12); and he has substituted a journey to Jerusalem involving the presentation of Jesus at the temple and the disclosure of Jesus' future universal mission by Simeon and Anna for the Matthean account of the journey into Egypt (Lk 2:22-39/Mt 2:13-21). At Lk 2:39a (as noted above), Luke delimits the end of an *inclusio* by introducing the words κατὰ τὸν νόμον κυρίου (cf. the beginning of the *inclusio* at Lk 2:22). The terminology also in Lk 2:39a ἐτέλεσεν πάντα sounds very much like the great formulaic statements ("and when Jesus finished all these things") at the end of Matthew's Discourses (Mt 7:28; 11:1; 13:53; 19:1; 26:1). Luke prefers ἐπιστρέφειν to the Matthean ἀναχωρεῖν, and Lk 2:39 echoes Mt 2:22b-23. At any rate, at Lk 2:39b Luke clearly echoed Mt. 2:22b-23 as the source for his composition. Indeed, the two-fold expression εἰς τὴν Γαλιλαίαν and εἰς πόλιν ἑαυτῶν Ναζαρέθ in Lk 2:39 echo εἰς τὰ μέρη τῆς Γαλιλαίας and εἰς πόλιν λεγομένην Ναζαρέτ in Mt 2:22-23. All of these features of Luke's text support the hypothesis of Luke's use of Mt 2:22-23 at Lk 2:39.

Lk 2:40. Just as the account of John's birth and disclosure of mission ends with a summary statement about the child growing and becoming strong in the Spirit, so Jesus is said to grow and become strong in wisdom. The reference to wisdom anticipates Jesus' actions in the temple in the next unit (Lk 2:41-52).

¶ 7. Jesus visits his father's house
Lk 2:41-52

When Jesus is twelve years old, he goes with his parents, as is their custom, to the temple in Jerusalem at the feast of Passover. The parents become separated from Jesus and begin their journey home thinking that he is with other relatives. After a day's travel, he is missed. They look for him unsuccessfully among their relatives and friends and find it necessary to return to Jerusalem to continue the search. Eventually, they find him in the temple with the teachers, listening to them and asking them questions. This scene depicts a typical student-teacher relationship that would be appropriate in either a Jewish or non-Jewish, Hellenistic setting. Here, Jesus excels. He is the model pupil and his actions impress all who are witnesses to his excellent performance. "All who heard him were amazed at his understanding and his answers." When his parents do find him, they express their anxiety. In response, Jesus offers a puzzling expression that his parents were not yet able to understand: "Did you not know that I must be in my Father's house?" The family then returns home together, and Mary, once more, "ponders these things in her heart."

General observations. This beautiful account, at home in the broad Hellenistic literary environment, is Lukan composition. In it, Luke demonstrates Jesus' excellence at a young age and, through the literary device of anticipation, prepares the reader for a time when Jesus will have numerous occasions to engage religious leaders, both friendly and hostile.

While there are many parallels in Hellenistic βίος literature in which the motif of the child prodigy may be found, perhaps the closest parallel to Luke's depiction of Jesus as a youth appears in Plutarch's *Cicero* II.2:

> ...when he was of an age for taking lessons, his natural talent shone out clear and he won name and fame among the boys, so that their fathers used to visit the schools in order to see Cicero with their own eyes and observe the quickness and intelligence in his studies for which he was extolled, though the ruder ones among them were angry at their sons when they saw them walking with Cicero placed in their midst as a mark of honor.[14]

As Cicero's demonstrated prowess in his studies as a youth serves Plutarch's portrait of Cicero's career as an orator; so Jesus' abilities, exemplified in this scene in the temple at the age of twelve, serve Luke as a prelude to Jesus' messianic career. Jesus' excellence is demonstrated by his command of Torah. This capacity will persist in his adult career and will continue in the lives of those who follow after him in Luke's account of the disciples and apostles in Acts.

Lk 2:41. The son of devout parents, Jesus makes the journey to Jerusalem to keep the Passover. The use of πορεύεσθαι with εἰς occurs 16 times in Luke. This is a Lukan linguistic characteristic (Collison 61) and an indicator of Lukan composition.

Lk 2:42-50. As noted above, the incident in the temple was composed by Luke in keeping with a description of excellence in Hellenistic literature. It functions as the first demonstration that Jesus has grown to enough maturity to recognize the validity of the earlier announcements of his divine origin. As the Son he now comes to claim appropriate recognition in his Father's House (Lk 2:49). He exercises this claim through his skill in

[14] Cf. Philo, *Mos.* I.5.21-23; Josephus, *Vita* 9; Philostratus, *Apol.*, I.7; Plutarch, *Alex.* 5.1.

teaching. The description of the Son's capacities is a vivid expansion of the role of the παῖς in Isa 53:2. We now learn how "the Servant" grew up. Later, in his ministry, he comes again to Jerusalem to claim his Father's house by teaching in the temple precincts (Lk 19:47; 20:1; 21:37). Tragically, the Servant-Son will be rejected by the temple leadership and handed over to Roman soldiers to be put to death.

Lk 2:42, 43. Καὶ ἐγένετο is a Lukan linguistic characteristic (cf. Lk 2:46; Collison 42-43). Collison 67 identifies ὑποστρέφειν in Lk 2:43 as a linguistic usage of Luke (cf. Lk 2:45). This is evidence for Lukan composition.

Lk 2:50, 51. Τὸ ῥῆμα is a linguistic usage of Luke (Collison 176-177). Καί + a form of ἔρχομαι + εἰς with a direct object in Lk 2:51 is well distributed in Luke (Lk 1:23; 2:15; 3:3; 4:16, 31; 5:25; 8:22, 31, 53; 4:1; 15:6; 16:28; 23:42). This is additional evidence of Lukan compositional activity.

Lk 2:52. After the annunciation to Hannah and her song of praise for the faith of Samuel, we learn in 1 Sam 2:26 (1 Kgdms LXX) that the child matured and found favor μετὰ κυρίου καὶ μετὰ ἀνθρώπων. Mary's life had followed a similar path and she has a similar result with her son.

PART TWO LK 3:1–4:16A

THE NEW ERA OF SALVATION ANNOUNCED BY JOHN AND JESUS

Overview

Before the major inaugural event of Jesus' ministry, the presentation of the Sermon in Nazareth (Lk 4:16b-30), Luke gave an account of a series of initial events that provides essential information for understanding Jesus' momentous announcement. As in Part One, Luke used the rhetorical technique of comparison to organize his narrative account. In Lk 3:1-20 the account of the mission of John is given.

In 3:21-4:16 the focus is on Jesus. John's mission is clearly the beginning of the fulfillment of the eschatological promises of Isaiah (Lk 3:4-6). Yet, as promising as the mission of John is, in comparison, it is clearly subsidiary to that of Jesus (Lk 3:16-17). Indeed, Luke went out of his way to demarcate John's mission from Jesus' entrance on the scene. Luke constructed the account of Jesus' baptism in such a way that John appears to be somewhere else, i.e. in prison (Lk 3:19-21). Baptized from Heaven as the Son of God, Jesus goes forth in the power of the Spirit to confront Satan (Lk 4:2-13).

¶ 8. John the Baptist announces that salvation is at hand

Mt 3:1-4 ===> **Lk 3:1-6**

For the benefit of his international audience, Luke situates the appearance of John the Baptist within several local Syrian and Jewish rulerships. He also supplies the overarching Roman imperial dates to specify the beginning of John's mission (cf. Lk 1:5 and 2:1-2). The quotation of John's message (taken from Isa 40:3-5) ends with the declaration: "all flesh shall see the salvation of God!"—an announcement which Jesus will echo when he gives his first sermon in Nazareth.

General observations. Luke is ready to begin the account of the ministry of John. He used the Matthean account as his basic source. Luke's opening verses reveal his intended audience and focus.

Lk 3:1-3a. Instead of Mt's very general statement "in those days" (Mt 3:1), words which indicate that Matthew took it for granted that *his* audience well knew when these things occurred, Luke identified in precise detail the names of the local kings and rulers necessary for readers in foreign lands to ascertain exactly when the events described in Luke's story actually occurred (Lk 3:1-3). Nothing could be a clearer indication of his basic desire to provide an accurate chronology of the events of Jesus' ministry "in order." Luke's account of the setting of John's ministry περίχωρον τοῦ Ἰορδάνου (Lk 3:3) appears to be taken from Mt 3:5. Luke has made this geographical reference the climax of his account of the setting for the beginning of his main story. Luke also used περίχωρος at the end of this part to mark Jesus' transition into Galilee (Lk 4:14). The word is preferred in Lukan composition (Collison 175).

Lk 3:3b-6. Luke selectively followed Mt in using the quote from Isa 40:3, adding Isa 40:4-5 which ends with the significant words quoted above relating to a universal revelation of salvation. Luke thus affirmed that "all flesh" would *see* —in the person and ministry of his Son, Jesus Christ—God's powerful salvation.

• Mt's description of John's strange clothing and lifestyle could have seemed to Luke's non-Jewish audience as detracting from his authoritative portrayal, so Luke omitted those details. Also, Matthew's description of John's clothing came from a description of Elijah (2 Kgs 1:8). Unlike Matthew, for Luke John is not Elijah *redivivus* (cf. Mal 4:5-6; Mt 17:10-13).

¶ 9. John rebukes the Judeans

Mt 3:7-10 ===> **Lk 3:7-9**

In harsh language, John warns the Judean multitudes that their supposed secure status as members of the elect nation of Israel will avail them nothing on Judgment Day because they have been so sinful. They must repent and make amends.

General observations. After providing a more general introduction than Matthew (Mt 3:5-7a/Lk 3:7a) Luke followed Matthew as closely here as anywhere in his entire narrative. On the Two *Source* Hypothesis, this is the first appearance of the hypothetical Q source in Luke. However, no studies of the hypothetical Q source have noticed that numerous characteristic Matthean words and phrases occur here in Luke's account. Goulder (1:13-14, 273-274, 279-280) notes that approximately 20% of the wording in Luke's report of John's proclamation (Lk 3:7-18) consists of words or phrases that are characteristic of Mt. Thus, rather than being evidence that Mt and Lk are here dependent upon another source, we have clear evidence for Luke's direct use of the canonical Gospel of Matthew.

Lk 3:7-9. Especially striking is γεννήματα ἐχιδνῶν (Mt 3:7//Lk 3:7) which only occurs here, at Mt 12:34 and at Mt 23:33 within the Synoptic Gospels. Similarly, the combination of ἐκκόπτειν with βάλλειν (Lk 3:9//Mt 3:10) followed by a reference to "fire" is also a Matthean characteristic (cf. Mt 7:19 and Tevis, Display 224). Again, the term "good fruit" (vs. "evil fruit") is a favorite of Mt (9 times), and it occurs only here and at Lk 6:43 in contexts clearly parallel to Mt's order. All of these words and phrases are characteristic Matthean linguistic formulations, and their presence here in parallel passages in Luke and nowhere else in Luke is clear evidence of Luke's direct utilization of the canonical Gospel of Matthew.

• On the other hand, Luke has slightly altered his Matthean source. His use of ἔλεγεν (Lk 3:7) is a typical Lukan linguistic usage (Collison 55).

Luke (3:8) likes ἄρχομαι plus the infinitive in a pleonastic sense (occurs 22 times; see Collison 39-40). Luke has substituted it for Matthew's δόξητε λέγειν (Mt 3:9).

¶ 10. The crowds ask John what they must do
Lk 3:10-14

Stricken by his words, the crowds ask John what they must do. John gives instructions to three groups of people: those who have enough to help the poor, the tax collectors, and the soldiers. To each John gives specific instructions on how to make amends.

General observations. This short passage has no parallel in Mt. However, it is doubtful that Luke drew upon a nonMatthean source for this segment of his narrative. We assume this is Lukan composition. There may be a structural motivation underlying his account of John addressing crowds, tax gatherers, and soldiers. In Part Three, Jesus also meets crowds (Lk 4:40-41; cf. Lk 3:10-11), then Levi the tax gatherer (Lk 5:27-32; cf. Lk 3:12-13); and a soldier—the centurion (Lk 7:2-10, cf. Lk 3:14). Could Luke have structured John's activity as a parallel to Jesus' ministry?

Lk 3:10-14. The phraseology τί...ποιήσωμεν that Luke used to open and close the unit (Lk 3:10, 14) is one of his favorite phrases (Lk 3:10, 12, 14; Acts 2:37; 4:16; cf. Lk 12:17; 16:3-4; 18:41; 19:48; 20:13. See also Lk 10:25=Lk 18:18).

• The grouping into three may also be characteristic of Luke (Goulder 1:274).

• The emphasis on "doing" closely resembles Luke's emphasis in the conclusion to the Sermon on the Plain (Lk 6:49) and his emphasis at the end of his restructuring of Matthew's Parables chapter (Lk 8:21; cf. also Lk 11:28).

• It is possible that Luke made a special effort to include soldiers in this list. Luke had an interest in the role of Roman soldiers (e.g., Lk 7:2-11; Acts 10:1-48; 22:22-29). At the end of his two-volume work, Paul is portrayed preaching the gospel precisely to soldiers, namely, the elite Praetorian Guard in Rome (cf. Acts 28:16-30).

• Note that although these demands are challenging they are not as stringent as the demands of Jesus. Jesus' true disciple will give away his *one* coat (Lk 6:29) and, in the case of Zacchaeus, he will return four-fold *everything* he has taken fraudulently (Lk 19:1-10, esp. 19:8). In this instance of comparison Jesus also emerges stronger than John.

¶ 11. John insists that he is not the Messiah

Mt 3:11-12 ===> **Lk 3:15-17**

The people are so overcome by John's spiritual authority that they begin to wonder if he might be the long-awaited Messiah sent to redeem Israel. But John warns them that he is not the Messiah. "I merely baptize you with water. The One coming after me will baptize you with the Holy Spirit and with fire!"

General observations. Although Luke resumes following Matthew in the same order at this point, in Lk 3:15 he prefaces his use of Mt 3:11-12 with a brief introduction. The introduction drives home a major Lukan theme: the subordination of John to Jesus.

Lk 3:15. The double use of the genitive absolute is characteristic of Luke (Collison 77-78), as is the use of the optative with indirect questions (Collison 85).

Lk 3:17. Quite astonishing is the appearance of Matthew's "gather his grain into the barn" (Mt 3:12//Lk 3:17). This is a distinctive Matthean phrase (cf. Mt 3:12 and 13:30), as is the use of συνάγειν (see Goulder 1:14). These linguistic characteristics of Mt in the parallel text of Lk are strong evidence that Luke copied from Mt and not a source such as Q.

¶ 12. Herod Antipas throws John in prison

(Mt 4:12a; 14:3) **Lk 3:18-20**

While the people are taking John's words to heart, suddenly Herod Antipas, enraged at John's criticism of his marriage to his brother's wife Herodias (Antipas had secretly had his brother murdered first), seizes John and throws him into prison. John's work as a prophetic messenger is brought rapidly to an end.

General observations. The appearance of this very important little pericope—clearly out of Mt's order at this point—requires an extended explanation on the Two Gospel Hypothesis. The series of parallel vignettes about John the Baptist and Jesus in Lk 1-2, followed by the full report of John's preaching in Lk 3:1-18 comes to an abrupt end here in Lk 3:19f. Why has Luke arranged matters in this way?

Luke is confronted by a series of closely related problems at this precise location in Mt's order of pericopes:

a) In Mt, the beginning of Jesus' ministry (mentioned in Mt 4:12-17) is apparently precipitated by John's imprisonment. To Luke's Hellenistic audience, this would have seemed an improbable, almost accidental way for the Savior of the World to begin his public activity.

b) Jesus is baptized by John in Mt's account (3:13-17). Luke probably omitted this since John's baptism was one of "repentance." Moreover, Jesus' request in Mt that John should baptize him could have seemed to give John too much authority—something Luke regularly avoided.

c) Mt's account leaves unanswered the question, was Jesus originally a disciple of John the Baptist or not? This ambiguity is only heightened when Mt says that after John was imprisoned, Jesus began to preach "repent for the kingdom of heaven is at hand"— precisely the same thing John had been preaching (Mt 4:17; cf. Mt 3:2).

For all these reasons, Luke had to make a number of drastic and closely coordinated modifications in Matthew's narrative. Generally speaking, Luke began with roughly parallel accounts of the two prophets' births; then in the account of John's preaching, Luke had John unequivocally state that he was not worthy to untie Jesus' sandal (much less be his teacher). Luke went on to suppress Mt's account of John's baptism of Jesus, inserting instead a brief report about John being thrown in prison—thus creating the impression that John was not even present when Jesus was baptized. By such means as these, John was clearly made to be subordinate to Jesus so that his ministry could not overlap or compete with Jesus' public ministry. Finally, in Lk 3:21f., in sharp contrast to Mt, Luke provided his narrative with a stirring account of the inauguration of Jesus' mission.

Lk 3:18-20. In contrast to most synopses, we think this pericope begins at Lk 3:18 (cf. Nestle-Aland[27]). The reason is that the μέν...δέ construction begins there and ends with Lk 3:20.

Lk 3:18-20 is a Lukan composition. There are a number of favorite Lukan words and phrases in this section indicating major Lukan composition (e.g., especially ἕτερος, εὐηγγελίζετο τὸν λαόν, προστιθέναι see Collison 184-185, 51, 173-174, 63-64).

¶ 13. Jesus is baptized by the Holy Spirit

Mt 3:16-17 ===> **Lk 3:21-22**

The scene switches. Large numbers are being baptized in the waters. After Jesus was baptized he was in prayer. Suddenly, God sends a divine portent from heaven: a beautiful dove flies over and lights upon Jesus as a great voice comes out of the sky, "You are my Son. Today I have begotten you!"

General observations. For the momentous account of Jesus' baptism Luke has returned to Matthew 3. As noted in the previous general observations, Luke chose to avoid Mt's ambiguous description of Jesus being baptized by John. Instead, Luke focused on the divine signs accompanying Jesus' baptism, signs that indicate that he is being anointed for a special mission as the Son of God.

Lk 3:21-22a. Note that Luke dropped the reference to the "Jordan River" in Mt 3:13. Yet he knew this was where Jesus' baptism occurred because later on he says Jesus "*returned* from the Jordan" (Lk 4:1). Luke's statement at Lk 4:1 requires knowledge of Mt 3:13 to make geographical sense. This is another subtle hint of Luke's familiarity with the text of Mt.

Lk 3:22b. Luke also revised Mt's version of the Voice from Heaven. However, there is a well-known textual difficulty here. The reading adopted by UBS^4 Σὺ εἶ ὁ υἱός μου ὁ ἀγαπητός, ἐν σοὶ εὐδόκησα is the wording of Mk 1:11, but it is probably not what Luke originally had. We think Lk 3:22 originally read ἐγὼ σήμερον γεγέννηκά σε, the quotation of Ps. 2:7. This reading is found in D it (numerous mss) Justin, Clement *et al.* The UBS reading is supported by $\mathfrak{P}^4$ ℵ A B L W Θ vg, sy, cop, arm, eth, Augustine *et al.* We find the UBS committee's reasoning for opposing the Western text difficult to understand. "The Western reading, 'This day I have begotten thee,' which was widely current during the first three centuries, appears to be secondary, derived from Psalm 2:7" (Metzger 1994, 112f.). We think that Luke's original reading was indeed *meant to be* a quotation from Ps 2:7, since Luke later explicitly quoted Ps 2:7 again in Acts 13:33, clearly looking back at this passage (N.B. the synopses of Boismard and Greeven who also adopt the Western reading). One can see why the later orthodox Fathers may have altered Luke's original reading to conform to Mk. For Luke, the emphasis is on the role of the Holy Spirit in Jesus' life. The Holy Spirit was active at his birth (Lk 1:35). Now the Holy Spirit confirms Jesus' divine sonship.

¶ 14. Jesus' lineage

(Mt 1:1-16) **Lk 3:23-38**

Heaven has proclaimed that Jesus is "the Son of God." In good Hellenistic style, Luke proceeds to reinforce this title by providing his audience with a genealogy tracing Jesus' historical lineage back through ancient noble families in his native country to "Adam," the first human, whom Luke pointedly calls "the son of God."

General observations. In his opening chapters Matthew was concerned to set forth the argument that Jesus was both Son of David and Son of God (Mt 1:1-18, 20, 23; 2:15; 3:17; 4:1-11). Luke was concerned to make the same argument. Jesus' Davidic origin was clearly intimated in Luke's birth account (Lk 1:27, 69; 2:4, 11); and the earlier promises that he would be called Son of the Most High were dramatically fulfilled at his baptism with the pronouncement of the divine *Bath Qol* (Lk 3:22). Now, by way of summary, Luke integrates the two titles into his narrative story by binding around his account of Jesus' Davidic ancestry a reference to Jesus' special origin as the divine son of the virgin (Lk 3:23). There were earlier precedents of divine sonship in the election of the Davidic family, but even more clearly in the action of God in the creation of Adam (Lk 3:38). Luke accomplished one of his literary goals by putting his account of Jesus' ancestry in a different order than Matthew.

Luke's genealogy is preceded by the *Bath Qol* and followed by his version of the testing of God's Son. Luke has used a source other than Matthew for his account of Jesus' genealogy. As is well known, Luke traced the descent of the Davidic family through Nathan and Zerubbabel. Richard Bauckham has plausibly shown that similar traditions were in circulation amongst Palestinian Jews in the first century.[1] It is possible that Luke derived his account of Jesus' ancestry from Palestinian Christians—perhaps the same sources that supplied him with some of the material in the Birth Narratives. In this case, Luke gave precedence to this source over the Matthean account.

Lk 3:23 appears to be mainly Lukan composition. The collocation of καὶ αὐτὸς ἦν is characteristic of the text of Lk (Goulder 2:801). Also, the use of the periphrastic imperfect (ἦν ἀρχόμενος) is characteristic of the text of Lk (Collison 73-74). The phraseology ὡς ἐνομίζετο echoes the earlier account of the virginal conception in Lk 1:27-30.

Lk 3:24-38. Luke's version traced Jesus' ancestry back beyond Abraham to Adam, "the son of God." Even though Luke did not minimize Jesus' Davidic ancestry, the reference to Adam is another indicator of Luke's international perspective (cf. Lk 3:6). There may be a Pauline concept in the background here (cf. 1 Cor 15:45; Rom 5:14).

¶ 15. Satan tempts the Son of God

Mt 4:1-11 ===> **Lk 4:1-13**

Luke carries on the theme of Jesus' endowment with the Holy Spirit in a dramatic scene where Jesus, immediately after his baptism and acknowledgment as the Son of God, is confronted by the Devil himself. The Devil tries to attack Jesus through hunger, through ambition, and finally through the desire for self-preservation. But Jesus remains firm in his trust in God. Temporarily thwarted, the Devil departs for a more opportune moment.

General observations. Luke resumed following Mt's order to obtain this story. However, he revised it, omitting the additional words in Jesus' answer to Satan in the first temptation: "but by every word that comes from the mouth of God" (Mt 4:4b//Dt 8:3b). Luke also rearranged the order of the temptations in Mt. Matthew had set forth a dramatic three-fold portrait of Jesus as prophet (bread); priest (temple); and king (view from the mountain). Matthew's structure might also reflect the order of the temptations of Israel in Exodus (bread in the desert, ch. 16; water at Massah, ch. 17; incident at the mountain, ch. 32). Mt's quotations from Deuteronomy (Mt 4:4 = Dt 8:3; Mt 4:6 = Ps 91:11-12; Mt 4:7 = Dt 6:16; Mt 4:10 = Dt 6:13) clearly referred to those temptations. On the other hand, Luke's version had the effect of focusing the story on the last temptation where Jesus is tempted to preserve his life *in Jerusalem*. By this

[1] See *Jude and the Relatives of Jesus in the Early Church* (Edinburgh: T & T Clark, 1990) 315-373.

rearrangement of Mt's Temptation Narrative, Luke dramatically foreshadowed Jesus' final confrontation with evil in Jerusalem.

Lk 4:1 expanded Mt 4:1 to stress that Jesus was now full of the Holy Spirit. The use of ὑποστρέφειν (Lk 4:1) is a favorite Lukan term occurring 24 times in Luke and not at all in Matthew (Collison 67). The description of persons in Luke-Acts as "full of the Holy Spirit" is also Lukan (Lk 1:15, 41, 67; 4:1; Acts 2:4; 4:8; 4:31; 9:17; 13:9).

Lk 4:2-13. Evidence of characteristic Lukan phraseology is strong throughout, even though Luke used Matthew as a source. See, for instance, in Lk 4:6, the reference to "all this authority" (Collison 173, 183-184) and Lk 4:13: πειρασμόν, ἀπέστη (cf. Collison 41). The term ἄχρι occurs only once in Mt (in source material), four times in Lk and 15 times in Acts. The phrase ἄχρι καιροῦ in Lk 4:13 is found again in Acts 13:11 but nowhere else in the New Testament.

EXCURSUS: THE IMAGE OF THE WANDERING SAGE IN GRECO-ROMAN LITERATURE AND ITS RELEVANCE FOR UNDERSTANDING LUKE'S COMPOSITION

Luke structured his narrative of Jesus' activity around a series of trips or journeys. With respect to the Galilee period, it is possible to discern two tours. One started from Capernaum at Lk 4:31 and ended back in Capernaum at Lk 7:1. Another series of journeys begins at Lk 7:11 when Jesus went to Nain, where a number of events took place. After that, Lk 8:1 says, "Soon afterwards he went on through the cities and villages [of Galilee] preaching and bringing the good news of the Kingdom of God." This second extended series of journeys contained the most important events of the Galilean ministry, culminating with the Transfiguration when a chosen few apostles saw "the Kingdom of God."

Shortly afterward, Jesus set his face to go to Jerusalem (Lk 9:51). This journey stretched over no less than ten chapters (Lk 9:51 to 19:27) as Luke created an extended teaching section. After arriving in Jerusalem (Lk 19:45), Luke narrated the final events of Jesus' last week, culminating in the trials, execution and resurrection of Jesus.

Interspersed among these longer journeys Luke located a number of smaller trips and tours involving other people: Jesus' parents went from Nazareth to Bethlehem and back (Lk 2:1-40); Mary visited Elizabeth and returned home (Lk 1:39-56); Jesus and his family went to Jerusalem when he was twelve (Lk 2:41-52). The Twelve disciples had their own missionary trip (Lk 9:1-10), as did the Seventy-two (Lk 10:1-17). After the resurrection, two associates walked to Emmaus and back to Jerusalem (Lk 24:13-35).

Is this use of journeys as a narrative device peculiar to Luke's Gospel? Hardly. In Acts, within the over-arching scenario of the proclamation of the gospel of Jesus Christ in Jerusalem, then to Judea and Samaria, and then to the ends of the earth, there are numerous trips and journeys. We all remember Luke's depiction of the first, second, and third "missionary journeys" of Paul, sketched by the author with a hind-sight that is more systematic than can be seen from Paul's letters. On these missionary tours

Luke hung numerous anecdotes and vignettes about the apostle Paul and his enemies and followers. In addition to these, there was Philip's trip to a "city of Samaria" and thence to Gaza where he met the Ethiopian eunuch, and from there he went on "through all the towns till he came to Caesarea" (Acts 8:40). This was followed by Peter's journeying through towns and villages, ending with Lydda, Joppa and Caesarea (Acts 9:32–10:1).

Other journeys could be mentioned, but this should be sufficient to show that the journey-motif is not unique to the Gospel of Luke. Indeed it must be said that journeys were the preferred narratological mechanism used by the author of Luke-Acts to structure his material into a seeming chronological sequence and give his whole narrative the constant impression of forward momentum (see Introduction, pp. 33f.).

Why would the author of Luke-Acts want to cast virtually his whole narrative in this mold? The answer is not far to seek. This model had many resemblances to the role of the wandering sage who was a well-known and respected figure in the cities and villages of the entire ancient eastern Mediterranean world. Springing from roots in the Greek Cynic-Stoic tradition and the far older tradition of the wandering holy man, we should say that Luke, in effect, created an act of homage to the Apostle Paul by casting his biography of Jesus and history of the early Christian leaders on the model which Paul had followed. By transforming nearly all of the central figures in his two-volume work into the type of the traveling sage and wise man, a figure familiar on the street corners of every Hellenistic town and city, Luke would have made his story seem much more accessible to his audience than was the case with the more eschatologically oriented image of Jesus in Matthew. As such, it was an extension of the brilliant attempt at enculturation of the Hebrew Gospel in Greek cultural terms pioneered by the Apostle Paul. Recent scholarship has thrown considerable light on this aspect of the writings of the Apostle Paul, as one who himself embodied the ideal of the wandering Cynic-Stoic sage.[2]

Who were these wandering sages and what did they look like? Dressed in the traditional philosopher's robe and sandals, having no visible means of support, they went from city to city and, taking a stand in the city square at the busiest time of day, exhorting the crowds to reform the manifest shortcomings of their city lest the gods swiftly come and punish them with blight or disease or worse. Such sages often healed the sick and gave instruction on the proper ways to conduct the local rituals. One of the most famous of these wandering sages in the first century in the eastern Mediterranean was the Cilician follower of Pythagoras, Apollonios of Tyana, a famous "divine man" who was sage, healer, seer, political advisor and prophet throughout the whole region, including Egypt and Rome.[3] For the classic description of this Cynic-

[2] See on this whole subject especially the classic study by Ragnar Hoïstad, *Cynic Hero and Cynic King* (Uppsala: C.W.K.Gleerup, 1948). More recently see Abraham Malherbe, *Paul and the Popular Philosophers* (Minneapolis: Fortress Press, 1989); also T. Engberg-Pedersen ed., *Paul in his Hellenistic Context* (Minneapolis: Fortress Press, 1995) for further bibliography.

[3] See Philostratus, "Life of Apollonios," in D. Cartlidge & D. Dungan, *Documents for the Study of the Gospels,* rev. ed. (Philadelphia: Fortress Press, 1994) 203-238.

Stoic wandering way of life, one can do no better than read Epictetus' famous description, "On the Calling of a Cynic" (*Discourses* 3:22).

With this pre-understanding in hand we are now prepared to work carefully through Luke's account of Jesus' Galilean ministry.

Interweaving Transitional Unit. Lk 4:14-16a

¶ 16. Jesus returns to Galilee

(Mt 9:26, 31, 35-36) Mt 4:12-13, 23-24 ====> **Lk 4:14-16a**

With John the Baptist now off center stage, Luke is ready to portray Jesus beginning his public ministry. Jesus triumphantly returns to Galilee in the "power of the Holy Spirit" and "teaches in their synagogues." Word of his activity quickly spreads to the surrounding regions.

General observations. After the story of Satan's temptation in Mt 4:1-11 comes Mt 4:12-17 in which the following items occur:

(a) Jesus hears that John the Baptist has been arrested.
(b) Jesus "withdraws" into Galilee.
(c) Then, leaving Nazareth,
(d) Jesus goes and lives in Capernaum, fulfilling the prophecy of Isa 9:1-2,
(e) Where he begins to preach, "repent for the Kingdom of God is at hand."

Luke adopted a number of closely related alterations regarding each of these items. As for (a), we pointed out above in our discussion of Jesus' baptism how Luke dealt with the account of John's arrest in Mt 4:12a and 14:3 by placing it at the time of Jesus' baptism. Here Luke took over the second part of Mt 4:12b: "and he withdrew into Galilee," adding that Jesus did so "in the power of the Spirit" (Lk 4:14a). The continuation in Lk 4:14b is a Lukan expansion based on the Matthean summaries in Mt 4:12, 23a, 24a and 9:26 to set the stage for the sermon in the synagogue at Nazareth.

After this brief introduction, Luke omitted item (e), Mt's brief description of Jesus' beginning to preach publically, "Repent, for the kingdom of heaven is at hand" (Mt 4:17), in favor of a generalizing account of the spread of Jesus' fame. Luke may have wished to avoid this phraseology for two reasons:

(1) being identical with John's message, it could have left the impression that Jesus really was, after all, no more than John's disciple—precisely the impression Luke will seek to avoid throughout his narrative.
(2) As an indication of Jesus' first public preaching, this summary would have seemed extremely meager and even unintelligible by Hellenistic historiographical standards. Something much more glorious was called for.

Finally, Luke decided to expand items (c) and (d), Mt's statement that Jesus "returned to Galilee and leaving Nazareth, went to Capernaum." Mt's terse account gave no explanation as to what happened in Nazareth or *why* Jesus might have left. Luke opened up Mt's narrative and inserted the account of Jesus' preaching in the synagogue at Nazareth and subsequent rejection by the people of Nazareth taken from Mt 13:54-58.

Possibly based on nonMatthean tradition, Luke meticulously revised Mt's narrative, inserting a carefully conceived tableau of the young Savior visiting his home town where his graceful words were at first greeted by his friends with admiration and praise, only to turn into envy and rage. In the process, Luke replaced Mt's prophecy-fulfillment quote of Isa 9:1-2, which was unsuitable for his compositional needs of the prophets' announcement of a new era, by another prophecy-fulfillment *sermon* based on the passages from Isa 61:1-2; 58:6. Luke portrayed Jesus using Isaiah to announce in unmistakable terms his own self-understanding as the anointed messenger who sets forth the major emphases of his entire public mission. By Hellenistic literary standards, the purposes for this important opening scene were accomplished; instead of Mt's abrupt shifts to Galilee/Nazareth/Capernaum, Luke provided the reader with a smoother narrative flow into the Nazareth scene where the chief themes of Jesus' mission were set forth.

Lk. 4:14a was taken from Mt 4:12b. The Lukan summary opens with a reference to Jesus' "return" ὑποστρέφειν. This is a favorite vocabulary item of Luke (Collison 67). On the Two Gospel Hypothesis, this Lukan vocabulary item replaced Matthew's equally characteristic ἀναχωρεῖν (Tevis, Display 15). But Luke has added "in the power of the Spirit" to emphasize continuity of the theme that began with the coming of the Holy Spirit at Jesus' baptism (Lk 3:22), and continued with Jesus being led out into the wilderness "full of the Holy Spirit" (Lk 4:1). Luke used two geographical references from Mt 4:12 "into Galilee" (εἰς τὴν Γαλιλαίαν) (Lk 4:14a) and "Nazareth" (Ναζαρά) (Lk 4:16) to frame this transition unit. This is further literary evidence for Luke's dependence upon Matthew. It also appears to be resumptive of Lk 2:39. This is further evidence that Luke is developing a coherent (orderly) narrative.

Lk 4:14b-15, as the synopsis below indicates, is based upon a collage of phrases taken from a number of Matthean summary passages. This is extremely significant source-critical evidence. These are not actual sayings or anecodotes of Jesus that Luke could have received by tradition: this is Matthean summary material, i.e., words and phrases that have the highest likelihood of coming from the hand of the final redactor of the Gospel of Matthew, not any of Mt's sources. For words and phrases from these Matthean summaries to appear in a parallel text in Lk's order is important evidence indicating Luke's direct literary dependence upon

Matthew (see further Introduction, pp. 21-24). Consider the underlined words in the following synopsis.

Synopsis of Lk 4:14-16

Illustrating Luke's utilization of redactional material from a number of different Matthean contexts to create this summary passage.

Mt 4:12-13a	Mt 4:23a, 24a	Mt 9:26 (cf. 9:31)	Lk 4:14-16
12 Ἀκούσας δὲ	**23** Καὶ		**14** Καὶ
ὅτι Ἰωάννης			
παρεδόθη			
ἀνεχώρησεν	περιῆγεν		ὑπέστρεψεν
			ὁ Ἰησοῦς
			ἐν τῇ δυνάμει
			τοῦ πνεύματος
εἰς τὴν Γαλιλαιαν			εἰς τὴν Γαλιλαίαν·
		26 καὶ	καὶ
		ἐξῆλθεν	
		ἡ φήμη αὕτη	φήμη
			ἐξῆλθεν
	ἐν ὅλῃ	εἰς ὅλην	καθ᾽ ὅλης
	τῇ Γαλιλαίᾳ,	τὴν γῆν ἐκείνην.	τῆς περιχώρου
			περὶ αὐτοῦ.
			15 καὶ αὐτὸς
	διδάσκων		ἐδίδασκεν
	ἐν ταῖς		ἐν ταῖς
	συναγωγαῖς		συναγωγαῖς
	αὐτῶν. . .		αὐτῶν,
	24 καὶ		
	ἀπῆλθεν		
	ἡ ἀκοὴ αὐτοῦ		
	εἰς ὅλην		
	τὴν Συριαν·		
			δοξαζόμενος
			ὑπὸ πάντων.
13 καὶ καταλιπὼν			**16** Καὶ ἦλθεν
τὴν Ναζαρὰ			εἰς Ναζαρά

Lk 4:15 "teaching in their synagogues." This is the only occurrence of this phrase in Luke. On the other hand, "in their synagogues" occurs at Mt 4:23; 9:35; and 10:17 (cf. Tevis, Display 6). This is an example of a "one-way indicator," i.e., a phrase occurring a number of times in Mt which occurs in Lk only in a parallel passage where there is evidence of copying.

Lk 4:16 εἰς Ναζαρά. This unique spelling of "Nazareth" is found in the New Testament only in this parallel synoptic context: Mt 4:13//Lk 4:16. Elsewhere, Luke consistently spells "Nazareth" differently (see chart on the next page).

Various Spellings of "Nazareth" in the Gospels

Illustrating Luke's customary spelling (including the adjectival forms)
with the unique spelling at Lk 4:16, which is a contextual parallel to Mt 4:13.

Lk 1:26 Γαβριὴλ ἀπὸ τοῦ θεοῦ εἰς πόλιν τῆς Γαλιλαίας ᾗ ὄνομα Ναζαρὲθ;

Lk 2:4 ἀπὸ τῆς Γαλιλαίας ἐκ πόλεως Ναζαρὲθ εἰς τὴν Ἰουδαίαν;

Lk 2:39 κυρίου, ἐπέστρεψαν εἰς τὴν Γαλιλαίαν εἰς πόλιν ἑαυτῶν **Ναζαρέθ.**

Lk 2:51 μετ᾽ αὐτῶν καὶ ἦλθεν εἰς **Ναζαρὲθ** καὶ ἦν ὑποτασσόμενος αὐτοῖς.

Lk 4:16 Καὶ ἦλθεν εἰς **Ναζαρά**, οὗ ἦν τεθραμμένος...

Lk 4:34 τί ἡμῖν καὶ σοί, Ἰησοῦ **Ναζαρηνέ**; ἦλθες ἀπολέσαι ἡμᾶς; (adjectival form)

Lk 24:19 Καὶ λεγεὶ αὐτῷ, Τὰ περὶ Ἰησοῦ τοῦ **Ναζαρηνοῦ...** (adjectival form)

Acts 10:38 Ἰησοῦν τὸν ἀπὸ **Ναζαρέθ,** ὡς ἔχρισεν αὐτὸν ὁ θεὸς πνεύματι ἁγίῳ...

The Gospel of Matthew has three different spellings:

Mt. 2:23 ἐλθὼν κατῴκησεν εἰς πόλιν λεγομένην **Ναζαρέτ**·

Mt 4:13 καὶ καταλιπὼν τὴν **Ναζαρὰ** ἐλθὼν κατῴκησεν εἰς Καφαρναοὺμ...

Mt 21:11 ἐστιν ὁ προφήτης Ἰησοῦς ὁ ἀπὸ **Ναζαρὲθ** τῆς Γαλιλαίας.

Cf. the Gospel of John:

Jn 1:45 προφῆται εὑρήκαμεν, Ἰησοῦν υἱὸν τοῦ Ἰωσὴφ τὸν ἀπὸ **Ναζαρέτ.**

Jn 1:46 εἶπεν αὐτῷ Ναθαναήλ, Ἐκ **Ναζαρὲτ** δύναταί τι ἀγαθὸν εἶναι;

Cf. the Gospel of Mark:

Mk 1:9 ἦλθεν Ἰησοῦς ἀπὸ **Ναζαρὲτ** τῆς Γαλιλαίας καὶ ἐβαπτίσθη...

Mk 1:24 λέγων· τί ἡμῖν καὶ σοί, Ἰησοῦ **Ναζαρηνέ**;

Mk 10:47 καὶ ἀκούσας ὅτι Ἰησούς ὁ **Ναζαρηνὸς** ἐστιν ἤρξατο κράζειν...

Mk 14:67 λέγει· καὶ σὺ μετὰ τοῦ **Ναζαρηνοῦ** ἦσθα τοῦ Ἰησοῦ.

Mark 16:6 ὁ δὲ λέγει αὐταῖς· ...Ἰησοῦν ζητεῖτε τὸν **Ναζαρηνόν...**

• The unique spelling of "Nazareth" in Lk 4:16//Mt 4:13, in combination with all of the other evidence of Luke's dependence upon several Matthean redactional contexts in Lk 4:14-16, suggests that Luke is directly dependent upon the canonical Gospel of Matthew in this context.

PART THREE LK 4:16B–7:15

THE INAUGURATION OF THE PROPHET–MESSIAH'S MISSION

Overview

Jesus, anointed by the Spirit, comes into his home territory and delivers a message rife with the major themes of his early Galilean ministry (Lk 4:16-30). These themes, which constitute the fulfillment of the Isaianic hopes, include: (1) the announcement of good news to the poor (Lk 4:18; cf. 6:20-30); forgiveness and healing from both sickness and social alienation (Lk 4:18; cf. 4:31-41; 5:12-6:11); and the extension of the benefits of the new era even to the most marginalized persons (Lk 4:24-27). The latter themes, with their direct references to particular incidents in the prophetic missions of Elijah and Elisha (1 Kgs 17:1-24; 2 Kgs 5:1-14) are especially significant since, at the end of this part, Jesus the Prophet-Messiah recapitulates these wonderful deeds of the earlier prophets (Lk 7:1-23). All of these marvelous happenings are structured by Luke into a lengthy trip from Capernaum to Capernaum that spans the greater part of this section (Lk 4:31-7:1).

Yet, already as early as Lk 2:34-35, an ominous tone of possible rejection by the venerable leaders of the established order within Israel is introduced. This is symbolized by the rejection of Jesus' message by the people of Nazareth (Lk 4:28-30); and later by the Pharisees and their scribes (Lk 5:21, 30; 6:2, 7).

In response to this rejection Jesus carefully calls an inner group of disciples who will be the vanguard of the people who accept the proposition that "Today, the salvation of the new era has arrived" (Lk 4:21). First, Simon, James, and John (Lk 5:1-12); then Levi (Lk 5:27-32); then the nucleus of the new Israel is made complete (Lk 6:12-16). Then, and only then, Jesus brings his early mission to a climax by a major address on the plain (Lk 6:20-29) which reiterates the major themes of his ministry. Combined with his deeds of healing (Lk 7:1-15), the people see the fulfillment of the Isaianic hopes (cf. Lk 4:18-19).

¶ 17. Jesus' first sermon at Nazareth

(Mt 13:54-58) Mt 4:13a ====> **Lk 4:16b-30**

Jesus goes to the synagogue and, after reading from the prophet Isaiah (Isa 61:1-2; 58:6), announces that the time of the fulfillment of this good news for the poor and oppressed has arrived. At first the words do not make a deep impact. But then, upon reflection, a home-town boy is making extraordinary claims and the occasion takes on ominous overtones. Jesus seems to become provocative, stating that his gracious reception will not last. "No prophet is acceptable in his own country," he says, underlining the point with two historical allusions to periods in Israel's history when prophets were prevented by Heaven (=God) from doing any miracles for Israel. They did heal Gentiles, that is, God's grace did continue to function toward foreigners; but not toward Israel. These words enrage the crowd and they try to kill Jesus, but he passes through them and goes away unharmed.

General observations. Luke, following Mt, is at Mt 4:13 where the text abruptly states that Jesus left Nazareth. No reason is given for this action in Mt 4:13-17, although it is later in Mt. 13:54ff. Similar to his reference to the account of John's imprisonment, Luke reached forward to Mt 13:54-58 and, using nonMatthean tradition as well, created an account of Jesus' first sermon in his home town of Nazareth, followed by the townspeople's hostility toward him. Luke did not use Mt's first sermon, the Sermon on the Mount, until Jesus has chosen *all twelve* disciples (unlike Mt). In the meantime, Jesus' sermon in Nazareth does two things: it states the major thematic emphases of Jesus' entire ministry and provides a reason why his activities in Galilee were centered in Capernaum and not in his home town. The following synopsis illuminates Luke's compositional activity.

Synopsis of Lk 4:16, 22-24, 31-32

Illustrating Luke's conflation of Matthew's account of the rejection of Jesus in Nazareth (Mt 13:54-58) with the compositional phrases before and after Matthew's Sermon on the Mount (Mt 5:2; 7:28-29) to provide a setting for his account of Jesus' inaugural sermon in Nazareth.

Jesus' rejection in his own country **Mt 13:53-55a; 57b-58**	**Jesus' first sermon in Nazareth** **Lk 4:16, 22-24**
Mt 13:53 Καὶ ἐγένετο ὅτε ἐτέλεσεν ὁ Ἰησοῦς τὰς παραβολὰς ταύτας, μετῆρεν ἐκεῖθεν.	
54 καὶ ἐλθὼν εἰς τὴν πατρίδα αὐτοῦ (cf. Mt 4:13)	**Lk 4:16** Καὶ ἦλθεν εἰς Ναζαρὰ οὗ ἦν τεθραμμένος, καὶ εἰσῆλθεν κατὰ τὸ εἰωθὸς αὐτῷ ἐν τῇ ἡμέρᾳ τῶν σαββάτων
ἐδίδασκεν αὐτοὺς ἐν τῇ συναγωγῇ αὐτῶν,	εἰς τὴν συναγωγὴν καὶ ἀνέστη ἀναγνῶναι...
ὥστε ἐκπλήσσεσθαι αὐτοὺς...	**22** Καὶ πάντες ἐμαρτύρουν αὐτῷ καὶ ἐθαύμαζον ἐπὶ τοῖς λόγοις τῆς χάριτος
Mt 5:2 Καὶ ἀνοίξας τὸ στόμα αὐτοῦ ἐδίδασκεν αὐτοὺς λέγων·	τοῖς ἐκπορευομένοις ἐκ τοῦ στόματος αὐτοῦ,
Mt 13:54b καὶ λέγειν: πόθεν τούτῳ ἡ σοφία αὕτη καὶ αἱ δυνάμεις;	**22** καὶ ἔλεγον·
οὐκ οὗτός ἐστιν ὁ τοῦ τέκτονος υἱός;...	οὐχὶ υἱός ἐστιν Ἰωσὴφ οὗτος;

Synopsis of Lk 4:16, 22-24, 31-32 (cont.)

	Lk 4:23 καὶ εἶπεν πρὸς αὐτούς·
	πάντως ἐρεῖτέ μοι τὴν παραβολὴν ταύτην·
	ἰατρέ, θεράπευσον σεαυτόν·
cf. Mt 4:13 and Mt 8:5	ὅσα ἠκούσαμεν γενόμενα εἰς Καφαρναοὺμ
cf. Mt 13:54a and Mt 13:57b	ποίησον καὶ ὧδε ἐν τῇ πατρίδι σου.
Mt 13:57b ὁ δὲ Ἰησοῦς εἶπεν αὐτοῖς·	**24** εἶπεν δέ·
	ἀμὴν λέγω ὑμῖν ὅτι
οὐκ ἔστιν προφήτης ἄτιμος εἰ μὴ	οὐδεὶς προφήτης δεκτός ἐστιν
ἐν τῇ πατρίδι	ἐν τῇ πατρίδι αὐτοῦ...
	καὶ ἐν τῇ οἰκίᾳ αὐτοῦ
καὶ οὐκ ἐποίησεν ἐκεῖ δυνάμεις πολλὰς	
διὰ τὴν ἀπιστίαν αὐτῶν.	
Jesus moves from Nazareth to Capernaum	**Introduction to healing of possessed man in Capernaum**
Mt 4:13	**Lk 4:31-32**
13 καὶ καταλιπὼν τὴν Ναζαρὰ	**31** Καὶ (cf. Lk 4:16)
ἐλθὼν κατῴκησεν	κατῆλθεν
εἰς Καφαρναοὺμ	εἰς Καφαρναοὺμ
τὴν παραθαλασσίαν	πόλιν τῆς Γαλιλαίας.
ἐν ὁρίοις Ζαβουλὼν	
καὶ Νεφθαλίμ...	
Conclusion to Jesus' Sermon on the Mount	
Mt 7:28-29	
28 Καὶ ἐγένετο	καὶ
ὅτε ἐτέλεσεν	
ὁ Ἰησοῦς	
τοὺς λόγους τούτους,	
	ἦν διδάσκων αὐτοὺς ἐν τοῖς σάββασιν·
ἐξεπλήσσοντο οἱ ὄχλοι	**32** καὶ ἐξεπλήσσοντο
ἐπὶ τῇ διδαχῇ αὐτοῦ·	ἐπὶ τῇ διδαχῇ αὐτοῦ·
29 ἦν γὰρ διδάσκων αὐτοὺς	
ὡς ἐξουσίαν ἔχων	ὅτι ἐν ἐξουσίᾳ
καὶ οὐχ ὡς οἱ γραμματεῖς αὐτῶν.	
	ἦν ὁ λόγος αὐτοῦ.

Lk 4:16b provides the framework for Jesus' entrance into the synagogue. The reference in Lk 4:15 ἐν ταῖς συναγωγαῖς αὐτῶν (cf. εἰς τὴν συναγωγήν in Lk 4:16) echoes directly ἐν τῇ συναγωγῇ αὐτῶν from Mt 13:54.

Lk 4:17-21 highlights the scriptural basis of Jesus' mission as being drawn from Isa 61:1-2a, slightly modified with a line from Isa 58:6. As John's mission emerged as the fulfillment of Isaianic hopes (Lk 3:3-6), likewise Jesus' mission brings to fulfillment the Isaianic promises. The motif of comparison between John and Jesus is continued. The use of "Today" to announce the new era of salvation (Lk 4:21) already echoes a major theme of Luke (Lk 2:11; 3:22). It will emerge in key places later in the narrative (Lk 19:9; 23:43; Acts 13:33). Lk is capable of weaving texts from the LXX into a very sophisticated construct (Lk 19:40-44; 21:20-26). It is very difficult to determine whether in Lk 4:17-21, Luke is using nonMatthean tradition as a basis for his composition or is composing freely.

Lk 4:22-24 echoes Mt 13:54-57. The reference to Capernaum in Lk 4:23 is puzzling. It is not in the Matthean parallel. Mt 4:13 says Jesus left Nazareth to go to Capernaum. Is the reference to Capernaum inserted into the Matthean account at Lk 4:23 simply a specification within the general description of Jesus' itinerary in Lk 4:14-15? Following the order of Mt 4:13, after giving the Sermon in Nazareth, Jesus went to Capernaum (Lk 4:31-41) where he performed mighty deeds. Is this a Lukan attempt at foreshadowing or a holdover from his use of nonMatthean source material?

Lk 4:25-30 provides the reason why the people of Nazareth were prepared to have Jesus put to death—presumably as a false prophet. His announcement that the blessings of the messianic age will be received by outsiders challenges the conventional opinion of the people of Jesus' home town and was unacceptable. There is not a great surfeit of linguistic characteristics of Luke in these verses. As with Lk 4:17-21, it is difficult to determine whether Luke is using tradition or composing freely.

¶ 18. Jesus goes to Capernaum and heals a demon-possessed man

(Mt 4:13) Mt 7:28-29 ====> **Lk 4:31-37**

Jesus leaves Nazareth and goes to Capernaum where he teaches in their synagogue. After the sermon, he encounters a man possessed by a demon. The demon is instantly fearful. "Aha!" it shouts in a loud voice. "Have you come to destroy us? I know who you are! You are the Holy One of God!" It is a deft ironic touch. The people of Jesus' own home town have no idea who he is and have just tried to kill him. In the very next town Jesus meets a demon who knows exactly who he is. Luke says that Jesus' words were spoken with great authority. As if to prove the point, Jesus sternly orders the demon out of the man, amazing the onlookers.

General observations. Luke is still carefully developing his narrative based on Mt 4:13 where Jesus goes from Nazareth to Capernaum. However, the account of the exorcism given here is unique to Luke, possibly coming from his nonMatthean tradition. The Matthean compositional phrases that come precisely before and after Mt's Sermon on the Mount also appear here in this parallel text of Luke. They indicate Luke's awareness of the Sermon on the Mount in Mt's text at this point; i.e., they are evidence that he is intentionally moving around it for the time being (see synopsis for the previous pericope).

Lk 4:31a is dependent upon Mt. 4:13. Luke has now brought Jesus to Capernaum which, following Mt, will serve as the major center for Jesus' ministry in Galilee.

Lk 4:31b. Parts of Mt 4:13 and 7:28f. appear in the text of Lk 4:31-32. The remainder of Lk 4:31b: "he was teaching on the Sabbath" is a Lukan phrase that occurs only here and at Lk 13:10.

• Many of the words that are found in the text of Luke are fragmentary preservations of characteristic Matthean transitional phrases—not sayings or actions of Jesus (see synopsis for the previous pericope). This material was created by Matthew to situate the Sermon on the Mount in his narrative. What we have here is clear evidence that Luke has carefully avoided all of the Sermon on the Mount (saving it for later use) and, following the Matthean transitional material around the Sermon on the Mount, has, through the paraphrase of Mt 7:28-29, created a new scene in Capernaum (cf. Mt 8:5), whose basic purpose was to provide ironic contrast to the disastrous ending to Jesus' visit to Nazareth. This appearance of redactional material from the Gospel of Matthew in Luke is strong evidence that the hypothetical Q source is unnecessary.

Lk 4:33-36 is nonMatthean material. It is used to emphasize the "authority" (Lk 4:32, 36), "teaching" (Lk 4:31, 32), and "power" (Lk 4:32, 36) that Jesus had over the demonic forces. The words of the demon not only remind Luke's audience of what has just happened in Nazareth, they also echo the Voice from Heaven at Jesus' baptism. Just as Jesus' endowment with the Holy Spirit led to an immediate confrontation with the Devil, so also his own announcement of who he was and what he will do elicits an immediate response from the forces of evil, both at Nazareth and at Capernaum. Being filled with the Spirit, Jesus meets both tests successfully.

Lk 4:37 along with Lk 4:14 form an *inclusio* around the two scenes in the synagogues which punctuate the beginning of Jesus' Galilean ministry. Both scenes stress the spread of Jesus' fame. One (Lk 4:16-30) ends with rejection; the other (4:31-36) ends in triumph. As we have already noted, the construction of *inclusios* appears to be a Lukan compositional strategy. The remaining portion of this Part of Luke is set within a first journey taken by Jesus out from Capernaum (Lk 4:31) and back to Capernaum (Lk 7:1).

¶ 19. Jesus heals Simon's mother-in-law and many others

Mt 8:14-17 ===> **Lk 4:38-41**

Immediately after the sermon in the synagogue, Jesus goes across the street into Simon Peter's house and, while there, sees that his mother-in-law is in the grip of a deathly high fever. His spiritual authority still with him, Jesus rebukes the fever demon and it leaves her. She immediately gets up and acts the hostess for her guests. As the day begins to wane, many bring their sick and ailing to Jesus and he heals them all. Some demons shout out his identity in the process: "You are the Son of God!" but Jesus silences them.

General observations. Luke, now at Mt 7:28-29, continued to move forward through Mt's account. He skipped the next two stories for different reasons. The healing of the leper (Mt 8:1-4), coming just after the Sermon on the Mount, did not occur in Capernaum which is where Jesus now is (according to Luke's plan). Thus Luke saved it for a place later in the narrative of this first great journey. Nor did Luke use the account of the healing of the Centurion's Servant (Mt 8:5-13) at this point because it would clash with his central purpose in this part of his narrative, which was to describe the process of calling the disciples, culminating in the great sermon given to them (Lk 6:20-7:1//Mt 5-7). Furthermore, in Matthew this sermon preceded Jesus' healing of the Centurion's Servant. So Luke also held this story in reserve, telling it immediately after his version of Mt's Sermon on the Mount (Lk 7:2-10). This brought Luke to the account of the healing of Peter's mother-in-law in Capernaum. Luke put this unit here to provide his audience with the beginning of an explanation as to why Peter might have immediately responded to Jesus' call to come and follow him in the very next story (Lk 5:1-11). The scene ends with a general summary of Jesus' healings.

Lk 4:38-41 paraphrased Mt 8:14-17. Luke characteristically skipped the Matthean fulfillment of prophecy + quotation in Mt 8:17. However, there are definite echoes of the omitted quotation, Lk 4:40 νόσοις // Mt 8:17 νόσους and Lk 4:40 ἀσθενοῦντας // Mt 8:17 ἀσθενείας.

EXCURSUS: THE SELECTION OF THE 12 AND THE MESSAGE OF NON-RETALIATION

In this part of his narrative, Luke devoted his attention to a question that would have had deep interest for his audience: when and how did Jesus attract his first disciples? Beyond the well-known fact that crowds came to Jesus from all the surrounding countryside, Luke's audience would have been particularly interested in learning how such famous Apostles as Peter and Paul and John first made the decision to drop everything else and become disciples of Jesus.

It was a question to which the Gospel of Matthew paid scant attention. After his account of the Temptation, the Gospel of Matthew abruptly mentions John's arrest and Jesus' hasty retreat to Galilee. Then Matthew's Jesus left Nazareth and moved to Capernaum where he began to preach John's message: "Repent for the kingdom of heaven is at hand." This terse summary of Jesus' activity, coming with little explanation at the beginning of his public activity, would have been less than satisfactory to Luke's audience. Indeed, we should go on to observe that Matthew's equally terse account of the way in which Jesus attracted the three most important disciples of the Twelve would probably have seemed equally inadequate to Luke's audience. No explanation or rationale for their decision to follow him is given in Mt 4:18-22. From a Hellenistic dramatic perspective, Mt's account borders on being perfunctory, almost trivial. Luke's audience would have desired to know far more about the amazing things that must have happened to convince these men to follow Jesus.

In Mt's order of pericopes, Jesus chose the Twelve Apostles and then gave a major speech to them and to the crowds that had gathered. Luke followed Matthew's basic order in narrating these two items, but considerably augmented the account of the selection of the Twelve Apostles to bring in all of them. He then made a careful selection from Mt's large (by Luke's standards) Sermon on the Mount, so that the speech Jesus gave in Luke was both a powerful follow-up to the inaugural sermon he gave in his home town of Nazareth and also a significant message to his new disciples (and the crowds) as to how they should comport themselves.

In this speech, Jesus began by stressing the central motif of good news to the poor, miserable and oppressed; God will lift you up. But then he shifts focus: those of you who wish to follow me, when you are mistreated, do not retaliate. After the words on retaliation, everything is explanatory images and concluding points.

How are we to account for this perhaps surprisingly narrow selection from among the rich and varied collection of sayings in Mt's Sermon on the Mount? The explanation might be seen in the way Luke chose to describe Jesus' ministry up to this point:

(a) the sermon in Nazareth is immediately followed by an attempt to kill Jesus, and

(b) in the first journeying mission out of Capernaum and back, Luke has collected precisely those accounts from Mt 9 and 12 that stress the hostile reaction of the Pharisees to what Jesus is doing.

This early stress on the opposition to Jesus in Luke's narrative would have caused in Luke's audience the growing response: "Why didn't Jesus do something to them? Why didn't he punish the wicked people who tried to kill him? Why didn't he see what the Pharisees were up to and punish them? He could have, couldn't he?"

The theme of non-retaliation in Luke's version of Mt's Sermon on the Mount was Luke's way of giving Jesus' answer to this reaction. In Mt's collection, the sweeping demands not to return evil for evil but to "turn the other cheek" are given no explanatory, historical setting.

However, Luke chose to put the the non-retaliation/non-condemnation sayings from Mt's Sermon on the Mount at this point in his narrative where they could become the focal point of a major theme throughout his Gospel. As part of his reconstruction, Luke took the story of the rejection at Nazareth from Mt 13:54-58 and placed it at the very beginning of his account of Jesus' public activity, to foreshadow the Jewish leaders' rejection of Jesus—in Luke's understanding of Scripture, a divine necessity before the Gospel could be preached to the Gentiles. (It should be noted that this is Paul's understanding of Scripture as well; cf. Rom. 11:7-11.) After this ominous beginning, Luke went on to create a second scenario—Jesus' first healing and teaching tour from Capernaum and back—made up of just those stories in Matthew that mentioned a hostile reaction by the Pharisees to something Jesus or his disciples did. Luke brought all of these accounts together and subtly heightened the references to the Pharisees' anger, thus augmenting the theme of deadly opposition to Jesus. With this as a new "historical" background, Luke's audience could understand why Jesus would instruct his new disciples on how to respond to evil; It was his own life-long practice! "Blessed are you who sorrow now, who hunger now—but do not fight evil with evil! Return good for evil! Be merciful even as your heavenly Father is merciful!" (Again, note that this is another Pauline theme, cf. Rom 12:14-21.)

In all respects, then, Luke's compositional activity vis-à-vis the Gospel of Matthew at this point makes perfect sense. Just as he amplified and deepened the story of the beginning of Jesus' ministry, so also he amplified and clarified the reason why his earliest disciples chose to follow him as their master. In addition, Luke carefully paved the way for his version of Matthew's Sermon on the Mount by a series of conflict vignettes that provided a clear-cut rationale for the precise choice of themes in this speech.

With this background, let us now turn our attention to the individual pericopes.

¶ 20. Jesus leaves Capernaum on his first missionary trip

(Mt 4:17, 23, 25) **Lk 4:42-44**

Having healed all who came to him the evening before, the residents of Capernaum throng to Jesus and want to be with him the next morning. But Jesus tells them that he must depart from Capernaum in order to "preach the good news of the kingdom of God to the other cities also." So, Jesus begins preaching in the synagogues.

General observations. As noted above, Luke will now focus on how the Twelve were chosen and why Jesus preached the sermon to them that he did. To provide a fitting chronological account of these things, Luke first created this brief summary of Jesus' preaching on the basis of linguistic clues found in Mt 4:17, 23, and 25. Luke now begins a second forward progression through Mt in order to prepare for the call of the disciples and Jesus' instructions to them.

Luke's previous pericope tells of the healing of Peter's mother-in-law which prepares the reader for Jesus' call of Peter to come and follow him. This short summary passage, therefore, is a bridge to the next story, the call of Peter, James and John. As such, although it echoes Matthew, it is mostly Luke's own creation and is full of Luke's characteristic terminology. See, for instance, Lk 4:42; the genitive absolute (Collison 77-78) πορεύεσθαι twice, πορεύομαι εἰς (Collison 60-61), and the telic use of the genitive of the articular infinitive (Collison 190). In Lk 4:43 there is the commonly used εὐαγγελίζεσθαι (Collison 51), κηρύσσων τὴν βασιλείαν τοῦ θεοῦ (Collison 169-170). The following synopsis reveals Luke's conflation of summary compositional language from Mt 4:17-25.

Synopsis of Lk 4:42-44

Illustrating Luke's conflation of Matthean redactional phraseology taken from Mt 4:17–25.

Mt 4:17, 23, 25	Mt 4:23, 25	Lk 4:42-44
17 Ἀπὸ τότε ἤρξατο		42 Γενομένης δὲ ἡμέρας
ὁ Ἰησοῦς		
κηρύσσειν	cf. Mt 4:23	cf. Lk 4:44
		ἐξελθὼν ἐπορεύθη εἰς
		ἔρημον τόπον·
		καὶ οἱ ὄχλοι ἐπεζήτουν
		αὐτόν
		καὶ ἦλθον ἕως αὐτοῦ
		καὶ κατεῖχον αὐτὸν
		τοῦ μὴ πορεύεσθαι ἀπ'
		αὐτῶν.
καὶ λέγειν,		43 ὁ δὲ εἶπεν πρὸς
		αὐτοὺς ὅτι
Μετανοεῖτε· ἤγγικεν γὰρ		
	23 Καὶ περιῆγεν	Καὶ
	ἐν ὅλῃ τῇ Γαλιλαίᾳ	ταῖς ἑτέραις πόλεσιν
	διδάσκων	
	ἐν ταῖς συναγωγαῖς αὐτῶν	cf. Lk 4:44
cf. Mt 4:17	καὶ κηρύσσων	cf. Lk 4:44
	τὸ εὐαγγέλιον	εὐαγγελίσασθαί με δεῖ
ἡ βασιλεία τῶν οὐρανῶν..	τῆς βασιλείας	τὴν βασιλείαν τοῦ θεοῦ,
	καὶ θεραπεύων πᾶσαν	
	νόσον	
	καὶ πᾶσαν μαλακίαν	
	ἐν τῷ λαῷ.	
		ὅτι ἐπὶ τοῦτο ἀπεστάλην.
cf. Mt 4:17	cf. Mt 4:23	44 καὶ ἦν κηρύσσων
	cf. Mt 4:23	εἰς τὰς συναγωγὰς
	25 καὶ ἠκολούθησαν αὐτῷ	
	ὄχλοι πολλοὶ	
	ἀπὸ τῆς Γαλιλαίας	
	καὶ Δεκαπόλεως	
	καὶ Ἱεροσολύμων	
	καὶ Ἰουδαίας	τῆς Ἰουδαίας.
	καὶ πέραν τοῦ Ἰορδάνου.	

Lk 4:42-43. Luke went out of his way to stress the eager clamoring after Jesus on the part of the crowds. The use of imperfect indicative verbs denoting continual or repeated action is noteworthy: οἱ ὄχλοι ἐπεζήτουν αὐτὸν καὶ ἦλθον ἕως αὐτοῦ καὶ κατεῖχον αὐτὸν τοῦ μὴ πορεύεσθαι ἀπ' αὐτῶν.

Lk 4:44. The reference to Jesus' preaching in the synagogues "of Judea" in 𝔓75 (although the manuscript is fragmentary) ℵ B C *et al.* is questionable (note Metzger's explanation that the UBS editorial committee basically relied on the "rougher reading" principle; Metzger 1994:114f.). The earlier Western text's "Galilee" may well be the original text (A D Δ Θ Ψ it [11 mss] vg, syr, cop, *et al.)*. The reading accepted by UBS, despite its attestation in otherwise reliable manuscripts, appears to be a harmonistic echo of Mt 4:25, intended to expand Jesus' field of activity. If it is genuine, it may be a Lukan anticipation of Jesus' conflict with the Pharisees. In Mt 3:5-7 the Pharisees come from Judea (cf. Lk 5:17).

¶ 21. Jesus calls Simon, James, and John to be disciples

(Mt 4:18-22) **Lk 5:1-11**

With the people pressing close beside him, Jesus sees an empty boat and asks Simon to take him out a short distance from shore so he can address the crowd better. When he is finished speaking, he tells Simon to put out to deeper water and let down his nets. Simon protests that they have fished all night to no avail. "But," he adds, "I will do as you say." Suddenly, the nets are full of fish. Calling to James and John to come help, they haul in an enormous catch. At this, Simon Peter falls down at Jesus' feet and cries out, "Lord, depart from me. I am an evil man!" But Jesus reassures him, offering the forgiveness promised in the sermon in Nazareth (Lk 4:18): "Do not be afraid, Simon. Henceforth, you will be catching men!" All are astonished at the miracle, and James and John and Simon leave everything and follow Jesus.

General observations. This story does not appear anywhere in Matthew and may come from Luke's nonMatthean tradition. Another version of this story is found in Jn 21:1-11. Luke may have chosen this account over the call of the four in Mt 4:18-22 because no explanation is given in Matthew as to why these great leaders should have left their work of providing for their families and become disciples of an itinerant prophet. Luke's account of the stay at Simon's house (Lk 4:38-39) and the miraculous catch of fish (Lk 5:1-11) not only provided reasons for the three disciples to follow Jesus, they anticipated Simon's leadership role in the early Christian community (Acts). Despite Simon's disclaimer of sinfulness (Lk 5:8), he is singled out by Jesus as the leader of the mission (Lk 5:10).

Lk 5:1 contains characteristic Lukan terminology: note the opening use of ἐγένετο δὲ with the articular infinitive, which is a linguistic characteristic of Luke (Collison 214).

Lk 5:6. The occurrence of πλῆθος πολύ, in Lk 5:6, to characterize the great catch of fish, may be consciously echoed again in Lk 6:17, where exactly the same phrase describes the enormous crowds gathered to hear Jesus prior to Luke's version of Mt's Sermon on the Mount: καὶ <u>πλῆθος</u> <u>πολὺ</u> τοῦ λαοῦ ἀπὸ πάσης τῆς Ἰουδαίας καὶ Ἰερουσαλὴμ καὶ τῆς παραλίου Τύρου καὶ Σιδῶνος, κτλ.

Lk 5:8. The presence of the dual name "Simon Peter" in Lk 5:8 and nowhere else in the Lukan writings seems to indicate dependence on Mt 4:18. More common for Luke is "Simon called Peter" (Lk 6:14 and four times in Acts).

Lk 5:11. Finally, Luke reflects a knowledge of Mt 4:22 at the end of the unit with the announcement that the disciples left all to follow Jesus:

Mt 4:22 'Αφέντες... ἠκολούθησαν αὐτῷ

Lk 5:11 ἀφέντες πάντα ἠκολούθησαν αὐτῷ

This verse also foreshadows the leaving of everything by Levi at Lk 5:28; and similar calls for discipleship in 14:33 and 18:22.

¶ 22. Jesus heals a leper

Mt 8:1-4 ====> **Lk 5:12-16**

Luke continues to describe Jesus moving through the cities of Galilee. In one of them, he encounters a leper, heals him, and, following the law meticulously, has the man report to the priest and obey the rules of Moses for full rehabilitation into the community. The result is that Jesus' fame continues to spread, and "great crowds" come to him. But, in characteristic Lukan fashion, Jesus withdraws for a time of prayer.

General observations. Luke now begins to develop further the theme of opposition to Jesus' mission. To accentuate the theme, Luke related an account where Jesus went out of his way to be sensitive to the scruples of Jewish piety. This will underscore the fact that when the opposition to him emerges it will appear unreasonable, quibbling and petty. This is the first of a series of pericopes stretching through Lk 6:11 that will focus on the developing Pharisaic opposition to Jesus.

With this pericope, Luke has brought into his narrative all the incidents in Mt between the Temptation and the Sermon on the Mount. As we noted above, there is evidence at Lk 4:44 that he was aware of Mt 4:25, just before the Sermon, and, at Lk 4:31-32, that he was aware of the end of the Sermon (cf. Mt 7:28-29). At this point, Luke resumed following Mt's order, taking up the first pericope after Mt's Sermon on the Mount (Mt 8:1-4): the healing of the leper.

Lk 5:12. In place of Mt's reference to coming down the mountain, Luke inserted a reference to his travel motif, keeping alive the theme that Jesus is on a journey. At Lk 5:12 he changed Mt's genitive absolute to his own familiar καὶ ἐγένετο with the articular infinitive to introduce the pericope (Collison 214).

Lk 5:12-14 is mostly very similar to Mt; the slight differences are all attempts to heighten the dramatic tone of Mt's account.

Lk 5:15-16 is an expansion of Mt 8:4 on what happened to the man after he visited the priest. As a summary passage, it has a number of verbal similarities with Lk 4:14-15; 4:36-37; and 7:16-17. Taken together, these four Lukan verses constitute a set of transitional passages created by Luke.

Here, not surprisingly, the number of Lukan linguistic characteristics in the story increases. Διήρχετο δὲ μᾶλλον ὁ λόγος περὶ αὐτοῦ is Lukan (Collison 214). The phrase πολλοὶ ὄχλοι is reminiscent of Mt 8:1 (cf. Tevis, Display 4). For a discussion of θεραπεύεσθαι ἀπὸ see Collison 124 (ἀπὸ with verbs of healing). For συνέρχεσθαι, cf. Goulder 1:330. Finally, for the theme of Jesus withdrawing in prayer see Lk 3:21; 5:16; 6:12; 9:18; 9:28-29; 11:1; 22:41; 22:42. Throughout his narrative, Luke will often portray Jesus as entering into prayer before major developments in the narrative. After the summary of Lk 5:15-16, another major development in the opposition to Jesus occurs.

¶ 23. The Son of Man can forgive sins

Mt 9:1-8 ====> **Lk 5:17-26**

One day Jesus is in a house teaching when suddenly a paralyzed man is lowered to him through a hole in the roof. The crowd of listeners prevented his friends from bringing him in the door. Impressed by their faith, Jesus tells the man, "Your sins are forgiven." A crowd of Pharisees is present, having come "from every village of Galilee and Judaea and Jerusalem." They are outraged and demand to know by what authority Jesus forgives sins. Jesus answers their objection with a question of his own: "Which is easier, to forgive sins or to heal?" They cannot answer such a strange question. So Jesus, showing that both are equally "easy" for him, orders the lame man to get up, roll his bed up and go home. He does so, glorifying God. Everyone is amazed.

General observations. Luke has followed Mt's order. However, the next story after the healing of the leper is the Centurion's Servant, which occurs in Capernaum. Reserving that for later in his narrative, when Jesus will come back to Capernaum immediately following the Sermon on the Plain (Lk 7:1), Luke moved to the next conflict account, the healing of the paralytic. Using this as his starting point, Luke provided several conflict stories describing the mounting hostility of the religious leaders to Jesus' announcement of forgiveness (cf. Lk 4:18).

Lk 5:17. Luke discarded Mt's introduction to the story (Mt 9:1) and created his own, opening with καὶ ἐγένετο ἐν μιᾷ τῶν ἡμερῶν (Collison 214). There are other signs of Luke's hand: καὶ αὐτός (Lk 5:17) occurs forty times in Lk (Collison 194-195). The periphrastic imperfect in this verse is also characteristic of Luke (Collison 73-74). Luke's use of νομοδιδάσκαλοι here is a *hapax legomenon*. The stress on the great number of "Pharisees and teachers of the law" present indicates Luke's intention to focus on the theme of their opposition to Jesus during the next several stories.

Lk 5:19. The setting of the healing in a house is not in the account in Mt. Nor is the detail about lowering the man to Jesus through a hole in the roof, i.e., the "(ceramic) tiles" διὰ τῶν κεράμων. Here is a good example of Lukan verisimilitude (cf. 5:19b), designed to prepare the reader for the expressions of great faith shown by those who bring the paralytic.

Lk 5:21. Whereas Mt had "some of the scribes" (Mt 9:3), Luke added, "and the scribes and the Pharisees began to question..." Also in this verse, Luke spelled out more clearly what blasphemy the scribes thought Jesus had committed.

Lk 5:22-26. Luke followed Mt's account closely. The only alterations are minor additions intended to make the account more dramatic.

¶ 24. Jesus calls Levi the tax-collector to be his disciple

Mt 9:9-17 ====> **Lk 5:27-39**

After this, Jesus goes out and sees a tax collector sitting at his table. "Follow me," he says to him. Dropping everything, the man invites Jesus to his house, where he prepares a sumptuous feast. Pharisees, who were watching all this, grumbled to Jesus' disciples: "Why do you eat with evil men and sinners instead of law-abiding citizens?" "Does a doctor visit healthy people?" Jesus asks.

General observations. Following the order of Mt, Luke picked up the next story of conflict between Jesus and the Pharisees (Mt 9:9-17) and presented it here without many changes. It is clear that Luke has gathered conflict stories for a reason. At the end of this unit (a second conflict story), Luke will move from Mt 9:17 to 12:1 to continue this sequence with the next two conflict stories in the order in which they appear in Mt. Luke may also have been drawn from Mt 9 to Mt 12 by the repeated quotation of Hos 6:6, "I desire mercy and not sacrifice," in Mt 9:13 and Mt 12:7.

Lk 5:27. According to Luke, the one whom Jesus called is named "Levi" and not "Matthew" (Mt 9:9). Luke lists Matthew as one of the twelve who will be chosen later (Lk 6:15). Possibly Luke gives the alternative name here to prevent confusion for his readers. Luke's major interest is in the meal to follow.

Lk 5:28. The redactional phrase καταλιπὼν πάντα echoes Lk 5:11 and anticipates Jesus' later calling of disciples to give up all and follow him.

Lk 5:29-32. In place of a rather pedestrian meal in the house of the new disciple (Mt 9:10-13), Luke described this as a δοχὴν μεγάλην ("great banquet"). This is the first instance in Luke of the recurring scene where Jesus taught at a meal (Lk 7:36-50; 10:38-42; 11:37-54; 14:1-24; 22:4-38; 24:29-32, 41-43). The use of γογγύζειν anticipates the use of the cognate in similar settings in Lk 15:2; 19:7. The reference to repentance is Lukan (cf. Lk 15:7; 24:47; Acts 5:31; 11:18; 13:24; 19:4; 20:21; 26:20).

Lk 5:33-37. The explanation of fasting and the saying about the patch (Lk 5:36) move in a different direction from Mt. In contrast to Mt, Luke stresses the incompatibility of mixing the "old" with the "new." For Luke, the "old" had validity (Lk 7:28), but now the new time of forgiveness of sins is here, it must be received, not resisted like the Pharisees do.

¶ 25. The Son of Man is lord of the Sabbath

Mt 12:1-8 ====> **Lk 6:1-5**

Luke continues the series of stories describing the constantly critical attitude of the Pharisees toward Jesus. One Sabbath, as they were walking through a grain field, Jesus' disciples pluck and eat some grains of wheat. As if hovering nearby just waiting for their chance to catch them out, some Pharisees immediately object, demanding to know why they are "working" on the Sabbath. Jesus' answer comes down to the statement that he, the "Son of Man," gave them permission to do so; "the Son of Man is lord of the Sabbath."

General observations. As noted above Luke went forward in Mt's order and moved down to Mt 12; Mt 12:1-8 is the source for this conflict story. Two features of the story may have prompted Luke to select it. First, this story in Mt 12:7 had precisely the same quote from Hos 6:6 as the one found in Mt 9:13. Second, this story further documented the opposition of the Pharisees to Jesus, a theme on which Luke carefully built throughout Part 3.

Luke 6:1-5. Luke followed Matthew's version of the story fairly closely, omitting the second rather obscure argument in Mt 12:5f. concerning work priests do in the temple and the direct reference to scripture (Mt 12:7). This would be opaque for Luke's Hellenistic readers. Luke had just finished a unit on the subject of wine. Still following the themes of food and opposition from the Pharisees, he took up a conflict story that involved a charge that the disciples both plucked the heads of wheat and, after rubbing the husks off, ate them. The act of eating was allowable, but the act of plucking the heads off the wheat was thought by some to be a violation of Sabbath Torah. To Luke's Hellenistic readers this sounded like Jesus and his followers were being charged with impiety. Jesus responded vigorously. He invoked the earlier precedent of David's action (Lk 6:4) in eating the bread of the Presence. After Luke passed over the second precedent (the priests eating the bread; Mt 12:5-7) he went directly to Mt 12:8 and had Jesus, the new David, claim to be the Son of Man, the Lord of the Sabbath (Lk 6:5).

¶ 26. Jesus heals a man's hand on the Sabbath

Mt 12:9-14 ===> **Lk 6:6-11**

On another Sabbath, after he had taught in a synagogue, Jesus sees a man with a crippled right hand. Aware that he is still under the hostile scrutiny of the scribes and Pharisees around him, Jesus realizes that they are concerned that he too will "work" on the Sabbath. So he asks them if Moses permitted doing good on the Sabbath. They do not answer. Taking the lack of a reply as proof that they knew the right answer, he immediately touches the man's hand and heals it. Frustrated and furious, the Pharisees begin to discuss with each other what they should do to Jesus.

General observations. Luke followed Mt's order to obtain this story. With this account Luke completed his series of conflict stories. He has now explained why the Pharisees had animosity towards Jesus. Luke has made several expansions to Mt's account to underscore the reasons for the actions of the Pharisees (cf. Lk 6:7-8). Also, a portion of Mt that Luke omitted here (Mt 12:11-12) is echoed later in Lk 14:4-6.

Lk 6:11. The link-word "Sabbath" (Lk 6:1, 5, 7, 9) binds this unit (Lk 6:7, 9) closely with the previous one (Lk 6:1, 5). Lk 6:11 contains Lukan modifications (Collison 216; πίμπλημι Collison 60; ἀλλήλων Collison 201-202; and τί ἄν with the optative, Collison 222, cf. Goulder 1:340), but the verse is basically similar to Mt 12:14.

¶ 27. Jesus chooses 12 Apostles; heals many who are sick and demon-possessed

(Mt 4:23-5:1; 9:35-10:4) Mt 12:15 ===> **Lk 6:12-20a**

In the face of mounting opposition, Luke portrays Jesus going aside into the mountains to pray. We have reached another major turning point in the story. After spending an entire night in prayer and supplication, Jesus gathers his many disciples together and chooses Twelve, whom he calls his "Apostles,"—those who will be sent to preach the Kingdom of God and heal. Then, coming down with them onto a level place, he is part of a huge crowd that has gathered from all parts of the country. Many are sick and possessed by unclean spirits. He heals them all. Then, he begins to explain the heart of the gospel to them and to his Twelve Apostles.

General observations. The following Synopsis shows how Luke, having arrived at Mt 12:15 (which is the beginning of a summary passage in Mt), moved back from Mt 12:15 to similar material in Mt 4:23–5:1, with its list of the names of the Twelve and the introduction to the Sermon on the Mount. With the following synopsis as a guide, let us examine the evidence for this compositional move on Luke's part in greater detail.

Synopsis for Lk 6:12-20a

Illustrating how Luke moved from one Matthean summary transitional passage (Mt 12:14-15) back to a similar summary passage (Mt 4:23-5:1) to create a healing summary and depict Jesus' choice of all twelve disciples.

Mt 4:23-5:1	**Mt 12:14-15, 9:35-10:4**	**Lk 6:11-20a**
	14 ἐξελθόντες	
	δὲ οἱ Φαρισαῖοι	**11** αὐτοὶ δὲ
		ἐπλήσθησαν ἀνοίας,
	συμβούλιον ἔλαβον	
		καὶ διελάλουν
	κατ᾽ αὐτοῦ	πρὸς ἀλλήλους
	ὅπως αὐτὸν ἀπολέσωσιν.	τί ἂν ποιήσαιεν τῷ Ἰησοῦ.
23 Καὶ περιῆγεν	**9:35** Καὶ περιῆγεν ὁ	
	Ἰησοῦς	
ἐν ὅλῃ τῇ Γαλιλαίᾳ,	τὰς πόλεις πάσας	
	καὶ τὰς κώμας,	
διδάσκων ἐν ταῖς	διδάσκων ἐν ταῖς	
συναγωγαῖς	συναγωγαῖς	
αὐτῶν καὶ κηρύσσων	αὐτῶν καὶ κηρύσσων	
τὸ εὐαγγέλιον τῆς	τὸ εὐαγγέλιον τῆς	
βασιλείας	βασιλείας	
καὶ θεραπεύων πᾶσαν	καὶ θεραπεύων πᾶσαν	See Lk 6:18
νόσον	νόσον	
καὶ πᾶσαν μαλακίαν	καὶ πᾶσαν μαλακίαν.	
ἐν τῷ λαῷ.		See Lk 6:17
24 καὶ ἀπῆλθεν ἡ ἀκοὴ		See Lk 6:18
αὐτοῦ		
εἰς ὅλην τὴν Συρίαν·		
καὶ προσήνεγκαν αὐτῷ		
πάντας τοὺς κακῶς		
ἔχοντας		
ποικίλαις νόσοις		See Lk 6:18
καὶ βασάνοις συνεχομένους		
καὶ δαιμονιζομένους		
καὶ σεληνιαζομένους		
καὶ παραλυτικούς,		
καὶ ἐθεράπευσεν αὐτούς.	**12:15b**	
25 καὶ ἠκολούθησαν αὐτω	καὶ ἠκολούθησαν αὐτω	
ὄχλοι πολλοὶ	ὄχλοι πολλοί,	See Lk 6:17
	καὶ ἐθεράπευσεν αὐτοὺς	
	πάντας	See Lk 6:19
ἀπὸ τῆς Γαλιλαίας		
καὶ Δεκαπόλεως		
καὶ Ἱεροσολύμων		See Lk 6:17
καὶ Ἰουδαίας		
καὶ πέραν τοῦ Ἰορδάνου.		
5:1 Ἰδὼν δὲ τοὺς ὄχλους	**9:36a** Ἰδὼν δὲ τοὺς	**6:12** ἐγένετο δε
	ὄχλους...	
ἀνέβη	see Mt 12:15a	ἐν ταῖς ἡμέραις ταύταις

Synopsis for Lk 6:12-20a (cont.)

Matthew 5	Matthew 10	Luke 6
	[Mt 9:36b-38 omitted]	**Lk 6:12** ἐξελθεῖν αὐτὸν
Mt 5:1 εἰς τὸ ὄρος·		εἰς τὸ ὄρος προσεύξασθαι
καὶ καθίσαντος αὐτοῦ		καὶ ἦν διανυκτερεύων
		ἐν τῇ προσευχῇ τοῦ θεοῦ.
	Mt 10:1	**13** Καὶ ὅτε ἐγένετο ἡμέρα,
προσῆλθαν αὐτω	Καὶ προσκαλεσάμενος	προσεφώνησεν
	τοὺς δώδεκα	τοὺς
οἱ μαθηταὶ αὐτοῦ·	μαθητὰς αὐτοῦ	μαθητὰς αὐτοῦ
καὶ ἀνοίξας τὸ στόμα		
αὐτοῦ		
ἐδίδασκεν αὐτοὺς λέγων,	ἔδωκεν αὐτοῖς	καὶ ἐκλεξάμενος ἀπ᾽αὐτῶν
	ἐξουσίαν πνευμάτων	See Lk 6:18
	ἀκαθάρτων	
	ὥστε ἐκβάλλειν αὐτὰ	
	καὶ θεραπεύειν πᾶσαν	See Lk 6:18
	νόσον	
	καὶ πᾶσαν μαλακίαν	
	2 Τῶν δὲ δώδεκα	δώδεκα
		οὓς καὶ
	ἀποστόλων	ἀποστόλους
	τὰ ὀνοματά ἐστιν ταῦτα·	ὠνόμασεν·
	Σίμων	**14** Σίμωνα
	ὁ λεγόμενος Πέτρος	ὃν καὶ ὠνόμασεν Πέτρον,
	καὶ Ἀνδρέας	καὶ Ἀνδρέαν
	ὁ ἀδελφὸς αὐτου	τὸν ἀδελφὸν αὐτοῦ,
	καὶ Ἰάκωβος	καὶ Ἰάκωβον
	ὁ τοῦ Ζεβεδαίου	
	καὶ Ἰωάννης	καὶ Ἰωάννην
	ὁ ἀδελφὸς αὐτοῦ,	
	3 Φίλιππος	καὶ Φίλιππον
	καὶ Βαρθαλομαῖος,	καὶ Βαρθολομαῖον
	Θωμᾶς	
	καὶ Μαθθαῖος	**15** καὶ Μαθθαῖον
	ὁ τελώνης,	
		καὶ Θωμᾶν,
	Ἰάκωβος ὁ τοῦ Ἀλφαίου	καὶ Ἰάκωβον Ἀλφαίου
	καὶ θαδδαῖος	
	4 Σίμων	καὶ Σίμωνα
	ὁ Καναναῖος	τὸν καλούμενον Ζηλωτὴν
		16 καὶ Ἰούδαν Ἰακώβου,
	καὶ Ἰδούδας ὁ Ἰσκαριώτης	καὶ Ἰδούδαν Ἰσκαριώθ,
	ὁ καὶ παραδοὺς αὐτὸν	ὃς ἐγενετο προδότης.
		17 Καὶ καταβὰς
		μετ᾽ αὐτῶν
		ἔστη ἐπὶ τόπου πεδινοῦ,
See Mt 5:1, 4:25	See Mt 9:36a, 12:15	καὶ ὄχλος πολὺς
	See Mt 10:1	μαθητῶν αὐτοῦ,
See Mt 4:23		καὶ πλῆθος πολὺ τοῦ λαου
See Mt 4:25		ἀπὸ πάσης τῆς Ἰουδαίας

Synopsis for Lk 6:12-20a (cont.)

		Lk 6:17 καὶ Ἰερουσαλὴμ
		καὶ τῆς παραλίου
		Τύρου καὶ Σιδῶνος,
See Mt 4:24		18 οἳ ἦλθον ἀκοῦσαι αὐτοῦ
See Mt 4:24	See Mt 9:35, 10:1	καὶ ἰαθῆναι ἀπὸ τῶν νόσων
		αὐτῶν·
		καὶ οἱ ἐνοχλούμενοι
	See Mt 10:1	ἀπὸ πνευμάτων ἀκαθάρτων
See Mt 4:24	See Mt 9:35, 10:1	ἐθεραπεύοντο.
		19 καὶ πᾶς ὁ ὄχλος
		ἐζήτουν ἅπτεσθαι αὐτοῦ,
		ὅτι δύναμις παρ᾽ αὐτοῦ
		ἐξήρχετο
	See Mt 12:15	καὶ ἰᾶτο πάντας.
See Mt 5:1b		**20a** Καὶ αὐτὸς ἐπάρας
		τοὺς ὀφθαλμοὺς αὐτοῦ
		εἰς τοὺς μαθητὰς αὐτοῦ
		ἔλεγεν,

Lk 6:12-20a. Luke (6:12) read in Mt 12:15a that Jesus ἀνεχώρησεν ("departed"). Luke interpreted this to mean that Jesus departed *to the hills to pray*; a characteristic Lukan theme (other occurrences: Lk 3:21; 5:16; 9:18; 9:28-29; 11:1; 22:41; 22:42). After that, as he had done with Mt 4:13 earlier, Luke "filled out" the Matthean narrative at this place. Luke had Jesus select *all twelve* disciples (Lk 6:13-16); and then had him *return* to a level place to accommodate a large crowd gathered for a sermon (Lk 6:17-19; perhaps avoiding Mt's impression of a crowd trying to listen on a mountain). Next, in Mt 12:15b, Luke found language echoing the context of Mt 4:23-5:1, where also "many crowds followed Jesus and he healed them." Luke added the references to Gentiles (cf. "Tyre and Sidon" in Lk 6:17) in combining the Matthean summaries from Mt 4:25 and 12:15. The use of Mt 4:23-5:1 and 12:14-15 also echoes Mt 9:35-10:2, the introduction to the Call of the Twelve (Mt 10:2-4), which may have prompted Luke to tell that story first (Lk 6:13-16). By this strategy, Luke has introduced all of the 12 Apostles, as well as the crowds, for Jesus' great sermon.

Thus conceived, Luke's setting for this momentous sermon is much more elaborately prepared for than Matthew's similar sermon (Mt 4:23-7:29). Moreover those Apostles, who were expected later on in the mission of the Church (in Acts) to authenticate the tradition of Jesus' teachings, were all present for this first great sermon in Luke, in contrast to Matthew.[1]

[1] On Luke's use of Mt in this entire introductory unit in Lk 6:11-20a, see David Barrett Peabody, "Repeated Language in Matthew: Clues to the Order and Composition of Luke and Mark," in *Society of Biblical Literature 1991 Seminar Papers*, SBLSP 30, ed. Eugene H. Lovering, Jr. (Atlanta: Scholars Press, 1991) 657-667.

• There is literary evidence that Luke avoided making Mt's Sermon on the Mount Jesus' first public sermon, and that he created instead a first public sermon in Jesus' home town, using parts of Mt's Sermon on the Mount later as Jesus' *second* public sermon. Luke used part of the concluding compositional phrases from Mt 7:28-29 to conclude Jesus' first speech in Nazareth and the rest to conclude Jesus' second speech "on the plain." The following synopsis will illustrate this point.

Synopsis of Lk 7:1; 4:31-32 // Mt 7:28-29

Illustrating Luke's use of the concluding phrasealogy at the end of Mt's Sermon on the Mount *twice*; first to conclude Jesus' speech in Nazareth and second to conclude Jesus' sermon to his disciples and crowds "on the plain."

Conclusion to Sermon on the Mount Mt 7:28-29	**Luke's first use: to end Jesus' sermon in Nazareth Lk 4:31f.**	**Luke's second use: to end Jesus' Sermon on the Plain Lk 7:1**
Καὶ ἐγένετο	καὶ	Ἐπειδὴ
ὅτε ἐτέλεσεν ὁ Ἰησοῦς		ἐπλήρωσεν
τοὺς λόγους τούτους		πάντα τὰ ῥήματα αὐτοῦ
		εἰς τὰς ἀκοὰςτοῦ λαοῦ,
		εἰσῆλθεν εἰς Καφαρναούμ.
	ἦν διδάσκων αὐτοὺς	
	ἐν τοῖς σάββασιν· καὶ	
ἐξεπλήσσοντο οἱ ὄχλοι	ἐξεπλήσσοντο	
ἐπὶ τῇ διδαχῇ αὐτοῦ·	ἐπὶ τῇ διδαχῇ αὐτοῦ·	
ἦν γὰρ διδάσκων αὐτοὺς		
ὡς ἐξουσίαν ἔχων	ὅτι ἐν ἐξουσίᾳ	
	ἦν ὁ λόγος αὐτοῦ.	
καὶ οὐκ ὡς οἱ γραμματεῖς αὐτῶν.		

EXCURSUS: HOW LUKE EXCERPTED MATTHEW'S SERMON ON THE MOUNT

With the setting for this great sermon thus skillfully prepared, Luke portrayed Jesus delivering a series of simple but powerful statements to his Twelve Apostles and all the rest of his "disciples" (i.e., Luke's audience). The series of themes begins with "good news to the poor" (an echo of the first public sermon in Nazareth; Isa 61:1-2), followed by warnings not to retaliate for evil, nor to act in a condemnatory way. The sermon concludes with a paraphrase of Matthew's famous "Two Ways" (Mt 7:5-27) exhortations to live according to his teachings, not just hear the words and then forget them.

Luke's version of this sermon begins with the Beatitudes and ends with the Parable of the Two Houses. Including the Beatitudes and the Two Houses, these seven units are in virtually the same order in Mt's sermon and in Luke's.

Mt 5:2-12	Beatitudes	Lk 6:20b-26
Mt 5:44; 7:12; 5:38-42	On retaliation	Lk 6:27-31
Mt 5:43-48	On love of enemies	Lk 6:32-36
Mt 7:1-5	On judging harshly	Lk 6:37-42
Mt 7:15-20	By their fruits	Lk 6:43-45
Mt 7:21-23	Lord, Lord	Lk 6:46
Mt 7:24-27	Two houses	Lk 6:47-49

It is, therefore, quite likely that Luke selectively appropriated material from Mt's Sermon on the Mount in order, including a similar beginning, middle, and ending. The rationale for each specific selection will be spelled out in greater detail below. In addition, Luke artfully linked together Jesus' inaugural sermon (Lk 4:16-30) at the beginning of this Part and the Sermon on the Plain at the end of this Part (Lk 6:20-7:1) by having both echo Isa 61:1-2, giving the effect of a tight thematic unity between Jesus' sermons and his ministry. Let us examine each of the pericopes in greater detail.

¶ 28. Good news to the poor, warnings to the rich

Mt 5:2-12 ===> **Lk 6:20b-26**

As at his first sermon in Nazareth, on this great occasion, Luke portrays Jesus unequivocally siding with the poor and oppressed of the world: "Blessed are you poor people, for yours is the Kingdom of Heaven!" And with the hungry of the world: "Blessed are you hungry people! You shall have plenty to eat!" And with the grief-stricken and sorrowful people of the world: "Blessed are you people who are weeping! Soon you shall be laughing!" Jesus' message is simple and far-reaching. God's great reversal will overturn all of the power, success and joy of the evil, rich and wicked people in power in this world. Soon it will be *they* who will weep, hunger and be sorrowful!

General observations. Luke has already made Isa 61:1-2 the basic text for the sermon in Nazareth (Lk 4:16-30). Here, Luke again returned to the central theme of Isaiah's message and recast the Matthean beatitudes along the lines of Blessings and Woes similar to the pattern of Deut. 27-28. Scholars have long noted the almost sociological tenor of Jesus' words in Luke's version of the Matthean Beatitudes. It is our view that this version is secondary to Mt and is to be explained by Luke's consistent reshaping of the entire Gospel account to emphasize God's mercy toward the poor, oppressed and sick of the world (as we saw in the birth and infancy accounts and the inaugural sermon in Nazareth; note also Luke's unique inclusion of the Parable of the Rich Fool, and The Rich Man and Lazarus). Mt has a traditional set of blessings addressed to "they" (Mt 5:3-10) which is linked to parables addressed to "you" (plural; Mt 5:13-15). The closing beatitude (Mt 5:11-12) shifts to the second person plural in a saying full of Matthean phraseology. On the other hand, Luke put the entire set of

Beatitudes into the second person plural, abbreviated them to four Beatitudes, but included the Matthean "transitional Beatitude" virtually unchanged. This use of a Matthean composition constitutes evidence for Luke's use of canonical Mt, not a source like "Q."[2]

Lk 6:20b. In Lk, first comes a set of four who have "chosen Life": the poor, the hungry, the sorrowful, and the hated. Luke's striking revision of Mt focuses on "you" actual πτωχοί (Lk 6:20) instead of Mt's more ambiguous phrase πτωχοὶ τῷ πνεύματι (Mt 5:3).

Lk 6:21. As for the πεινῶντες, these poor are really hungry, cf. Mt's πεινῶντες...τὴν δικαιοσύνην (Mt 5:6). Lk's κλαῖοντες– these poor and hungry are "crying out" to God in their overwhelming suffering; cf. Mt's more restrained πενθοῦντες (Mt 5:4). As befits the Son of God who has come in the spirit of Isa 61:1-3, Jesus affirms their safety and security in God's love.

Lk 6:22. Luke expanded Mt's eighth beatitude (Mt 5:11) into another four-fold structure (Lk 6:22) to describe the enmity that the poor and despised receive "on account of the Son of Man" (cf. Mt 5:11 "on my account"). Finally, by adding ἐν ἐκείνῃ τῇ ἡμέρᾳ (Lk 6:23) to Mt 5:12, Luke echoed the blessings of the Day of the Lord announced earlier by Jesus in Nazareth (Lk 4:21). Thus, as noted above, Jesus' first two sermons as narrated by Luke are tightly bound together.

Lk 6:23-26. Matthew has no contrasting set of Woes. These have been added by Luke in keeping with his theme of the great eschatological reversal (cf. Lk 1:53-55; 16:19-31; 18:9-14; 14:11//18:14; 9:24//17:33; 13:30).

¶ 29. Do not retaliate for evil but have mercy

(Mt 5:39-42; 7:12; 7:1-5) Mt 5:43-44, 46-48 ====> **Lk 6:27-36**

So far, Jesus has basically reiterated and deepened what he said in his first sermon. Now Luke portrays Jesus moving into a completely new area: the necessity for all who would be his disciples to practice non-retaliation toward those who crush and oppress them. The extension of compassion is to be their life's goal, not vengeance.

General observations. Luke has just finished a carefully constructed series of vignettes in which Jesus is attacked by influential religious leaders. A powerful dramatic irony has been building up. If Jesus had so much authority, the reader could be wondering, why didn't he retaliate against his enemies' evil schemes? Now Luke is prepared to explain Jesus' actions fully. He gives Jesus' answer to "his disciples." All those who will follow him will suffer hatred and exclusion as he has (and will). The answer is carefully arranged into four basic units that are all framed by

---

[2] C. H. Dodd, "The Beatitudes: a Form-Critical Study," in *More New Testament Studies*, ed. C. H. Dodd (Manchester: Manchester University Press, 1968)1-10; see further Goulder 1:157.

the fundamental admonition: "love your enemies" (Lk 6:27/Lk 6:35a). First, there are four admonitions to love, do well, bless, and pray for your enemies (Lk 6:27-28). Then come two dual admonitions on the theme of giving to others (Lk 6:29-30) summarized by the famous "Golden Rule" (Lk 6:31). Next comes a series of admonitions to practice unrestricted love (Lk 6:32-34). This whole series is then given a brief summary (Lk 6:35a) ending with what was called in Hellenistic rhetoric an αἰτία, a *summary rationale or explanation*: "if you do these things you will be like God who is merciful to all!" (Lk 6:35b-36), which is Luke's very significant revision of Mt's strikingly Semitic conclusion at Mt 5:48. This entire theme is to be found repeatedly in Paul's letters, most notably Rom 12:14-21. Jesus' message is structured to be directly applicable to the church in the wider Greco-Roman world.

Lk 6:27-36. Luke's characteristic vocabulary is visible throughout; e.g. τύπτειν (Lk 6:29) for ῥαπίζειν (Mt 5:39), κωλύειν (Lk 6:29) for ἄφες (Mt 5:40), and χάρις (Lk 6:32) for μισθός (Mt 5:46).

¶ 30. Do not condemn others; look to your own faults

(Mt 15:14; 10:24-25; [6:12]) Mt 7:1-5 ====> **Lk 6:37-42**

Then Luke portrays Jesus' warning against finding fault in others, using four short sayings focused on the idea of *blindness*: Do not condemn (Lk 6:37-38); the parable of the "blind guides" (namely, the Pharisees who condemn, Lk 6:39); "blind" students (who condemn, i.e., look down on their teacher, Lk 6:40); and finally the condemnatory person who can see only the faults in others, but is "blind" to his own (Lk 6:41-42).

General observations. The use of Matthew is complex but understandable, as Luke wove together a four-fold set of sayings around the theme of warning against condemnation. Here is an instance where Luke drastically "re-ordered" Matthew's narrative in the interest of creating a common theme.

Lk 6:37-42. Luke began by taking the passage from Mt 7:1-2, "Judge not...." The Matthean passage was expanded considerably in Lk 6:37b-38 by the addition of further prudential advice on getting along with others. Then Luke (6:39) echoed the brief saying in Mt 15:14 where Jesus likens the Pharisees (who have, in Mt's *wider context*, just condemned Jesus for his teaching on cleanliness) to "blind guides" (a major Matthean concept; see Mt 15:14; 23:16, 17, 24, 26); that is, blind teachers of the Law (cf. Lk 5:27-6:11). Then, by an association of ideas, to continue the theme, Luke used another reference to teachers from the missionary discourse in Mt 10:24-25, the point of which was, again, "blind" students who consider themselves above their teacher (i.e., above Jesus) and condemn him. Finally, Luke came back to the context in Mt 7:1-5 and finished with the parable about being blind to one's own faults.

Lk 6:39a εἶπεν δὲ καὶ παραλβολὴν αὐτοῖς, if it is part of the original text, is Lukan redaction (cf. Lk 5:36; 12:16; 13:6; 14:7; 15:3; 20:9, 19; 21:29).

¶ 31. The good disciple will produce good fruit

Mt 7:16-28 (Mt 12:33-35) ====> **Lk 6:43-49**

For the conclusion, Luke portrays Jesus drawing a decisive comparison: everyone is either a good or an evil plant or tree. The one produces good fruit (figs, grapes); the other produces rotten fruit. Do not expect that merely mouthing "Jesus is Lord!" while doing evil will fool God! Then comes a metaphor: be like the person who builds his life upon a solid foundation of good deeds. He or she will stand on the Day of Judgment before God and be blessed.

General observations. Luke skipped over a number of sayings in Mt 7:6-15 and came to Mt 7:16-21 where he combined the saying about a tree known by its fruits with the similar saying in Mt 12:33-35. This brought him to the conclusion of the Sermon in Mt 7:21, 24-27//Lk 6:46-49: the Parable of the Two Houses, with its Matthean emphasis on hearing and doing. Luke made "hearing and doing" a major feature of his conclusion (Lk 6:46-47, 49). This emphasis on hearing and doing is an anticipation of a major theme in Luke's account of Jesus' ministry later on (Lk 8:19-21; 11:27-28).

¶ 32. Back in Capernaum, Jesus heals a centurion's servant

Mt 7:28; 8:5-13 ====> **Lk 7:1-10**

The traditional "Mount of Beatitudes" is a short distance around the shore of the Sea of Galilee from the village of Capernaum. Interestingly enough, Luke says, "After finishing his great sermon, Jesus entered Capernaum" as if it were close by. In doing so, Jesus ends his first journey with its goal to preach "in other cities." A centurion residing in Capernaum hears of his return and sends a request to Jesus to heal his sick servant. He reveals his awareness to Jewish susceptibilities by not requesting the Jewish teacher to come under his roof personally, lest he incur ritual impurity. The centurion only asks that Jesus say the word and his servant will be healed. Jesus marvels at this foreigner's faith in him.

General observations. Having completed this first utilization of Mt's Sermon on the Mount (other parts will be used later on), Luke (7:1a) acknowledged this fact by echoing Mt 7:28. Then, having already utilized Mt 8:1-4 (cf. Lk 5:12-16), Lk turned to the *next* pericope in Mt's order, "The Healing of the Centurion's Servant" (Mt 8:5-13). The centurion (a God-fearer) fit perfectly into Luke's concept of the faithful Gentile (cf. Acts 10:1-11:18). Since the story occurs, in Mt's version, in Capernaum, Luke could use it as the end-piece to his construct of Jesus' first missionary journey.

Luke was now nearing the end of his account of the first half of Jesus' Galilean ministry. To prepare for the second half of the Galilean ministry, Luke created a transitional, interwoven unit linking the Healing of the Centurion's Servant (Lk 7:1-10) with the raising of the dead son of the widow of Nain (Lk 7:11-15) to round out this portion of his narrative. These two accounts echo the exploits of the two great prophets, Elijah and Elisha (see below), that were mentioned in Jesus' opening Sermon in Nazareth (Lk 4:25-27). As the one who embodied in himself the prophetic tradition, Jesus was bringing to full realization the hope expressed in Lk 4:14-16.

Lk 7:1. Here Luke has clearly re-written Mt 7:28a in his own idiom (cf. Goulder 1:376). At the conclusion to his version of Jesus' inaugural sermon, Luke paraphrased Mt 7:28b-29a: "they were amazed at his teaching because his word was with authority" (Lk 4:31-32). The presence of this terminology drawn from a *redactional* section of Mt, both at the end of Luke's inaugural Sermon (Lk 4:31-32) *and again* at the end of the Sermon on the Plain (Lk 7:1), is strong evidence for Luke's direct use of canonical Mt.

Lk 7:3-6. Luke, by the use of verisimilitude, has expanded the Matthean account of the centurion's request to Jesus to show his great respect for Jesus' power and the extent of the centurion's faith in Jesus. The centurion does not approach Jesus directly but relays his request through elders of the Jews (Lk 7:3). The elders speak highly of the benefits bestowed by the centurion (Lk 7:4-5). There *are* worthy outsiders! A second embassy (Lk 7:6-7) represents the centurion as being a man of extraordinary faith: "But say the word, and let my servant be healed" (Lk 7:7). Surely this man with his great faith is one who "hears and does the word of God" (Lk 6:47, 49).

Lk 7:10 Ὑποστρέψαντες εἰς τὸν οἶκον is characteristic of the text of Luke. A form of ὑποστρέφειν occurs over thirty times in Lk-Acts and never in Matthew. Luke omitted Mt 8:11-12; but he will use it later at Lk 13:28-29.

Interweaving Transitional Unit (First Part). Lk 7:11–15

At this point, Luke was ready to begin a new series of stories that would complete his account of Jesus' Galilean mission. According to his customary compositional procedure (see Introduction pp. 33f., 44), Luke created a carefully crafted transitional pericope that continued themes related to the immediately preceding stories and, at the same time, introduced themes that would follow. We place the beginning of this transitional pericope here, as a conclusion to Part Three and we will locate the conclusion of the pericope as an introduction to Part Four (see p. 113). In this way we attempt to be faithful to the transitional nature of the pericope and to call attention to retrospective parts of it here and prospective parts of it there.

¶ 33. Jesus goes to Nain and brings the son of a widow back to life

Lk 7:11-15 (interweaving transitional pericope, first part)

Not long afterward, Jesus sets out with his Twelve Apostles to go to a nearby village called Nain. A large crowd accompanies them. As they near the city, they encounter a long funeral cortège slowly leaving Nain. It seems that a young man has died, the only son of a widow. The crowd is wailing over the tragedy that has befallen the widow and son. Jesus immediately feels compassion for the woman and tells her to dry her tears. Gently stopping the pall bearers, he speaks to the young man, "Arise!" The dead man instantly sits up and begins speaking. Jesus helps him down and gives him back to his mother.

General observations. This story is not in Mt. Indeed, as we will see later in the general observations for the account of John's Question to Jesus (Lk 7:18-35), Luke is now in the act of moving forward a considerable distance in Mt's order. Hence, we may conclude that this story has been introduced here, possibly from Luke's nonMatthean tradition, to prepare for Luke's use of Mt's account about John the Baptist's question. At the same time, Luke shaped this story so that it continued themes closely related to the story of the Centurion's Servant. He has just told of the healing of a servant near death (Lk 7:1-10; cf. ἤμελλεν τελευτᾶν at Lk 7:2). He now appended an even more impressive account, the resuscitation of a young man from death itself (cf. τεθνηκώς in Lk 7:12). These two stories can be seen as balanced: one deals with the dying son of a man and the second with the dead son of a woman; one contrasts a powerful, Gentile soldier with a powerless, Jewish widow.

Lk 7:11-15. The account reflects an implicit Elijah-Elisha motif that was made explicit by Luke at Lk 4:25-27. The account of the healing of the centurion's servant (Lk 7:1-10) has many formal similarities to the account of Elisha's healing of Naaman, the leper, in 2 Kgs 5:1-14 to which Luke had made explicit reference in Lk 4:27. Although this story (Lk 7:11-15) has certain verbal similarities to the Elijah story in 1 Kgs 17, the similarities are not numerous enough to lead one to the conclusion that Luke has composed this account primarily on the basis of 1 Kgs 17:17-24 (*pace* Goulder 1:383-384).

• There are numerous Lukan stylistic characteristics in this pericope: καὶ ἐγένετο to open a new unit (Lk 7:11) is a certain linguistic usage of Luke (Collison 43), as is the use of πορεύομαι followed by εἰς (Collison 61). Similarly, "the articular participle of καλέω used as an appositive usually to a proper noun" is a Lukan characteristic (Collison 80), as are ὡς (Collison 121), ὡς δὲ ἤγγισεν (Collison 228), and Μὴ κλαῖε (Collison 231). Even though Luke may have found the story in his nonMatthean tradition, he has used it in an adept manner for his own compositional purposes.

PART FOUR LK 7:16–9:50

JESUS IS SHOWN TO BE THE SON OF GOD

Overview

In Part Four of his narrative, Luke related the final, most miraculous events in all of Jesus' Galilean ministry. Basing his narrative primarily on Matthew, but including significant material from nonMatthean tradition, Luke carefully constructed a gradually ascending series of events that led to the final luminous manifestation, directly from heaven, of none other than Israel's lawgiver, Moses, as well as the great prophet Elijah, while Jesus was transfigured into pure light and a heavenly voice proclaimed: "This is my Son. Listen to him!" This scene represented the zenith and apex of all of the rising action in Luke's Gospel from the birth of Jesus up through the whole story of his public activity in Galilee. After this, Luke moved on to the next major part in his chronological history, Jesus' "long march" to Jerusalem, during which he taught his disciples how to live the Christian life.

If Luke focused in Part Four on the increasingly powerful miracles performed by Jesus, culminating in the manifestation of his divine sonship, Luke also wove a second theme around the first that stood in powerful ironic tension with it: the increasingly negative portrayal of the twelve disciples. Beginning with a description of the Mission of the Twelve that ended up being surprisingly inconsequential, this theme was brought to its own climax immediately after the Transfiguration scene in a series of five anecdotes where they are shown to be incompetent, blind, petty, exclusive and vengeful. Within the opening units of Part Five, Luke continued to suggest not only the inadequacy of the original twelve disciples, but went on to challenge the fitness of three more anonymous, would-be disciples. At that point Luke introduced an account (found nowhere in Matthew) that told how Jesus suddenly chose 72 other disciples and sent them out on a *second* preaching and healing mission. When they got back, they told Jesus how successful they had been, and Jesus gave them praise and blessings far beyond anything he had said to the original Twelve when they returned. It is a very intriguing section in Luke's Gospel, one worthy of much more analysis and discussion.

Having said that Part Four is where Luke narrated the climax of Jesus' Galilean ministry, we should add that there seem to be four pronounced divisions or sections within it.

In the first section, "A mighty prophet has arisen?" (Lk 7:16-50), Luke introduced the theme which we take to be central to all of Part Four: Who or what is Jesus?

In the second section, "Be mindful how you respond to the Word of God!" (Lk 8:1-21), the central theme linking these three pericopes together is the warning: "Take heed how you hear the Word of God!" This section begins with Jesus and the Twelve setting off on yet another tour "through the cities and villages of Galilee."

In the third section, "Jesus travels about performing a series of great miracles and then sends out the Twelve Apostles to do the same" (Lk 8:22-9:11), Luke paved the way for the story of the sending of the Twelve by selecting three miracle stories from Mt 8 and 9 that Luke had not already utilized. This section of miracle stories served to demonstrate Jesus' divine powers which he then conferred on the Twelve prior to sending them out.

In the fourth section, "The conclusion to Jesus' Galilean ministry" (Lk 9:12-36), the final events of the Galilean ministry are at hand. Luke portrayed Jesus miraculously producing enough food for more than five thousand people, after which he asked his disciples who the people were saying he was. They told him and then he asked who they, his own disciples, said he was. Peter's answer prompted Jesus to warn them immediately to tell no one what they have just heard, lest the authorities—fearing he may well be "the Christ of God," not proceed against him as the Scriptures predict they will. Then, in the final scene of Part Four, before three select disciples, God himself answers the question of who Jesus is once and for all: God's Elected Son. After that, Luke began a carefully constructed transitional section (Lk 9:37-62) which not only focused on Lk 9:51, the beginning of Luke's account of Jesus' last journey to Jerusalem (Lk 9:51–19:27), but also provided a rationale for Luke's distinctive story of the call, commissioning and return of the 72 other disciples (Lk 10:1ff.).

Let us now turn to a more detailed consideration of Part Four.

Section One: A Mighty Prophet Has Arisen? Lk 7:16–50

Luke is now prepared to describe the remainder of Jesus' activities in Galilee. To do this, he will make careful use of his major source, Matthew, and include, where appropriate, nonMatthean tradition. As noted at the end of Part Three, Luke connected these two Parts together by means of an interweaving transitional story. We treated the beginning of this story at the end of Part Three (Lk 7:11-15). We discuss the conclusion (Lk 7:16-17) here because it introduces the central theme that will recur throughout Part Four: Who is this Jesus?

This first section of Part Four consists of three stories. Following his practice of juxtaposing narratives about John the Baptist with parallel narratives about Jesus, Luke moved forward in Matthew's order to Mt 11:2-19, John's question to Jesus. Here Jesus gives a very carefully nuanced final appraisal of John the Baptist to the crowd. After this, John the Baptist is mentioned in the Gospel of Luke only in passing, almost always to highlight the supremacy of Jesus to him (see, e. g., Lk 9:7-9, 19; 11:1; 16:16; 20:3-8).

As we noted above, the starting point for this section is the reaction of the onlookers in Nain. That will lead to John's Question, and then to the incident of the Woman with thransitionalstion: Is Jesus a mighty *prophet?*

¶ 34. Fame of Jesus spreads everywhere. He is God's mighty prophet
Lk 7:16-17 (interweaving transitional pericope, second part)

When the people see the dead son of the widow rise up and begin speaking, they are amazed and terrified. "A great prophet has arisen!" some shout. Others say, "God has visited his people!" These statements quickly spread throughout Judea and all the surrounding country.

General observations. As noted in the general observation for the final story in Part Three, "Jesus brings a widow's son back to life," Luke did not get that story from Matthew. Luke is in the process of moving forward in Mt from the Sermon on the Mount (Mt 4:23-7:29//Lk 6:20-7:1a) to the story of the Centurion's Servant (Mt 8:5-13//Lk 7:1b-10), and then to the account of John the Baptist sending a question to Jesus (Mt 11:2-9//Lk 7:18-35). Much of the material that intervenes between these Matthean stories has already been used by Luke. Luke is concerned to introduce this summary (Lk 7:16-17) at this point in his larger narrative, since he will make the issue of the identity of Jesus of Nazareth the centerpiece of Part Four. That theme is struck in this Lukan "fame summary" by the crowd which proclaims, "A mighty prophet has arisen!" and "God has visited his people!" (cf. Lk 4:14-15, 37 and 5:15-16 for similar Lukan summary passages.)

Lk 7:16. The report of what the crowds actually say in direct speech is significant. The specific terms echo pronouncements from the infancy material about John the Baptist. Cf. Zechariah's speech: "Blessed be the Lord God of Israel for he has *visited* and redeemed *his people*" (Lk 1:68); "And you, child, will be called *prophet* of the Most High" (Lk 1:76). The reaction of the crowd at Nain *makes Jesus appear to be perceived as a prophet in the tradition of John the Baptist*. In this way, Luke set the stage for Mt's story in which John the Baptist sent two disciples (he cannot go in person since he is in prison) to ask Jesus: *who are you?* And *that* question will resonate throughout Part Four, until it is answered by God directly from Heaven. Then, once it is crystal clear who Jesus really is, Luke can devote *ten chapters* to teachings of the Lord Jesus (Part Five).

Lk 7:17. The reason Luke stressed the wide area in which this report spread was to make the next verse plausible: "the disciples of John [heard and] told him all these things."

• These verses are replete with signs of Lukan compositional activity. Lukan linguistic characteristics include: ἐδόξαζον τὸν θεόν (Collison 46), λαός (Collison 173-174), περὶ αὐτοῦ of Jesus (Collison 140), περίχωρος (Collison 175), the collocation of καί + a verb meaning "to go out" with ἦχος/φήμη/λόγος + ὅλος/πᾶς + περὶ αὐτοῦ + περίχωρος (Collison 214).

¶ 35. John the Baptist sends an inquiry to Jesus
Mt 11:2-19 ====> **Lk 7:18-35**

John's disciples hear of the miraculous event in Nain and tell their master. He immediately seeks to verify the report from Jesus himself. Sending two messengers, he asks Jesus who he is. Jesus tells the messengers to report to John what they have seen and heard: the blind see again, lame people walk again, lepers are cured, dead are raised, and the poor have good news announced to them. After the messengers are gone, Jesus tells the crowds that John was thought to be a prophet, but he was much more than just another prophet. Luke adds in a parenthetical aside, "the Pharisees and lawyers rejected him and thus rejected God's purpose for them."

General observations. The reason Luke concluded the story of the raising of the dead boy at Nain the way he did is now clear: the crowds in Lk 7:16 speak of Jesus as if he were like John the Baptist: a mighty prophet. This association of ideas paves the way for Luke to move forward in Mt's order to the account of John's question to Jesus. He took this story (including Jesus' comment on John) largely intact, omitting only Mt 11:12-13, which he will use later, at Lk 16:16. Why did Luke want this story here in his order? Because it gave Luke a decisive opportunity to answer, in the most powerful way possible, these foundational questions: "was Jesus no more than a follower of John the Baptist? Was Jesus just a prophet? Who *was* he really?"

Lk 7:18-20. These verses correspond closely to the account in Mt, except that Luke *repeats* the question of John. Where Mt simply has John send the question to Jesus, Luke has John do that ("Are you he who is to come?") and then has the messengers of John repeat the same statement in the presence of Jesus: "Are you he who is to come?" The effect in Luke is to underscore the question so that it is impossible to miss. On the other hand, there is a vague quality to this question which Luke finds helpful, just as Jesus' answer back to John is also curiously indirect (more on this in a moment).

• Lk 7:19 says that John sent *two* disciples to Jesus in contrast to Mt's "sent word by his disciples" (Mt 11:2). Dual messengers are characteristic of Lukan delegations (Lk 10:1; 19:29; 22:8; Acts 23:23).

• Lk 7:19-20 (cf. Mt 11:3) "Are you he who is to come?" is curiously and wonderfully vague. John did not come right out and ask, "Are you Elijah?" or "Are you the Messiah?" Whatever the question meant in Mt's context, Luke used this pericope to bring to the forefront the question of Jesus' identity. This is the precise reason why Luke moved forward from the story of the Centurion's Servant (Mt 8:5-13) to John's Question to Jesus (Mt 11:2-6). In the process of retelling this account, Luke could begin dealing with the question of Jesus' true identity (it will come up many more times in the stories to come). In Luke's retelling, this story relegated

John the Baptist to his important, but clearly secondary, status relative to Jesus.

Lk 7:21. "In that hour", etc. is a Lukan composition added to Mt's account, being inserted between Mt 11:3 and 11:4, so that Jesus' answer, "Go and tell John *what you have just seen and heard*" could be based on the messengers' own personal, eye-witness experience. This is another example of the strikingly *literal* character of Luke's understanding of the history of Jesus' ministry.

Lk 7:22. Most of the activities that Jesus lists in his response to John seem to reflect the prophecies of Isaiah: "the blind receive their sight" (cf. Lk 4:18; 7:21-22//Isa 61:1-2; Isa 29:18; 35:5), "the lame walk" (cf. Lk 11:14; 7:22//Isa 35:6), "the deaf hear" (7:22//Isa 29:18; 35:5), and "the poor have the good news preached to them" (Lk 4:18; 6:20//Isa 29:19). The activities that do not reflect the prophecies of Isaiah (i.e., "the lepers are cleansed" and "the dead are raised") echo the actions of the prophets Elisha ("the lepers are cleansed" cf. Lk 4:27//2 Kgs 5) and Elijah ("the dead are raised"; cf. Lk 4:25-26//1 Kgs 17:17-24). Note that these same prophetic figures are mentioned in Jesus' inaugural sermon (Lk 4:16-30) and it is precisely these two stories (2 Kgs 5 and 1 Kgs 17:17-24) from the entire Elijah-Elisha cycle (1 Kgs 17:1–2 Kgs 13:21) that are specifically mentioned there. All of this discloses a striking thematic unity in Luke's compositional activity.

Lk 7:23. The appearance of σκανδαλίζειν in the text of Luke (Lk 7:23//Mt 11:6) is clear evidence of Luke's literary dependence on the canonical Gospel of Matthew. This word occurs 16 times in Mt in widely separated literary contexts. It is found in Lk only twice, always in contexts parallel to Mt: Mt 18:6//Lk 17:2; and Mt 18:7 (three times)//Lk 17:2 (once). This is a case where a frequently occurring, widely dispersed term in Mt appears in the Gospel of Luke only in passages parallel to Mt's order. As such, it is a "one-way indicator" of Luke's direct dependence on the canonical Gospel of Matthew, not a source such as "Q" (for an explanation of this term, see Introduction, pp. 21-24; for another example, see our discussions at Lk 8:40-56).

Lk 7:24-28. Jesus' comments on John the Baptist to the crowd in Lk are virtually identical to Mt 11:7-11. However, Luke omitted the key statement, "For all the prophets and the law prophesied until John came..." from Mt 11:12-14 at this stage in his narrative. We see two reasons for this. First, although Luke was careful to claim that John was a great prophet (Lk 7:26-28), John was not, in Luke's view—in contrast to Matthew—the "Elijah who is to come" (Mt 11:14). Second, Luke will use a modified form of Mt 11:12-14 later (Lk 16:16), but again omit the reference to John the Baptist as Elijah in Mt 11:14. Note that Luke also omitted Mt 17:10-13 which contains the same Matthean concept. This is clearly a tradition that Luke intentionally avoided each time he encountered it.

Lk 7:29-30 is an example of a "narrative aside," i.e., where Luke the narrator slips out from behind the curtain to address a word to the audience directly. As such, it is of course an addition to the Matthean account, replacing what is in Mt's version at this point, namely Mt 11:12-16, which Luke will use later at Lk 16:16. Why did Luke insert this negative comment about the Pharisees here? We think that it is an example of his interweaving style of composition (see Introduction, pp. 30-33). He is preparing for his next story about a Pharisee who rejects Jesus. That this addition is a Lukan composition, perhaps created on the basis of Mt 11:19c, is evident from the numerous Lukan linguistic characteristics in it: ἅπας/πᾶς ὁ λαός (Collison 174), βαπτίζω (Collison 42) and νομικός (Collison 174-175). The statement by Luke, that Pharisees and the lawyers did not submit to John's baptism (cf. Lk 3:3-22) and thus rejected God's βουλή, uses a technical term that occurs ten times in Lk-Acts but never in any of the other canonical gospels.

Lk 7:31-34 is fairly close to the account in Mt 11:16-19. The use of "sinners" at Lk 7:34 helps Luke unite this story with the next one in Luke which is about a woman whom Luke describes as a "sinner." There may be a link behind the scenes as well: note that in Mt 21:31-32 there is another story about John the Baptist that mentions τελῶναι <u>καὶ πόρναι</u>. Luke has no explicit parallel to that story in his narrative.

Lk 7:35. This unit ends with the Lukan version of the saying about Wisdom, who is "justified (ἐδικαιώθη) by all her *children*," in contrast to Mt's account, which says that "Wisdom is justified by her *works*." Whatever the enigmatic statement may mean in Mt's context, Luke interprets it quite specifically and locally. For Luke, "Wisdom's *children*" refer to "the people and the tax-collectors" in this story who "justified God" (ἐδικαίωσαν τὸν θεόν), in contrast to the Pharisees. As such, the verse becomes a typical Lukan interweaving transition to the next account, the story of a Pharisee who is utterly blind and opposed to Jesus while one of Wisdom's children (the sinful woman) fully vindicates God's purposes.

¶ 36. Jesus forgives a sinful woman

(Mt 26:6-13) **Lk 7:36-50**

Then one of the Pharisees comes up and invites Jesus to dine with him. Jesus accepts the invitation and goes to his house. While they are reclining at table, a woman of the city who had apparently committed adultery comes in uninvited and, weeping, washes Jesus' feet with her tears and dries them with her hair. Then she rubs his feet with ointment. The Pharisee host is furious. "He's no *prophet!*" he says to himself. "If he were, he'd *know* what kind of woman she is! How *dare* he let her touch him!" Reading his thoughts, Jesus tells the Pharisee a story about two men who each owed money, one a little and the other a great amount. Both had their debts forgiven. "Which one will feel greater love toward the person who forgave their debts?" asks Jesus. The Pharisee replies, "Obviously the one forgiven the most." Pointing to the woman, Jesus says that, grateful to be forgiven for a crushing burden of guilt, she is expressing her love for him, "but as for *you*, what love have *you* expressed toward me?" Turning to the woman, Jesus says, "Woman, your sins are forgiven." Now the guests are shocked. "Who is this who even forgives sins?" But Jesus ignores them. "Your faith has saved you," he tells the woman. "Go in peace."

General observations. This story does not occur in Mt at this point. A similar account is found in Mt 26:6-13, traditionally known as The Anointing at Bethany. Luke did not use it at that parallel point in his narrative. We suggest that this story may be a variant of that account (cf. also Jn 12:1-8), which Luke introduced here, accompanied by extensive modifications. Jesus has just been described in Lk 7:34 as one who comes eating and drinking, a friend of tax gatherers and sinners. Luke now gives this story about Jesus eating and being friendly to a sinful woman. As such, the story is a vivid illustration of Pharisees who reject God's βουλή for themselves, while tax collectors and sinners accept it (see again the previous account at Lk 7:29-30).

Lk 7:36. The meal setting as a locale for Jesus' controversial teaching is encountered frequently in Lk and Mt. In this case, it is part of the tradition he received.

Lk 7:37. In this verse Luke may have meant to suggest that the woman waited until Jesus was being entertained by the Pharisee and then crashed the party to see him, when it would have been maximally embarrassing. Why couldn't she have waited until afterward? Surely, there is a strain of humor in this account, given middle-eastern standards of etiquette.

Lk 7:39. The Pharisee contemptuously says to himself, "Ha! This man is no prophet!" thus revealing why he invited Jesus to his home—namely, to see if, in fact, this Jesus really is what the crowd said at the conclusion of the previous story about the Widow's Son at Nain: "A great prophet has arisen!" (Lk 7:16). This is why we put Lk 7:16f. as the beginning of this section: "Is Jesus (just) a prophet?" The larger question: "Who is this Jesus?" is precisely the question the guests ask at the close of this story. It will be repeated again and again in the stories to come.

Lk 7:40ff. The Pharisee's silent contempt is instantly perceived by Jesus, who answers his thoughts as if they had been spoken outright. *This proof of Jesus' prophetic ability* is a marvelous ironic touch in view of the Pharisee's contemptuous dismissal of him.

Lk 7:40-43. Jesus' example is not a parable. Rather, it is typical of Luke's exemplary stories that look like parables but actually are quite different from the parables in Mt 13.

Lk 7:47. The theme "women who are forgiven much love much" links this account directly to the next pericope, Lk 8:1-3 (see further below), and from that point we look forward in the story to the women who stood by Jesus in the hour of his death, in sharp contrast to all of his male disciples.

Lk 7:48-49. Jesus forgives the woman causing the guests to become mightily incensed: "Who is this who even forgives sins?" they ask. This question harks back to John's question, "Are you he who is to come?" and it also looks forward to further repetitions of this question: "Who is this?" As for the reaction of the guests, there are close verbal similarities with the reaction of the Pharisees when Jesus forgave the sins of the paralyzed man Lk 5:17-26. This creates the suspicion that this pericope may have been heavily edited by Luke.

Synopsis illustrating similarities between Lk 5:20f. and Lk 7:48f.

Lk 5:20-21	**Lk 7:48-49**
20 καὶ ἰδὼν τὴν πίστιν αὐτῶν	
εἶπεν, Ἄνθρωπε,	**48** εἶπεν δὲ αὐτῇ,
ἀφέωνταί σοι αἱ ἁμαρτίαι σου.	Ἀφέωνταί σου αἱ ἁμαρτίαι.
21 καὶ ἤρξαντο διαλογίζεσθαι	**49** καὶ ἤρξαντο
οἱ γραμματεῖς καὶ οἱ Φαρισαῖοι	οἱ συνανακείμενοι
λέγοντες,	λέγειν ἐν ἑαυτοῖς,
Τίς ἐστιν οὗτος	Τίς οὗτός ἐστιν
ὃς λαλεῖ βλασφημίας;	ὃς καὶ
τίς δύναται	
ἁμαρτίας ἀφεῖναι	ἁμαρτίας ἀφίησιν;
εἰ μὴ μόνος ὁ θεός;	

Lk 7:50. This phrase enunciates a major Lukan theological and christological theme in language of the Pauline kerygma, cf. Rom 1:16 and its OT source, Hab. 2:4 (see also Rom 10:9-10). Its appearance here is clearly due to Luke's compositional activity. Other occurrances of this phrase (for which there is one parallel in Mt) are:

Lk 7:50	εἶπεν δὲ πρὸς τὴν γυναῖκα, Ἡ πίστις σου σέσωκέν σε· πορεύου εἰς εἰρήνην.
Lk 8:48	ὁ δὲ εἶπεν αὐτῇ, Θυγάτηρ, ἡ πίστις σου σέσωκέν σε· πορεύου εἰς εἰρήνην.
Lk 17:19	καὶ εἶπεν αὐτῷ, Ἀναστὰς πορεύου· ἡ πίστις σου σέσωκέν σε.
Lk 18:42	καὶ ὁ Ἰησοῦς εἶπεν αὐτῷ, Ἀνάβλεψον· ἡ πίστις σου σέσωκέν σε.
Mt 9:22	ὁ δὲ Ἰησοῦς στραφεὶς καὶ...εἶπεν, Θάρσει, ...ἡ πίστις σου σέσωκέν σε.

Section Two: Be Mindful How You Respond to the Word of God! Lk 8:1–21

Following the principle that we have adopted elsewhere of taking references to tours or trips as indicators of how Luke provided structure to his narrative (see Introduction, pp. 33f.), the next section goes from Lk 8:1 to 8:21 and includes three stories. Central to this section is Luke's use of the parable collection in Mt 13 and the allegory on the Word of God. This concept—faithful obedience to the Word of God—forms the core of this section. Let us now examine these pericopes in greater detail.

¶ 37. Jesus and the Twelve go on another journey through Galilee

(Mt 9:35; 11:1; 27:55-56) **Lk 8:1-3**

Soon afterward, Jesus and the Twelve Apostles set off on a preaching tour through cities and villages in Galilee. Jesus wants to show them how it is done, since he will soon send them out on their own. Accompanying them are certain women of means whom Jesus has forgiven. In gratitude, these women supply provisions for Jesus and the Twelve.

General observations. This short summary, indicating that another tour is about to begin, is a Lukan composition intended to signal to his audience that one segment of the narrative is finished and another is about to begin. Luke is following the order of Mt loosely here, moving forward toward Mt 13, the collection of parables. The picture we have is the typical Lukan one of Jesus teaching, while on the road, first to the crowds and then privately to his disciples.

Synopsis of Lk 8:1

Illustrating Luke's conflation of Mt 9:35 and 11:1, the beginning and ending of Mt's Missionary Discourse, to introduce a new section of his narrative in which Jesus and the Twelve set out on a missionary journey.

Mt 9:35	Lk 8:1	Mt 11:1
Καὶ περιῆγεν	Καὶ ἐγένετο	Καὶ ἐγένετο
	ἐν τῷ καθεξῆς	ὅτε ἐτέλεσεν
ὁ Ἰησοῦς		ὁ Ἰησοῦς διατάσσων
		τοῖς δώδεκα μαθηταῖς αὐτοῦ,
	καὶ αὐτὸς διώδευεν	μετέβη ἐκεῖθεν
τὰς πόλεις πάσας	κατὰ πόλιν	
καὶ τὰς κώμας	καὶ κώμην	
διδάσκων		τοῦ διδάσκειν
ἐν ταῖς συναγωγαῖς αὐτῶν		
καὶ κηρύσσων	κηρύσσων και	καὶ κηρύσσειν
		ἐν ταῖς πόλεσιν αὐτῶν.
τὸ εὐαγγέλιον	εὐαγγελιζόμενος	
τῆς βασιλείας	τὴν βασιλείαν τοῦ θεοῦ	
καὶ θεραπεύων πᾶσαν νόσον	καὶ οἱ δώδεκα σὺν αὐτῷ,	
καὶ πᾶσαν μαλακίαν.		

Lk 8:1. Luke says that Jesus and the Twelve set out on a tour, "city by city and village by village." These words echo Mt 11:1 and Mt 9:35, the verses which serve to open and close Matthew's Missionary Discourse (Mt 9:35-11:1). The preceding synopsis indicates the parallels.

Lk 8:2-3. Luke skillfully composed this transition by mentioning other women who accompanied Jesus and the Twelve as identical in kind to the woman who has just been forgiven and who wanted to do something for Jesus out of her deep gratitude and love. Luke says explicitly that "Mary, called Magdalene, [had] seven demons [driven out of her.]" Presumably the other women also had been "forgiven much."

These women will play a prominent role later, at the time of Jesus' death and burial. They reappear at Lk 23:49, watching Jesus' crucifixion after his male disciples have fled, and again at Lk 23:55, where they help to prepare Jesus' body for burial, regardless of the danger involved. These are the same women who will report the angels' words to the Eleven male Apostles (who, Luke notes, don't believe a word they say). In other words, Luke here introduces a theme, long in advance, that consists of an explicit *contrast* between the love, courage and loyalty of Jesus' closest women disciples and the confusion, cowardice and betrayal by the Twelve.

Lk 8:3. The reference to "Joanna, the wife of Chuza, Herod's steward", is striking. Not mentioned in any part of Matthew, her appearance here in company with Mary Magdalene and "Salome" begs for an explanation. The reader has already encountered Herod Antipas at Lk 3:1 and again in the reference to Herod's arrest of John the Baptist at Lk 3:18-20. The next reference to Herod after this pericope will contain mention of his curiosity about Jesus (Lk 9:7-9). Then, after the execution of John the Baptist, certain Pharisees warn Jesus that Herod wants to kill him too (Lk 13:31). Finally, Luke will describe Herod's pleasure at fulfilling his desire to see Jesus, about whom he had heard so many reports (Lk 23:7-8; cf. Lk 9:7-9). In the ensuing trial, Herod Antipas finds no crime worthy of death in Jesus and sends him back to Pilate. In other words, Herod Antipas is a significant, if ambiguous, figure throughout Luke's narrative. This reference to his palace manager's wife—considering her husband's position, she would have been relatively wealthy—and her faithful assistance to Jesus and the Twelve from this point to the end is one of many indications in Luke-Acts that there was a sizable and socially complex entourage of faithful women and men followers around Jesus beyond the Twelve Apostles. Some of these disciples, according to Luke, were drawn from households that had the backing of Roman authority.

• The conclusion that this pericope is a Lukan composition is strengthened by the presence of numerous Lukan stylistic characteristics. Collison 220 lists "an imperfect plus a prepositional phrase with κατά plus two participles" as a collocation that appears three times within the Gospel of Luke (Lk 8:1; 9:6; and 13:22). Other Lukan linguistic characteristics include καὶ αὐτός of Jesus (Collison 194), εὐαγγελίζομαι (Collison 51), ἡ βασιλεία τοῦ θεοῦ (Collison 169-170), οἱ δώδεκα (Collison 168), ὅς + εἶναι + participle (Collison 226), θεραπεύω ἀπό (Collison 124), the collocation of a person ἀφ' οὗ/ἧς + δαιμόνιον and ἐξέρχομαι (Collison 219), articular participle of καλέω used as an appositive, usually to a proper noun (Collison 80), δαιμόνιον (Collison 171), ἀπό with verbs of healing (Collision 124), ἕτερος (Collison 184), and ὅστις in a demonstrative sense (Collison 208).

¶ 38. Jesus teaches his disciples to take heed how they hear the Word of God

(Mt 5:15; 10:26) Mt 13:2-9, 18-23 ====> **Lk 8:4-18**

Soon a large crowd gathers, drawn from all the towns round about, and Jesus tells them a parable. "Once there was a sower who cast his seed on the field. Some of the seed fell on rocky ground and died, some fell on a path where it was eaten by birds, some was choked by weeds, and some fell in good soil and bore much grain." Later, his disciples ask him what the parable means. He tells them that they are among the elect few to whom the secrets of the Kingdom of God will be explained. For everyone else, all will remain a riddle, so that they will not understand. Then he goes on to explain the parable. "The seed is the Word of God," he says, telling how each type of soil represents a certain kind of person. The last, good soil represents those "who hold the word fast in an honest and good heart, bringing forth fruit with patience." In conclusion, Jesus exhorts his disciples to let their good deeds shine forth like beacon lights, not to cover them up where no one can see them. "Take heed then how you hear and respond!" he warns them.

General observations. Luke moved from John's Inquiry (Mt 11:2-19) to the parable collection (Mt 13), skipping over a number of stories and pericopes, some of which he has already used and others of which he will use later. What is guiding his selection process at this point? The answer emerges clearly in the modifications he made to the Matthean material that caused his narrative to focus on the theme: "The Word of God and responses to it." This concept will feature prominently in this and in the next pericope, tying the two together.

EXCURSUS: EXPLANATION OF WHY LUKE SELECTED ONLY ONE PARABLE FROM MT'S COLLECTION

The following chart indicates what Luke took from Matthew's parable collection and what he left behind. It also shows the other Matthean material that Luke inserted into this context to round out his message. This section ends with the next pericope, which Luke took from Mt 12, to re-emphasize its main point: "Take heed how you hear the Word of God!" (Lk 8:18a).

Matthew's Parables	Luke's Parables
Mt 13:1-9 Parable of Sower	Lk 8:4-8 Parable of Sower
Mt 13:10-11, 13-15 Request for explanation	Lk 8:9-10 Request for explanation
Mt 13:16-17 Blessed are you	**[Luke will use this later, after the 72 return; see Lk 10:23f. At this point, he went on with]**
Mt 13:18-23 Interpretation of Sower	Lk 8:11-15 Interpretation of Sower
	[Then Luke inserted two sayings]
(Mt 5:15) Lamp	Lk 8:16 How to use a lamp
(Mt 10:26) Nothing will stay hidden	Lk 8:17 Nothing will stay hidden
	[To which Luke added this warning (not in Mt)]
---------------	Lk 8:18a Take heed how you hear.
	[Then Luke went back in this context and added]
(Mt 13:12) Dual recompense	Lk 8:18b The dual recompense saying
Mt 13:24-30 Parable of Weeds	---------------
Mt 13:31-32 Parable of Mustard seed	**[Lk will use this later at Lk 13:18-19]**
Mt 13:33 Parable of Leaven	**[and this at Lk 13:20-21.]**
Mt 13:34-35 Prophecy fulfillment	---------------
Mt 13:36-43 Interpretation of Weeds	---------------
Mt 13:44-46 Parables of Treasure and Pearl	---------------
Mt 13:47-50 Parable of Net and interpr.	---------------
Mt 13:51-52 Householder	**[To conclude this section, Luke brought forward and modified Mt's account of]**
(Mt 12:46-50) Jesus' true relatives	Lk 8:19-21 Jesus' true relatives

The most obvious fact to observe from this chart is that Luke selected to use at this point only one parable out of the seven or eight available in Matthew's collection: the Parable of the Sower. Why precisely this one? One explanation could be that in Lk 8:10 Jesus had said to the Twelve Apostles "to you it has been given to know the secrets of the Kingdom of God..." In contrast to the rest, this parable is one (of two) where Jesus actually gives the secret meaning to them.

Luke used two more of Mt's parables in the Central Section (Lk 13:18-20). He never uses the rest. On the other hand, Luke has a number of parables unique to his Gospel, but they are unlike most of the Matthean parables, being more story-like and picturesque. It would also appear Luke preferred to utilize his collection instead of Matthew's set, that emphasized accountability and judgment.

What did Luke do with the one parable he brought into his narrative at this point? To answer this question we must first observe that Luke combined with it a saying taken from Mt 5 on how to use a lamp, and another saying taken from Mt 10:26, a warning that nothing will remain hidden. Why did Luke combine these sayings with the Interpretation of the Parable of the Sower? We suggest that, aside from a clever play on the theme of light, the clue for all three compositional moves on Luke's part is the words found at the conclusion to the Interpretation of the parable: "Take heed then how you hear" (Lk 8:18a). This warning echoes the stock saying at the conclusion to Mt's Parable of the Sower: "He who has ears, let him hear" (Mt 13:9). Luke's revised version of this stock saying has been inserted at Lk 8:18a by Luke *out of Mt's order*. As such, it might be a good indicator of Luke's intentions in constructing this whole speech.

The other main clue is the way Luke used the technical term "word of God" in the context of this whole section. In the next pericope in Luke, the story about Jesus' mother and brothers (drawn from Mt 12:46-50), Luke has changed the final statement of Jesus from Matthew's "whoever does the *will of my Father in heaven* is my brother" to "my mother and my brothers are *those who hear the word of God and do it*." This shift in terminology echoes the beginning of Luke's version of the Interpretation of the Parable of the Sower, where Luke has Jesus say: "The seed is *the Word of God*"—which is not what Matthew says (although the idea is there in Mt 13:19ff. "word of the kingdom"). This alteration binds Luke's version of the account of Jesus' relatives to his Interpretation of the Parable of the Sower.

What are the reasons for these changes? The clue may be seen in the only other place in the Interpretation of the Parable of the Sower where Luke has altered Matthew's version: at the conclusion. Consider the following chart (Luke's differences are in italics):

Mt's Conclusion 13:23	**Lk's Conclusion 8:15**
As for what was sown on good soil, this is he who hears the word and understands it; he indeed bears fruit and yields in one case a hundredfold, in another sixty, and in another thirty.	And as for that in the good soil, they are those who, hearing the word, *hold it fast in an honest and good heart* and bring forth fruit *with patience.*

It seems evident that Luke's revision of Matthew's Interpretation of the Parable of the Sower has *moralized* it. In Matthew's account, Jesus exuberantly announces God's surprising eschatological overabundance. In Luke's revision, Jesus holds out a moral standard for the Church to adhere to: Jesus' disciples must "hold [the Word] fast in an honest and good heart, patiently bringing forth good fruit."

Finally, Luke's re-wording in turn clarifies the meaning of the warning Luke inserted later in v. 18a—after the example of how to use a lamp and the warning that nothing is hidden from God — "take heed *how you hear* the Word of God!"

If we step back from the immediate context for a moment, we may glimpse Luke's larger agenda. In Part Three, Luke had described Jesus' selection of the Twelve Apostles, followed by the great sermon in which Jesus laid out core values and teachings for his new disciples as well as the eager crowds. In Part Four, Jesus took the Twelve on a missionary journey during which he gave another speech consisting of a warning to heed how they hear the Word of God. Of course this warning was intended for Luke's wider audience, but it also played an important part in the development of the plot. This warning put the Twelve on notice. It served as the opening curtain on a series of vignettes in which the Twelve will be described in terms of failure to hear or abide by the word of God. The depths of their perfidy will culminate in Judas' betrayal and Peter's denial, followed by Jesus' crucifixion at the hands of his enemies.

Lk 8:4. This is Lukan composition which sets the stage for the following speech.

Lk 8:5-8. The parable largely followed Matthew's version in Mt 13:3-9.

Lk 8:9-10. The request for an explanation followed Matthew's version closely, except for a characteristic alteration of "kingdom of heaven" to "kingdom of God," and the equally characteristic omission of the OT proof text in Mt 13:14-15. Luke omitted Mt 13:12 at this point, but inserted it later at Lk 8:18b. He also omitted Mt 13:16-17 at this point and used it in a most striking manner later at Lk 10:23f., the Return of the 72.

Lk 8:11-15. The first most important difference in Luke's account is the emphatic statement at the beginning: "The seed is the Word of God" (Lk 8:11)—a statement which is not in Matthew as such, although it is present at several places in Matthew's context. The other significant difference is the moralization of the conclusion: "Hold [the Word] fast in an honest and good heart and bring forth fruit with patience" (Lk 8:15; cf. Mt 13:23). This alteration radically de-eschatologizes Matthew's version, which is typical of Luke, making this parable more useful for preaching and catechesis in the Church's ecumenical mission.

• The references to "heart" at Lk 8:12, 15 reflect Mt 13:15, 19 respectively. In Matthew these references stem from a sophisticated pattern of interpretation of Isa 6:9-10 (cf. Mt 13:15). Luke has fragmentarily preserved this pattern. On the assumption that a clear, sharp pattern is more original than a fragmented pattern, we see this as evidence of Luke's literary dependence upon the text of the canonical Gospel of Matthew.

Lk 8:16. At this point in Jesus' explanation, Luke introduced material taken from Mt 5:15 about how to use a lamp properly. Luke's point is that all who hear God's word should be like a lamp placed on a stand that enables all those entering "to see" or be enlightened. Luke's liking for this image is shown by his use of it again at Lk 11:33.

Lk 8:17. Next Luke introduced a fragment from Mt's Mission Discourse (Mt 10:26) which served to underline a similar point: there is nothing which will not be brought to light. Luke also reused Mt 10:26 at Lk 12:2.

Lk 8:18a. This is Luke's summary, bringing together all Jesus has said up to this point into a final warning to the Twelve Apostles. It contains an implicit reference back to the way the "good soil" responded to the Word of God (cf. Lk 8:15).

Lk 8:18b reintroduces the verse Luke passed over earlier (Mt 13:12) . Its role here is to warn about what might be termed the principle of eschatological dual recompense: to those who truly have more will be given, while from those who have not enough, even what they have will be taken away. This concludes Luke's use of Matthew's parable collection for now.

Lk 8:16-18 intervenes between Lk 8:4-15 and Lk 8:19-21. Why has Luke done this? Luke's major sources for the whole of Lk 8:4-21, according to the

Two Gospel Hypothesis, were Mt 12:46-50 and Mt 13:1ff., two contiguous literary units in Mt, the order of which Luke reversed. One may note further that Lk 8:16-18 is composed of exactly one verse from each of the first three discourses of Jesus in Mt in order:

Lk 8:16 is // Mt 5:15: the Sermon on the Mount

Lk 8:17 is // Mt 10:26: the Mission Discourse

Lk 8:18 is // Mt 13:12: the Parables Discourse

Luke continued to use these same verses later. Luke combined Mt 5:15f. with Mt 6:22-23 at Lk 11:33-36 (cf. Lk 8:16). And Luke combined Mt 10:26f. with Mt 16:6 at Lk 11:53-12:3 (cf. Lk 8:17).

In short, Lk 8:16-18 is related to Lk 11:33-36 by the common use of Mt 5:15, while Lk 8:16-18 is related to Lk 11:53-12:3 by the common use of Mt 10:26.

Moreover, Lk 8:16 and Lk 11:33 both differ from Mt 5:15 in exactly the same way. Luke changed Mt's "and it shines on all those in the house" to "in order that those who go in should see the light." Luke, thereby, changed Mt's focus away from passive residents in a house upon whom the light shines to active persons who must go into the house in order to see the light. Compare Luke's "punchline" for this section of his Gospel: Jesus' true relatives are "those who hear the word of God *and do it*" (Lk 8:21). Earlier in his Gospel, Luke had ended the Sermon on the Plain with the contrast between those who hear *and do* Jesus' words with those who hear *but do not do* (Lk 6:46-49). Later in Luke's Gospel, Jesus will also respond to a blessing on his mother with the words, "Blessed rather are those who *hear the word of God and keep it*" (Lk 11:28).

Given the interrelationships among these three Lukan literary contexts (Lk 8:16-18, 11:33-36, and 11:53-12:3), the clearly Lukan redaction of Mt 5:15 at both Lk 8:16 and Lk 11:33, and the presence of Lukan themes within them all, it is most likely that all three of these Lukan literary contexts are compositions of the author. And all three are composed of verses, sometimes even the same verses, from different literary contexts in Mt.

This complex pattern of data is strong evidence for Luke's direct literary dependence upon the text of the canonical Gospel of Matthew. That is, this complex pattern of data is difficult to explain as the accidental result of Matthew and Luke independently making use of a common source, such as "Q." On the Two Gospel Hypothesis, one would conclude that Luke transposed and revised Lk 8:16-18 to insert between his use of Mt's Parable of the Sower (Mt 13:1-23) and the account of Jesus' mother and brothers (Mt 12:46-50) in order to stress a theme of central interest to his entire Gospel.

¶ 39. Jesus' true mother and brothers are those who do the Word of God

Mt 12:46-50 ====> **Lk 8:19-21**

Suddenly, Jesus' mother and brothers appear on the scene. However, they cannot get to him because the crowd around Jesus is too dense. So they send word in to Jesus to come out, but he refuses, saying, "My mother and my brothers are those who hear the Word of God and do it!"

General observations. Two units on the family in Matthew frame the Matthean Parable Discourse (Mt 12:46-50; 13:54-58). Luke has already utilized Mt 13:54-58 much earlier, at Lk 4:16-30. Luke now brings Mt 12:46-50 from its position immediately prior to Matthew's parable collection to a position immediately following Luke's equivalent of it. Its use in this new position serves to underscore the main point in the speech Jesus has just given to the Twelve regarding the Word of God.

Lk 8:21. The main difference between Luke's version and the one in Mt 12:46-50 comes at the very end. Mt 12:50 reads: "For whoever does the will of my Father in heaven is my brother and sister and mother." Luke has changed that to: "My mother and brothers are those who hear the Word of God and do it." (Lk 8:21; cf. Lk 11:28). This ties this vignette back directly to the Lukan version of the Interpretation of the Parable of the Sower and is the last evidence we need to indicate that these three pericopes, Going on a Tour (Lk 8:1-3), the Parable of the Sower and its Interpretation (Lk 8:4-18), and Jesus' True Relatives (Lk 8:19-21), form a thematic unity.

• Luke's compositional activity is quite visible in this unit, as can be seen from the use of παραγίνεσθαι with πρός (Lk 8:19; cf. Collison 96-97). The use of τυγχάνειν (Lk 8:19: six times in Luke-Acts, but never in Mt or Mk) may also be a Lukan characteristic (so Goulder 1:419). Ακούειν τὸν λόγον τοῦ θεοῦ (Lk 8:21) and εἶπεν with the preposition are characteristic Lukan expressions (Goulder 1:419).

Section Three: Jesus Travels About Performing Miracles and Then Sends out the Twelve Apostles to Do the Same. Lk 8:22–9:11

What is our explanation for selecting Lk 8:22–9:11 as the next major section in Luke's narrative? The next pericope in Lk's order is Lk 8:22-25, traditionally known as Stilling the Storm. If Mt was Luke's major source, that Luke should have chosen to relate this account next in his order of events is not obvious, since to do so, Luke had to *go back* in Mt's order to Mt 8:18, 23-27 to get this story. Why did Luke do this? We propose two explanations.

(a) Having presented two foundational teaching sessions to the Twelve Apostles at the beginning (Lk 4:16b-32) and toward the end of Part Three (Lk 6:20-7:1a), Luke may have decided that the next, chronologically appropriate account to narrate was

Matthew's account of Jesus' Sending Out of the Twelve to do their own preaching and healing.

(b) In leading up to that event, in order to provide further evidence of Jesus' power and authority, Luke needed several important healing stories from Mt 8-9 that he had not used yet. Thus at Lk 8:22, Luke constructed a brief journey for Jesus and the Twelve that ended back in Capernaum. This tour included four deeds of power by Jesus, the Stilling of the Storm (Lk 8:23-27), the Healing of the Gerasene Demoniac (Lk 8:28-34), the Healing of Jairus' Daughter (Lk 8:40-42a, 49-56) and the Healing of the Woman with the Issue of Blood (Lk 8:42b-48).

In other words, we see the central event in this Section of Luke's Part Four to be the Sending Out of the Twelve (Lk 9:1-6). Luke related the miracle accounts which come before it as a way of demonstrating Jesus' authority and power to commission the Twelve Apostles to do as he had done. In fact, a close reading of Luke suggests that he intended for his audience to visualize all of these miracles, from Lk 8:18-56, to have taken place on the same day! (cf. Lk 24:1-53). Following these demonstrations of divine power, Jesus sends the Twelve Apostles out to go and do likewise (Lk 9:6).

One final point. The opening miracle story, Jesus' calming of the storm on the way over the Sea of Galilee to the land of the Gerasenes, concludes with the Apostles' astonished cry: "*Who is this* who can command even the winds and the sea and they obey him?" This is the third time this question has been asked since the beginning of Part Four. It will be asked three more times in subsequent stories until the question: "Who is Jesus?" is definitively answered by God directly from Heaven in the Transfiguration (Lk 9:35).

¶ 40. Jesus crosses the Sea of Galilee

Mt 8:18, 23-27 ====> **Lk 8:22-25**

One day Jesus and the Twelve Apostles get into a boat and begin to cross the Sea of Galilee. On the way, Jesus falls asleep. Suddenly a storm blows in and the waves threaten to sink the boat. Terrified, they wake Jesus and beg him to save them. He immediately orders the winds to cease, which they do. "Where is your faith?" he asks his men. But they ask each other, "Who is this who can order even the winds and the sea to do his bidding?"

General observations. As noted in the comments above, Luke has gone back in Mt's order from the pericope on Jesus' True Relatives (Mt 12:46-50) to pick up this story in Mt 8:23ff. (including Mt 8:18). His purpose is to lead into the account of the Sending Out of the Twelve (Lk 9:1-6) by means of the immediately preceding miracle accounts. Once he selected this story, he related it without major modifications of his Matthean source.

Lk 8:22. This verse is a conflation of Mt 8:18 with Mt 8:23. It is a Lukan conflation intended to clearly indicate that Jesus and the Twelve are setting off on yet another journey. This time they are going across the Sea of Galilee to the "country of the Gerasenes" on the other side. The introductory, transitional and temporal reference in Lk 8:22 accords with Luke's style: 'Εγένετο δὲ ἐν μιᾷ τῶν ἡμερῶν (cf. Lk 5:17; Collison 132-133, 214). Note that Mt 8:13 is where Luke stopped utilizing Mt at Lk 7:10. Luke had already utilized Mt 8:14-17 at Lk 4:38-41 which would bring Luke to Lk 8:18. Luke now returns precisely to Mt 8:18 to begin composing this miracle story unit from Matthew's first collection of miracle stories in Mt 8-9. Luke will return to those few verses he omitted from Mt 8:18-27, i.e., Mt 8:19-22, to conclude a well-structured "interweaving transitional section" (Lk 9:37-62) that he will use to introduce the call and commissioning of the 72 Other Disciples (Lk 10:1ff.)

Although Lk 8:22 does echo Mt 8:18 (δέ + a compound of ἔρχομαι + εἰς τὸ πέραν), Lk 8:22 also shares a number of features with Mt 8:23.

Lk 8:22 καὶ ἐνέβη εἰς πλοῖον καὶ οἱ μαθηταὶ αὐτοῦ

Mt 8:23 καὶ ἐμβάντι αὐτῷ εἰς τὸ πλοῖον... οἱ μαθηταὶ αὐτοῦ

The appearance of verbal parallels in Lk 8:22 to both Mt 8:18 and to Mt 8:23 is all the more intriguing since the intervening material—Mt 8:19-22, a story about two unprepared would-be followers of Jesus—is later utilized by Luke to compose a series of three vignettes depicting the faults of would-be disciples in Lk 9:57-62. This evidence of meticulous utilization of Mt's *redactional* phraseology, stripped from around a specific pericope (Mt 8:18 and 23), supports our contention that Luke made direct use of the canonical Gospel of Matthew (for further discussion, see the Introduction, pp. 21ff.).

• Luke usually refers to the "lake" (λίμνη) of Galilee (e.g., Lk 8:22-23), rather than to the "sea" (θάλασσα) of Galilee, which is Mt's typical term (e.g., Mt 8:24, 26, 27; cf. Collison 182).

Lk 8:23-25. Within the story of the stilling of the storm, Matthew has Jesus rebuke his disciples *before* Jesus calms the storm, but Luke records that Jesus questioned the faith of the disciples *after* the storm has been calmed. The emphasis is on lack of faith in Lk 8:25.

¶ 41. Jesus heals an incurable demoniac near Gerasa
Mt 8:28-34 ====> **Lk 8:26-39**

Landing in foreign territory, Jesus is immediately accosted by a ragged demoniac long possessed by demons. "What have you to do with me, O Jesus, Son of the Most High God?" cries the man. Jesus orders the demons to reveal their name. "We are legion!" they boast, for there were thousands of demons inhabiting the man. No one had ever been able to cure him. When Jesus begins to exorcize them, they beg him not to cast them into the uttermost hell, so he orders them to enter a herd of swine gathered nearby. They leave the man and suddenly the pigs rise up and rush pell-mell over the cliff into the waters below, where they drown. Terrified, the local herdsmen flee, spreading word everywhere about what had happened. People stream out of the city to see, and they find Jesus and the former demoniac, sitting at Jesus' feet, clothed and in his right mind. "Go away!" they shout. So Jesus and his disciples leave. The healed demoniac begs Jesus to let him go with them, but he sends him back, saying, "Go tell your kinsmen how much the God of Israel has done for you today!" This he does, telling everyone what Jesus of Nazareth did for him.

General Observations. This is the next story in Matthew's order and Luke utilized it, considerably altering and elaborating upon it.

Lk 8:26. There is a famous textual problem in this verse. We accept the reading "Gerasenes," for the reasons the UBS editorial committee has given. It is apparent that Luke has modified Matthew's little-known, but probably accurate place name "Gadara" to "Gerasa" (= Heb. Jerash), even though this involved Luke in a geographical incongruity. The large and famous trading center of Gerasa/Jerash was situated on the plateau east of the Jordan Valley more than 50 km from the Sea/Lake of Galilee.

Lk 8:27. Although Luke reduced Matthew's two demoniacs to one (cf. Mt 8:28), possibly for simple narrative reasons, he has this one demoniac filled with, not two, but a whole legion (= 6000) of demons. As we can see from the ending, Luke concluded by describing the one healed man as the ideal disciple (see below).

Lk 8:28. The cry of the demon(s) proving that they know perfectly well who Jesus is, causes, in Luke's context, a powerful ironic contrast with the cry of the disciples not two verses earlier: "Who then is this?!" The demoniacs in Mt 8:29 called Jesus "Son of God," but in Luke's account, the demons call him υἱὲ τοῦ θεοῦ τοῦ ὑψίστου (D omits τοῦ θεοῦ), which resembles Lk 1:32 where Gabriel announces to Mary that the child in her womb "will be called the Son of the Most High" (cf. Lk 2:14).

Lk 8:29-31 is a considerable expansion of Mt. Lk 8:29 is clearly added to give a reason for the challenge, otherwise unmotivated, in Mt 8:29. The elaborate description of the severity of the demoniac's illness is a stock element in Hellenistic healing accounts. Providing the demon(s) with a name like "legion" is a brilliant, but secondary, touch.

Lk 8:35. At this point, Luke provided a more fitting conclusion to the healing, in the sense that the bystanders received vivid proof of the complete cure of the previously incurable maniac. The phrase παρὰ τοὺς πόδας τοῦ Ἰησοῦ (Lk 8:35) is a characteristic Lukan phrase descriptive of the ideal disciple (cf. Lk 8:41; 10:39; 17:16).

Lk 8:37-39. The people, probably Gentiles, begged Jesus to leave, since his God was destroying their property. Jesus, in turn, urged the man not to go with him but to tell his fellow countrymen what Jesus' God had done for him—something that none of their gods could do. The demoniac gives credit to Jesus for his healing (a Lukan Christological affirmation?). In the very next story, Jesus tells the Jewish parents of the girl raised from the dead not to tell anyone in their city what has happened (Lk 8:56). Actually,

Peter, James, and John, the ones who saw Jesus transfigured (Lk 9:28) were present when Jesus raised the little girl as well. In anticipation of the Resurrection event, the healing of Jairus' daughter is, like the transfiguration, too sacred an event to be spread abroad at the present stage of Jesus' ministry.

¶ 42. Jesus returns to Capernaum and heals two women

Mt 9:18-26 ====> **Lk 8:40-56**

When Jesus arrives back at Capernaum, everyone is waiting for him. Just then, Jairus, the ruler of Capernaum's synagogue, comes up and, falling to his knees, begs Jesus to come see his little daughter who is at that very moment about to die. They head for his house when a woman in the crowd, who has had an incurable flow of blood for twelve years, touches the hem of his garment and is healed instantly. Jesus stops and asks who has touched him. "The crowd is pressing on us!" says Peter. But the woman, realizing that she will be found out, comes forward and admits that she touched Jesus' garment and was cured instantly. While they are speaking, a man comes from Jairus' home to announce that his daughter is dead. "She will be well," answers Jesus. When they arrive at Jairus' house, Jesus takes Peter, James and John and the girl's parents inside, putting everyone else outside, for the crowd is loudly lamenting her death. Going up to the girl, Jesus calls to her, "Little girl, arise!" The little girl's spirit returns and she gets up. Jesus tells her parents to give her nourishment, but warns them not to tell anyone what has happened.

General observations. Luke followed Matthew's order to get this dual account. That is, at the end of the previous healing account Luke had come to Mt 8:34. The next three pericopes in Matthew, the Healing of the Paralytic (Mt 9:1-8), the Call of Levi (Mt 9:9), and the Dispute about Fasting (Mt 9:10-17), Luke had already used earlier in Lk 5:17-39. The *very next unit* is Mt 9:18-26 and this is exactly where Luke got this story. This kind of precise, pericope by pericope utilization of the material in Matthew in widely separated contexts of Lk's order supports the hypothesis of Luke's direct literary dependence upon the canonical Gospel of Matthew, not a source like "Q."

Lk 8:40-56. Luke's account of these two healings is fuller and more detailed than those of Mt (cf. the Lukan expansions in the previous story). On the eve of Jesus' commissioning of the Twelve, Luke wished to accentuate the power and authority of Jesus. He did this through frequent use of verisimilitude and novelistic expansions of his Matthean source. See, especially, Lk 8:43b, 44b, 45-47, 49-50c, 51b-52a, 53b, 54b-56. The theme of faith as a response to the great demonstrations of power is stressed (cf. Lk 8:46, 48).

• Goulder (1:424-425) has noted two examples of unusual phraseology from Mt echoed here in Luke. See ἄρχων εἷς from Mt 9:18 also found in Lk

8:41 and τοῦ κρασπέδου τοῦ ἱματίου αὐτοῦ from Mt 9:20 repeated in Lk 8:44. The distinctively Jewish term κρασπέδον appears three times in Mt, once in this parallel passage in Lk and once in a Markan parallel, but nowhere else in the NT (Mt 9:20//Lk 8:44; Mt 14:36//Mk 6:56 and Mt 23:5). We believe this to be "one-way" evidence of the literary dependence of Luke (and Mark) on Mt. By that we mean the occurrence of a word or phrase characteristic of the text of Mt appearing *only* in the other Synoptics in passages parallel to the order of Mt. (For further discussion of this term, see the Introduction, pp. 21-24. For another example of this phenomenon, see above, at Lk 7:23.)

• The concluding admonition of Jesus to the parents, μηδενὶ εἰπεῖν τὸ γεγονός (Lk 8:56), stands in opposition to the ending of the story in Mt 9:26, καὶ ἐξῆλθεν ἡ φήμη αὕτη εἰς ὅλην τὴν γῆν ἐκείνην. It also contrasts with the conclusion of the previous story where Jesus explicitly instructed the healed demoniac to return home and "proclaim what God has done for" him (Lk 8:39). See the discussion of this difference in the note to Lk 8:37-39 above.

¶ 43. Jesus sends the Twelve Apostles out on a preaching tour

Mt 9:35-10:16; 11:1 ====> **Lk 9:1-6**

Finally Jesus commissions the Twelve Apostles, giving them the same authority he has just demonstrated over demons and illness and death, and sends them out to preach the Kingdom of God and to heal. He instructs them to take no provisions for the road, since people will provide them with whatever they need. "But if anyone does not receive you," he adds, "shake the dust off of your feet as a witness against them." And the Twelve depart, going through villages preaching the gospel and healing everywhere.

General observations. Luke has reached the account which forms the climax of this section: the Mission of the Twelve Apostles. However, to get to this account, Luke passed over (for now) the Healing of Two Blind Men (Mt 9:26-31), which Luke will use in combination with its Matthean "doublet" (Mt 20:29-34) later in Lk 18:35-43. Luke also passed over the Healing of a Dumb Demoniac (Mt 9:32-34) for the moment, but will also eventually conflate this story with its Matthean "doublet" (Mt 12:22-30) at Lk 11:14-23. These temporary omissions from Mt bring Luke to the Sending of the Twelve in Mt 9:35-10:16. Luke presents a greatly abbreviated version of it here (Lk 9:1-6).

Luke's utilization of the missionary instructions in Mt 10 reveals a complex but perfectly systematic pattern which has not been captured by existing synopses (see our synopsis below, pp. 160-164). In Mt, immediately after Jesus calls the Twelve and gives them their traveling instructions, he launches into a lengthy series of warnings and instructions about the mission. This long speech Luke utilized in a number of different contexts, just as he did with Mt's Sermon on the Mount. *All but one verse* of Mt's Missionary Instructions were used in different literary settings in Lk (Lk 6, 9, 10, 12, 14, 17 and 21). A more detailed discussion will be provided when the relevant pericopes are discussed below.

Lk 9:1-2 contains language not typical of Luke's Gospel elsewhere. We believe these are fragmentary preservations of typically Matthean linguistic characteristics. See, for example, Mt 4:23, 9:35 and 10:1. Luke has fragmentarily preserved pieces of these most distinctively Matthean redactional passages at Lk 9:1 νόσους θεραπεύειν, and Lk 9:2 κηηρύσσειν τὴν βαλισείαν and τούς ἀσθενεῖς (reading τούς ἀσθενεῖς with ℵ A D L alii). This is again "one-way" evidence of Luke's direct literary dependence upon Mt. Some of these Matthean literary characteristics seem to have come to him from one of the prophetic texts that the first Evangelist used so often to shape his narrative (See Mt 8:17//Isa 53:4 Αὐτὸς τὰς ἀσθενείας ἡμῶν ἔλαβεν καὶ τὰς νόσους ἐβάστασεν cf. Mt 10:8). Note also Luke's earlier and typical omission of the prophetic proof text which probably supplied Matthew with these literary characteristics at Mt 8:16-17 (cf. Lk 4:40-41).

• Luke did not give the names of the twelve disciples here (cf. Mt 10:2-4), since he has already done so at Lk 6:13-16.

Lk 9:3. This verse repeated the instructions in Mt 10:9-10 except that Luke omitted the rationale for the instruction, given by Mt in 10:10b: "the workman deserves his food." This removes the whole reason for these instructions. Nevertheless, it is obvious that Luke understood their intent, since later on, during the Last Supper, Lk 22:35 portrays Jesus explicitly asking the Twelve, "When I sent you out [with no provisions], did you lack anything?" and they reply, "Nothing."[1]

Lk 9:5. Goulder argues that the phrase, ἐξερχόμενοι ἀπὸ τῆς πόλεως ἐκείνος τόν κονιορτόν...ἀποτινάσσετε, at Lk 9:5, is triply characteristic of Matthew: [1] the participle, ἐξερχόμενοι; [2] two locations joined by "or," such as "town or village," and [3] a phrase beginning with an article and ending with ἐκεῖνος, such as τῆς πόλεως ἐκείνης. Lk 9:5 reflects all three of these typical Matthean literary characteristics (Goulder 1:431).

Lk 9:6. Lk 9:1-2, 6 seem to echo both the opening of Matthew's missionary discourse and its ending.

¶ 44. Herod Antipas wonders who Jesus is

Mt 14:1-2 ====> **Lk 9:7-9**

Meanwhile, Herod Antipas, the ruler of Galilee, heard of all these events and wondered who it was that was doing them. People told him that John the Baptist had come back from the dead; others said Elijah or one of the other old prophets had

[1] On this subject, see David L. Dungan, *The Sayings of Jesus in the Churches of Paul. The Use of the Synoptic Tradition in the Regulation of Early Church Life* (Oxford: Basil Blackwell, 1971) 41-80.

reappeared. But Herod said, "John's head I cut off, so who is this?" And he desired to meet Jesus in person.

General observations. Luke had used the compositional framework of Matthew's Mission Discourse (Mt 9:35 and 11:1) to frame the previous pericope (Lk 9:1-2, 6). From Mt 11:1, Luke moved forward in Mt, headed toward the climax of Jesus' Galilean ministry which, for Luke, was the Transfiguration (Mt 17:1-13//Lk 9:28-36). In his final utilization of Mt prior to the beginning of the Lukan Travel Narrative (Lk 9:51), Luke used a number of pericopes from Mt to underscore the theme, Who is Jesus? This was his way of preparing the reader for the climactic event of the Transfiguration.

How has Luke gone about using his major source Mt at this point? Luke moved forward from the conclusion of Mt's Mission Discourse (Mt 11:1) to the end of Matthew's parable chapter (Mt 13:53, note the verbal similarities to Mt 11:1). Most of the intervening accounts have already been utilized by Lk (Mt 11:2-19//Lk 7:18-35; Mt 12:1-21//Lk 6:1-19; Mt 12:46-13:53//Lk 8:4-21). The two accounts between Mt 11:1 and Mt 13:53 that Luke has not yet utilized will appear in the Travel Narrative (Mt 11:20-30//Lk 10:13-22; Mt 12:22-45//Lk 11:14-32). In this way Luke moved forward in Mt from 11:1 to 13:53, bringing him to the "Rejection at Nazareth" (Mt 13:54-58). Parts of this account Luke used early on in his version of Jesus' inaugural sermon at Nazareth (Lk 4:16-30, esp. Lk 4:24//Mt 13:57). Next in Mt comes an incident with Herod (Mt 14:1-11), some details of which Luke had also already narrated at Lk 3:18-20 (cf. Mt 14:3-4). Luke now makes use of other parts of this story (Mt 14:1-11) to raise a further question about the identity of Jesus.

This Lukan incident serves three functions in this context:

1) It provides a dramatic interlude while the Twelve are away.
2) It is an anticipation of Herod's encounter with Jesus later (Lk 23:6-15; cf. Lk 13:31-33), just the kind of thing Luke likes to do: weave into earlier parts of his narrative themes and persons who will play a prominent role later on (cf. the earlier references to Herod at Lk 3:1; 3:19; and 8:3).
3) It returns to the major theme running throughout Part Four: Who is Jesus? This theme that involves John, Elijah, and the prophets will appear again shortly at Lk 9:19.

Lk 9:7-8 is Luke's expansion of Mt 14:1-3 and 10, which Luke has supplemented with phrases from a similar story in Mt 16:13-16 (see esp. ἄλλος + δέ +Ἠλίας + προφήτης in Lk 9:8//Mt 16:14). He does this again at Lk 9:19, another example of Luke "creating a doublet." In the chart on the next page, the underline/dotted words are parallels; the words in bold in Lk 9:8 and Lk 9:19 have no equivalent in Mt and are from Luke.

Chart illustrating Luke's creation of a doublet

#1. Lk 9:7-8 (the report to Herod) καὶ διηπόρει διὰ τὸ λέγεσθαι ὑπό τινων ὅτι Ἰωάννης ἠγέρθη ἐκ νεκρῶν, ὑπό τινων δὲ ὅτι Ἠλίας ἐφάνη, ἄλλων **δὲ ὅτι προφήτης τις τῶν ἀρχαίων ἀνέστη.**

Mt 14:2 (Herod's comment) καὶ εἶπεν τοῖς παισὶν αὐτοῦ, Οὗτός ἐστιν Ἰωάννης ὁ βαπτιστής· αὐτὸς ἠγέρθη ἀπὸ τῶν νεκρῶν καὶ διὰ τοῦτο αἱ δυνάμεις ἐνεργοῦσιν ἐν αὐτῷ.

Mt 16:14 (answer of Jesus' disciples) οἱ δὲ εἶπαν, Οἱ μὲν Ἰωάννην τὸν βαπτιστήν, ἄλλοι δὲ Ἠλίαν, ἕτεροι δὲ Ἰερεμίαν ἢ ἕνα τῶν προφητῶν.

#2. Lk 9:19 (answer of Jesus' disciples) οἱ δὲ ἀποκριθέντες εἶπαν, Ἰωάννην τὸν βαπτιστήν, ἄλλοι δὲ Ἠλίαν, ἄλλοι **δὲ ὅτι προφήτης τις τῶν ἀρχαίων ἀνέστη.**

Lk 9:9. Luke revised Matthew's account (Mt 14:1-2) so as to avoid Herod's supposition that Jesus was John the Baptist raised from the dead. After all Luke has done to separate the two up to this point, he has no intention of getting them mixed up in the reader's mind here.

¶ 45. The return of the Twelve; crowds gather

Mt 14:12-14 ====> **Lk 9:10-11**

When the Twelve Apostles return from their mission, they report all of their activities to Jesus. This report elicits no response from Jesus except to withdraw with these disciples around the coast to a city called Bethsaida. But since the crowds knew that Jesus had gone to Bethsaida, they followed him there. Upon their arrival, Jesus welcomed the crowds, spoke to them about the Kingdom of God and healed those in the crowds who had need of healing.

General observations. This short summary brings closure to the preaching and healing tour of the Twelve that was commissioned by Jesus in Lk 9:1-6. Luke now says that Jesus and his disciples go on another tour to Bethsaida. The mention of crowds gathering sets the stage for the momentous Feeding of the Five Thousand, which comes next. In short, this literary unit is a characteristic Lukan interweaving, transitional pericope. Luke has already mentioned John's imprisonment (Lk 3:18-20) and so he has no need to repeat the content of Mt 14:3-9 and 11 here.

Lk 9:10-11. In contrast to Matthew, who nowhere tells of the return of the Twelve, Luke says that they came back and reported all they had done to Jesus. Nevertheless, Luke portrays a strikingly muted response by Jesus to the achievements of the Twelve. Indeed, nothing is recounted. On the other hand, Jesus will make a more positive response later, when the seventy-two other disciples return from their comparable mission (Lk 10:17-20, no parallel in Mt). We will discuss the possible implications of this surprising difference below.

The mention of "going apart privately" reflects the wording of Mt 14:13, where Jesus is reacting to the report that Herod Antipas has just executed John the Baptist. This causes Jesus to go into hiding in Matthew's account. However, Luke does not leave it at that. He adds "....withdrew apart to a city named Bethsaida." Luke's reason for mentioning this city is to prepare the grounds for Jesus to curse Bethsaida later on in Lk 10:13 (cf. Mt 11:21). As the rich number of variants in the manuscript tradition indicates, however, this reference to Bethsaida introduced serious strains in Luke's account. Under the influence of Matthew's version, the disciples say in Lk 9:12 that they are "in a desert place" (cf. Mt 14:13, 15), and the crowds are told to "go get food from villages" round about (Lk 9:12, cf. Mt 14:15) despite the fact that, according to Luke's account, they were in the city of Bethsaida. Noticing this anomaly, scribes have tried to resolve it by a variety of textual emendations.

• That Mt's story lies behind Luke's version is demonstrated by the appearance of a number of Matthean literary characteristics in the parallel account in Lk: ὑπεχώρησεν (cf. the Matthean ἀνεχώρησεν at Mt 14:13; Tevis, Tables 13 and 15), κατ ' ἰδιαν (Mt 14:13//Lk 9:10; cf. Tevis, Table 28); οἱ ὄχλοι ἠκολούθησαν αὐτῷ (cf. Mt 14:13; Tevis, Table 4) and θεραπεία cf. ἐθεράπευσεν at Mt 14:14 (cf. Tevis, Tables 5 and 8).[2] The presence of Matthean linguistic characteristics within the text of Luke in contexts where Lk is parallel with Mt's order, combined with the presence of Lukan linguistic characteristics where Lk differs from Mt in the same contexts, is strong evidence that Luke is literarily dependent upon the canonical Gospel of Matthew, not "Q." (For examples of other "one-way indicators" see our discussions at Lk 7:23; 8:40-56; Introduction, pp. 21-24.)

• Lukan modifications to the Matthean text include: "he spoke to them of the Kingdom of God," which is a typical Lukan expression (cf. Acts 1:3; Collison 169-170); ὑποστρέφειν (Collison 67); the absolute use of οἱ ἀπόστολοι (Collison 168), and the participle of κάλεω (Collison 179).

Section Four: The Conclusion to Jesus' Galilean Ministry. Lk 9:12–36

Luke is now ready to describe the final climactic events of Jesus' activities in Galilee, prior to his departure for Jerusalem. In this final Section, the question of the identity of Jesus that appeared at the beginning of Part Four and came up repeatedly during it, will come to center stage until it is answered by God himself on the Mount. This is the high point and conclusion of Luke's whole Galilean narrative. After this, with Jesus' true identity now made crystal clear to Jesus' disciples (i.e., to Luke's audience), the stage is set for Luke's masterpiece of parenesis: the great Central

---

2 See also M. E. Boismard, "Introduction au Premier Récit de la Multiplication des Pains [Mt 14:13-14; Mc 6:30-34; Lc 9:10-11] in *The Interrelations of the Gospels. A Symposium led by M. E. Boismard - W. R. Farmer, - F. Neirynck Jerusalem 1984,* BETL 45, ed. David L. Dungan (Leuven: Leuven University Press/Uitgeverij Peeters, 1990) 244-258, esp. 245f.

Teaching Section (Lk 9:51–19:27) — Jesus' teachings to his disciples on how to create and maintain the Christian community.

¶ 46. Jesus miraculously feeds five thousand

Mt 14:15-21 ====> **Lk 9:12-17**

That evening, the crowds were still with Jesus and they were getting hungry. His Apostles said, "Send them away to get lodging and provisions." But Jesus said, "You give them something to eat." They replied that they had no more than five loaves and two fish. How could they feed such a large multitude with them (for there were about five thousand men)? Jesus said, "Tell them to sit down," so they did. Taking the loaves and fish, Jesus looked up to heaven and blessed and broke them and gave them to the disciples to give the people. And there was plenty for everyone. Indeed, no less than twelve baskets of leftover pieces were collected afterwards.

General observations. Luke followed Mt 14 closely at this point. His account of the Feeding of the Five Thousand is very similar to Mt's with only slight modifications. The role this story plays in Luke's narrative is to set the stage for the next story: having performed this incredible miracle, Jesus then confronts the Apostles: "Who do these people say I am?" Then he asks, "Who do you say I am?" The latter dialogue, in turn, sets the stage for the definitive answer from Heaven in the climactic scene where Jesus is revealed in glory.

Lk 9:12-17. As noted about the previous pericope, Luke's statement that they went to Bethsaida clashes head-on with the next statement, which he got from Mt 14:15, that they were "in a lonely place." This peculiar situation seems to us to be a rare example of an inadvertent collision between Luke's source Mt and his compositional result. Normally, Luke's appropriation of the Matthean material is precise, subtle and intelligible—dovetailing flawlessly with his theological/ecclesiological agenda.

• The additional mention of companies of fifty in Lk 9:14 is precisely the kind of secondary addition one would expect from a later retelling of Matthew's more economical account.

• As usual, the literary features that distinguish the text of Luke from the text of Matthew within this pericope turn out to be literary characteristics of Luke: πορεύομαι (Collison 60-61), ἅπας/πᾶς ὁ λαός (Collison 174), ὡσεί, especially with numerals and with the noun preceding the numeral (Collison 112), and the collocation of οὕτως and ποιέω (Collison 230, cf. οὕτως, Collison 160).

¶ 47. Peter says Jesus is the Christ of God

Mt 14:22-23; 16:13-20 ====> **Lk 9:18-20**

Not long after this, Jesus is praying alone with the disciples. And he asks them what the crowds they just fed are saying about him. They reply, "They say you are

John the Baptist back from the dead or one of the old prophets like Elijah." Jesus says, "Who do you say I am?" Peter answers, "You are the Christ of God!"

General observations. Luke followed Matthew's general order here, although his method requires some explanation. Indeed, the move from Matthew's account of the Feeding of the 5000 (Mt 14:15-23//Lk 9:12-17) to Peter's Confession (Mt 16:13-20//Lk 9:18-20) is an intriguing one for what it reveals about Luke's perception of the Apostle Peter. Luke has conflated two stories about Peter by moving from Mt 14:23 to Mt 16:13. More precisely, Lk 9:18 begins with Jesus "praying alone," which is taken from Mt 14:23 (it is the kind of image Luke likes). In Matthew's account, this situation indicator sets up the story of Jesus' walking on the water and Peter's attempt to do the same (Mt 14:24-33). Luke omitted these stories and, instead, moved forward in Mt to the next major story about Peter (Mt 16:13-20; between Mt 14:33 and 16:13, Peter is mentioned by name only at Mt 15:15). Lk 9:18, a conflation of Mt 14:22-23 and Mt 16:13, then provided the introduction to Jesus' dialogue first with the disciples and then with Peter (Lk 9:18-20). Luke's dominating interest is the identity of Jesus; Mt's account of Peter's confession is critical in this regard. This dialogue echoes Lk 9:7-9, which is clearly hovering in the background of both the Matthean and Lukan accounts. Luke omitted the passage about Peter receiving the keys to the kingdom of heaven in Mt 16:17-19 because he will give the Lukan equivalent at the Last Supper (Lk 22:31; see the discussion on this below). Finally, as we will see in the next pericope, Luke will omit Matthew's account of Jesus' rebuke of Peter entirely (Mt 16:22-23). Since Peter has given the right answer about Jesus' identity (the Lukan theme for this Section of his Gospel), Luke would find such a rebuke inappropriate for his purposes in this context.

Lk 9:18a. Luke's introduction to this unit resembles Lk 11:1 (Collison 218).

Lk 9:18 Καὶ ἐγένετο ἐν τῷ εἶναι αὐτὸν προσευχόμενον

Lk 11:1 Καὶ ἐγένετο ἐν τῷ εἶναι αὐτὸν ἐν τόπῳ τινὶ προσευχόμενον

Lk 9:20. If Luke changed Matthew's formulation: "you are the Messiah, the Son of the Living God," (Mt 16:16) to "the Christ of God," τὸν Χριστὸν τοῦ θεοῦ (Lk 9:20), the phrasing, though perhaps odd, is paralleled by χρίστον κυρίου at Lk 2:26.

¶ 48. Jesus predicts his suffering and death

Mt 16:20-23 ====> **Lk 9:21-22**

Having heard Peter's answer, Jesus charges his disciples to be silent. For the first time Jesus predicts his suffering, death, and resurrection.

General observations. This pericope in Lk is a continuation of the preceding story. Jesus' messiahship will be connected with his death and resurrection. As there was previously at Lk 4:41; 5:14; and 8:56, there is a charge here to maintain silence (Lk 9:21-22).[3]

Lk 9:22. The wording of this first Passion Prediction in Luke is particularly close to the wording of another Passion Prediction passage at Lk 17:25 (Collison 217).

¶ 49. The cost of discipleship; assurance that some will see the Kingdom of God

Mt 16:24-28 ====> **Lk 9:23-27**

Jesus goes on. "If any man would be my disciple, let him deny himself and take up his cross each day and follow me! For what have you gained if you acquire the whole world, but lose your soul? No, whoever is ashamed of me will be condemned by the Son of Man when he comes in glory on Judgment Day. But I say to you right now, some of you will not die before you see the Kingdom of God!"

General observations. Luke continued to follow Matthew's order and wording closely for this pericope. The alterations are minor, but bring out significant aspects of Luke's theology. Luke is interested in maintaining the Matthean order because it highlights the theme of discipleship. This anticipates a central emphasis of Luke in Part Five, the Travel Narrative.

Lk 9:23-27. Luke has Jesus say that his disciples should "take up their cross *every day,*" giving greater specificity to Matthew's somewhat vague, once-for-all statement (Mt 16:24; cf. Lk 14:27). Luke makes it a daily requirement. καθ' ἡμέραν is a Lukan linguistic characteristic (Collison 137). Furthermore, whereas Matthew says "Jesus told <u>his disciples</u>" (Mt 16:24), Luke's Jesus addresses this admonition "to all" (Lk 9:23).

• Luke's conclusion in Lk 9:26-27 seems to differ only slightly from Matthew's "they will see the Son of Man coming in his Kingdom" (Mt 16:28). Actually, there is more here than meets the eye. Luke is de-eschatologizing Matthew's prediction, so that it will refer to an event that takes place eight days later (in the very next story), where three select disciples see a divine manifestation of Moses and Elijah and Jesus in glory. In other words, when Jesus predicts that "some standing here ... will see the Kingdom of God," Jesus' prediction is literally fulfilled about a week later. This is another instance of Lukan interweaving and foreshadowing. Although this prediction is fulfilled with the Transfiguration, Luke also anticipates a return of Jesus after the resurrection to bring the kingdom to fulfillment.[4]

---

[3] For a detailed discussion of the passion prediction passages in the Synoptic Gospels and how the literary evidence within them provides support for the Two Gospel Hypothesis, see William R. Farmer, "The Passion Prediction Passages and the Synoptic Problem: A Test Case," *NTS* 36 (1990) 558-570.

[4] For ways in which the prophetic saying in Lk 9:27 and all similar prophetic sayings within the Synoptic tradition provide evidence for solving the synoptic problem, see David Peabody, "A Pre-Markan Prophetic Sayings Tradition and the Synoptic Problem," *JBL* 97 (1978) 391-409.

• Other minor differences between Matthew and Luke can be explained on the basis of Lukan redaction. Lukan linguistic characteristics within this context include ἔλεγεν δέ (Collison 56), καθ' ἡμέραν (Collison 137), the anaphoric use of οὗτος (Collison 202-203), the collocation of the interrogative pronoun τίς with the inferential particles/conjunctions ἄρα, γάρ, and οὖν (Collison 210), λέγω δὲ ὑμῖν (Collison 57), cf. λέγω δὲ ὑμῖν ἀληθῶς (Collison 225), βασιλεία τοῦ θεοῦ (Collison 170), and Luke's classical usage of αὐτοῦ as a substitute for ὧδε.

¶ 50. Jesus Christ is shown to be the Son of God

Mt 17:1-13 ====> **Lk 9:28-36**

About eight days after Jesus predicted that "some of you standing here will see...the Kingdom of God," Jesus takes Peter, James, and John up onto the mountain where his prediction is fulfilled. During the night, Jesus begins communing with God and suddenly his face loses its mortal appearance and his robes begin to shine with God's glory. Two "holy messengers" emerge out of brilliant light; they are Moses and Elijah—God's most important prophets. They converse with Jesus about the glorious departure (ἔξοδος) which "he was soon to accomplish in Jerusalem." Peter and the others, although sleepy at first, behold everything. The two prophets begin to disappear. Peter jumps up and asks Jesus if they should make three enclosures to house them, in hopes of enticing them to stay longer. Suddenly a thick, terrifying cloud envelops them and a great Voice says, "THIS IS MY SON! MY CHOSEN ONE! LISTEN TO HIM!" Abruptly the vision disappears and the disciples find themselves standing alone with a very human Jesus. They are so stunned they remain silent for days, telling no one what their eyes have seen.

General observations. Luke followed the order of Matthew to obtain this account. However, unlike Matthew, Luke has been carefully building toward this crowning revelation of Jesus' divine status since earlier in his narrative. A number of key figures, beginning with John the Baptist, asked the question repeatedly, "Who are you? Are you he who is to come?" Simon the Pharisee's guests asked: "Who is this who even forgives sins?" The disciples asked each other: "Who is this who can command the wind and the sea and they obey him?" Herod Antipas said, "John the Baptist I beheaded, but who is this who does all these things?" Finally, Jesus himself asks his disciples who they think he is. Peter answers: "You are the Christ of God." The true answer at last. But then, eight days later, Peter and James and John are taken up on "the mountain" where they witness a divine verification of the answer: Jesus is changed into pure light before their very eyes. They hear God's Voice proclaim: "THIS IS MY SON! LISTEN TO HIM!" On this high note, Luke concludes his rich and nuanced history of Jesus' Galilee ministry.

This vignette also sets the stage for the next part of his narrative: the lengthy account of Jesus' journey to Jerusalem, during which—with "listen to him!" still echoing in the background—Jesus teaches the Twelve and the crowds many things about the Christian life. We will discuss this more fully in the introductory Overview of Part Five.

Lk 9:28. ἐγένετο δὲ μετὰ τοὺς λόγους τούτους is one of Luke's typical transitional formulas (cf. Collison 42-43) referring to the words of Jesus in Lk 9:23-27.

• Luke changes "and after six days" (Mt 17:1) to "about eight days after these sayings." In early Christian tradition there is a linkage between the eighth day and the final resurrection appearance of Jesus in his glory (cf. Jn 20:26; *Epistle of Barnabas* 15).

Lk 9:31. This verse contains important additional composition inserted by Luke. Instead of the vague Matthean "and they spoke with him," Luke explains what Moses and Elijah spoke about: Jesus' *exodus*—his departure from the human world: ἔλεγον τὴν ἔξοδον αὐτοῦ, ἣν ἤμελλεν πληροῦν ἐν Ἰερουσαλήμ. This is an explicit anticipation of the climactic events in the Holy City, the net effect of which is to convey to Luke's audience that Jesus' passion and death in Jerusalem had full divine sanction and Jesus' prior knowledge.

Lk 9:32. This verse continues Luke's additional composition. In context, it seems curiously pointless. Our suggestion is that it was added for the single detail that *Peter* almost fell asleep, but didn't. This may be an intentional allusion to the next time Peter is with Jesus during prayer (Gethsemane) and he does fall asleep. If this be correct, then this is meant to be a negative aside regarding Peter, added to Matthew's story. As we will see in the subsequent pericopes, Luke is about to begin a series of stories which he has carefully brought together that will display all of the Twelve to be blind, arrogant and incompetent.

Lk 9:33. As he has done before, Luke modified Matthew's κύριος "lord" (Mt 17:4) to his own preferred ἐπιστάτης, "master" (cf. Lk 5:5; 8:24bis; 8:45; see also Lk 9:49 and Collison 181).

Lk 9:33 contains a curious addition to Matthew's report of Peter's offer to build three enclosures (Mt 17:4): "not knowing what he said." This is the second insertion of a negative note about Peter, in our opinion, by Luke. Its purpose is the same as the one above: to begin the series of stories depicting the Twelve in a negative light.

Lk 9:34-36. The details of Mt 17:5-7 are slightly modified by Luke. There is a textual problem. UBS^4 argues that the Voice in Lk 9:35 said: Οὗτός ἐστιν ὁ υἱός μου <u>ὁ ἐκλελεγμένος</u> "This is my Son, the Chosen One" (see Metzger, 1994:124). The witnesses in support of this reading include $\mathfrak{P}^{45, 75}$ ℵ B L vgst sy^{s,hmg}. In support of versions closer to Matthew's text, there are: ὁ ἀγαπητός supported by A C* R W it vg^{ww} sy$^{(c).p.h}$ Mcion Cl; and ὁ ἀγαπητός, ἐν ᾧ εὐδόκησα —fully parallel with Mt's text: C^3 D. We are inclined to agree with UBS^4, despite the powerful support of the "Western" witnesses for a text similar or identical to Mt, and despite our hypothesis which says Luke was working directly from Matthew's text (so we view "harmonizations" in a different light than the UBS committee). In this case, we believe Luke changed Mt's "my beloved" (Mt 17:5) to "my chosen one" in anticipation of the voice of the crowd at Lk 23:35 ὁ Χριστὸς τοῦ θεοῦ ὁ ἐκλεκτός "Let him save himself, if he is the Christ of God, the Chosen One!"

• Luke omitted Mt 17:9-13 because the identification of John the Baptist with Elijah conflicted with Luke's own belief that John was *not* Elijah (cf. Luke's omission of this same Matthean claim about the identity of John and Elijah from Mt 11:14 at both Lk 7:30-31 and Lk 16:16). Luke has already given his definitive statement on the relationship of Jesus and John in Lk 7:24-35.

EXCURSUS: THE FUNCTIONS OF LUKE'S INTRODUCTION (LK 9:37-62) TO HIS LENGTHY COLLECTION OF JESUS' TEACHINGS (LK 10:1-19:27)

In Luke's account, Jesus' Galilean ministry culminated with the glorious vision of Jesus' full divine status as God's chosen Son (Lk 9:28-36). In that story, Elijah and Moses prophetically discussed Jesus' "departure, which he was about to fulfill in Jerusalem." Looking back to events that had built up to this moment of divine revelation (at least from Lk 7:16 through Lk 9:27), and looking forward down the long road to Jerusalem (Lk 9:51-19:27), the Transfiguration serves as a turning point in Luke's narrative as well as being the conclusion of the Galilean ministry.

After this story, Luke's Jesus prepares for "departure in Jerusalem." And Luke's readers have this shining revelation—including the divine words, "Listen to him!"—in mind as Jesus later gives teaching after teaching on Christian discipleship: about prayer, true leadership, overcoming fear and anxiety, and so on (Lk 10:1-19:27). Then, when this great compendium of lessons about discipleship has been completed, Jesus enters Jerusalem for the final, climactic events of the Gospel (Lk 19:28-24:53). Viewed in this way, Luke's whole Gospel is a beautifully crafted, orderly, ecclesiastically-oriented portrait of the Lord Jesus Christ and his instructions, not just to the Twelve, but to all of his disciples, both those who preceded Luke as well as contemporaries, like Theophilus (cf. Lk 1:1-4). Having clarified the role of the Transfiguration scene in Luke's Gospel as a whole, let us return to our immediate context.

Following the transitional section under discussion here (Lk 9:37-62), Luke adopted a literary strategy for utilizing material from Mt that differs from the process of cyclic progression he utilized prior to this. In the earlier part of his Gospel, Luke adopted material from Mt, almost always in Matthew's order, in a succession of forward progressions through Mt (see the explanatory chart and explanation in the Introduction, pp. 13-21). But, after this transitional section, Luke took over material from Mt in a different, but also orderly, manner. Let us explain what we mean.

Prior to the beginning of Luke's Central Section (Lk 9:51ff.) Luke made some initial use of Jesus' teachings from each of Matthew's first four discourses (Mt 4:23-7:29, cf.

Lk 6:20-7:1; Mt 9:35-11:1, cf. Lk 9:1-6 and sections of the Sermon on the Plain [Lk 6:12-16, 37-42]; Mt 13:1-53, cf. Lk 8:4-21; Mt 18:1-19:1 cf. Lk 9:46-48). Having made these earlier uses, Luke utilized much of the remaining material from these Matthean discourses in newly constructed Lukan literary contexts within the Travel Narrative.

Luke combined the remaining materials from Matthew's first four discourses with material from Matthew's last discourse (Mt 23:1-25:46), and with nonMatthean tradition. Luke blended all of these disparate materials together into a carefully constructed series of teachings within the Travel Narrative (Lk 10:1-19:27).

But even as Luke combined materials from many different literary contexts in Mt, his orderly use of Mt can still be seen. Luke was careful to make *sequential* use of the remaining sayings materials from Matthew's Parables Discourse, Matthew's Mission Discourse, and the Woes to the Pharisees (Mt 23). On the other hand, having utilized more of Matthew's Sermon on the Mount than any other Matthean discourse *prior* to Lk 9:51, Luke seems less able (or perhaps less concerned) to maintain Matthew's order when utilizing further material from this discourse within the Travel Narrative. But even when selecting remaining material from the Sermon on the Mount, Luke did not proceed in a random manner.

To prepare for this change in the way he utilized Mt beginning at Lk 10:1ff. (discussed above), and to set the stage for the lengthy teaching section within the middle of his Gospel narrative, Luke created a complex, interweaving transitional section, Lk 9:37-62 (on "interweaving," see the Introduction, pp. 30-33). How did he do it?

First, we noted that the most important early story within the Lukan Travel Narrative is the account of the "Mission of 72 others." How did Luke justify Jesus undertaking a *second* call and commissioning of disciples? There is no mention of such an event in Mt (or John or Mark for that matter). Nevertheless, Luke gives this event an extraordinarily deliberate preparation. Indeed, we might be surprised by the way in which Luke chose to account for Jesus' sending out a whole second mission after the first. Be that as it may, the fact is, Luke justified the need for a second call and commissioning of disciples by constructing a series of vignettes in which the original Twelve were shown to be less than admirable. Beyond that, Luke described three more anonymous, would-be disciples as equally unsuited to be disciples of Jesus.

In all, Luke brought together no less than *eight stories,* three taken from Mt in Matthew's order (Lk 9:37-48), two from nonMatthean tradition (Lk 9:49-56), followed by two more from Mt 8:18-22 that Lk had previously passed over at Lk 8:22 (Lk 9:57-60), and finally one composed by Lk himself on the basis of Mt 8:18-22 (Lk 9:61-62). With this collection of eight stories, four immediately prior to Lk 9:51 and four immediately thereafter, Luke provided a concrete, "historical" rationale for Jesus' decision to send out "72 others" on a second missionary tour. It then turned out to be far more glorious and successful than the one undertaken by the Twelve earlier. This perhaps surprising outcome will be discussed more fully below.

Let us conclude by outlining Luke's compositional activity in composing this interweaving transitional section. Immediately following Matthew's story of the Transfiguration of Jesus, which Luke subtly retouched twice to deprecate Simon Peter,

Luke then picked up the next story in Mt's order, which described the inability of all of the disciples to heal an epileptic boy (Mt 17:14-21//Lk 9:37-43a).

The next story in Matthew's order described Jesus' repeating his warning about his death (Mt 17:22-23). Luke took it into his narrative (Lk 9:43b-45), but changed Matthew's conclusion about the disciples' despair at hearing Jesus' prediction into a very different statement, namely, that none of the disciples could understand *because God had concealed its meaning from them,* and they were too afraid to ask him to explain it.

Luke omitted the next story in Mt's order: Payment of the Temple Tax (Mt 17:24-27); it would have had little meaning for his international audience.

He then picked up the next story in Mt's order, about the disciples arguing over who would be the greatest in the Kingdom of Heaven (Mt 18:1-5//Lk 9:46-48). But Luke changed this into a more mundane squabble: who among them *at present* was "the greatest" (cf. the Lukan "doublet" at Lk 22:24-30). This quarrel takes on sharp irony in view of the current record of their failures and shortcomings.

In other words, what we see happening at this point in Mt's order is that *Luke systematically used only stories that told of the failures and shortcomings of the disciples.* Note that he began this motif with two slight additions to the Transfiguration account that effectively placed Simon Peter in an ambiguous, not to say foolish, light. In doing so, Luke started this series of stories already *within* the last story of the *previous* series, a classic illustration of Luke's compositional technique of interweaving two major parts of his narrative by means of anticipations in preceding material (see Introduction, pp. 30-33).

In addition to these three accounts taken from Mt, Luke *added two more negative stories about James and John* from his nonMatthean tradition describing:

(a) an occasion when John told Jesus that they had stopped someone else who was *successfully* healing in Jesus' name (even though they could not)—prompting a reprimand from Jesus (Lk 9:49-50), and

(b) an occasion when James and John asked Jesus if they should call fire down from heaven onto a Samaritan village and burn it up because it had refused to receive Jesus—prompting another scolding by Jesus (Lk 9:51-56).

Immediately after this series, the impact of which is to leave the reader/audience with the impression that *Jesus' Twelve Apostles—beginning with the three leaders—were inadequate,* Luke went on in the same vein and *reached back* to Mt 8:19-22, which he had previously passed over at Lk 8:22, for *more* negative material about would-be disciples (cf. Lk 9:57-62). Luke drew the two stories of would-be disciples from Mt *and composed a third* using phrases taken from them. This suite of four vignettes about other would-be disciples who volunteered their services is introduced here to fill the gap left by the now seemingly useless Twelve. But even these would-be disciples prove to be unfit.

At precisely this point, Luke portrayed Jesus suddenly choosing "72 other" disciples with the comment, "The harvest is plentiful but—as everyone can now see—the true laborers are few. Pray God, the Lord of the Harvest, to send out *the right kind of laborers* into the bountiful harvest" (Lk 10:2). That is exactly what Luke portrays Jesus doing next, with resounding success (Lk 10:1-20).

Let us go back to the point where we began. It is our view of the general outline of Luke's Gospel that Luke intended to present the scene of Jesus in divine glory, with the Voice of God announcing him as his Son, as the culmination and climax of Jesus' Galilean activities, preparing the reader/audience to be receptive to a long central teaching section. By this point, Luke had used most of the material in Mt down through ch. 17. This means that Luke located his great Central Section in the Matthean order of events at *Mt 18:1-19:1, Matthew's version of Jesus' Community Regulations*. Then within this Central Section, Luke combined this collection of sayings on the community (Mt 18:1-19:1) with material drawn from all of Jesus' other long speeches in Mt (Mt 4:23-7:29; Mt 9:35-11:1; Mt 13:1-53; Mt 23:1-26:1), and other material from his nonMatthean tradition.

Why did Luke go to such pains to combine all of these sayings from the speeches of Jesus in Mt? As we noted in the Introduction, Luke undoubtedly viewed the speeches in Mt as far too long (see p. 32 item <1>). Second, we assume that Luke did want to provide the Christian churches in the wider, ecumenical mission areas with an effective compendium of the Lord's teachings, carefully rephrased to be useful for their situations and needs. We will discuss more fully the rationale for Luke's fundamental compositional decision in our Overview at the beginning of Part Five.

But why did Luke begin that Part of his Gospel with this series of negative stories about the Twelve Apostles? There may be many different ways to account for this striking feature. For our part, we take as our starting point the fact that Luke began his great compendium of Jesus' teachings (the "Travel Narrative") with a glorious account of the mission by 72 spirit-led disciples other than the Twelve (an obvious echo of the account in Num 11 where the Lord appoints 72 elders to share the "spirit of Moses"). Nor is it accidental that Luke based Jesus' motivation for this second, much more successful mission, upon a series of stories told at the expense of the "Pillar Apostles," beginning with their leader, Simon Peter. Luke is strikingly explicit, naming names and giving specific details.

We suggest that Luke's predecessor in this was none other than the Apostle Paul, himself not one of the original Twelve, nor an apostle who always stood in good graces with the Twelve or the Jerusalem leadership where members of Jesus' family still remained in authority when Luke composed his Gospel. Without wishing to overstate our case, for the Twelve are definitely rehabilitated by Luke later on in Acts, the fact remains that Luke's general perspective was focused not on the Jerusalem leadership but on the *oikoumene* and the leadership among those churches who brought them into being and faithfully guided them. Hence, in this passage and in much of the rest of Luke's narrative, the Twelve Apostles are not the most admirable of figures. Such is our understanding of the complex series of motivations involved in this key section of Luke's Gospel.

In keeping with our view, Lk 9:51 remains an important turning point in Luke's narrative, forming the dividing point between the Galilean ministry and the Journey to Jerusalem. Leading up to it on the one side are four accounts portraying the Twelve as incompetent, uncomprehending, boastful and exclusive. Then comes Lk 9:51a, the announcement that Jesus has decided to go to Jerusalem. Immediately after that, in Lk 9:51b-62, are four more stories, the first depicting James and John as vengeful and three more depicting would-be disciples as frivolous, distracted, and unprepared.

We propose to call this series of eight stories an *interweaving transitional section* between Parts Four and Five. This section exemplifies Luke's literary skill in the way he stitches together different parts of his narrative, so that one part seems to flow seamlessly into the next. In an attempt to acknowledge Luke's literary artistry in this case, we have chosen to divide our discussion of this Lukan unit in half, discussing the first half here at the end of Part Four (Lk 9:37-50) and the second half at the beginning of Part Five (Lk 9:52-62), in spite of the literary unity which we have attempted to describe in this excursus on Lk 9:37-62. We now turn to the four stories in this Lukan unit which conclude Part Four.

Interweaving Transitional Section (first half) Lk 9:37-50

¶ 51. The disciples fail to heal a demon-possessed boy

Mt 17:14-18 ====> **Lk 9:37-43a**

On the next day, a great crowd comes out to Jesus and a man rushes up to him and cries, "Teacher, I beg you! Please heal my son! Demons are destroying him! I asked your disciples to heal him but they couldn't do it!" Angered, Jesus exclaims, "What kind of faithless generation is this?! How long should I put up with it?!" Going to the boy, Jesus casts out the demon and gives the boy back to his father. The crowd is astonished at God's greatness.

General observations. Luke continued to follow Mt's order for this story. However, he made some minor alterations to heighten the dramatic impact. The most important difference is found at the end, where Luke has omitted Mt's conclusion (Mt 17:19-20) and substituted his own (Lk 9:43a).

Lk 9:37. This verse is a Lukan construct based upon a conflation of Mt 17:9 and 14. Since a first prediction of Jesus' resurrection already appeared in Lk 9:22 and announcement of what will happen to the Son of Man will occur at Lk 9:44, Luke lost little by the omission of Mt 17:10-13. These verses in Mt also include a reference to John the Baptist as Elijah, a concept that Luke rejected (see Luke's similar editing and omission of Mt 11:14 at Lk 7:24-28 and again at Lk 16:16).

Lk 9:38 καὶ ἰδού is a probable characteristic of Lukan style which he has added to Mt 17:14. The same applies to ἀνήρ which replaces Mt's ἄνθρωπος (cf. Collison 167). δέομαί σου is introduced into the story by Luke and repeated for dramatic effect in 9:40. The striking phrase ἐπιβλέψαι ἐπὶ τὸν υἱόν μου, ὅτι μονογενής μοί ἐστιν is Luke's equivalent for Mt's "have mercy" and is parallel to the "only begotten" son of the widow of Nain in Lk 7:12. And just as the son of the widow in Nain is "returned to his mother" in Lk 7:15, the "only begotten son" is "returned to his father" in Lk 9:42 (cf. Goulder 1:445).

Lk 9:39-42 are similar to Mt 17:15-18 with a few additional dramatic flourishes (cf. Lk 9:42).

Lk 9:43 is Luke's replacement of Mt's report of the downcast disciples coming to Jesus to ask why they could not heal the boy (Mt 17:19-20). Note that Luke suppressed all mention of the disciples' desire to learn from their failure, leaving them instead in the harsh glare of abject failure. Another bit of evidence that this ending came from the hand of Luke may be found in the use of the term "and all were astonished at the *majesty* of God" (μεγαλειότητος τοῦ θεου). This term is found only here and in Acts 19:27: "(Artemis) may be deposed from her magnificence μέλλειν τε καὶ καθαιρεῖσθαι τῆς μεγαλειότητος αὐτῆς (scil. Ἀρτέμιδος), she whom all Asia and the world worship." Otherwise, the word does not occur in the NT except at 2 Pet 1:16. Outside the NT it was a widely-used Hellenistic attribute of divinity, cf. the cry of the Ephesian silversmiths: ἔκραζον λέγοντες, Μεγάλη ἡ Ἄρτεμις Ἐφεσίων (cf. Liddell-Scott-Jones, s.v. μεγαλειότητος). Its presence here is likely because of Luke's rewriting the ending of this story.

¶ 52. The disciples fail to understand Jesus' prediction of his suffering

Mt 17:22-23 ====> **Lk 9:43b-45**

But, even as the crowd and disciples are marveling at Jesus' power, he warns his disciples that it won't last long. Soon he is to be delivered by God into the power of evil men. The disciples stare at him uncomprehendingly. They cannot understand a word he is saying because God has mysteriously hidden full understanding from them. They are too frightened to ask him to give additional explanations.

General observations. This story occurs next in Matthew's order and Luke took it over, making major alterations in the process.

Lk 9:43b. Mt's version begins with a geographical detail: "as they were gathering in Galilee," which Luke skipped, the better to dovetail this story into the conclusion of the previous story for purposes of ironic contrast. Clearly, Luke is juxtaposing the amazing display of Jesus' power in the previous unit (cf. Lk 9:43a) with an announcement that he must suffer. Jesus' true glory will come in the cross. It is noticeable that Luke omitted any reference to resurrection from the dead here (cf. 17:22).

Lk 9:44. Luke abbreviated Matthew's version of Jesus' saying, but then he added the emphatic words, "let these words sink into your ears." This touch can only be explained as dramatic irony, since the very next sentence states that God was preventing the disciples from understanding Jesus.

Lk 9:45. This is mostly a Lukan creation. He omitted Mt's detail about the disciples' distress (Mt 17:23b) and instead stressed the disciples' inability to understand.

¶ 53. The disciples quarrel over who is the greatest

Mt 18:1-2, 5 (Mt 10:42) ====> **Lk 9:46-48**

Continuing his negative theme and illustrating just how "darkened" their minds are, Luke portrays the disciples stupidly breaking out into an argument as to who is the "greatest" among them. Jesus patiently brings a child into their midst and says, "Whoever is willing to be accepting of everyone—even a little child like this—for my sake, *truly* accepts me and the God who sent me. Only the truly humble among you Twelve Apostles should presume to be the leader of the rest."

General observations. Luke skipped the next account in Matthew's order after Mt 17:23, the Payment of the Temple Tax (Mt 17:24-27) since it held little meaning for his Gentile audience. At that point, Luke reached the speech of Jesus traditionally known as "Community Regulations" (Mt 18:1-35). This Matthean collection was apparently chosen by Luke as the place where he would stop following the narrative order of the Gospel of Matthew and create a central section containing teaching material from the major speeches in Mt as well as other material from his own sources, thereby creating his own much larger and more effective compendium of the Lord's Teaching for the Christian Churches in the wider ecumenical mission areas.

The first anecdote in Matthew's Community Regulations chapter is this story, where the disciples quarrel over who will be the greatest in the kingdom of heaven (Mt 18:1). Pursuant to his theme in this Transitional Section of the shortcomings and failures of the Twelve Apostles, Luke picked up this story and told it here.

Luke created a doublet, with precisely this same conjunction of prediction of suffering followed by a quarrel over who is greatest, at the Last Supper in Lk 22:21-26. That account helps us understand what may be hovering in the background here: Luke interpreted this story in Mt 18:1-5 so that it would address the shameful infighting in his (i.e., Luke's) own day as to who was the most powerful in the community after Jesus. That this may be what is in Luke's mind can be seen from the change in Lk 9:47 (see below).

Lk 9:46. In Luke's narrative, this disagreement breaks out immediately after Jesus has predicted his impending death. The disciples are prevented from understanding. As a sign of the "darkness of their minds," they begin quarreling over who among them is the greatest. Luke retained the question and answer format of Jesus in Mt 18:1,4 (Lk 9:46; 48), but for Luke the question arose among the disciples themselves.

Lk 9:47-48. These verses are based on Mt 18:2, 5 Ὃς ἐὰν δέξηται τοῦτο τὸ παιδίον ἐπὶ τῷ ὀνόματί μου, ἐμὲ δέχεται. The meaning of "receiving a child in Jesus' name" (RSV) is difficult to understand in Luke's context at this point. Mt's fuller version is clearer; it is about arrogance and pride: "whoever humbles himself like this child..." (Mt 18:4a). But Mt's version began with the question "Who will be the greatest in the *Kingdom of Heaven*?" Luke has removed "heaven" from the story entirely, changing the point of the squabble among the Twelve Apostles into a contest over pre-eminent status in the present.

Lk 9:48b-c is a conflation of Mt 18:5 and Mt 10:40: "whoever accepts you accepts me and he who accepts me accepts Him who sent me."

Synopsis of Lk 9:48b-c

Illustrating how Luke conflated Mt 10:40 and 18:5.

Matt 10:40	**Luke 9:48b-c**	**Matt 18:5**
Ὁ δεχόμενος	Ὃς ἐὰν δέξηται	καὶ ὃς ἐὰν δέξηται
ὑμᾶς	τοῦτο τὸ παιδίον	ἓν παιδίον τοιοῦτο
	ἐπὶ τῷ ὀνόματί μου,	ἐπὶ τῷ ὀνόματί μου,
ἐμὲ δέχεται	ἐμὲ δέχεται·	ἐμὲ δέχεται·
καὶ ὁ ἐμὲ δεχόμενος	καὶ ὃς ἂν ἐμὲ δέξηται,	
δέχεται	δέχεται	
τὸν ἀποστείλαντά με.	τὸν ἀποστείλαντά με.	

Mt 10:40 is also a very close parallel to Lk 10:16: "He who hears you hears me and he who rejects you rejects me and he who rejects me rejects Him who sent me." All of this suggests that Luke has added a version of this saying in Mt to the end of the story in Mt 18:5. It is one which he used in more than one context.

• The central thrust of this story in Luke's version is to restrict the meaning of the saying on humility to a warning against infighting among the church's leaders. "To accept a child means to accept me and the One who sent me" should be interpreted: you leaders must be humbly willing to accept anyone into your trust, even the lowest members of the community. If you cannot accept even the lowliest, then you have not truly accepted me nor the God who sent me."

¶ 54. John stops someone who can heal in Jesus' name

(Mt 12:30) **Lk 9:49-50**

No sooner has Jesus rebuked the Twelve for their arrogance than John proudly informs him that he stopped a stranger who was successfully healing people in Jesus' name. Again, as if patiently speaking to children, Jesus tells his disciples: be more inclusive! Whoever is not explicitly opposed to us can heal in my name.

General observations. This story is not found in Mt anywhere. This indicates to us that Luke intentionally put together a series of negative stories about the disciples. This one is explicitly about the Apostle John. It completes the set of four stories of the shortcomings of the Twelve before the momentous announcement in Lk 9:51 that Jesus was going to Jerusalem. As such it constitutes the climax to the first section of the transitional unit from the Galilean ministry to the Travel Narrative. Immediately following, as the first pericope of the second section of the transitional unit (Lk 9:52-56), Luke will insert another negative story, this time about John and his brother James. They urge Jesus to call fire down from heaven on some recalcitrant Samaritans, thereby earning another rebuke from Jesus.

Lk 9:49 Luke's indictment of John could not be more ironic. Jesus has barely stopped speaking when John tells him that he made an outsider stop using Jesus' name to heal, even though he was successful at it, while the Twelve were not.

Lk 9:50. Jesus' answer seems to be the opposite of Mt 12:30: "He that is not with me is against me and he who does not gather with me scatters," which Luke will use in a later context (Lk 11:23). This is another instance where Luke used a Matthean saying more than once.

PART FIVE LK 9:51–19:27

JESUS JOURNEYS TOWARD JERUSALEM

Overview

Part Four of Luke's orderly narrative of Jesus' life ended in a climactic moment on the Mount where Jesus was declared the elect Son of God by divine pronouncement (Lk 9:35). The inner circle of Jesus' followers who were privileged to witness this event were told bluntly at the time, "Hear him!" Within Part Five we "hear Jesus" (Lk 9:51-19:27).

Part Five begins with Luke's momentous announcement that Jesus has decided to take the road toward Jerusalem, with all that that would mean. While on the way, Jesus teaches his disciples, his friends, his opponents, the crowds who follow him and all who would "hear him" about many important topics. These include what and how to pray, the sources of spiritual power, what and whom to fear or be anxious about, the need to avoid hypocrisy, the costs of discipleship, who is judged and who is saved, the need for undivided loyalty, the nature of the Kingdom of God and who is included within it, and the need for faith and good works. Especially the disciples would need all of these teachings if they were to be prepared for the coming events in Jerusalem (Lk 19:28-24:53) and for the continuing mission of the Church following those events (Acts). Toward the end of the Travel Narrative, Jesus promises his disciples that everything that they may have left behind to follow him, even members of their own family, will be restored in this age and that eternal life is the promise of the age to come (Lk 18:28-30; cf. Lk 12:51-53; 14:25-26). Yet in the interim, innocent people, even God's prophets, must die in Jerusalem (Lk 13:1-5, 31-35; 18:31-34; and Lk 19:28ff.).

PROCEDURAL NOTE. In Part Five, Luke's utilization of Mt followed a more complex path than was the case in Lk 3 through 9, or 20-24. For this reason, we adopted a new category for Part Five that will appear, when necessary, immediately after the narrative summary for each Section. They have been called "source-critical observations," and will explain our reasons for grouping the following pericopes into a larger whole, or Section.

Source-critical observations. For this Part, Luke again utilized the typical Hellenistic motif of the wandering teacher going on a journey. This last journey of the earthly Jesus is toward Jerusalem (Lk 9:51-19:28) where, as the divine Son/King, he will enter the city to claim the allegiance of the people (Lk 19:28-48). Throughout this journey, however, Luke included recurrent anticipatory notes that contrast with Jesus' forthcoming glorious entry into Jerusalem and foreshadow his rejection by the Jerusalem leadership once he reaches the city (Lk 9:51-53; 11:15-16; 13:1-5, 31-35; 17:25; 18:31-34).

• When he composed Lk 9:18-50, Luke followed the sequential order of pericopes in Mt 16:13-18:5. By Lk 9:51, therefore, Luke has come into contextual parallel with Jesus' Discourse on Community Regulations in Mt 18:1-19:1 (cf. Mt 18:1-2, 4-5//Lk 9:46-48). The Lukan Travel Narrative provides a literary context, similar to Matthew's discourses, where longer collections of teachings of Jesus may be narrated. But within the Travel Narrative, Luke's Jesus is able to give even more teachings to a later church than any one of Jesus' speeches in Mt contains. Compare Mt 9:35-11:1 or Mt 18:1-19:1 with Lk 9:51-19:27. In fact, within the Travel Narrative, Luke made use of material from *all* of the long speeches of Jesus in Mt, both those which Luke had already drawn upon to some extent and the one or two Luke had not yet reached in his use of Mt (cf. Mt 23:1-26:1). Here, Luke's Jesus gives a very extensive collection of teachings within the type of narrative context Luke prefers. Matthew, by way of contrast, allows each long discourse of Jesus to interrupt the flow of his narrative.

• For the content of Part Five, Luke has drawn from the following sources:

(1) material that Luke, for the most part, had not already utilized from each of Mt's Great Discourses of Jesus;

(2) material drawn from Mt 11:20-12:50 and a few other Matthean narrative contexts;

(3) nonMatthean tradition—especially parables.

Luke blended these materials into sections on major themes of Jesus' teaching. Luke probably chose themes that would be of direct benefit to Christians throughout the Hellenistic world. But even when Luke has combined material from different literary units in Mt with teachings drawn from *nonMatthean* tradition, Luke's text still reflects remarkable agreement with the order of sayings *within* each of the speeches in Matthew. For a detailed graphic display of these agreements consult the Appendix: Chart C. The Travel Narrative.

• The two Lukan sections on Prayer (Lk 11:1-13 and 18:1-14) frame most of that part of Luke's Travel Narrative where Luke's text agrees with the order of most of the sayings within each of Mt's speeches of Jesus (Lk 10:23-18:14). After Lk 18:14, Luke returned to the sequential order of pericopes in Mt and followed it to the account of the Empty Tomb (Lk 18:15-24:11), where he branched off to form his own conclusion (Lk 24:12-53).

Organization of the Lukan Travel Narrative (Lk 9:51-19:27)

Luke's Travel Narrative seems to have been arranged under a number of general themes or subjects. We have identified these by means of the following Sections within Lk 9:51-19:27. Luke's demonstrable skill in weaving his narrative into a fine, apparently seamless, literary tapestry often made identifying the dividing line between the Sections rather difficult. Again, considerable reflection was often required to identify Luke's supposed reasons for combining certain sayings from Mt's speeches of

Jesus with other sayings material from his nonMatthean tradition—under a given theme or subject. Here is an outline of Part Five.

Starting point: Lk 9:51. Jesus sets out for Jerusalem.

Interweaving Transitional Section to Part Five (second half): Lk 9:52-62. Ineptitude in Discipleship. (See first half in Lk 9:37-50)

Section 1: Lk 10:1-42. The Great Mission.

Section 2: Lk 11:1-13. To the Disciples: On Prayer.

Section 3: Lk 11:14-32. To the People: On Spiritual Power.

Section 4: Lk 11:37-52. To Pharisees and Lawyers: On Hypocrisy.

Section 5: Lk 12:4-34. To Friends and Disciples: Reject Fear and Anxiety. Trust God.

Section 6: Lk 12:35-53. To the Disciples and Others: Appropriate Conduct Before the Lord's Coming.

Section 7: Lk 12:54-13:30. To the Multitudes: Who Is Truly Judged?

Section 8: Lk 14:1-35. To a Dinner Audience: The Messiah's Banquet Instructions.

Section 9: Lk 15:1-32. To Scribes and Pharisees: God Seeks and Saves the Lost.

Section 10: Lk 16:1-31. To Disciples and Pharisees: You Cannot Serve God and Money.

Section 11: Lk 17:1-19. To the Disciples: On Faith and Works.

Section 12: Lk 17:20-37. To Pharisees and Disciples. Where is the Kingdom?

Section 13: Lk 18:1-14. To the Faithful and the Self-Righteous: On Prayer.

Section 14: Lk 18:15-30. To the Disciples, a Ruler and Hearers: On the Kingdom of God.

Section 15: Lk 18:31-43. To the Twelve and a Man: True Blindness.

Interweaving Transitional Section to Part Six (first half): Lk 19:1-27. Preparation for the King to Come into His City

A noteworthy structural feature of the Travel Narrative is the way in which many of the themes introduced at the beginning reappear toward the end. These include:

Ineptitude in Discipleship: Lk 9:37-62 and Lk 18:31-34.

Receiving Jesus and His Disciples: Lk 9:51-56; 10:1-12; and Lk 19:1-10.

What Must I Do to Inherit Eternal Life?: Lk 10:25-28 and Lk 18:18-23.

A Good Samaritan: Lk 10:29-37 and Lk 17:11-19.

The Would-Be Disciple Who Hears and Does: Lk 10:38-42 and Lk 19:1-10.

The Loss/Restoration of Family Unity: Lk 12:52-53; 14:25-27; and Lk 18:28-30

Prayer: Lk 11:1-13 (Section Two) and Lk 18:1-14 (Section Thirteen).

Seeking and Saving the Lost: Lk 15:1-32 and Lk 19:1-10.

With these preliminary clarifications completed, let us begin our detailed examination of the Lukan Travel Narrative.

¶ 55. Jesus sets out for Jerusalem
Lk 9:51

Realizing that the time had come for him to "fulfill the Scriptures," Jesus turns his face toward Jerusalem and sets out on the road with his disciples.

General observations. At Lk 9:51, the author writes, "When the days of [Jesus'] ἀναλήμψεως were completed, he set his face to go to Jerusalem." With this, Luke began a major new Part in his narrative which lasts almost ten chapters. This momentous verse is entirely Lukan composition. It appears at the center of Luke's carefully constructed transitional unit from the Galilean Ministry to the Journey to Jerusalem (Lk 9:37-62).

Lk 9:51a. The usual translation of ἀναλήμψις as "assumption" may be questioned, since the assumption of Jesus will not be mentioned until Lk 24:50-51 and repeated in Acts 1:9-11. Hence, Jesus' assumption was not "fulfilled" or "completed" (συμπληροῦσθαι) prior to Lk 9:51, as current translations of this verse imply. On the other hand, to interpret ἀναλήμψις as "death" is equally questionable because the death of Jesus is also still ahead in the Lukan Gospel (cf. Lk 23:26-56). It is possible that the reading here should be ἀναλάμψεως rather than ἀναλήμψεως. According to Liddell and Scott, ἀναλάμψις was a variant spelling of ἀναλήμψις in the Hellenistic period, and a translation of ἀναλάμψεως at Lk 9:51 may make better sense of the Lukan narrative than the alternative translations just mentioned. Lk 9:51 could be translated, "And it happened, when the days of Jesus' *shining forth* were fulfilled, he set his face to go to Jerusalem." The sentence in Lk 9:51 would then refer back to the story of "Jesus in Glory" (Lk 9:28-36) which concluded Jesus' ministry in Galilee.

• On the other hand, if we should accept the usual reading of Lk 9:51, Luke would here be making one more comparison between Jesus and Elijah, both of whom were taken up into heaven (cf. Lk 24:50-51//Acts 1:9-11 and 2 Kgs 2:9-12).

Interweaving Transitional Section (Second Half). Ineptitude in Discipleship. Lk 9:52-62

¶ 56. The failure of John and James to be forgiving
(Mt 9:32-10:16)
Lk 9:52–56

Jesus now begins his already foreshadowed and anticipated journey toward Jerusalem and certain death. He sends a few messengers on ahead to a Samaritan village, but the Samaritans tell them to go away. John and James vengefully ask Jesus to burn the village with fire from heaven (like Sodom and Gomorrah). Jesus chastises them for suggesting such a thing and they move on to another village.

General observations. This pericope has no direct parallel in the Synoptic tradition. Luke may have intended the rejection of Jesus by the Samaritans to indicate that they took offense that Jesus was going to Jerusalem rather than into Samaria. This unit introduces the theme of the Samaritans into the Travel Narrative and prepares the reader for the impact of Lk 10:25-37, the Parable of the Good Samaritan, and perhaps also for Lk 17:11-19, the Good Samaritan Leper.

Lk 9:52-56. On the reaction of John and James, compare the similar statement, also made by John, on behalf of himself and some other disciple(s), at Lk 9:49-50. There John reports to Jesus that he and some other apostle(s) had prevented someone who did not follow Jesus and his apostles from doing Jesus' healing work. In Lk 9:52-56, as in Lk 9:49-50, Jesus must correct his disciples. In this second story about the disciple, John, along with James, Jesus rebukes the vengeful attitude of these two apostles toward a Samaritan village that had failed to "receive" Jesus (Lk 9:53, οὐκ ἐδέξαντο αὐτόν). Compare Lk 9:46-48//Mt 18:1-2, 4-5 and Mt 10:40 and especially Lk 9:48. See synopsis above, p. 148).

Luke apparently constructed a saying complementary to Lk 9:48 at Lk 10:16, Ὁ ἀκούων ὑμῶν ἐμοῦ ἀκούει, καὶ ὁ ἀθετῶν ὑμᾶς ἐμὲ ἀθετεῖ· ὁ δὲ ἐμὲ ἀθετῶν ἀθετεῖ τὸν ἀποστείλαντά με to serve as the conclusion of his unit about the mission of the seventy-two other disciples at Lk 10:1-16.

• Again, within this pericope, Luke may be calling attention to a similarity between the story of Jesus and the story of Elijah. See the similar story of Elijah calling down fire on Ahaziah's messengers at 2 Kings 1:1-18.

• On the Two Gospel Hypothesis, Luke certainly returned to the context of Mt 9:35-10:16 in order to compose Lk 10:1-12, the literary unit only six verses ahead in Luke's text. If Luke did plan to return to Mt 9:35-10:16, as he clearly did at Lk 10:1ff., he might well have consulted this context in Mt prior to composing Lk 9:51. There are a number of echoes and parallels to Mt 9:35-10:16, not only in Lk 10:1-12, but also in Lk 9:52-56. Two of these echoes of Mt 9:35ff. within Lk 9:52-56 are

(1) the use of ἀπέστελειν to refer to Jesus' sending out disciples and

(2) the use of a form of εἰσέρχομαι + εἰς + "house/village of the Samaritans," both within Lk 9:52 and Mt 10:5.

It would appear that Luke explicitly chose to respond to the tradition about Jesus preserved in Mt 10:5-6 in his "parallel" at Lk 9:52. According to Mt 10:5-6, Jesus specifically told the twelve disciples, when they were commissioned, "Do not go in the way of the Gentiles and do not enter into a city of the Samaritans, but go rather to the lost sheep of the House of Israel." By contrast, Luke had Jesus *explicitly* send his disciples into a Samaritan village at Lk 9:52.

Be that as it may, the effect on the ministry of Jesus and his disciples was the same. At this point in Mt and in Lk, Jesus and his disciples do not associate with the Samaritans. However, according to Lk, this lack of association was not because Jesus rejected the Samaritans, but rather because "they did not receive him." The theme of "receiving" or "not receiving" Jesus and/or his disciples recurs throughout the Lukan Gospel (see Lk 8:4-21; 9:1-6; 9:48-49; 9:51-56; 10:1-16; 16:1-9; and 18:15-17).

• The teachings of Jesus contained in Mt 10:5-6 found no place in Luke's version of the Mission of the Twelve (Lk 9:1-6) nor did they find any place within Luke's distinctive story of the Mission of Seventy-Two Other Disciples (Lk 10:1-12). If Luke has responded to Mt 10:5-6 within Lk 9:51-56, that would help to explain the absence of a parallel to Mt 10:5-6 within either Lk 9:1-6 or Lk 10:1-12. The statements made about Gentiles and Samaritans within Mt 10:5-6 are contrary to Luke's own views, of course, so that is the basic reason for these Lukan omissions.

¶ 57. The failure of a first would-be disciple to be realistic

Mt 8:19-20 ====>**Lk 9:57-58**

As Jesus and his disciples continue on their journey toward Jerusalem, a certain man meets them on the way and offers to follow Jesus wherever he might go. Jesus corrects this man's naive idea of what is required of being a follower of his. Every creature in the sky or on the earth has a home, but Jesus, the Son of Man, doesn't even have a place to lay his head at night. The would-be disciple goes away.

General observations. Already within Lk 9:49-50, John had explained to Jesus that he and some other apostle(s) had forbidden an exorcist from doing Jesus' healing work "because he did not *follow* with us." This statement may help explain why Luke next returned to Mt 8:19-22 where he found a unit about two would-be "followers" of Jesus. Earlier, Luke had passed over Mt 8:19-22 in composing Lk 8:22-25. Here Luke incorporated his earlier omission. Luke composed the whole of Lk 9:57-62 on the basis of Mt 8:19-22. Mt 8:19-22 is the first of only three Matthean units (Mt 8:19-22, Mt 9:27-31 and Mt 9:32-34) between the end of Jesus' first great discourse in Mt (Mt 7:29) and the beginning of his second (Mt 9:35) that Luke had not yet used.

Lk 9:57-58. This and the next two pericopes in Luke clearly anticipate Jesus' instructions to the seventy-two other disciples. Within the cities and villages to which the seventy-two will be sent, the newly commissioned disciples will have to depend upon the hospitality of others to provide for their needs, including meals and temporary lodging (Lk 10:1ff.).

• In contrast to Matthew, Luke did not identify these would-be disciples.

• The spectrum of failure ranges from the Twelve even to these prospective disciples.

¶ 58. The failure of a second would-be disciple to proclaim the Kingdom of God

Mt 8:21-22====>**Lk 9:59-60**

Jesus next encounters a second man. Unlike Jesus' encounter with the first man, this man does not volunteer to follow Jesus, but, rather, is called by Jesus. And unlike the naive enthusiasm of the first man, this man expresses reluctance to become one of Jesus' disciples, saying that he first has to go away and bury his father. Jesus replies to this man's more reluctant attitude, beginning with a metaphorical admonition, "Let the dead people bury their own dead." But that does not conclude Jesus' response to this second man. Contrasting the man's expressed desire "to go away first to take care of his father's burial" Jesus continues with the words, "But when you do go away, you must proclaim the Kingdom of God."

General observations. Luke continued to follow the order and basic content of Mt in recording this shocking announcement that loyalty to Jesus takes precedence over the most basic of responsibilities to one's own family. Luke well knew that discipleship in his day could and did lead to divisions within the family (Lk 12:49-53), but, before the Travel Narrative concludes, Luke's Jesus will affirm that families will be re-united even in this age (Lk 18:28-30).

Lk 9:59-60. Luke's modifications of Mt 8:21-22 included his adding a requirement for this man's discipleship. Specifically, he must "go away," not to bury his father, but rather "to proclaim the Kingdom of God." This Lukan addition is similar to one Luke may have made to his nonMatthean tradition in Lk 9:62. Jesus' two responses, one at Lk 9:60 and one at Lk 9:62 are both concerned with "the Kingdom of God" and this is a demonstrable Lukan interest (Collison 169-170).

¶ 59. The failure of a third would-be disciple to be fit for the Kingdom of God

(Mt 8:21-22) **Lk 9:61-62**

Jesus now encounters a third and final would-be disciple. Like the first one, this man volunteers to follow Jesus. But like the second, he wishes to delay his departure until he can make arrangements for those in his family. As was the case with the first two men, Jesus responds to this third would-be disciple with a metaphorical admonition, "No man who puts his hand on the plow and walks forward looking backward is fit for the Kingdom of God!"

General observations. This pericope either came from Luke's non-Matthean tradition or it is a Lukan composition. Luke included it because it forms the fourth unit on inadequate followers after the momentous announcement of Lk 9:51. As such, it balanced the four units on inadequate followers at the end of the Galilean ministry (Lk 9:37-50). This pericope brings closure to the interweaving transitional section that began at Lk 9:37 (Lk 9:37-62).

Lk 9:59-62 represents yet another parallel between the story of Jesus in Lk and the story of Elijah in 1-2 Kings. See 1 Kgs 19:19-21 where Elisha says, in response to Elijah's calling of him as a disciple, "Let me kiss my father and my mother, and then I will follow you." This statement by Elisha is somewhat closer to the request made to Jesus by Luke's third would-be disciple in Lk 9:61-62 than it is to the request made by Luke's (and Mt's) second would-be disciple in Lk 9:59-60//Mt 8:21-22. In this case, on the Two Gospel Hypothesis, Luke would have made the allusion to this story about Elijah more explicit than the source material he had used in Mt.

Section One. The Great Mission. Lk 10:1–42

Immediately following the display of the shortcomings of the Twelve Apostles and three other would-be disciples, Jesus calls forth and commissions a group of 72 other disciples. The need for this new cadre is now abundantly clear. Using another familiar farmer's dilemma, Jesus explains: "The harvest is ready but there aren't enough workers to bring it in!"

Jesus selects 72 new disciples and instructs them how they are to proceed. They are to rely on others for everything they need during their mission. He goes on to berate the villages of Chorazin, Bethsaida and Capernaum which had apparently not welcomed Jesus and his disciples earlier. The disciples will be Jesus' agents, even as Jesus is God's agent. Those who hear the disciples hear Jesus and those who hear Jesus hear the Word of God. Similarly, those who reject the disciples reject Jesus, and those who reject Jesus reject God.

When the 72 disciples return from their mission, they receive much greater praise from Jesus than the original 12 apostles had received from him on their return. As part of the rejoicing associated with this return, Jesus prays, as is his custom. Jesus then blesses his disciples for what they see and hear.

A lawyer from the crowd then asks what he must do to inherit eternal life. Jesus asks him what he reads in the Law and the Prophets. The lawyer responds with the double commandment to love God and love neighbor and Jesus commends him. But the lawyer wants to pursue the question; "Who is my neighbor?" he asks. Jesus responds with the Parable of the Good Samaritan with which he makes at least two points. First, the neighbor is whoever needs your help, i.e., to whom are *you* willing to be the neighbor? Second, the Samaritan saw someone in need and *did* something about it.

Luke's narrative goes on to depict a visit by Jesus in the home of two sisters. Here again, the theme of choosing the more important thing—listening and hearing the Word of God—over all competing claims for our attention, is stressed.

Source-critical observations. We will briefly outline Luke's compositional procedures here. See the Excursus below (with the synopsis) for a more complete account.

To compose this new mission, Luke returned to the context of Mt 9:35-10:16, which he had used for the Mission of the Twelve earlier (Lk 9:1-6).

We noted above that Mt depicted the Mission of the Twelve, but said nothing of their return. Nor is there any mention of a Mission of Seventy-two Others in Mt. Luke composed that account (Lk 10:1-20) mainly on the basis of Mt 10:1-16, taking into account the need for appropriate closure of the mission of the Seventy-two. The prayer in Mt 11:25-27 is the first unit following Mt's Mission Discourse that Luke had not utilized. Luke used it for the composition of Jesus' prayer upon the return of the Seventy-two in Lk 10:21-22. Then Luke moved forward to Mt's Parables Collection (Mt 13:1-23), which he had partly utilized in his presentation of the Parable of the Sower (Lk 8:4-18). From Mt's explanation for using parables (which he had skipped) Luke took the blessing in Mt 13:16-17 and appended it to the prayer as a blessing on the Seventy-two (Mt 13:16-17//Lk 10:23-24).

For the next unit, Luke moved to Mt's Great Commandment Question (Mt 22:34-39), but substituted the *question* from Mt's Rich Young Man story (Mt 19:16-22) which is about what one must *do* to have eternal life. Thus the stress on *ears that hear* in Lk 10:24 leads naturally to what one must *do* in Lk 10:25. Having made that connection, Luke was able to use the Great Commandment question to introduce its illustration from his nonMatthean tradition, the account of the Good Samaritan (Lk 10:29-37), followed by the Mary/Martha story as another disciple who *hears*.

¶ 60. Jesus sends 72 others on a second mission

(Mt. 9:35-10:16; 11:20-24; 10:40) **Lk 10:1-16**

After the shortcomings of the Twelve Apostles and other would-be followers are made manifest, Jesus decides to send out a second group composed of 72 missionaries because "the harvest is ready but the laborers are few." Jesus gives this second group the same instructions he gave the first twelve about taking no provisions for their journey, as well as what to do when they enter the towns where they will preach and heal. Jesus concludes his instructions with a series of woes to the three Jewish villages in the area that have proved less than receptive to him: Chorazin, Bethsaida and Capernaum. Jesus' message is grim: tell these villages they have one last chance to receive him or risk divine retribution.

General observations. In the series of eight vignettes contained in the transitional section linking together Parts Four and Five (Lk 9:37-62), Luke provided a literal basis for Jesus' statement in Lk 10:2, "The harvest is great, but the [*qualified*] workers are few." Jesus now commissions new workers who greatly expand the scope and effectiveness of his mission. Luke used Mt 9:35-10:16; 11:20-24; and 10:40 to create this very significant unit, standing prominently at the beginning of the Travel Narrative. Mt 9:35-10:16 and Mt 10:40-11:l are the beginning and ending of Mt's Mission

Discourse. Hence, Luke's conflation of these two passages from Mt here. The doublet in Mt 10:15 and Mt 11:24 could help to explain why Luke brought Mt 9:35-10:16 and Mt 11:20-24 together in this Lukan context, but Luke's move down from Mt 11:1 to 11:20 could also be explained by the fact that Luke had already utilized the intervening material, Mt 11:2-19, at Lk 7:18-35. Details of how Luke accomplished his literary task within Lk 10:1-12 are found in the Excursus below.

EXCURSUS: THE MISSION OF THE 12 AND THE 72: A COMPARATIVE ANALYSIS

Luke used Mt's account of the Mission of the Twelve for his own parallel account of that event, and then here again, to describe the Mission of the Seventy-two. As such, it is an example of Luke creating a doublet instead of removing one.

As Moses had sent out twelve scouts across the Jordan and later selected seventy-two other elders to help him, Luke first described Jesus sending out the Twelve in Lk 9:1-6, and then, in Lk 10:1-16, sending out seventy-two other disciples.

Luke had made use of Mt's story of the mission of the twelve disciples in Mt 9:35-10:16 at least three times by the time Luke reached Lk 10:16 (cf. Lk 6:12-16, Lk 9:1-6, and Lk 10:1-16). However, a close comparison of the differences between the two major Lukan uses of this material (Mission of the Twelve, Lk 9:1-6 and Mission of the Seventy-two, Lk 10:1-16) will throw considerable light upon Luke's missionary agenda. For this purpose, we have provided a synopsis. We ask the reader's patience, however, since to present the parallels adequately has taken several pages. But we thought it was important to locate the synopsis here rather than in the Appendix, so that the literary data we discussed would be close at hand. After the synopsis, there is an analysis of Luke's account of the Mission of the Twelve, followed by a comparative analysis of the Mission of the Seventy-two.

Synopsis of Lk 9:1-6 and 10:1-16

Illustrating the way Luke used many Matthean Mission passages to create two mission accounts: the Mission of the Twelve and the Mission of the Seventy-two.

Mt 9:35-10:16; Mt11:20-24; Mt10:40//Mt 18:5	**Lk 9:1-6 Mission of the 12**	**Lk 10:1-16 Mission of the 72**
9:35 Καὶ περιῆγεν		**10:1** Μετὰ δὲ ταῦτα
ὁ Ἰησοῦς τὰς πόλεις πάσας		ἀνέδειξεν
καὶ τὰς κώμας	cf. Lk 9:5	ὁ κύριος ἑτέρους
		ἑβδομήκοντα [δύο]
διδάσκων		
ἐν ταῖς συναγωγαῖς αὐτῶν		
καὶ κηρύσσων	cf. Lk 9:2, 5	καὶ ἀπέστειλεν αὐτοὺς
τὸ εὐαγγέλιον τῆς βασιλείας	cf. Lk 9:2	ἀνὰ δύο [δύο]
καὶ θεραπεύων	cf. Lk 9:2	πρὸ προσώπου αὐτοῦ

The Synoptic Mission Instructions (cont.)

Mt 9:36 (cont.) πᾶσαν νόσον	**Lk 9:1-6**	**Lk 10:1 (cont.)** εἰς πᾶσαν πόλιν
καὶ πᾶσαν μαλακίαν.	cf. Lk 9:4	καὶ τόπον
Ἰδὼν δὲ τοὺς ὄχλους		
ἐσπλαγχνίσθη περὶ αὐτῶν,		οὗ ἤμελλεν αὐτὸς ἔρχεσθαι.
ὅτι ἦσαν ἐσκυλμένοι		
καὶ ἐρριμμένοι		
ὡσεὶ πρόβατα		
μὴ ἔχοντα ποιμένα.		
37 τότε λέγει		**2** ἔλεγεν δὲ
τοῖς μαθηταῖς αὐτοῦ,		πρὸς αὐτούς,
Ὁ μὲν θερισμὸς πολύς,		Ὁ μὲν θερισμὸς πολύς,
οἱ δὲ ἐργάται ὀλίγοι·		οἱ δὲ ἐργάται ὀλίγοι·
38 δεήθητε οὖν		δεήθητε οὖν
τοῦ κυρίου		τοῦ κυρίου
τοῦ θερισμοῦ		τοῦ θερισμοῦ
ὅπως ἐκβάλῃ ἐργάτας		ὅπως ἐργάτας ἐκβάλῃ
εἰς τὸν θερισμὸν αὐτοῦ.		εἰς τὸν θερισμὸν αὐτοῦ.
10:1 Καὶ προσκαλεσάμενος	**9:1** Συγκαλεσάμενος δὲ	
τοὺς δώδεκα μαθητὰς αὐτοῦ	τοὺς δώδεκα	
ἔδωκεν αὐτοῖς	ἔδωκεν αὐτοῖς	
ἐξουσίαν	δύναμιν καὶ ἐξουσίαν	
πνευμάτων ἀκαθάρτων	ἐπὶ πάντα τὰ δαιμόνια	
ὥστε ἐκβάλλειν αὐτὰ		
καὶ θεραπεύειν πᾶσαν νόσον	καὶ νόσους θεραπεύειν	
καὶ πᾶσαν μαλακίαν.		
5 Τούτους τοὺς δώδεκα		**3** ὑπάγετε·
ἀπέστειλεν ὁ Ἰησοῦς	**2** καὶ ἀπέστειλεν αὐτοὺς	ἰδοὺ ἀποστέλλω ὑμᾶς
παραγγείλας αὐτοῖς λέγων,		
Εἰς ὁδὸν ἐθνῶν		
μὴ ἀπέλθητε		
καὶ εἰς πόλιν Σαμαριτῶν		
μὴ εἰσέλθητε·		
6 πορεύεσθε δὲ μᾶλλον		
πρὸς τὰ πρόβατα	cf. Mt 10:16	ὡς ἄρνας ἐν μέσῳ λύκων.
τὰ ἀπολωλότα οἴκου Ἰσραήλ.		
‹10:7› πορευόμενοι δὲ		
κηρύσσετε λέγοντες ὅτι	κηρύσσειν	
Ἤγγικεν ἡ βασιλεία	τὴν βασιλείαν	cf. Lk 10:9
τῶν οὐρανῶν.	τοῦ θεοῦ	
	καὶ ἰᾶσθαι	
8 ἀσθενοῦντας	[τοὺς ἀσθενεῖς],	
θεραπεύετε,	cf. Lk 9:1	
νεκροὺς ἐγείρετε,		
λεπροὺς καθαρίζετε,		
δαιμόνια ἐκβάλλετε·		
δωρεὰν ἐλάβετε,		
δωρεὰν δότε.		
	3 καὶ εἶπεν πρὸς αὐτούς,	
9 Μὴ κτήσησθε	Μηδὲν αἴρετε	**4** μὴ βαστάζετε

The Synoptic Mission Instructions (cont.)

Mt 10:9 (cont.) χρυσὸν	**Lk 9:3 (cont.)**	**Lk 10:4 (cont.)** βαλλάντιον,
	εἰς τὴν ὁδόν,	
	μήτε ῥάβδον	
μηδὲ ἄργυρον		
μηδὲ χαλκὸν		
εἰς τὰς ζώνας ὑμῶν,		
10 μὴ πήραν	μήτε πήραν	μὴ πήραν,
εἰς ὁδὸν		
	μήτε ἄρτον	
	μήτε ἀργύριον,	
μηδὲ δύο χιτῶνας	μήτε [ἀνὰ] δύο χιτῶνας	
	ἔχειν.	
μηδὲ ὑποδήματα		μὴ ὑποδήματα,
μηδὲ ῥάβδον·		
		καὶ μηδένα
		κατὰ τὴν ὁδὸν
cf. Mt 10:12		ἀσπάσησθε.
ἄξιος γὰρ ὁ ἐργάτης		cf. Lk 10:7
τῆς τροφῆς αὐτοῦ.		
11 εἰς ἣν δ᾽ ἂν	**4** καὶ εἰς ἣν ἂν	**5** εἰς ἣν δ᾽ ἂν
πόλιν ἢ κώμην εἰσέλθητε,	οἰκίαν εἰσέλθητε,	εἰσέλθητε οἰκίαν,
ἐξετάσατε		
τίς ἐν αὐτῇ ἄξιός ἐστιν·		cf. Lk 10:7
κἀκεῖ μείνατε	ἐκεῖ μένετε	
ἕως ἂν ἐξέλθητε.	καὶ ἐκεῖθεν ἐξέρχεσθε.	
12 εἰσερχόμενοι δὲ		
εἰς τὴν οἰκίαν	cf. Lk 9:4	
ἀσπάσασθε αὐτήν·	cf. Lk 10:4	πρῶτον λέγετε,
		Εἰρήνη τῷ οἴκῳ τούτῳ.
13 καὶ ἐὰν μὲν ᾖ		**6** καὶ ἐὰν ἐκεῖ ᾖ
ἡ οἰκία ἀξία,	cf. Lk 10:5	
ἐλθάτω ἡ εἰρήνη ὑμῶν		υἱὸς εἰρήνης,
		ἐπαναπαήσεται
ἐπ᾽ αὐτήν,		ἐπ᾽ αὐτὸν
ἐὰν δὲ μὴ ᾖ ἀξία,		
ἡ εἰρήνη ὑμῶν	cf. Lk 10:5	ἡ εἰρήνη ὑμῶν·
		εἰ δὲ μή γε,
πρὸς ὑμᾶς ἐπιστραφήτω.		ἐφ᾽ ὑμᾶς ἀνακάμψει.
		7 ἐν αὐτῇ δὲ τῇ οἰκίᾳ
cf. Mt 10:11-12		μένετε
		ἐσθίοντες καὶ πίνοντες
		τὰ παρ᾽ αὐτῶν·
cf. Mt 10:10		ἄξιος γὰρ ὁ ἐργάτης
		τοῦ μισθοῦ αὐτοῦ.
		μὴ μεταβαίνετε
		ἐξ οἰκίας εἰς οἰκίαν.
cf. Mt 10:11		**8** καὶ εἰς ἣν ἂν πόλιν
		εἰσέρχησθε
		καὶ δέχωνται ὑμᾶς,

The Synoptic Mission Instructions (cont.)

Mt 10:13 (cont.)	**Lk 9:4 (cont.)**	**Lk 10:8 (cont.)**
		ἐσθίετε τὰ παρατιθέμενα ὑμῖν
cf. Mt 9:35 and 10:1		**9** καὶ θεραπεύετε
cf. Mt 10:8		τοὺς ἐν αὐτῇ ἀσθενεῖς
		καὶ λέγετε αὐτοῖς,
cf. Mt 10:7		Ἤγγικεν ἐφ' ὑμᾶς
		ἡ βασιλεία τοῦ θεοῦ.
14 καὶ ὃς ἂν	**5** καὶ ὅσοι ἂν	**10** εἰς ἣν δ' ἂν
cf. Mt 10:11		πόλιν εἰσέλθητε
μὴ δέξηται ὑμᾶς	μὴ δέχωνται ὑμᾶς,	καὶ μὴ δέχωνται ὑμᾶς,
μηδὲ ἀκούσῃ		
τοὺς λόγους ὑμῶν,		cf. Mt 10:9
ἐξερχόμενοι	ἐξερχόμενοι	ἐξελθόντες
		εἰς τὰς πλατείας αὐτῆς
ἔξω τῆς οἰκίας	ἀπὸ	
ἢ τῆς πόλεως ἐκείνης	τῆς πόλεως ἐκείνης	
ἐκτινάξατε		εἴπατε,
τὸν κονιορτὸν	τὸν κονιορτὸν	**11** Καὶ τὸν κονιορτὸν
		τὸν κολληθέντα ἡμῖν
		ἐκ τῆς πόλεως ὑμῶν
τῶν ποδῶν ὑμῶν.	ἀπὸ τῶν ποδῶν ὑμῶν	εἰς τοὺς πόδας
	ἀποτινάσσετε	ἀπομασσόμεθα ὑμῖν·
	εἰς μαρτύριον ἐπ' αὐτούς.	
	6 ἐξερχόμενοι δὲ	
cf. Mt 9:35	διήρχοντο κατὰ τὰς κώμας	
		πλὴν
		τοῦτο γινώσκετε ὅτι
cf. Mt 9:35 and 10:7	εὐαγγελιζόμενοι	ἤγγικεν ἡ βασιλεία τοῦ θεοῦ.
cf. Mt 9:35 and 10:1	καὶ θεραπεύοντες πανταχοῦ.	
15 ἀμὴν λέγω ὑμῖν,	Mt 11:24 = Mt 10:15	**12** λέγω ὑμῖν ὅτι
ἀνεκτότερον ἔσται		
γῇ Σοδόμων καὶ Γομόρρων		Σοδόμοις
ἐν ἡμέρᾳ κρίσεως		ἐν τῇ ἡμέρᾳ ἐκείνῃ
		ἀνεκτότερον ἔσται
ἢ τῇ πόλει ἐκείνῃ.		ἢ τῇ πόλει ἐκείνῃ.
16 Ἰδοὺ ἐγὼ		
ἀποστέλλω ὑμᾶς		cf. Lk 10:3
ὡς πρόβατα		
ἐν μέσῳ λύκων·		
γίνεσθε οὖν φρόνιμοι		
ὡς οἱ ὄφεις		
καὶ ἀκέραιοι		
ὡς αἱ περιστεραί.		
Matt 11:20-24		
20 Τότε ἤρξατο		
ὀνειδίζειν		
τὰς πόλεις ἐν αἷς ἐγένοντο		

The Synoptic Mission Instructions (cont.)

Mt 11:20 (cont.)		Lk 10:12 (cont.)
αἱ πλεῖσται δυνάμεις αὐτοῦ,		
ὅτι οὐ μετενόησαν·		
21 Οὐαί σοι, Χοραζίν,		13 Οὐαί σοι, Χοραζίν,
οὐαί σοι, Βηθσαϊδά·		οὐαί σοι, Βηθσαϊδά
ὅτι εἰ ἐν Τύρῳ καὶ Σιδῶνι		ὅτι εἰ ἐν Τύρῳ καὶ Σιδῶνι
ἐγένοντο αἱ δυνάμεις		ἐγενήθησαν αἱ δυνάμεις
αἱ γενόμεναι ἐν ὑμῖν,		αἱ γενόμεναι ἐν ὑμῖν,
πάλαι ἂν ἐν σάκκῳ		πάλαι ἂν ἐν σάκκῳ
καὶ σποδῷ		καὶ σποδῷ καθήμενοι
μετενόησαν.		μετενόησαν.
22 πλὴν λέγω ὑμῖν,		14 πλὴν
Τύρῳ καὶ Σιδῶνι		Τύρῳ καὶ Σιδῶνι
ἀνεκτότερον ἔσται		ἀνεκτότερον ἔσται
ἐν ἡμέρᾳ κρίσεως ἢ ὑμῖν.		ἐν τῇ κρίσει ἢ ὑμῖν.
23 καὶ σύ, Καφαρναούμ,		15 καὶ σύ, Καφαρναούμ,
μὴ ἕως οὐρανοῦ ὑψωθήσῃ;		μὴ ἕως οὐρανοῦ ὑψωθήσῃ;
ἕως ᾅδου καταβήσῃ·		ἕως τοῦ ᾅδου καταβήσῃ.
ὅτι εἰ ἐν Σοδόμοις		
ἐγενήθησαν		
αἱ δυνάμεις αἱ γενόμεναι		
ἐν σοί,		
ἔμεινεν ἂν μέχρι τῆς		
σήμερον.		
24 πλὴν λέγω ὑμῖν ὅτι	Mt 11:24 = Mt 10:15	
γῇ Σοδόμων ἀνεκτότερον		
ἔσται		
ἐν ἡμέρᾳ κρίσεως ἢ σοί.		

Matt 10:40	Matt 18:5	
40 Ὁ δεχόμενος		16 Ὁ ἀκούων
ὑμᾶς		ὑμῶν
ἐμὲ δέχεται,		ἐμοῦ ἀκούει,
	5 καὶ ὃς ἐὰν δέξηται	καὶ ὁ ἀθετῶν
	ἓν παιδίον τοιοῦτο	ὑμᾶς
	ἐπὶ τῷ ὀνόματί μου,	
	ἐμὲ δέχεται.	ἐμὲ ἀθετεῖ·
καὶ ὁ ἐμὲ δεχόμενος		ὁ δὲ ἐμὲ ἀθετῶν
δέχεται		ἀθετεῖ
τὸν ἀποστείλαντά με.		τὸν ἀποστείλαντά με.

Lk 9:1-6. The mission of the Twelve

Lk 9:1. Συγκαλεσάμενος δὲ τοὺς δώδεκα, Luke gets from Mt 10:1. The scope of the "power and authority" is similar in both versions. Luke just removed Mt's redundancies.

• Luke omitted the names of the Twelve here because he had already used them in composing his version of their call at Lk 6:13-16.

• Luke also omitted the injunction to go into no city of the Samaritans or road of the Gentiles (Mt 10:5-6b). Luke even took pains to correct this tradition by having Jesus send (ἀπέστειλεν) his disciples into Samaria in Lk 9:52-56.

Lk 9:2. Luke had already utilized something similar to the Matthean injunction to "preach as you go, saying 'the Kingdom of Heaven is at hand.' Heal the sick, etc." (Mt 10:7-8) at Lk 7:22//Mt 11:5.

• Luke's use of "Kingdom of God" in Lk 9:2 is clearly secondary to Mt's more Jewish "Kingdom of the Heavens" in Mt 10:7 et passim.

Lk 9:3. Luke omitted "You received without pay, give without pay" from Mt 10:8 as well as the similar statement at Mt 10:10b, "The worker is worthy of his food," although these statements in Mt provide the rationale for the instructions about taking no provisions which Luke did utilize (Lk 10:4). Mt's version says that disciples should not worry about payment because they will not need to buy anything along the way. Luke used a modified form of this in Lk 10:7 which justifies eating at the host's expense, but its absence in Lk 9:3 is clearly a sign of the secondary nature of Lk 9:1-6 to the parallel material in Mt 9:35-10:16.

• Contrary to most current interpretations, the instructions to take nothing for their journey have nothing whatever to do with personal abstinence or an ascetic lifestyle. It is therefore inappropriate to attempt to reconstruct an earlier "Q" version on this basis. These instructions are simply an anticipation of the hospitality that the disciples may expect along the way. That Luke himself understood these instructions precisely in this fashion is obvious from the retrospective question of Jesus and the disciples' answer in Lk 22:35, followed by Jesus' new instructions in Lk 22:36-38. Lk 22:35-38 finds no parallel anywhere within the Gospel of Matthew. To think that "Q" had this explanation of Lk 9:1-6 in this very different literary context (Lk 22:35-38), and that Matthew combined these two contexts, using a Jewish scriptural argument, when he recreated Mt 9:35-10:16, is most improbable.

Lk 9:4-5. Mt's "city or village" at Mt 10:11, followed by "house" at Mt 10:12, is shortened by Luke to "house" at Lk 9:4. But Lk 9:5 adopted "city" and dropped "house". (cf. Mt 10:14). Again, these modifications reflect the secondary nature of Lk 9:1-6 // Mt 9:35-10:16.

Lk 9:6 is composed of elements taken from the introduction to Mt's account, Mt 9:35.

• Summary of Lk 9:1-6 and its use of Mt 9:35-10:16. The most noteworthy thing to observe about Luke's version of Mt 9:35-10:16 at Lk 9:1-6 is the across-the-board reduction of the material in Mt 10. The reason for this will become clearer later, but essentially, Luke's purpose was to place greater emphasis upon the mission of the 72 than on the mission of the Twelve. Evidence of the disparity between the two missions in Luke's view can be seen in the difference between what happens when the two groups return. When the Twelve return (Lk 9:10), all Lk says is "they told Jesus what they had done" (half a verse) and the narrative moves on immediately to tell of the great Feeding of the Five Thousand in Bethsaida (Lk 9:10-17). But when the 72 return (Lk 10:17-24), they report how successful they have been; Jesus ecstatically proclaims that he has seen Satan fall like lightning (a proleptic eschatological announcement); he gives them an amazingly comprehensive blessing ("nothing will ever hurt you"). The contrast between the two missions could not be sharper.

10:1-16. The mission of seventy-two other disciples

Lk 10:1. The second commissioning, that of the 72, is a Lukan creation intended to hearken back to two passages in Numbers.[1] In Num 13, Moses appoints 12 scouts, one from each of the tribes of Israel, to go across the Jordan and scout out the land. They come back filled with stories of a land flowing with milk and honey, but populated by giants too powerful for the Israelites to conquer. In Num 11, God appointed 70 (or 72) elders and says, "I will take some of the spirit that is on you and put it on them, so they will share the burden of this nation, and you will no longer have to carry it by yourself" ἀφελῶ ἀπὸ τοῦ πνεύματος τοῦ ἐπὶ σοὶ καὶ ἐπιθήσω ἐπ' αὐτούς, καὶ συναντιλήμψονται μετὰ σοῦ τὴν ὁρμὴν τοῦ λαοῦ, καὶ οὐκ οἴσεις αὐτοὺς σὺ μόνος (Num 11:17 LXX).

• The confusion between "70" and "72" reflected in the history of Luke's text probably stems from the fact that God ordered Moses to bring 70 elders before him to share his spirit, which he did. Later, two other elders (Eldad and Medad) were also found to have received some of Moses' spirit back in the camp (Num 11:26-30), raising the total to 72. So is the number 70 or 72? The manuscripts of Luke could have been "corrected" in either direction, but the later manuscripts tend to agree on 70. We agree with the conjecture of UBS[4], principally following 𝔓[75] B D the Diatessaron, itala, and Origen, that it should be "72," because the somewhat more complicated, literal use of these materials from the book of Numbers by Luke seems the more difficult reading, and therefore more original.

Lk 10:1. This verse contains the phrase καὶ ἀπέστειλεν αὐτοὺς. This is the same way that Luke modified Mt 10:5 at Lk 9:2.

• Luke's omission of Mt 10:5-6 from Lk 10:1ff. is explained by Luke's previous inclusion of Lk 9:51-56. Within Mt 10:5-6, Jesus forbids his disciples to go into the way of Gentiles and to enter any city of the Samaritans. By contrast, in Lk 9:51-56, Jesus is depicted as actually sending some messengers into a Samaritan village. The group Jesus sent apparently included James and John, two of the Twelve Apostles.

• The words πρὸ προσώπου αὐτοῦ within Lk 10:1 would seem to reflect back to similar words in Lk 7:27//Mt 11:10 that are derived from Mal 3:1 and that were applied to John the Baptist. These words also seem to reflect the earlier wording of Lk 9:51-53, those verses that serve as a major transition within the Lukan Gospel and as an introduction to Luke's central Travel Narrative.

• The words οὗ ἤμελλεν αὐτὸς ἔρχεσθαι in Lk 10:1 are also reminiscent of similar words in Lk 9:31. They also seem to reflect Lk 9:51-52, via Lk 9:31, forward through Luke's travel section (Lk 9:51-19:27) and to the events which follow in Lk 19:45ff.

Lk 10:2. This verse was composed from Mt's introduction to the Mission of the Twelve (Mt 9:35-38, esp. Mt 9:37-38).

Lk 10:3. The statement "Go! Behold, I send you out as sheep in the midst of wolves",

---

[1] Cf. D. Tiede, *Prophecy and History in Luke-Acts* (Philadelphia: Fortress Press, 1980) 60-61.

occupies the location of the rationale for taking no provisions for the road in Mt (Mt 10:8e). Luke's relocation causes Mt 10:16//Lk 10:3 to mean precisely the same thing as Mt 10:8e: "you received without pay, give without pay." The disciples will be given anything they need, so they do not need to work for wages or to take too many provisions on their mission journey. Luke's reference to "lambs among wolves" at Lk 10:3 means that the disciples will be completely safe. This, of course, is the exact opposite of what the parallel words in Mt 10:16 mean in Mt's original context. For Matthew, these words mean that the disciples were headed for persecution, suffering and death. But Luke's transposition and use of this saying as the rationale for the instructions for non-provision reveals his implicit awareness of the other saying (Mt 10:6) that was originally standing in his source at this point. In other words, Luke's version is clearly secondary to Matthew's. The common references to "sheep" in Mt 9:36; 10:6; and 10:16 may help to explain Luke's relocation of Mt 10:16 to an earlier context in Lk (Lk 10:3, cf. Mt 10:16). This earlier context in Lk is close to Luke's other parallels to Mt 10:5-6 in Lk 10:3, but Luke, of course, omitted much of Mt 10:5-6 from Lk 10:3 because he had already responded to this material by utilizing the story now found in Lk 9:52-56.

Lk 10:4b. The phraseology "Greet no one on the road", is unique to Lk 10, and these words are probably intended to convey an impression of urgency and speed (but compare the word "Greet" in Mt 10:12).

Lk 10:5-6. The remaining instructions involve many small details.[2]

Lk 10:7-16. However, it should be noted that the injunctions in Lk 10:7 to remain in "the same house" and "do not go from house to house," both missing from the parallel in Mt, are possibly indications of abuses current in Luke's missionary context. They hardly reflect the time of Jesus' activity.

• Likewise, the injunction to "eat and drink whatever they set before you" (Lk 10:8b, ἐσθίετε τὰ παρατιθέμενα ὑμῖν; cf. Lk 10:7, ἐσθίοντες καὶ πίνοντες τὰ παρ' αὐτῶν) which is missing completely from Mt's version, is quite similar to Paul's recommendation "if an unbeliever invites you to his house. . . eat whatever is put in front of you" εἴ τις καλεῖ ὑμᾶς τῶν ἀπίστων. . . πᾶν τὸ παρατιθέμενον ὑμῖν ἐσθίετε (1 Cor 10:27). For these and other reasons, we conclude that Lk 10:1-16 also gives evidence of being a secondary version of Mt 9:35-10:16, just as Lk 9:1-6 did.

• The saying about Sodom in Lk 10:12 is the same as in Mt 10:15. And Mt 10:15 provided a link for Luke to bring in the woes against Chorazin, Bethsaida and Capernaum from Mt 11:20-24 because Mt 11:24 is the doublet to Mt 10:15.

Lk 10:13-16. For the warning of the cities of Chorazin, Bethsaida and Capernaum, Luke used Mt 11:21-23. Luke seems to have composed Lk 10:16 as a complement to the saying he created in Lk 9:48 by conflating Mt 10:40 and 18:5. Luke could also have been influenced in constructing Lk 10:16 by the opening words of Mt 10:14, καὶ ὃς ἂν μὴ δέξηται ὑμᾶς. Luke used this Lukan composition at Lk 10:16 to conclude Jesus' speech to the newly chosen 72 others in Lk 10:1-16.

---

[2] For a fuller discussion, see D. L. Dungan, *The Sayings of Jesus in the Churches of Paul* (Oxford: Basil Blackwell, 1971) 41-80.

¶ 61. Blessing of the disciples on their return Lk 10:17-20

The 72 others come back from their missionary journey with glowing reports and are greeted by an exceptionally exuberant Jesus. He has seen Satan fall like lightning out of heaven! Jesus has given authority to his disciples to tread over snakes and scorpions. Nothing will hurt them! But the disciples do need some correction. Jesus says that they should rejoice that their names are written in heaven rather than over the fact that the demons/spirits obey them. This prophecy and promise to the missionaries is immediately followed by an ecstatic prayer in which Jesus thanks God for hiding all these things "from the wise and understanding" of the world. When they are alone, Jesus assures all of his disciples that "many prophets and kings" desired to see what they see and didn't.

General observations. There is no parallel to this material in Mt. Lk 10:17 is clearly Lukan composition. Most likely, Lk 10:18-20 is also Lukan composition.

•Notes about the presence or absence of Satan play a role in the total narrative of Luke-Acts.

Lk 10:17-20. This pericope contains many Lukan redactional elements (ὑποστρέφω, Collison 67; δαιμόνιον, Collison 171; ἐξουσία, Collison 173; ἐπάνω in a metaphorical sense, Collison 152-153; double negative, Collison 164-165; πλήν, Collison 120-121). As he had done following the Sending of the Twelve (Lk 9:1-9), so also here, following the Sending of the Seventy-two other disciples (Lk 10:1-16), Luke created a subsequent unit describing their return (Lk 10:17, cf. Lk 9:10).

• The report of the returning 72 other disciples about their *successful* subjection of the demons/spirits "in Jesus' name" is a counterbalance to the unsuccessful attempt by the Twelve to cast out a spirit from a boy that Luke reported in Lk 9:39-40 (cf. Lk 9:49-50).

• Jesus' report that he had seen Satan falling down from heaven at Lk 10:18 may echo Capernaum's being "brought down to Hades," a few verses earlier at Lk 10:15. It also contrasts with the request made to Jesus by James and John to be permitted to call down fire (lightning?) from heaven on that Samaritan village which had rejected Jesus (Lk 9:52-56).

• The mentioning of "serpents" in Lk 10:19 echoes the comment about serpents in Mt 10:16. This provides some evidence that Luke knew the text of Mt at this point.

• Luke's choice to make explicit the power of the 72 other disciples over both "snakes" and "scorpions" also anticipated Luke's modifications of Mt 7:9-10 at Lk 11:11-12, within a Lukan unit that deals with prayer (Lk 11:1-13). Within Lk 11:11-12, Luke accepted Mt's "fish" and "snake" images (Mt 7:10//Lk 11:11; cf. Lk 10:19), but modified Mt's "loaf" image into "an egg" and his "stone" image into "a scorpion" (Mt 7:9; cf. Lk 11:12 and 10:19). In the process, Luke destroyed the visual similarities between the loaf and the stone that contribute to the meaning of Jesus' words in Mt 7:9 in the same way that the visual images of the "fish" and the "serpent" contribute to the meaning of Jesus' words in Mt 7:10. Lk 11:11-12, thus, displays its secondary nature to the parallel text of Mt 7:9-10. Since Lk 10:19 seems to anticipate these Lukan modifications at Lk 11:11-12, one could judge Lk 10:19 also to be secondary to the text of Mt 7:9-10.

Lk 10:19 also seems to reflect the text of Ps 91:13: "You will tread on the lion and the adder, the young lion and the serpent you will trample under foot." This verse from Ps 91, of course, immediately follows verses 11-12 of Ps 91, and Luke recorded the words of Ps 91:11-12 on the lips of Satan in the course of recounting the third and final temptation of Jesus by Satan (cf. Lk 10:18) in the wilderness (Lk 4:10-11 = Ps 91:11-12 = Mt 4:6). The words from Ps 91:11-12 appear on the lips of Satan during Jesus' second temptation in Mt. They appear on the lips of Satan during the third Lukan temptation. Luke seems to have reversed the order of the last two temptations in Mt in order to conclude with a temptation in Jerusalem on the pinnacle of the temple (Lk 4:9-13, cf. Lk 9:51-53 and Lk 19:45ff., esp. Lk 19:45-47, in the wake of Lk 9:51-53; 13:33-34; 17:11; 18:31; 19:11; and 19:28). Luke's use of Mt 4:1-11 in composing Lk 4:1-11, where a quotation of Ps 91:11-12 is to be found, may have suggested to Luke that he utilize an allusion to Ps 91:13, the next verse in Ps 91, in composing his own redactional unit at Lk 10:17-20. And that decision, in turn, somewhat effected Luke's clearly secondary modifications of Mt 7:9-10 at Lk 11:11-12.

¶ 62. Jesus praises God

Mt 11:25-27 ====> **Lk 10:21-22**

Rejoicing in the Holy Spirit, Jesus thanks his "Father, the Lord of heaven and of earth" because He hid his truth from the wise and understanding and revealed it to "infants." Jesus rejoices that God, his Heavenly Father, delivered all things to him. Since no one knows who the Son of God is except God himself and no one knows who God is except the Son of God, it is up to the Son of God, Jesus, to reveal God, the Father, to whomever he wishes to reveal Him.

General observations. Just prior to his insertion of Lk 10:17-20, Luke had been following the text of Mt 11:21-23 (cf. Lk 10:13-16). Mt 11:24 would have been repetitive in Lk since Luke copied the doublet to Mt 11:24, just a few verses earlier at Lk 10:12 (cf. Mt 10:15). Therefore, Luke could skip Mt 11:24 between Lk 10:16 and 21 by introducing Lk 10:17-20, which seems to be mostly of Lukan composition. For Lk 10:21-22 Luke continued to follow Mt 11:25-27.

Lk 10:21-22. In Lk 10:21, the phrase "rejoicing in the Holy Spirit" reflects an important Lukan motif: the activity of the Holy Spirit (Collison 176).

• The content of this passage has long intrigued interpreters for its "Johannine" ring. Its purpose in this context is to provide the basis for the blessing of the disciples in Lk 10:23-24.

• Luke omitted Mt 11:28-30 because, for him, Jesus' "yoke" is by no means "light."

• This unit in Lk contains a significant prayer of Jesus (Lk 10:21-22) which Luke used to anticipate the next Lukan unit on prayer (Lk 11:1-13). Within the introduction to that unit (Lk 11:1), the narrator says that Jesus was in prayer "as was his custom." This anticipatory example of prayer by Jesus in Lk 10:21-22 supplements what the narrator of Lk often says about Jesus within redactional verses of his Gospel (Lk 3:21; 5:16; 6:12; 9:18; 9:28-29; 11:1; 22:40; and 22:45-46, i.e., "he was in prayer").

• The address to God in Lk 10:21 as "Father" also prefigures Jesus' address to God in prayer simply as "Father" in Lk 11:2 (cf. Mt 11:25; 6:9-10). The more extensive direct address to God in prayer at Lk 10:21 as "Lord of heaven and of the earth" (= Mt 11:25; cf. Mt 6:9) represents Luke's fragmentary preservation of a literary feature that is repeated within the text of Mt. This constitutes further evidence of the secondary nature of Luke to Mt.

• The reference to how things have been "hidden" to "the wise and understanding" in Lk 10:21 may reflect Luke's knowledge of Mt 10:16b, "Be wise as serpents and innocent as doves." If it does, this may provide one more reason why Luke might have omitted Mt 10:16b, in the process of relocating Mt 10:16 to a context close to Mt 10:6 (Lk 10:3). If Luke planned to denigrate "the wise and understanding" and to lift up "the infants" by comparison at Lk 10:21, and then have Jesus bless his disciples by comparing them with the many (wise and understanding?) "prophets and kings" (cf. "righteous men" in Mt 13:17) in Lk 10:12-24, an admonition to the 72 other disciples to be "wise as serpents" would have produced considerable irony, if not an inconsistency. On babes/infants/children, cf. Lk 18:15-17.

• The comparison between what is "hidden" or "dark" and what is "revealed" or "light" that is featured in Jesus' prayer in Lk 10:21-22 is also clearly a Lukan theme (See, for example, Lk 1:79; 2:26-35; 8:16-18; 11:33-36; 11:53-12:3; 15:8; 16:8; 17:30; 18:34; 19:42; 22:53; 23:44-45).

¶ 63. Blessed are the disciples for what they see and hear

(Mt 13:16-17) **Lk 10:23-24**

After this, Jesus turns to his disciples privately, blesses their eyes for what they have seen, and assures them that many prophets and kings had wished to see what they are seeing but did not see it, and to hear what they have heard but did not hear it.

General observations. Luke used Mt 12:46-13:23 earlier in composing Lk 8:4-21, but Mt 13:16-17 were some of the verses within Mt 12:46-13:23 that Luke had omitted from the parallel context in Lk 8:4-21. Luke now used these two previously omitted verses (Mt 13:16-17) as part of his introductory material (Lk 10:23-29) for the Parable of the Good Samaritan (Lk 10:30-37) and the story of Mary and Martha (Lk 10:38-42). Luke used the story of the Good Samaritan (Lk 10:30-37) to illustrate the disciple who "sees and does." (See esp. Lk 10:33 and 37; cf. Lk 10:23).

Lk 10:23-24. Luke destroyed the meaning the beatitude had in Mt 13:16. For Matthew, the people of Israel have been hardened (hence the combination of "prophets and righteous men"), but *the disciples* do "see" and "hear." Luke disturbed this Matthean understanding by substituting "Kings" for Mt's "righteous men." What precisely the disciples have "seen" (Lk 10:23) is ambiguous in the Lukan version as compared with Mt. It is simpler to understand Lk 10:23-24 as Luke's own excerpt and revision of part of the larger Matthean pericope (Mt 13:1-23) rather than Mt's use of an original, vague "Q" saying, to which Matthew later carefully appended the necessary Scriptural quotation (Mt 13:14-15) to clarify its meaning.

¶ 64. The Good Samaritan—one who sees and does

(Mt 5:43-48; 19:16-30; 22:34-40) **Lk 10:25-37**

Now that the disciples are all together and have received Jesus' eschatological blessing, Luke's narrative turns to those outside the inner group and describes their reactions. A lawyer stands up and wants to know how he too can inherit eternal life, how he too can have his name "written in Heaven," like Jesus' disciples. Since this person is a "lawyer," he is by definition one of the "wise and understanding." The lawyer and Jesus engage in a question-and-answer session, after the manner of lawyers and those they interrogate. The lawyer asks Jesus a "deep" question, and Jesus challenges him to answer it himself, which he skillfully does, quoting Deut 6:5 and Lev 19:18, "love your neighbor as yourself." When Jesus commends him on his reply, he has another question ready: "And who is my neighbor?" This prompts Jesus to tell the story of a certain Samaritan, who, unlike certain members of the Judean elite, showed some mercy to a beaten and robbed traveler. Then Jesus asks him, "Which of these three was a neighbor to the victim?" When the lawyer again gives the correct answer, Jesus says, "Go and do like this Samaritan!"

General observations. Prompted by the emphatic reference to "hearing" in the blessing in 10:24, Luke rephrased Mt 19:16 (τί ἀγαθὸν ποιήσω ἵνα σχῶ ζωὴν αἰώνιον to Lk 10:25 τί ποιήσας ζωὴν αἰώνιον κληρονομήσω;) and combined it with the Great Commandment answer (Mt 22:37-39//Lk 10:27) to set the scene for the Parable of the Good Samaritan. "Hearing" in Luke's theology is regularly associated with doing (cf. Lk 6:47-48; 8:21; 11:28; and, for the negative example of "hearing and *not doing*," cf. Lk 6:49). Luke used the Parable of the Good Samaritan and the story of Mary and Martha as examples of two good disciples, one who *sees and does,* and one who *hears* (cf. Luke's eight stories about inadequate disciples and would-be disciples in Lk 9:37-62). Luke had just introduced these concepts into Lk 10:23-24 by relocating Mt 13:16-17, which he had omitted earlier from Mt 13:1-23 at Lk 8:4-21. The Good Samaritan story contains two examples, that of the priest and that of the Levite, of "seeing and not doing" (Lk 10:31 and 32; cf. Lk 6:49), and one example, that of the Samaritan, of "seeing and doing" (Lk 10:33; cf. Lk 6:47-48; 8:21; and 11:28). The story of the Good Samaritan ends with the question, "Which of these three does it seem to you to have *become a neighbor* to the victim?" The response is "the one who *did* the mercy with him" (ὁ ποιήσας τὸ ἔλεος μετ᾽ αὐτοῦ). Jesus replies, "Go! You *do* likewise." Thus, at the outset of the Travel Narrative, Jesus makes emphatically clear one of the foundational principles of discipleship: one who does mercy is the neighbor.

Lk 10:25-37. Note that Luke reversed the roles in the story and had the lawyer give the appropriate answer to (Lk's version of) the question taken from Mt 19:16. By having the lawyer answer correctly twice (Lk 10:27, 37) Luke expresses his guardedly optimistic view toward the outsider.

• This positive view toward the outsider is increased with the shocking point that it was not one of the religious elite (priest, Levite) who showed mercy, but a "foreigner" (the Samaritan).

¶ 65. The story of Mary and Martha—one who hears the word
Lk 10:38-42

Luke tells another story, echoing the theme of "seeing and hearing." As Jesus goes further on his road to Jerusalem, he encounters two sisters. He begins to teach and one of them sits at Jesus' feet listening to what he has to say. The other is burdened with taking care of so many guests and complains that has been left to do all the chores.

General observations. Luke used here the second of two stories from his nonMatthean tradition. The story of Mary and Martha illustrates the importance of giving priority to "hearing" the Word of God. Luke balanced these two stories, one about a man and the other about a woman, in a way that is reflected elsewhere within the Lukan Gospel. See, for instance, the Lukan account of the healing of the powerful, Gentile, male Centurion's Son, followed by the healing of the poor, Jewish, female widow's son (Lk 7:2-17). See further the parable of the *male* shepherd who seeks one lost sheep out of 100 followed by the parable of the *female* who seeks the one lost coin out of 10 (Lk 15:1-10).

Lk 10:38-42. In a message clearly intended for Luke's audience, he tells of those who had the privilege of "seeing" Jesus, such as Martha, but did not give it top priority and, thereby, did not "choose the good portion."

• Martha busied herself with "many things," but only "one thing was needed": to be obedient to God's word. In apparent disregard of the rules of hospitality, Jesus told Martha that it was Mary, who had "heard the Word" of the Lord (Lk 10:39; cf. Lk 8:21 and 11:28), who "chose the good portion" (Lk 10:42; cf. Mt 19:16-17) "which would not be taken from her."

• We may note here, as something of an aside, that the distinctively Lukan composition at Lk 11:28: "Blessed are those who hear the word of God and guard it (φυλάσσοντες)", also shares something with Mt 19:20. When the lawyer in Mt 19:17 is told "which" commandments to keep (τήρησον), he responds, "I have guarded/kept (ἐφύλαξα) all these."

Section Two. To the Disciples: On Prayer. Lk 11:1–13

At the request of his disciples to be taught to pray, even as John the Baptist had taught his disciples to pray, Jesus first teaches his disciples a model prayer. He follows this with a parable about persistence in prayer and general advice on confident prayer.

Source-critical observations. Luke introduced this unit on prayer with a typically Lukan setting, "Jesus at Prayer," and a characteristically Lukan comparison of John the Baptist with Jesus. Luke turned to the most striking of Mt's units on prayer, Mt 6:5-15, to shape his own story. Then he presented an abbreviated version of the Lord's Prayer. In place of the brief Matthean commentary on the prayer (Mt 6:14-15), Luke substituted a parable from his nonMatthean tradition about a persistent neighbor (Lk 11:5-8) to illustrate persistence in prayer. Then Luke closed this section with material drawn from Mt 7:7-11 which serves Luke to affirm that God answers optimistic prayers with the gift of the Holy Spirit (cf. Acts 2). The reason for Luke's return to this Matthean context within the Sermon on the Mount is easy to provide. Mt 6 contains Mt's first collection of Jesus' teachings on prayer (Mt 6:5-15), including Mt's version of the Lord's Prayer (Mt 6:9-13//Lk 11:2-4). Luke had omitted the whole of Mt 6 when he composed the Sermon on the Plain. Luke has abbreviated the model prayer in accord with demonstrable Lukan interests (Lk 11:2-4). After the inclusion of the parable, Luke moved forward in Mt's Sermon on the Mount and chose Mt 7:7-11 (Lk 11:9-13), also about petitioning God and which he had also not used in the Sermon on the Plain, to conclude this Section on prayer.

¶ 66. Jesus' prayer

(Mt 6:1-18) **Lk 11:1-4**

Jesus' prayer in the presence of his disciples in Lk 10:21-22 occasions a question on how to pray. Jesus' disciples say they want to be taught to pray, just like John taught his disciples. Jesus responds to this request with a model prayer for his disciples.

General observations. Luke adapted the Lord's Prayer from Mt 6:9-13. In so doing, he put it in a context where the disciples, as precursors of disciples in a later church, are taught the foundations of prayer.

Lk 11:1 καὶ ἐγένετο and Jesus at prayer are Lukan features (Collison 42-44).

Lk 11:2-4. The secondary character of Luke's version of this prayer is manifest. He shortened the opening address (omitting ὁ ἐν τοῖς οὐρανοῖς, contrast Lk 10:21//Mt 11:25), omitted the entire phrase γενηθήτω τὸ θέλημά σου, ὡς ἐν οὐρανῷ καὶ ἐπὶ γῆς (but again, contrast Lk 10:21), changed "give (δός) us the ἐπιούσιον bread today (σήμερον)" to "give (δίδου) us the ἐπιούσιον bread daily (καθ' ἡμέραν)," clearly breaking the eschatological tenor of Mt's version in favor of a de-eschatologized, ongoing (Imperfect) giving of "daily bread."

• The term καθ' ἡμέραν is frequently used elsewhere by Luke (Collison 137). In Lk 9:23 Luke altered Mt 16:24 by adding καθ' ἡμέραν (cf. further Lk 16:19; 19:47 and Acts 2:46; 2:47; 16:5 and 17:11).

• Luke also changed Mt's more Jewish and euphemistic "debts" to its more generally recognized meaning, "sins" (clearer to Gentiles). Compare Lk 13:1-5. At Lk 11:4, Luke changed Mt's first use of "debts" to "sins" and then adopted Mt's second and parallel usage of "debts." Once Luke had explained the metaphor by changing the first metaphorical usage of "debts" to its non-metaphorical equivalent, "sins," he could then adopt the equivalent metaphorical term, when it appeared at a comparable point within a second parallel clause (cf. Mt 6:12 and Lk 11:4). In a similar way, within Lk 13:1-6, the term "sinners" appears first in Lk 13:2, and then the term "debtors" is used in a subsequent and parallel clause (Lk 13:4).

• Luke also omitted the reference to "the evil one" (another euphemism?) at the conclusion of Mt's version. Luke thereby made the prayer end on a note, not of the eschatological test, as in Mt's version (so Jeremias), but with a de-eschatologized, this-worldly conclusion: "lead us not into (everyday) temptation," i.e., help us ward off sinful actions.[1]

¶ 67. When are we to pray? - pray persistently!

Lk 11:5-8

Now that the disciples know what to pray, Luke explains *when* they are to pray by having Jesus tell a story, the point of which is to pray persistently.

[1] See W. Farmer, *The Gospel of Jesus: The Pastoral Relevance of the Synoptic Problem* (Louisville: Westminster/John Knox Press, 1994) 41-51.

General observations. Lk 11:5-8 is nonMatthean tradition that contains teachings about prayer. Another parable, perhaps from the same collection, with the same theme, occurs in Lk 18:1-8 where there is, again, no parallel in Mt.

¶ 68. How are we to pray? - pray optimistically!

(Mt 7:7-11) **Lk 11:9-13**

Jesus now explains *how* the disciples are to pray. If they have been told to pray persistently, now they are told to pray confidently, in hope and trust to a Father who loves them.

General observations. Lk 11:9-13 comes from Mt 7:7-11, with dramatic embellishments added by Luke ("egg-scorpion"). His egg-scorpion exchange for loaf-stone kept the idea but ruined the similarity of images in Mt. See the more extensive note within the discussion of Lk 10:17-20 above. Luke clearly used the principle of thematic association to pull together Matthean and nonMatthean tradition into a coherent body of teaching.

Lk 11:9-13. The conclusion softened the Matthean materialism and came straight out of Lukan theology: what we are really supposed to ask for is the Holy Spirit, not *things* (contrary to Mt). Luke's change of Mt's "good things" to "Holy Spirit" is clearly redactional. It set the stage for the teaching in the next section about how to respond when one is challenged as acting under the power of false spirits (i.e., demons).

Section Three. To the People: On Spiritual Power. Lk 11:14–32

After Jesus casts a demon out of a mute person, some accuse Jesus of casting out demons by the power of Beelzebul, the prince of demons. Others demand a sign from heaven, legitizing Jesus. Jesus responds to the charge of casting out demons by Beelzebul with a counter-argument. If he really is using demonic power to cast out demons, Satan is wounding himself, which is nonsense. A woman interrupts to bless Jesus' mother, but he deflects the blessing toward disciples who *hear and do* the Word of God. Taking up the demand for a sign, Jesus recalls the demand of the prophet Jonah for a sign to Nineveh, concluding that one far greater than Jonah, and far wiser than Solomon, is here.

Source-critical observations. Prior to the introduction of his unit on prayer (Lk 11:1-13), Luke had last made use of Mt at Mt 11:25-30//Lk 10:21-22, a prayer of Jesus. After his unit on prayer, Luke returned to Mt 11:30. Luke had already utilized the immediately following controversy stories in Mt 12:1-21//Lk 6:5-19, so Luke began following Mt again with the very next story in Mt, the Beelzebul controversy (Mt 12:22-45//Lk 11:14-32).

Since Luke also had not previously utilized the Matthean doublet to the introduction to the Beelzebul controversy (Mt 9:32-34//Mt 12:22-24), Luke conflated these two different but closely related Matthean literary units.

After introducing in a characteristic anticipatory way the people's demand for a sign from heaven from Jesus (Mt 12:38//Lk 11:16), Luke continued to follow the text of Mt 12:25-32 for Lk 11:17-23. Then, since Luke had already conflated Mt 12:33-35 about "trees and their fruits" with its Matthean doublet at Mt 7:15-20 to compose Lk 6:43-45 in the Sermon on the Plain, Luke moved forward in Mt. He deliberately skipped Mt 12:36-42 in order to use it as the conclusion of this Section.

Luke then followed Mt for the account of a man who had one demon cast out, but, by not filling the void caused by its departure, was later filled with seven demons worse than the first (Lk 11:24-26//Mt 12:43-45).

At Lk 11:27-28, Luke arrived at Mt 12:46-50 for a second time. Here he substituted a story about a woman in the crowd blessing Jesus' mother. Luke concluded this vignette in a way that is almost identical to Luke's ending of the story of Jesus' family at Mt 12:46-50//Lk 8:19-21; namely, the distinctively Lukan affirmation of "those who hear the word of God and do/keep it." (Compare also the last half of Section One of the Travel Narrative).

Luke had temporarily omitted the unit on the demand for a sign in Mt 12:36-42 (cf. Lk 11:23-24). But he returned to those verses to conclude Section Three of the Travel Narrative, by conflating Mt 12:38-42 with its doublet on "the evil generation that seeks signs" (Mt 16:1, 4). Recall that Luke had already anticipated this conclusion by inserting the demand for a sign at the beginning of the Section (Lk 11:16). So the end of Section Three returns to a theme introduced at its beginning. Though Jonah the prophet was himself a sign to the Ninevites, and Solomon the king attracted great crowds to hear his wisdom, one greater than both prophet and king has come in the person of Jesus, since his spiritual power is of divine origin (cf. Lk 3:21-4:15 and Lk 9:28-36).

¶ 69. The crowds demonize Jesus

(Mt 9:32-34; 12:22-30; 16:1//12:38; 12:43-45) **Lk 11:14-26**

In Luke's dramatic presentation, the great mission of the 72 and the teachings that followed it now provoke a counter-reaction. First Jesus casts out a "mute demon." Suddenly opposition to Jesus begins to manifest itself. Some in "the crowd" accuse Jesus of using Satanic powers to perform his miracles. Jesus argues back by means of the question: "How can Satan conquer Satan?" and uses the analogy of a strong man's "palace" being overthrown by one more powerful. "If I, by means of the finger of God cast out these demons, Satan's power has come to an end. But if I do it by means of Beelzebul (= the Devil), then his house is divided and will collapse from within. Either way, he is destroyed!"

General observations. Once Luke had made use of Mt 7:7-12//Lk 11:9-13 in concluding the preceding Lukan section on prayer (Lk 11:1-13), there were at least three ways that Luke might have been prompted, in his orderly use of Mt, to move from Mt 7:12 to Mt 12:22ff. for the beginning of the next Lukan section "To the People: On Spiritual Power," Lk 11:14-32.

•First, at Lk 10:21-22, Luke utilized Mt 11:25-30, the very end of Mt 11. Lk 10:21-22 was a prayer by Jesus that anticipated the subsequent unit on prayer at Lk 11:1-13. Now, having written Lk 11:1-13, and having already utilized the conflict accounts and the healing summary in Mt 12:1-21 (cf. Lk 6:1-19), Luke would come precisely to Mt 12:22ff.//Lk 11:14ff. for the beginning of the next unit in the Lukan Travel Narrative (Lk 11:14-32).

Second, there is literary evidence within the text of Lk 11:14-15 that Luke conflated Mt 9:32-34, "on casting out demons by Beelzebul," with the Matthean doublet at Mt 12:22-24. Not long before Lk 11:14, Luke had made use of Mt 9:35-10:16 in composing Lk 10:1-12. The Matthean unit that immediately precedes Mt 9:35-10:16 is, of course, Mt 9:32-34. And, since Mt 9:32-34 is a doublet to Mt 12:22-24, this could have taken Luke precisely to Mt 12:22ff. at Lk 11:14ff.

Third, Luke had already made use of Mt 7:15-20, which follows Mt 7:12 by only a few verses, in composing Lk 6:43-45. Toward the conclusion of the Sermon on the Plain (Lk 6:20-7:1), Luke had conflated Mt 7:15-20 (on "trees and their fruits") with its Matthean doublet at Mt 12:33-35, to produce Lk 6:43-45. This Lukan shift of material from Mt 12:33ff. into the context of Mt 7:15ff. demonstrates that Luke knew the way from Mt 12:33ff. to Mt 7:15ff., so he might have made the return trip here. And from Mt 12:33, it is not far to Mt 12:22, which is the verse in Mt that Luke utilized to begin his new unit at Lk 11:14.

Any one of these three paths to Mt 12:22//Lk 11:14 would be sufficient to justify the view that Luke made rational and orderly use of Mt in this context. But this network of three paths that all lead to the context of Mt 12 (two paths leading precisely to Mt 12:22) strongly supports the hypothesis of Luke's direct use of the canonical text of Mt. How would advocates of the "Q" hypothesis refute this web of evidence?

Lk 11:14. Lukan redactional changes are not difficult to ntoice here. Luke consistently (but not always) omitted "Son of David" (Mt 12:23, cf. Lk 11:15). This Lukan omission from Mt 12:22-28 may also be explained by the fact that Luke utilized not only Mt 12:22-26 but also the Matthean doublet in Mt 9:32-34 to compose Lk 11:14-18, i.e., there is no reference to "Son of David" in Mt 9:32-34. As evidence of Luke's dependence upon Mt 9:32-34, as well as on Mt 12:22-28, note particularly Mt 9:33a.

Lk 11:16. Luke moved "while others, to test him, sought from him a sign from heaven" (Lk 11:16) into this context from its location in Mt's *next* story (Mt 12:38). The reason for doing so seems to have been to introduce a similar collateral theme, namely, an evil generation wants proof from God ("a sign from Heaven") before they will lift a finger to respond to Jesus. This is another example of the frequently encountered Lukan compositional technique; insertion of a phrase or story in the immediately preceding pericope to prefigure, or set the stage for, a theme about to come up.

Lk 11:20. On the phrase "finger of God," compare Mt 12:28, "spirit of God."[2]

Lk 11:22. The phraseology "his armor in which he trusted" is a Lukan addition, reinforcing the theme of "trusting in the wrong thing" (here strength, military power; next, one's family lineage; third, wealth).

Lk 11:23. Luke followed Mt 12:30 exactly at this point: "The one who is not with Jesus is against Jesus and the one who does not gather with Jesus, scatters." But contrast Lk 9:50: "The one who is not against the disciples is with them." The apparent tension between these two teachings of Jesus in Lk could be explained by Luke's use of two different sources: Mt for Lk 11:23 and nonMatthean tradition for Lk 9:50.

Lk 11:24-26. Luke stopped following the account in Mt at Mt 12:31-32, the sin against the Holy Spirit. He used it later in a mission context where it receives an interpretation more in line with Luke's mission theology (see Lk 12:10).

• Luke already used Mt 12:33-35 at Lk 6:43-45. Luke skipped Mt 12:36-37; he was interested in actions not words. Luke will soon use Mt 12:38-42 in Lk 11:29-32. This brought Luke to Mt 12:43-45, which Luke used at Lk 11:24-26 in order to continue the Beelzebul/evil spirit theme in a very understandable way. Those who taunt Jesus by claiming that he is acting by the agency of demonic powers, or who demand he show signs to validate his activity, had better be sure they do not make their own converts worse than better. Jesus can place the benefits of the Kingdom of God in the hearts of his converts. What do his opponents place in the hearts of theirs?

¶ 70. Do not trust in family lineage

(Mt 12:46-50) **Lk 11:27-28** (cf. Lk 10:23; 23:29)

Dramatically, "While he is saying these things," a woman suddenly interrupts to bless Jesus' mother. But Jesus emphatically shifts the focus to the real issue, saying to her–and everyone–that the one who is truly blessed is the one who hears the word of God and keeps it.

General observations. Continuing to follow Mt 12, Luke now came a second time to Mt 12:46-50 (cf. Lk 8:19-21). Lk 11:27-28 is Luke's dramatic

[2] See the discussion by W. D. Davies and D. C. Allison on "Finger of God/Spirit of God" in *A Critical and Exegetical Commentary on the Gospel according to St. Matthew*, International Critical Commentary, 2 vols. (Edinburgh: T & T Clark, 1988) 2:339-340.

redaction of Mt 12:46-50. It anticipates the opposite and contrasting affirmation at Lk 23:29, which has no parallel in Mt and is best explained as Lukan composition. The following synopsis is the basis for our analysis.

Synopsis of Lk 11:27-28

Illustrating how Luke created a doublet based on Mt 12:46-50,
first at Lk 8:19-21 and again here in Lk 11:27-28.

Mt 12:46-50	Lk 8:19-21	Lk 11:27-28
46 Ἔτι	**19** Παρεγένετο δὲ	**27** Ἐγένετο δὲ
αὐτοῦ λαλοῦντος	πρὸς αὐτὸν	ἐν τῷ λέγειν αὐτὸν ταῦτα
τοῖς ὄχλοις ἰδοὺ		
ἡ μήτηρ	ἡ μήτηρ	ἐπάρασά τις φωνὴν γυνὴ
καὶ οἱ ἀδελφοὶ αὐτοῦ	καὶ οἱ ἀδελφοὶ αὐτοῦ	
εἱστήκεισαν ἔξω	καὶ οὐκ ἠδύναντο	
ζητοῦντες αὐτῷ λαλῆσαι.	συντυχεῖν αὐτῷ	
	διὰ τὸν ὄχλον.	ἐκ τοῦ ὄχλου
47 εἶπεν δέ τις αὐτῷ,	**20** ἀπηγγέλη δὲ αὐτῷ,	εἶπεν αὐτῷ,
Ἰδοὺ ἡ μήτηρ σου	Ἡ μήτηρ σου	Μακαρία ἡ κοιλία
		ἡ βαστάσασά σε
		καὶ μαστοὶ
		οὓς ἐθήλασας.
καὶ οἱ ἀδελφοί σου	καὶ οἱ ἀδελφοί σου	
ἔξω ἑστήκασιν	ἑστήκασιν ἔξω	
ζητοῦντές σοι λαλῆσαι.]	ἰδεῖν θέλοντές σε.	
48 ὁ δὲ ἀποκριθεὶς	**21** ὁ δὲ ἀποκριθεὶς	
εἶπεν τῷ λέγοντι αὐτῷ,	εἶπεν πρὸς αὐτούς,	**28** αὐτὸς δὲ εἶπεν,
		Μενοῦν μακάριοι
Τίς ἐστιν ἡ μήτηρ μου		
καὶ τίνες εἰσὶν οἱ ἀδελφοί		
μου;		
49 καὶ ἐκτείνας		
τὴν χεῖρα αὐτοῦ		
ἐπὶ τοὺς μαθητὰς αὐτοῦ		
εἶπεν, Ἰδοὺ		
ἡ μήτηρ μου	Μήτηρ μου	
καὶ οἱ ἀδελφοί μου.	καὶ ἀδελφοί μου	
50 ὅστις γὰρ ἂν	οὗτοί εἰσιν οἱ	οἱ
		ἀκούοντες
	τὸν λόγον τοῦ θεοῦ	τὸν λόγον τοῦ θεοῦ
	ἀκούοντες	
ποιήσῃ	καὶ ποιοῦντες.	καὶ φυλάσσοντες.
τὸ θέλημα τοῦ πατρός μου		
τοῦ ἐν οὐρανοῖς		
αὐτός μου ἀδελφὸς		
καὶ ἀδελφὴ καὶ μήτηρ		
ἐστίν.		

Lk 11:27-28. This pericope echoes the story in Mt 12:46-50, which Luke had already used in an edited form at Lk 8:19-21. At this point, Luke wanted a way to reply to the accusation of "some in the crowd" about Jesus being in league with Beelzebul. In Mt 9:32-34 and Mt 12:22ff. this accusation comes from the Pharisees (cf. Mt 10:24-25). To create his account, Luke continued following the Matthean order: "the crowds demonize Jesus," (Mt 12:22-37//Lk 11:14-26) is followed by "the demand for a sign" (Mt 12:46-50//Lk 11:27-28), in the course of which Luke reused the reference to Jesus' mother (cf. Mt 12:46-50//Lk 8:19-21).

• Mt 12:46 begins: "while he was still speaking", which is similar to the transitional phrase used by Luke at 11:27 ἐγένετο δὲ ἐν τῷ λέγειν αὐτὸν ταῦτα ἐπάρασά τις φωνὴν γυνὴ ἐκ τοῦ ὄχλου. The phrase ἐγένετο δὲ ἐν τῷ plus the infinitive is a favorite Lukan stylistic characteristic (cf. Collison 42-44). Luke merely changed the character in Mt 12:47 from "someone" into "some woman" who then "raises her voice" to bless Jesus' mother.

• Mt 12:46-50, as modified by Luke at 11:27-28, raised the same fundamental issue as the story in Mt 12:46-50, as modified by Luke at Lk 8:19-21: Jesus' family is confusing the situation. This results in precisely the same concluding statement on the lips of Jesus at Lk 11:28 as appeared there at Lk 8:21: Blessed "are those who hear the Word of God and do/guard it!" Thus, this story is another instance where Luke has *created a doublet* from material he has used elsewhere in his account. No synopsis currently in print shows these connections.

¶ 71. This evil generation wants a sign from Heaven

(Mt 12:38-45; 16:1-2a, 4) **Lk 11:29-32**

Seeing the crowds increasing, apparently drawn by Jesus' preaching and the evident signs of conflict all around him, Jesus lectures to the issue of signs, "Are you waiting for some great sign from Heaven? Well there isn't going to be any! You want a sign? Jonah was the sign for the city of Nineveh! So the Son of Man will be your sign! The queen of the South responded to the Wisdom of Solomon, and the Ninevites repented at the preaching of Jonah. But the Queen of the South and the Ninevites will arise and stand in judgment on the present generation because someone greater than both Solomon, the king, and Jonah, the prophet, has appeared. And what has been the response?"

General observations. Luke continued to make use of Mt 12 by incorporating Mt 12:38-42 (seeking a sign). This unit has a doublet in Mt 16:1-2a and 4. Luke already utilized Mt 12:43-45 at Lk 11:24-26, as noted above; and Mt 12:46-50 was used by Luke for a second time in composing Lk 11:27-28 (cf. Lk 8:19-21). Just prior to the discussion on Jesus' family at Lk 8:19-21 there is Lukan thematic summary (Lk 8:16-18). A similar Lukan thematic summary appears in the next Lukan unit (Lk 11:33-36).

Lk 11:29-32. In creating Lk 11:29-32 Luke first continued with his source material in Mt 12:38-42 (seeking a sign), which comes after Mt's version of the Beelzebul controversy (Mt 12:22-30). Although in Mt 12:38f. the interlocutors continue to be "scribes and Pharisees," Luke changed it to "crowds" (parallel with the previous attack, Lk 11:14-26). That Luke was aware of the larger Matthean context (Mt 12:38) and that the story about seeking a sign involved scribes and Pharisees (Mt 16:1) was what led Luke to introduce material from the woes against the scribes and Pharisees in Mt 23 in the very next section (Lk 11:37-52). Luke's version of Mt 23 consists of two parts, a critique of the *Pharisees* (Lk 11:37-44) *and scribes* (in this case, a "lawyer," Lk 11:45-52).

• Luke omitted the reference to Jonah being "3 days and nights in the belly of the fish" (Mt 12:40), if it was in his text of Matthew, so as not to contradict his passion predictions which say that the resurrection will happen *on* the third day (Lk 9:22; 18:31-33; cf. Lk 24:7, 21).

• The response of Jesus to the charge that he is possessed by demons is a perfect *segue* into a similar thematic unit on controversy. Only here, instead of being on the defense, Jesus goes on the attack against hypocrisy (cf. Lk 12:1).

¶ 72. Lukan thematic summary

(Mt 5:14-16; 6:22-23) **Lk 11:33-36**

Jesus ends his address to the crowds with some examples. "No one lights a lamp and then puts it under the table where it can't give any light to the room! By the same token, if your eyes—which are supposed to be 'lamps' to give light to your body—are 'dark,' that is, if you can't see what I am talking about, then your whole body is 'dark.' And if you really are completely 'in the dark' about me, you are truly doomed!"

General observations. Since Luke had come to the beginning of Mt's Parables Discourse for a second time (Mt 12:46-50//Lk 8:19-21//Lk 11:27-28), he needed a way to proceed in his use of Mt. As a beginning of this transitional process, Luke composed a thematic summary at Lk 11:33-36. As he had done at Lk 8:16-18, so at Lk 11:33-36, Luke composed this summary from verses drawn from Mt, in Mt's order. It contains metaphors that Luke used here to express some of his ideas about discipleship (Lk 11:33//Mt 5:15; Lk 11:34-36//Mt 6:22-23): disciples coming into the church must see the light (the good works of others). They themselves must not only hear the word of God, but also do it. They must take care *how they hear the word of God*, lest what they seem to have gained be taken from them. Disciples must not hide their convictions but provide shining examples for others. What they hear in private should be made known to others in public, even if this causes divisions within their own families. The following synopsis will reveal how Luke conflated Mt 5:14-16 and 6:22-23 to create a transitional, thematic summary.

Synopsis of Lk 11:33-36

Illustrating the way Luke conflated material from Mt 5:14f. and 6:22f.

Mt 5:14-16	**Mt 6:22-23**	**Lk 11:33-36**
14 Ὑμεῖς ἐστε		
τὸ φῶς τοῦ κόσμου.		
οὐ δύναται πόλις κρυβῆναι		
ἐπάνω ὄρους κειμένη·		
15 οὐδὲ		**33** Οὐδεὶς
καίουσιν λύχνον καὶ		λύχνον ἅψας
		εἰς κρύπτην
τιθέασιν αὐτὸν		τίθησιν
		[οὐδὲ
ὑπὸ τὸν μόδιον		ὑπὸ τὸν μόδιον]
ἀλλ' ἐπὶ τὴν λυχνίαν,		ἀλλ' ἐπὶ τὴν λυχνίαν,
καὶ λάμπει πᾶσιν		ἵνα
τοῖς ἐν τῇ οἰκίᾳ.		οἱ εἰσπορευόμενοι
16 οὕτως λαμψάτω		
τὸ φῶς ὑμῶν		τὸ φῶς
ἔμπροσθεν τῶν ἀνθρώπων,		
ὅπως ἴδωσιν		βλέπωσιν.
ὑμῶν τὰ καλὰ ἔργα		
καὶ δοξάσωσιν		
τὸν πατέρα ὑμῶν		
τὸν ἐν τοῖς οὐρανοῖς.		
	22 Ὁ λύχνος	**34** ὁ λύχνος
	τοῦ σώματός ἐστιν	τοῦ σώματός ἐστιν
	ὁ ὀφθαλμός.	ὁ ὀφθαλμός σου.
	ἐὰν οὖν ᾖ ὁ ὀφθαλμός σου	ὅταν ὁ ὀφθαλμός σου
	ἁπλοῦς,	ἁπλοῦς ᾖ,
	ὅλον τὸ σῶμά σου	καὶ ὅλον τὸ σῶμά σου
	φωτεινὸν ἔσται·	φωτεινόν ἐστιν·
	23 ἐὰν δὲ	ἐπὰν δὲ
	ὁ ὀφθαλμός σου πονηρὸς ᾖ,	πονηρὸς ᾖ,
	ὅλον τὸ σῶμά σου	καὶ τὸ σῶμά σου
	σκοτεινὸν ἔσται.	σκοτεινόν.
	εἰ οὖν	**35** σκόπει οὖν μὴ
	τὸ φῶς τὸ ἐν σοὶ	τὸ φῶς τὸ ἐν σοὶ
	σκότος ἐστίν,	σκότος ἐστίν.
		36 εἰ οὖν
		τὸ σῶμά σου
		ὅλον φωτεινόν,
		μὴ ἔχον μέρος
	ὁ σκότος πόσον.	τι σκοτεινόν,
		ἔσται φωτεινὸν ὅλον
cf. Mt 5:15		ὡς ὅταν ὁ λύχνος
		τῇ ἀστραπῇ
		φωτίζῃ σε.

• On the earlier occasion when Luke made use of Mt 5:14-16, it was to construct a transitional passage (Lk 8:16-18) to unite most of Mt 13:1-23//Lk 8:4-15 with Mt 12:46-50//Lk 8:19-21. Luke had reversed the order of these two blocks of contiguous material in Matthew in order to be able to end the unit he created (Lk 7:36-8:21) with words similar to those he utilized at Lk 11:28. This reversal in the sequence of these two contiguous Matthean units within the parallel text of Lk is to be explained by the fact that Luke wanted to end Lk 7:36-8:21 with the Lukan punch line, "My mother and brothers are those who hear the word of God and do it" (Lk 8:21; cf. Mt 12:49-50). To do this, Luke needed to have Mt 12:46-50 follow Mt 13:1-23. Luke has a somewhat related conclusion at the end of the Sermon on the Plain (Lk 6:46-7:1). Luke also concluded Lk 11:27-28 with words of Jesus similar to those Luke described him as speaking at Lk 8:21.

Lk 11:28 "Blessed are those who hear the word of God and keep it!

Compare Lk 8:21 "My mother and my brother, these persons are those who hear the word of God and do it."

Since Luke made two uses of Mt 12:46-50 (Lk 8:19-21 and Lk 11:27-28), perhaps we should expect that the two thematic summaries that Luke would create to unite Mt 12:46-50 with other material from Mt would be similar (Lk 8:16-18; Lk 11:33-36). But there is more. When Luke concluded his use of Mt 23:1-36//Lk 11:37-52, he constructed yet another interweaving transitional passage from fragments taken from two different literary contexts in Mt (Lk 11:53-12:3). At Lk 8:16-18, Luke made use of Mt 5:14-16; 10:26-27; and Mt 13:12. Luke moved Mt 13:12 from its original location in Mt 13 precisely for the purpose of including this verse, along with Mt 5:14-16 and 10:26-27, within the thematic summary Luke created.

When Luke composed the second thematic summary we are currently discussing (Lk 11:33-36), he made a second use of Mt 5:14-16; but this time, he combined Mt 5:14-16 with Mt 6:22-23.

When Luke composed his even later related interweaving transitional passage (Lk 11:53-12:3), he made a second use of Mt 10:26-27, along with other fragments from Mt such as Mt 16:6.

These three Lukan constructions (Lk 8:16-18; 11:33-36; and 11:53-12:3) form a network among themselves. This network can be simply described. The first thematic summary (Lk 8:16-18) is related to the second (Lk 11:33-36) by the common use of Mt 5:14-16. And the first thematic summary is related to the interweaving transitional pericope (Lk 8:16-18 and 11:53-12:3) by the common use of Mt 10:26-27.

Surely we are in touch with the hand of the author of Lk within these three networked Lukan constructions. No earlier redactor of Lk would have been in a position to relate so intricately such different literary contexts within the Lukan Gospel. The redactor responsible for Lk 8:16-18; 11:33-36, and 11:53-12:3 was the redactor who composed the Gospel of

Luke. And this redactor has clearly utilized different passages from Mt in composing these patently Lukan constructions. This network of Lukan constructions is strong evidence of Luke's use of canonical Mt.

Lk 11:33. Luke altered the Matthean wording: Where Mt's version describes an absurd act (lighting a lamp and then putting it out again), Luke describes an act of *secrecy:* "No one lights a lamp and then puts it εἰς κρύπτην 'in the secret place'" (ancient homes often had a sort of secret cellar called the κρύπτη, hence the word *crypt;* cf. Liddell-Scott s.v.). "No. They light a lamp and put it on a lamp stand where everyone can see it." Moral? Let all your actions be like that! Out in the open. Luke's point within Lk 11:33 is the same point he made earlier at Lk 8:16. No one lights a lamp and places it in some place where it cannot be seen. According to Luke, a lamp is placed on a lamp stand "so that those who come in may see the light." Luke's emphasis on lamps being placed where they can be easily seen by those coming in may help to explain why Luke omitted so much of Mt 6:1-18 (cf. Lk 6:20-7:1 and Lk 11:1-13). The admonitions within this section of Mt 6 are for righteous behavior "in secret." Luke's understanding of the nature of discipleship was different from what one might understand from reading much of Mt 6:1-18.

Lk 11:33-36. Lk 11:33-36 not only summarized Jesus' response to the charges against him, but, by taking up such images as darkness versus light and secret versus public, Luke prepared the reader for similar motifs which occur in ensuing sections.

• The saying about the "divided eye" ("let your eye be ἁπλοῦς single") is also a metaphor for honesty in Lk as it is in Mt. Luke has altered the first saying slightly in order to bring it together with Mt 6:22-23.

• Although all of Lk 11:33-36 is a Lukan creation, Luke seems to have created Lk 11:35 almost *de novo.* Lk 11:35 seems to be Luke's not altogether successful attempt to cement the two sayings from different literary units in Mt. This causes Luke's text to make reference to a strange sort of lamp that has *dark parts,* rather than being wholly bright.

• As noted in the General Observations above, these sayings, with their contrasts between inner and outer prefigure the numerous contrasts in the next pericope to cups that are clean on the outside but filthy inside, and secret graves that look like regular ground so that men walk over them without realizing it. These metaphors also figure prominently in Jesus' advice to his "friends" to repeat from the housetops what they have heard in private.

Section Four. To Pharisees and Lawyers: On Hypocrisy. Lk 11:37–52

Jesus accepts a dinner invitation from a Pharisee who rudely criticizes Jesus for not washing before eating. This Pharisee's criticism elicits from Jesus a series of comments about Pharisees' behavior in general. He begins by noting their hypersensitivity regarding external cleanliness. After that comes a scathing observation on their disproportionate attention to public almsgiving, which serves them as a kind of self-aggrandizement. Jesus concludes by ironically comparing the outwardly extra clean but inwardly filthy Pharisees to invisible graves that people unwittingly walk on, causing defilement.

Hearing this, a lawyer complains that Jesus has reproached lawyers, too. This complaint calls forth an even longer critique from Jesus than the series he addressed to the Pharisees. Like the Pharisees, lawyers, too, are hypocritical. They load down others with heavy burdens but will not so much as touch such burdens themselves. They condemn those who killed the prophets, but they build the tombs of the prophets. Again, ironically, by building such tombs in an attempt to honor the prophets, the lawyers actually participate with their ancestors who murdered them. Finally, these lawyers have rejected the Wisdom of God but kept the key of knowledge to themselves, so that others cannot unlock and enter the door to true Wisdom.

Source-critical observations. Luke began the Travel Narrative in contextual parallel with Mt's Discourse on Community Regulations (Mt 18:1-19:1). The Travel Narrative served Luke as a literary device for presenting long collections of Jesus' teachings within a narrative context. Prior to the beginning of the Travel Narrative, Luke had made use of parts of each of Mt's first four discourses of Jesus, always including the opening verses (Mt 5:2-7:29, cf. Lk 6:20-7:1; Mt 9:35-11:1, cf. Lk 6:12-16, 9:1-6; Mt 13:1-53, cf. Lk 8:4-18; Mt 18:1-19:1, cf. Lk 9:46-48). Since Luke's Travel Narrative falls into contextual parallel with Mt 18:1-19:1, Luke's narrative had not yet come into contextual parallel with the last long collection of Jesus' teachings in Mt 23:1-26:1. But Luke intended to draw materials from *all* of Jesus' long discourses in Mt into the Travel Narrative. Luke, therefore, now moved forward in Mt to incorporate material from this last long collection of sayings of Jesus in Mt 23:1-26:1. As he had done with all four of the discourses he had utilized from Mt prior to the Travel Narrative, Luke began his use of Mt 23:1-26:1 with the opening verses from this discourse, Mt 23:1-36. Luke considerably reshaped these verses from Mt, as we see in the detailed notes to the pericopes within this section, but it was just these verses that Luke utilized to construct Section Four of the Travel Narrative.

¶ 73. Speech against Pharisees: you focus on external rites while neglecting important issues—justice and the love of God

(Mt 23:1-36) **Lk 11:37-44**

While Jesus was tongue-lashing the crowds, one of the "powerful" invites him to eat with him. But the Pharisee is shocked to observe that Jesus does not wash his hands first. This provokes an angry reply from Jesus against all Pharisees for their hypocrisy and indifference to the most important things in life: justice and the love of God. Jesus goes on to warn them that all of the sins of their fathers will be required of *them*. His bitter words outrage the Pharisees who gather around and berate him, hoping to catch him in some way.

General observations. At this point in Mt, Jesus is involved in a debate with Pharisees and scribes (cf. Mt 16:1 and 12:38). Luke now introduced the Pharisees and turned to Mt 23, selectively utilizing this material here (Lk 11:37-44) and in the next Lukan pericope (Lk 11:45-52). This is the second banquet scene created by Luke to critique the Pharisees (cf. Lk 7:36-50). Of the seven proclamations of woe in Mt 23, Luke took three and applied them to the Pharisees (Lk 11:37-44). He took three others and applied them to the lawyers (Lk 11:45-52).

Lk 11:37-38. These verses are Lukan composition to set up the speech of Jesus.

Lk 11:39-41. Here Luke picked up Mt 23:25-26 to assert the correlation between an inner pure life and an outer life of good deeds. Mt 23:25-26 says, "You cleanse the outside of the cup and side dish, but inside they are full of extortion and rapacity. Blind Pharisee, cleanse first the inside of the cup, so that its outside may also become clean." At Lk 11:39, Luke modified Mt to read, "Now you Pharisees cleanse the outside of the cup and platter, but *your* inside is full of extortion and wickedness. You fools, did not he who made the outside also make the inside?" By means of his modifications of the text of Mt, Luke corrected a perceived confusion in the Matthean text to a form of the sayings that can be directly applied to the Pharisees. Luke also made a different point than Matthew had made. Luke's point is that God made both inside and outside. Therefore, if God is the creator, then internal alms are just as good as the external ones (contrast Mt 6:1-4 which Luke omitted at Lk 6:20-7:1 and again at Lk 11:1-13). And since God created all things, everything is clean, not just some things, as the Pharisees in Mt might have claimed. These are the basic principles by which the Lukan Jesus assessed the Pharisees.

Lk 11:42. Luke edited Mt 23:23 to give the first of the three woes against the Pharisees. The Pharisees are too concerned with technicalities about alms and tithes and neglect the more important issues of justice and the love of God.

Lk 11:43. Luke's editing of Mt 23:6-7 for the second woe directed at the

Pharisees (Lk 11:43) focused on two points, "first seats" and "greetings in the markets." The first point prepared the way for Luke's parable in Lk 14:7-11 (see esp. Lk 14:7-8 and the use of Mt 23:12 at Lk 14:11 to conclude Lk 14:7-11). The first and the second points both prepare for Jesus' warning to his disciples (cf. Lk 20:45 and Mt 23:1) about the scribes in Lk 20:45-47. Thus, Luke dealt with the scribes mentioned in Mt, but in a different place.

Lk 11:44. The content of Mt 23:27 had to do with differences between the inside and the outside, which Luke used for his *third* woe against the Pharisees. This is similar in theme to Mt 23:25-26, which Luke had just utilized for his *first* woe against the Pharisees. The Pharisees are like concealed graves that unwittingly defile. Again the point is made that the outer appearance and inner life are not in proper relationship.

¶ 74. Speech against lawyers: do not abuse your authority

(Mt 23:4, 29-32, 34-36,13) **Lk 11:45-52**

Luke next depicts Jesus introducing a new interlocutor, a lawyer, who provides Jesus with an additional range of subjects on which to expound. The lawyer complains that what Jesus has just said against the Pharisee strikes at lawyers also. But Jesus changes the subject and berates the lawyer for three different abuses: (1) lawyers use their knowledge and authority to place impossible burdens on others, while refusing in any way to help bear them. (2) They build memorials. By building memorial tombs for the prophets, these lawyers become witnesses to their murder. And by building memorials to their own ancestors, they implicitly consent to or approve of the lives and works of their ancestors, who killed the prophets. Finally, (3) these lawyers use their great learning to block all knowledge of God. They do not want to know God themselves and they keep others from it as well.

General observations. Although Luke was still following Mt 23 where Jesus addressed the Pharisees throughout, here Luke created a second speech, this time addressed to a "lawyer." Part of Luke's rationale for selecting various parts of Mt 23 was his usual one of consolidating his material into common themes. However, other changes have to do with the fact that Luke's revisions always had one eye on the needs of the struggle of the church in the wider Greco-Roman world with those who demand strict allegiance to Torah.

Lk 11:46. For his first woe against the lawyers, Luke used Mt 23:4 to say they place intolerable legal burdens on others.

Lk 11:47-51. These verses are dependent on Mt 23:29-32, 34-36. Lk 11:49 contains a striking alteration of Mt 23:34. Luke says a statement attributed to Jesus in Mt comes rather from "the wisdom of God." Luke apparently decided that what Jesus said in Mt 23:34 was a prophecy of some sort; i.e., Luke seems to have decided that the "I" in Mt 23:34a could not have been Jesus speaking, so Luke created a speaker: "the Wisdom of God." But who is this "Wisdom of God"? (cf. Lk 2:40, 52; 7:35; 11:49 and 21:15 and certain contexts in the OT such as Prov 1:20; 7:4; 8:1, 11-12, etc.).

• For the reasons mentioned above, Luke's other alterations of Mt 23:34 are not difficult to understand: "kill and crucify" in Mt becomes "kill and persecute" in Lk.

• Mt's "I send you prophets and wise men and scribes" (Mt 23:34) becomes "I will send prophets and *apostles*" (Lk. 11:49). Note that the twelve "apostles" are explicitly said to be with Jesus along with several women at Lk 8:1-3.

Lk 11:51. Luke omitted the description of Zechariah as son of Berachiah in Mt 23:35. Nevertheless he anticipated the rejection of Jesus and destruction of the city with the statement that "this generation" will be accountable for its dismissal of the prophetic witness.

Lk 11:52. Luke changed Mt's "scribes and Pharisees" (Mt 23:13) to "lawyers" — they are the target of this second speech.

• Luke changed Mt's "you shut the kingdom of heaven against people" (Mt 23:13) to "you have taken away the *key of knowledge*" (Lk 11:52). This last change conforms with Luke's introduction of the figure of "the Wisdom of God" in Lk 11:49, who is said there to have sent all of God's prophets and apostles.

¶ 75. Interweaving transitional pericope

(Mt 23:1-2; 10:26-27; 16:1, 6) **Lk 11:53-12:3**

After this, Jesus suddenly breaks off, and attempts to leave the scene. However, his angry criticisms have made the Pharisees and scribes furious and they all begin shouting at him at once, challenging him to answer them. Meanwhile, the crowds have continued to grow, drawn by the uproar, and chaos breaks out as people begin trampling upon one another. Jesus goes off with his disciples and teaches them to have nothing to do with the hypocrisy of the Pharisees. Everything they think is in secret will one day come to light.

General observations. Luke terminated the banquet scene with a transitional interlude depicting the violent outbursts from the Pharisees and Scribes (Lk 11:53-54). This is Lukan redaction. Luke's reference here to Pharisees *and scribes* confirms that Luke has just been utilizing Mt 23 (Lk 11:37-52). Luke composed this scene to set up the next section of the Travel Narrative (Lk 12:4-34) that consists of a series of closely related speeches; first, to Jesus' own disciples (Lk 12:1) who are addressed again in closure at Lk 12:22, then to his friends (Lk 12:4-12), then to at least two brothers in the crowd (Lk 12:13-21), and finally back to his own disciples (Lk 12:22-34). See "Section Five. To Friends and Disciples: Reject Fear and Anxiety. Trust and Treasure God!, Lk 12:4-34."

Lk 12:1-3. The reference in Lk 12:1a to the crowds increasing goes back to the original focus on "the crowds" at Lk 11:29 and may constitute a closing member of an *inclusio* that began at Lk 11:29. If so, this may indicate that Luke was, in some sense, still working within one scene (Lk 11:29-12:3). Luke's technique of interweaving sections of his narrative into a smoothly flowing tapestry is impressive. Contrast the text of Mt where transitions are (perhaps intentionally) obvious and where the text's breaks may suggest a composite of earlier sources.

• To set the scene for the composition in Lk 12:4ff., Luke utilized the saying against the Pharisees from Mt 16:6. The doublet to Mt 12:38-42 at Mt 16:1-6, which had been conflated by Luke already at Lk 11:29-32, caused Luke to include pieces of Mt 16:1-6, not only here (Lk 12:1//Mt 16:1, 6), but also within at least two other Lukan contexts (see not only Mt 16:1, 4//Mt12:38-42//Lk 11:29-32 discussed above, but also Luke's careful use of the intervening verses from Mt 16:1-4, i.e., Mt 16:2-3, at Lk 12:54-56 discussed below.)

After making use of Mt 16:6 (cf. Lk 12:1) and modifying it to explain the meaning of "leaven" as "hypocrisy" for his readers who have just heard about this hypocrisy in Lk 11:37-45, Luke again turned to Mt 10:26-33, from Mt's mission instructions (Mt 9:35-11:1). Luke had already utilized Mt 10:26-27 to construct a thematic summary at Lk 8:16-18. Here Luke used Mt 10:26-27 to help construct an interweaving transition (Lk 11:53-12:3) that served to unite Luke's versions of Jesus' two previous speeches, one to the Pharisees (Lk 11:37-44) and one to the lawyers (Lk 11:45-52) with a third speech of Jesus, to his friends and disciples (Lk 12:4-34). Within Lk 11:53-12:3, Luke has combined Mt 10:26-27 at least with Mt 23:1-2; 16:1, 6 and perhaps some other verses from Mt. Compare the composite Lukan constructions at Lk 8:16-18 and Lk 11:33-36.

Section Five. To Friends and Disciples: Reject Fear and Anxiety; Trust and Treasure God! Lk 12:4–34

Jesus now teaches his friends and disciples not to fear or be anxious about non-ultimate matters. There will be much to be fearful about once they arrive in Jerusalem. Anxiety and fear of civil rulers who can kill the body is understandable. But, true fear should be reserved for God alone. In public trials, disciples should bravely confess their faith in Jesus, without worrying about how to say it. The Holy Spirit will aid them. The only truly dangerous sin is opposing the Holy Spirit.

He goes on. Excessive attention to this-worldly matters is foolish; death will strip them away. In fact, no "thing" in this life is really worth any anxiety, not even food or clothing. God feeds the creatures of the heavens and clothes the plants of the earth; why are we anxious about such things? Are we not more important than they? Let us be anxious about the Kingdom of God; everything else will be provided.

Source-critical observations. For Section Five of the Travel Narrative, Luke used two similar segments from two different speeches of Jesus in Mt as the basis for his composition. These similar segments are Mt 10:28-33, drawn from the Mission Discourse, and Mt 6:25-34, drawn from the Sermon on the Mount. The first segment from Mt 10 focused on the theme of anxiety and the second, from Mt 6, on the related theme of fear. Bringing these two segments of Mt together into a single section of the Travel Narrative fit Luke's concern for order.

Lk 12:4-34//Mt 10:28-33. Luke began this section of the Travel Narrative by incorporating Jesus' teachings on "fear" from Mt 10:28-33. Luke led into this material within the immediately preceding interweaving pericope (Lk 11:53-12:3) by closing that transitional unit with a second use of Mt 10:26 (Lk 12:2-3//Mt 10:26-27). Luke made an earlier use of Mt 10:26 within the thematic summary he composed from three verses from Mt in Mt's order at Lk 8:16-18 (Lk 8:16//Mt 5:15; Lk 8:17//Mt 10:26; Lk 8:18//Mt 13:12). Luke began this section at a verse in Mt he has already utilized (Mt 10:26).

Lk 12:10//Mt 12:32. To these teachings on fear, Luke attached the sayings about "a word against the Son of Man" and "blasphemy against the Holy Spirit" from Mt 12:32 as an example of the distinction between fears that have some basis and those that do not.

Lk 12:11-12//Mt 10:19-20. Luke also attached Mt 10:19-20 to the verses he was using from Mt 10 because Mt 10:19-20 already anticipates the theme of "anxiety" central to Mt 6:25-34 which Luke will use to end the main body of Section Five of the Travel Narrative.

Lk 12:13-21. Between the similar units on fear and anxiety drawn from Mt 10:26-33 and Mt 6:25-34, Luke sandwiched a parable from his non-Matthean tradition about a farmer whose anxiety is misplaced. He is anxious about the wrong things, material possessions.

Lk 12:22-32//Mt 6:25-34. Immediately following this appropriate parable, Luke made use of the second of his two basic sources for Section Five of his Travel Narrative, Mt 6:25-34, on anxiety.

• Luke rounded off his combined use of Mt 10 and Mt 6 within Lk 12:4-32 with the very telling editorial change of the word "anxiety" in Mt 6:34 to the word "fear" in the Lukan parallel (Lk 12:32). With this deft touch, Luke brought his readers back to the beginning point of Section Five and back from the text of Mt 6 to the text of Mt 10, Luke's main sources for Section Five of the Travel Narrative.

Lk 12:33-34//Mt 6:19-21. To create this interweaving transitional unit, Luke attached teachings on "true treasures" also drawn from the literary context in Mt 6 that Luke was using (Mt 6:19-21). These verses also relate back to the closing admonition of the sandwiched parable, "So is he who lays up treasure for himself, and is not rich toward God" (Lk 12:21). The reference to "thieves who break in and steal" in Mt 6:19 was rewritten by

Luke to emphasize that heaven is a place that "the thief does not draw near." With this revision, Luke anticipated the beginning of Section Six, with its metaphorical reference to "the thief in the night." This image ties together Luke's use of Mt 6:19-21//Lk 12:33-34 with Luke's use of 24:42-51 in the next Lukan literary unit, Lk 12:35-46//Mt 24:42-51; cf. Mt 25:1-13. Here Luke's own composition fits hand in glove with his use of Mt.

¶ 76. To Jesus' friends: Do not fear; do not be anxious.

(Mt 10:28-33; 12:32; 10:19-20) **Lk 12:4-12**

Do not fear. Do not be anxious. These are the themes of this speech of Jesus to his friends that opens this section of the Travel Narrative. Do not fear those who can kill the body. Fear instead those who can cast one's soul into Hell. Public confession of faith in Jesus will result in divine approval, yet open opposition to Jesus will be forgiven. But when called upon to repent, do not resist the Holy Spirit's prompting; that cannot be forgiven. And if public confession leads to persecution, do not be anxious about what to say under pressure; the Holy Spirit will help you.

General observations. Having made use of Mt 10:26-27 for a second time in constructing a Lukan interweaving transition (Lk 11:53-12:3; cf. Lk 8:16-18), Luke continued with Mt 10:28-33 (Lk 12:4-10). This was supplemented with material drawn from Mt 12:32 (Lk 12:10) and 10:19-20 (Lk 12:11-12). Luke used Mt 10:19-20 which contains the admonition, "Do not be anxious," to close this speech (Lk 12:11-12). It anticipates the longer segment on "Do not be anxious" that concludes this segment of the Travel Narrative (Lk 12:22-34). See the note to Lk 12:11-12 below.

Lk 12:4-9. After initial redaction in Lk 12:4a, Luke followed Mt 10:28-33 fairly closely for Lk 12:4-9. Lk 12:4a emphasizes Jesus' kinship with the disciples in public confession, torture, and death.

Lk 12:10. To this material from Mt 10:26-33, Luke attached one verse (Mt 12:32) from the context of Mt 12:31-36. Luke's theme in Lk 12:4-9 is the same as Mt's: fearless confession during persecution. Mt's version contains a rigorous admonition not to deny Jesus when on public trial; whoever does so will be denied by Jesus on the Day of Judgment (12:31-36). However, Lk 12:10 says precisely the opposite, introducing a similar saying from Mt 12:32: "whoever speaks a word against the Son of Man *will be forgiven*..." Why this abrupt shift? Luke could be laying the ground for the position to be taken by Peter in Acts. In his speech in the Temple he says, "when you killed Jesus the Holy and Righteous One, you and your rulers acted in ignorance. But now repent and turn back to God, that your sins may be forgiven" (paraphrase of Acts 3:14-19). In this view, the continuation of Lk12:10b, "to blaspheme against the Holy Spirit" would refer to the refusal to repent, now that it is evident who Jesus wasw.

Lk 12:11-12. While he was using a series of verses from Mt's Mission

Discourse in Mt's order within this context (Lk 12:2-12//Mt 10:26-33), Luke also chose to attach Mt 10:19-20 to them (Lk 12:11-12). In choosing to utilize Mt 10:19-20 here (Lk 12:11-12), Luke provided another skillful anticipation. From the theme of "Do not fear" (Lk 12:4-10), Luke moved into the related theme of "Do not be anxious" (Lk 12:11-12, 22-32//Mt 6:25-34). Only Luke's unique Parable of the Rich Fool, which also teaches the folly of misplaced anxiety, intervenes between Lk 12:4-12 and Lk 12:22-32. Note how Luke also altered, in a complementary way, "Do not be anxious" (Mt 6:34) to "Do not fear" (Lk 12:32), in order to begin to conclude this section (Lk 12:4-34).

With this alteration, Luke moves his readers to think back from the concluding theme of "Do not be anxious" (Lk 12:11-34) to the original theme of the Section "Do not fear" (Lk 12:32). Once Luke had inserted the Parable of the Rich Fool into this context, he introduced "treasure" sayings drawn from Mt 6 (Mt 6:19-21//Lk 12:33-34). The connection of Lk 12:33-34 with what precedes is also back to Lk 12:13-21, "Thus it is for the one who stores up treasures for himself and is not rich toward God." The reference to "almsgiving" (Lk 12:33; cf. Mt 6:1-4) may indicate that Luke is looking for any material within the Sermon on the Mount appropriate to this theme that he had not yet utilized.

What remained of Mt 5:2-7:29 that Luke found appropriate to use later includes only six more pericopes:

(1) Mt 5:21-26	Lk 12:57-59
(2) Mt 7:13-14	Lk 13:23-24
(3) Mt 5:13	Lk 14:34-35
(4) Mt 6:24	Lk 16:13
(5) Mt 5:17-20	Lk 16:17
(6) Mt 5:31-32	Lk 16:18

• Note that Luke changed "*I* will acknowledge" in Mt 10:32-33 to "the *Son of Man* will acknowledge" in Lk 12:8-9 to prepare for the next saying Luke used from Mt about the Son of Man (Lk 12:10//Mt 12:32). For Luke, the "Son of Man" always meant Jesus. The evidence for this claim occurs in three forms.

1. Luke substituted "Son of Man" for Mt's "I" four times.

   Mt 5:11//Lk 6:22
   Mt 10:32//Lk 12:8
   Mt 16:21//Lk 9:22
   Mt 26:50//Lk 22:48

2. Luke changed "Son of Man" in Mt to a personal pronoun referring to Jesus twice.

   Mt 16:13//Lk 9:18
   Mt 20:28//Lk 22:27

3. Luke omitted "Son of Man" from Mt 16:28 and made the "Kingdom of God" the subject of the same verb as "Son of Man" in Mt at Lk 9:27.

• The strict parallelism of Mt's wording has been kept, but the persons before whom Jesus (or the Son of Man) will testify have been changed by Luke (Lk 12:10) to "the angels of God." He had already used the full reference in his negative version of this saying at Lk 9:26, "of them the Son of Man will be ashamed when he comes in his glory and the glory of the Father and of the holy angels" (from Mt 16:27). There are a number of other associations of the Son of Man and the angels in Matthew (Mt 13:41; 16:27; 24:30-31; and 25:31; cf. Dan 7:13 LXX).

• Luke concluded this speech with Mt 10:19-20 (Lk 12:11-12) for the compositional reasons already discussed in the General Observations. Luke added references to "synagogues and the rulers and the authorities" to Mt's version, clearly intending to provide a sweeping, all-inclusive forecast regarding the kinds of situations in which Jesus' "friends" might find themselves called to testify.

¶ 77. Don't be anxious about material things

(Mt 6:25-33, 19-21) **Lk 12:13-34**

Suddenly a man interrupts Jesus with a request to help him obtain his rightful portion of his father's inheritance. Jesus refuses and goes on to use the man's request as a spring-board for telling the story of a man who was anxious about his material well-being. Then he turns to the disciples and repeats the teaching, using the natural world as a point of comparison. "Don't worry about material possessions! Seek the real treasure," says Jesus: "God's eternal blessing!"

General observations. The two stories in Lk 12:13-21 have no parallel in Mt. The first story (Lk 12:13-15) was used by Luke as an introduction to the following parable (Lk 12:16-21). The verses following this parable (Lk 12:22-32) display literary dependence on Mt 6:25-34. The similarities in main themes (anxiety and fear) and other thematic and verbal similarities (cf., Mt 10:29-31 with Mt 6:26-27) probably led Luke to combine Mt 10:26-33, as a beginning of this section (Lk 12:2-9), with Mt 6:25-34, as part of the ending (Lk 12:25-32) of this whole Section of Lk (Lk 12:4-34).

The conclusion of this section of the Travel Narrative (Lk 12:32-34) makes use of Mt 6:19-21, verses which precede Mt 6:25-34. Having used nothing from Mt 6 in his Sermon on the Plain, Luke first made use of material from Mt 6 in his unit on prayer at Lk 11:1-13//Mt 6:5-15; 7:7-11. The Matthean unit immediately following Mt 6:5-15 is Mt 6:16-18 which Luke omitted from his Gospel altogether, probably because of the secrecy advocated in this teaching on how to fast. This is in line with Luke's earlier omission of "secret" almsgiving (Mt 6:1-4) and his editing of Mt 6:5-

15 to omit the secrecy motif from his parallel in Lk 11:1-4. The author of Luke-Acts advocated *public* confession and discipleship (cf. Lk 8:16-18 and Lk 11:33-36).

Luke's prior use of Mt 6:5-15 at Lk 11:1-4 and his omission of Mt 6:16-18 from his Gospel altogether brings Luke to Mt 6:19-21, "Treasure in Heaven," which he used here (Lk 12:32-34). Luke had also used Mt 6:22-23, "On the Sound Eye," within the Lukan thematic summary at Lk 11:33-36.

This brings Lk to Mt 6:24, "On Serving Two Masters" which Luke will use as the last in a series of *aitiae* to the Parable of the Unjust Judge (Mt 6:24//Lk 16:13). And *that* brought Luke to Mt 6:25-34, "On Anxiety," which, as already noted, Luke combined with similar material from Mt 10:26-33 as the two basic building blocks for the Lukan Section, Lk 12:4-34. With the exception of the single verse noted (Mt 6:24//Lk 16:13) these uses of Mt 6 in Lk 12 complete Luke's uses of material from Mt 6. See other redactional details discussed below.

Lk 12:13-21. This unit has some interesting parallels with the story of Mary and Martha. See, for instance, this man's request, "*Teacher, tell my brother to* divide the inheritance with *me*" (Lk 12:13), and Martha's request, "*Lord*, do you not care that *my sister* has left *me* to serve alone? *Tell her* then *to* help *me*" (Lk 10:40). Further, notice Lk 10:42, "One thing is necessary. For Mary elected the <u>good portion</u> which will not be taken from her" Compare to this Lk 12:18: "all my <u>good things</u>" and the ending: "Fool, on this night your soul will be taken from you" (Lk 12:20). Is this another example of balance in Luke: two warning stories involving a woman and a man about missing the most important thing?

Lk 12:22-34. Having introduced the theme of a person's value in the sight of God, Luke went back to Mt's Sermon on the Mount for similar sayings about excessive concern for wealth, food, and clothing, concluding with the saying about "treasure" (Lk 12:33-34//Mt 6:19-21), an echo of Lk 12:21.

Lk 12:32 is a skillful alteration of Mt 6:34 to round out this section of Luke's Travel Narrative (Lk 12:4-34), as noted above. It is certainly the work of the author of Lk. It provided Luke's typical rationale for not being concerned with one's lowly estate in this world: soon there will be the great eschatological reversal.

Lk 12:33, "give alms," is a favorite Lukan theme; an alteration of the text of Mt 6:19-21 (perhaps in light of Mt 6:1-4). None of the differences between Lk and Mt within Lk 12:22-34 requires positing a source for Luke apart from Mt 6:25-34 and Mt 6:19-21.

• Note that the verses that fall between Mt 6:19-21 and Mt 6:25-34 used by Luke here are just the verses (i.e. Mt 6:22-23) less one (Mt 6:24) that Luke included within his interweaving transitional passage at Lk 11:33-36. Should we be surprised, then, that Luke utilized the verses on both sides of Mt 6:22-23 as source material for Lk 12:13-34? And should we be surprised to find the one remaining verse from Mt 6:19-34, i.e., Mt 6:24, appearing at last at Lk 16:13? Luke's use of Mt 6:19-34 is creative, clear and remarkable.

Section Six. To the Disciples and Others: Appropriate Conduct Before the Lord's Coming. Lk 12:35–53

Luke next turns to an area of major concern to the churches in the wider ecumenical mission: the seeming delay in Jesus' return. In this Section, Jesus teaches his "followers" to be watchfully expectant, like servants waiting for their master who is away attending a wedding feast. When the servants finally greet their returning master, to their surprise he gets busy and brings them something to eat.

Then the metaphor changes, to talk about a robbery while the master is out of the house. If the master had known that a thief was going to break into his house while he was away, he would not have left home. "And so it should be for you," says Jesus. "Be ready for the unexpected coming of the Son of Man."

This causes Peter to inquire, "Lord, are you telling this parable for us or for all?" Jesus responds indirectly to Peter's question. "Who is the faithful and wise steward who has been given charge of his master's household staff, to feed them at the proper time?" If this steward does what he has been assigned to do, this will surely lead to even greater responsibilities. But, should the master be delayed in returning and the steward begin to neglect his duties and abuse the servants, then he will be severely punished when the master returns.

Source-critical observations. Luke clearly thought that freedom from fear and anxiety was the appropriate state of mind while waiting for the coming of the Lord. This view is emphasized in all three of the Lukan eschatological discourses, this being the first (cf. Lk 21:34). This conduct characterizes not only the faithful servants, but the householder, and ultimately "you," the disciples.

•Once Luke had concluded his beautifully constructed Section Five, he was again at a turning point in the composition of the Travel Narrative. What should be narrated next? His decision at Lk 12:35 was the same as it had been at Lk 11:32ff.; namely, to move forward to the last long speech(es?) of Jesus in Mt 23:1-26:1 and to make some further use of that material (cf. the earlier usage at Mt 23:1-36//Lk 11:37-52 = Section Four of the Travel Narrative). Section Six, beginning with these uses of material from Mt 23:1-26:1, deals with various costs of discipleship:

(1) the cost of being watchful (Lk 12:35-40),
(2) the rewards of watching (Lk 12:41-44) and the costs of not watching (Lk 12:45-48), and
(3) the specific cost of family division (Lk 12:49-53).

Lk 12:35-36//Mt 25:1-13. To begin Section Six, Luke at least made allusions to the Parable of the Wise and Foolish Virgins (Mt 25:1-13). That story in Mt is central to the theme of this Lukan section. Luke will make (a second?) clearer use of this same parable later within the context of Lk 13:22-27.

Lk 12:37-40//Mt 24:42-44. Luke next made use of the doublet in Mt 24:42//Mt 25:13, "Watch, therefore, because you do not know the day. . ." to move to that segment of Mt that immediately precedes Mt 25:1-13, the Parable of the Wise and Foolish Virgins. That section is Mt 24:42-51. Luke first utilized Mt 24:42-44 for the balance of the teachings on the need and the costs of watchfulness.

Lk 12:41-46//Mt 24:45-51. After introducing a question from Peter, "Lord, do you say this parable for us or also for all?" Luke continued to utilize Mt 24:45-51 for instructions about distinguishing faithful disciples from others. The antecedent to "all" is unclear, but may refer to the later leaders of the Church who follow the apostles.

Lk 12:47-48 is either drawn from nonMatthean tradition or it is parenesis created by Luke himself on the basis of the teachings in Mt 24:45-51 and Mt 25:1-13. The teachings of Lk 12:47-48 about "knowing the will of one's Lord and not doing it" or "not knowing the Lord's will, but, nevertheless doing it" certainly conform with Lukan interests expressed at Lk 6:46-7:1, the ending of the Sermon on the Plain, and within other passages that seem to be Lukan compositions (Lk 8:16-18; Lk 11:27-28) even though all three of these passages are based on material from Mt (Lk 6:46-7:1//Mt 7:21-29; Lk 8:16-18//Mt 5:15//Mt 10:26//Mt 13:12; Lk 11:27-28//Lk 8:19-21//Mt 12:46-50). "Blessed are those true members of Jesus' family who hear the Word of God and do/keep it."

Lk 12:49-53//Mt 10:34-37. At this point Luke turned again to Mt 10 and continued to follow Mt 10:34ff., verse by verse, as he had been doing since the beginning of the Travel Narrative.

Mt 9:35-10:16	Lk 6:12-16; Lk 9:1-6; and Lk 10:1-2
Mt 10:26-33	Lk 12:2-9 (cf. Lk 8:17//Mt 10:26)
(Mt 10:19-20)	Lk 12:11-12
Mt 10:34-37	Lk 12:49-53

• Luke's move back to Mt 10:34ff. in Section Six emphasized that one of the major potential costs of discipleship is divisions among members of the family (cf. Lk 12:49-53 and Lk 14:25-26).

• Following Luke's use of Mt 10:34-37//Lk 12:49-53, only two major segments of Mt's Mission Discourse remained, Mt 10:17-25 and Mt 10:37-39. Luke had used the ending of the Mission Discourse in Mt 10:40-11:1 already at Lk 9:46-48 where Luke conflated it with the very beginning of Mt's Community Regulations (Mt 18:1-2, 4-5). The latter of these two segments of Mt 10, Mt 10:37-39, Luke continued to utilize, following the order of these sayings in Mt verse by verse throughout the remainder of the Travel Narrative.

Mt 10:37-38 ====> Lk 14:25-27

Mt 10:39 ====> Lk 17:33

Luke substituted most of the former of these two segments of Mt (Mt 10:17-22) for the Matthean doublet at Mt 24:8-14 when Luke came into contextual parallel with Mt 24:8-14 at Lk 21:12-19.

¶ 78. Watch and wait! Do not be dismayed that the Lord has not returned!

(Mt 25:1-13; 24:42-51) **Lk 12:35-48**

Having discussed false anxieties and fear, including the distractions of wealth, Luke now turns to discuss a distraction of a different sort: the difficulty of maintaining an attitude of expectant hope in the Lord's return. The disciples are told to remain vigilant, a word underlined by Peter's pointed question, "Lord, are you telling this parable for us (Twelve Apostles) or also for everyone?" (Lk 12:41). Luke concludes with a grave admonition to all those in authority.

General observations. Lk 12:35-48 modulates into another theme, but a related anxiety: the "Lord" did not return when everyone thought he would (cf. Lk 12:45). Indeed, this disappointment might well have been an underlying cause of growing "anxiety" among the "little flock" (Lk 12:32). To obtain the material for this compound unit, Luke reached far ahead to the long speech of Jesus contained in Mt 24-25. Here Luke first adopted Mt 25:1-13, "the parable of the ten bridesmaids." Luke abbreviated it and conflated it with the immediately preceding verses of Mt; i.e., Mt 24:42-51. The doublet within these two contiguous Matthean pericopes, "Watch, therefore, because you do not know the day" (Mt 25:13//24:42), provided the point at which Luke ceased to use Mt 25:1-13 and began to use Mt 24:42-51.

• The admonition to have "lamps lit" in Lk 12:35 conforms to a Lukan interest, demonstrable in two summaries Luke composed from widely separated verses in Mt (Lk 8:16-18//Mt 5:15//Mt 10:26//Mt 13:12 and Lk 11:33-36//Mt 5:15//Mt 6:22-23). This may be the reason why Mt 25:1-13 appears here. For the source of this image, see Mt 6:22, ὁ λύχνος and, more importantly, Mt 5:14-16, particularly Mt 5:15, καίουσιν λύχνον. Compare the repeated use of the word, λαμπάς in Mt 25:1, 3-4, 7-8.

• Luke inserted Peter's question into Lk 12:41 to break up Mt's mixture of ideas and to move to a related theme: judgment will be heavier on the leadership than the laity at the Last Day. The idea is there in Mt's text, but Luke brought it out more clearly.

Lk 12:36. The reference to attendance at weddings in Lk 12:36 (cf. Mt 25:10) is the first mention of a theme that will recur many times in the meal scenes that will come later in Lk. The reference to knocking and opening may be reminiscent of Mt 7:7, which Luke utilized in composing his section on prayer in Lk 11:1-13 (cf. the request to "open the door" at Mt 25:11).

Lk 12:46. This is an understandable alteration of Mt's "hypocrites" (Mt 24:51) to "unfaithful" (Lk 12:46).

Lk 12:47-48. The phraseology is Luke's own creation. It contains a curiously casuistic elaboration of the severity of punishments. It also reflects Luke's concern for "hearing the word of God and doing/guarding it" (Lk 8:21 and 11:28; cf. Lk 6:46-7:1) in the words, "But that servant who knew the will of his master and did not prepare or act according to it..."

¶ 79. Don't even be anxious about divisions within the family

(Mt 10:34-37; 19:3-9[?]) **Lk 12:49-53**

Breaking into an exclamation, Jesus exhorts his disciples not to be distracted by anything. Now the subject is family ties. Breaking them—for the sake of the Gospel—will be painful.

General observations. Luke utilized Mt 10:26-27 in composing two earlier passages (Lk 11:53-12:3 and Lk 8:16-18). He then made use of Mt 10:28-33 at Lk 12:4-9. Now Luke again turned to Mt 10 exactly where he left it. Lk 12:49-53 is parallel to Mt 10:34-37. Later Luke continued to use the text of Mt 10:26-39, in order, at Mt 10:37-38//Lk 14:26-27, and Mt 10:39//Lk 17:33. Having already utilized Mt 9:35-10:16 at Lk 6:12-19, Lk 9:1-6, and Lk 10:1-12, and having used a conflation of Mt 10:40-11:1 and Mt 18:5 within Lk 9:46-48, all that remained for Luke to utilize of Mt's second great discourse of Jesus, after Lk 14:26-27//Mt 10:37-38, was Mt 10:17-22.

We will see later that Luke substituted Mt 10:17-22 for the parallel material in Mt 24:8-14 when he composed Lk 21:12-19. By that point in his Gospel (Lk 21:19), *Luke had used every verse of Mt's Mission Discourse,* with the possible exception of Mt 10:23. But Mt 10:23 may have provided Luke with the seminal idea of depicting Jesus and his disciples on journeys, including the whole Central Travel Narrative: "When they persecute you in this city, flee into the other. For truly I say to you, you will not have completed the cities of Israel until the Son of Man comes."

Lk 12:49. Luke had Jesus suddenly interject the statement about "coming to cast fire upon the earth" (Lk 12:49; cf. Mt 10:34). This is a veiled allusion to the great fiery trial of the Day of Judgment and Jesus says that he himself can hardly wait until that day—in this context referring to the time of deliverance for all those who have been faithfully waiting.

Lk 12:50-51. Jesus says he has "a baptism to be baptized with," which is an allusion to his impending suffering aqnd death. This he is "enduring" συνέχομαι until it is "finished" or "accomplished" τελεσθῇ. Together both phrases serve as startling but fitting commentaries on Mt 10:34: "*Do not* *think that I came to* cast peace upon the earth, *I did not come to* cast peace, *but* a sword." Mt 10:34 has a formal parallel in Mt 5:17, *"Do not think that I came to* destroy the law or the prophets. *I did not come to* destroy, *but* to fulfill." It could be that Mt 10:34 was linked by Luke with the reference at the end of Mt 24:51 to the master who "cut in pieces" the wicked servant; he διχοτομήσει αὐτόν, presumably with a sword.

Lk 12:52-53. Luke's variation of the number of divisions in the household (Lk 12:52), and the curiously literal, indeed awkward, way in which Luke elaborated the six possible combinations (Lk 12:53), is not in Mt 10:35, when taken alone, as most synopses print the parallels. But all of the elements for Luke's six pairs can be found within Mt 10:35-37. See the needed "son" in Mt 10:37. Of course, for Matthew, these kinds of divisions within the family are grounded in the prophetic text of Mic 7:5-6. Luke's reworking of this material indicates that he either did not recognize Mt's allusions to Micah here or he did not want to preserve them. In either case, these Lukan modifications are more easily explained on the basis of Luke's use of Mt rather than the other way around.

• A reader of the difficult sayings about family divisions in Lk 12:49-53 (cf. Lk 14:26) should also note Jesus' promise of the restoration of family unity, and in *this* age rather than the next, toward the end of the Travel Narrative at Lk 18:28-30.

Section Seven. To the Multitudes: Who is Truly Judged? Lk 12:54–13:30

Having issued warnings about the costs of discipleship, Jesus next teaches about several kinds of judgment. First, although it is certain that the time of God's judgment is at hand and one needs only read the signs of the times to know this, civil magistrates bring on a severity of human judgment that could be easily avoided if members of the human community would only "judge for themselves" and settle their own disputes.

But it is a mistake to see signs of God's judgment in the deaths of innocent people in Jerusalem, whether those who died there were Galilean visitors, as Jesus and his disciples soon will be, or natives to the city. God does not send death as a punishment for sin, although everyone should repent of sin. God is rather as gracious as a farmer who takes extra time to tend to a fruitless tree, lest it be destroyed prior to bearing good fruit. Crippled people do not stand under the judgment of God. God is as concerned about crippled women and men as most humans are about their animals. Like God, people should show mercy whenever it is needed, even if that means "working on the Sabbath." The kingdom of God is not made up of the rich and the powerful. It grows from seemingly humble beginnings: a crippled woman, a grain of mustard, a bit of leaven.

While Jesus continues his journey through towns and villages toward Jerusalem, someone in the crowd asks, in light of the coming judgment, "Will those who are saved be few?" Jesus replies with a metaphor about the need to enter through the narrow door. Although some will knock, thinking they will be granted entrance because they presume to be acquainted with the Lord, the Lord will deny all knowledge of these would-be house guests and leave them outside. All members of God's family, joined by people from every corner of the earth, will dine together in God's Kingdom. All workers of iniquity will be shut out and watch the feast from outside. Some who think they will be first will actually be last while some who now are last will be first.

Source-critical observations.

Lk 12:54-56//Mt 16:2-3. Earlier, Luke made use of Mt 16:1, 6 under the influence of the contextual doublet he was then utilizing at Mt 12:38-42//Lk 11:29-32. At that point in Luke's text, Luke made use of Mt 16:1 and Mt 16:4. To begin Section Seven of the Travel Narrative, Luke returned to this previously utilized context in Mt 16:1-4 and now uses the intervening verses to begin this unit (Mt 16:2-3//Lk 12:54-56).

Lk 12:57-59//Mt 5:21-26//Mt 18:23-35. As we have frequently noted, Luke is contextually parallel to Mt 18:1-19:1 throughout the Travel Narrative, and the Parable of the Unforgiving Servant which ends Mt's chapter on Community Regulations (Mt 18:1-19:1) concludes with the dire note, "And in anger his lord delivered him to the jailers, till he should pay all his debt." And to this, Mt's Jesus adds, "So also my heavenly Father will do to every one of you, if you do not forgive your brother from your heart" (Mt 18:34-35). In a similar manner, Mt's first antithesis within the Sermon on the Mount that deals with murder (Mt 5:21-26) concludes with the words, "Make friends quickly with your accuser, ...lest your accuser hand you over to...be put in prison; truly, I say to you, you will never get out till you have paid the last penny." The similarities of these two different literary contexts in Mt led Luke from his contextual parallel for the Travel Narrative in Mt 18 to the verbal parallel he uses in Mt 5:25-26 for Lk 12:57-59.

Lk 13:1-5. This is nonMatthean tradition that Luke appropriately incorporated within this unit dealing with judgment. These two anecdotes, about innocent Galileans and natives of Jerusalem who died there, also served Luke well in prefiguring coming events in his narrative, after Jesus and his disciples reach the goal of their journey.

Lk 13:6-9. The Parable of the Fig Tree, also from nonMatthean tradition, fits just as well as Lk 13:1-5 does in a Lukan Section dealing with issues of judgment.

Lk 13:10-17. The story of the crippled woman healed on the Sabbath reflects many of the themes of Mt 12:9-14, which Luke already utilized at Lk 6:6-11. But this story also might have come to Luke from nonMatthean tradition. Here, however, it serves as a Lukan transitional pericope. It looks back on events narrated earlier, such as the similar story in Lk 6:6-

11//Mt12:9-14 and looks forward to the next Sabbath healing in Lk 14:1-6 which shares not only some of the same themes, but even some of the same wording with Lk 13:10-17.

Lk 13:18-21//Mt 13:31-33. At Lk 8:4-18, Luke had made earlier use of Mt 13:1-23. The next parable in Mt's Parable Chapter is that of the Weeds and the Tares (Mt 13:24-30). The interpretation of this parable follows in Mt, but not immediately (Mt 13:36-43). Luke omitted this highly eschatological parable and its interpretation from his Gospel. But in between the Parable of the Weeds and the Tares and its interpretation are the twin parables of the Mustard Seed and the Leaven (Mt 13:31-33). It is just these two parables in just this order that Luke selected to conclude this division of Section Seven of his Travel Narrative, just prior to the related question, "Will those who are saved be few?" and its answer (Lk 13:22-30).

Lk 13:22-25//Mt 7:13-14a is Lukan composition, but the words of the important question that helps to inaugurate this unit find their source in Mt 7:13-14.

Lk 13:25-27//Mt 25:1-13//Mt 7:21-23. At Lk 12:35-50, Luke made some earlier use of Mt 25:1-13, conflating those verses in Mt with the immediately preceding verses, Mt 24:42-51. Here at Lk 13:23-27, Luke returns to Mt 25:1-13, this time conflating these verses in Mt with similar teachings to be found in Mt 7:13-14, 21-23. Although Luke made an earlier use of Mt 25:1-13 (cf. Lk 12:35-50) and Mt 7:21-23 (cf. Lk 6:46), indicating the importance of these teachings for Luke, he had not, until now, made any use of Mt 7:13-14. With the use of Mt 7:13-14 and Mt 7:21-23 in sequence at Lk 13:22-27, Luke completed his use of Mt 7. *Luke thus utilized in an orderly way every verse in Mt 7* except for the potentially offensive, "Don't give what is holy to dogs, nor cast your pearls before swine. . ." (Mt 7:6).

Mt 7:1-5	=	Lk 6:37-42
(Mt 7:6)		(never used by Lk)
Mt 7:7-11	=	Lk 11:9-13
Mt 7:12	=	(Lk 6:31)
Mt 7:13-14	=	Lk 13:23-24
Mt 7:15-20//12:33-35	=	Lk 6:43-45
Mt 7:21-23	=	Lk 6:46 and Lk 13:26-27
Mt 7:24-27	=	Lk 6:47-49
Mt 7:28-29	=	Lk 7:1 plus Lk 4:32.

Lk 13:28-29//Mt 8:11-12. Mt 8:11-12 are two verses that Luke omitted from Mt 8:5-13 at Lk 7:2-10. Luke may have chosen to include these previously omitted verses here in anticipation of the Parable of the Rich Man and Lazarus which is coming up at Lk 16:19-31 (cf. Lk 13:28-29//Mt 8:11-12).

Lk 13:30//Mt 19:30//Mt 20:16. This is another saying which points to the great eschatological reversal and is, therefore, appropriate here as a conclusion to this section (cf. Mt 19:30 and Mt 20:16). In Mt, this duplicated logion frames the Parable of the Laborers in the Vineyard which Luke omitted (Mt 20:1-15; cf. Lk 18:30-31).

¶ 80. See the signs! Judgment is near!

(Mt 16:2-3; 5:25-26) **Lk 12:54-59**

Turning to the crowds once more, Jesus berates them for being able to tell the signs of the weather, but they seem unable to know what "this time" is. The time of ultimate judgment is coming. Petty disputes within the community should be settled there rather than taking them to the civil authorities.

General observations. Lk 12:54-56 made use of Mt 16:2-3, verses from Mt 16 that fall between those Luke previously utilized. Luke had previously utilized Mt 16:1 and Mt 16:4 at Lk 11:29-32 in combination with the Matthean doublet and contextual parallel, Mt 12:38-42. Luke then used Mt 16:6 at Lk 12:1. Lk 12:57-59 made use of ending verses (Mt 5:24-26) of the Matthean unit at Mt 5:21-26 and may also reflect at least the ending of the parable in Mt 18:23-35, which Luke did not use. Mt 5:25-26 and Mt 18:34-35 both contain references to persons being "handed over" (παραδίδωμι) to authorities until (ἕως) they should pay up (ἀποδίδωμι) everything owed. Lk 12:57-59 concludes with these same words and ideas.

Lk 12:54-56. Mt's signs of the weather in Mt 16:2-3 have been altered by Luke. Whereas Mt 16:2-3 has the familiar "red sky at night, sailor's delight; red sky in the morning, sailors take warning," Luke has altered the weather completely (Lk 12:54-56). He first mentioned the west wind which brings rain (only true in Palestine), and the south wind which brings drought and "burning heat"—true of Palestine and the entire northern Mediterranean coast. Luke's change of Mt's "east and west" to "south and west" may anticipate the expansion of "east and west" in Mt 8:11-12 to "north, south, east, and west" at Lk 13:28-29.

Lk 12:56, "Why don't you know how to interpret *this time?*" (cf. Mt 16:3 "*signs* of the times"?) is a strange Lukan modification since the motif of *signs* does appear within earlier Lukan contexts (cf. Lk 11:16, 29-30). Are these earlier references to "signs" simply accidental preservations by Luke of a motif that Matthew cared about, but Luke really did not?

Lk 12:57-59//Mt 5:21-26. Mt 5:(21)25-26 has been attached to Mt 16:2-3 on the principle of a common theme of judgment. The similarity of the conclusion to the parable in Mt 18:23-35 and the conclusion at Mt 5:21-26 (Mt 18:34-35; cf. Mt 5:26), probably accounts for the omission of Mt 18:23-35 from the text of Luke. This is an important explanation to note for our general thesis, that *the whole of Lk 9:51-19:27* is Luke's sequential parallel to Mt 18:1-19:15, Mt's Discourse on Community Regulations. That is, it may have been the conclusion of Mt 18:23-35, the contextual parallel to

Luke's Travel Narrative, that took Luke back to his verbal parallel at Mt 5:21-26.

¶ 81. But death in Jerusalem need not be God's judgment for sin! Lk 13:1-9

Jesus' admonitions prompt a question from the crowd. "What about those Galilean people who were killed by Pilate while they were sacrificing to God in the Temple in Jerusalem? Or the natives of Jerusalem who died when that tower fell on them? Were they killed because they were more sinful than others?" Jesus answers in the negative, but adds that everyone needs to repent. And people who do repent, like the fig tree that eventually bears good fruit when properly cultivated, will not be faced with the wrath of God.

General observations. Lk 13:1-9 is composed entirely of nonMatthean tradition. In Lk 13:1-5, Luke first provided two examples, one about Galilean visitors to Jerusalem who came to worship in the temple and one about innocent natives of Jerusalem. All of these righteous and innocent people died in Jerusalem. But Jesus teaches that none of these deaths in Jerusalem was a consequence of sin, even though everyone does need to repent of sin. To these two examples of innocent death in Jerusalem, Luke added a parable about a fig tree which, until it was properly cultivated, also faced imminent destruction.

Lk 13:1-5. Luke has made clear throughout his Travel Narrative that Jesus is journeying toward Jerusalem. Foreshadowing allusions to Jesus' suffering and death are common in Lk. Luke included these two exemplary stories here to prepare his readers for Jesus' own death in Jerusalem (Lk 19:28ff.) as a righteous (Lk 23:47; Acts 3:14; 7:52; 22:14) Galilean visitor. Like these others' deaths, Luke's text affirms that Jesus' own death in Jerusalem should not be construed as a sign of God's judgment for sin. Jesus dies a righteous man (Lk 23:47). Compare Paul's apparent struggle with some who would interpret Jesus' death as God's curse in Gal 3 and contrast Mt 27:54 where Jesus' death elicits the affirmation from the Centurion, not that Jesus was "righteous," but rather that Jesus was "Son of God" (an affirmation that Luke also makes, but elsewhere). An explicit threat to Jesus' life combined with the affirmation that prophets die in Jerusalem will soon be made at Lk 13:31-35.

• The attachment of a narrative account to a parable (Lk 13:5-6f.) appears elsewhere in Lk where Luke seems to be utilizing nonMatthean tradition.

• This unit is loosely united to the next one, in part, on the basis of the *Stichwort*, "eighteen" (Lk 13:4, 11, 16). But the theme of true judgment also continues.

¶ 82. Even an eighteen-year crippling condition is not God's ultimate judgment! God's Kingdom is all-inclusive.

(Mt 12:9-14; 13:31-33) **Lk. 13:10-21** (cf. Lk 6:6-11; 14:5)

To illustrate that people are not crippled by God as a punishment for sin and that people, like the fig tree, can be set straight with care, Luke tells of an occasion when Jesus healed a bent and crippled woman on the Sabbath. This Sabbath healing angered the president of the synagogue, who attacked Jesus on a technicality, accusing him of "working" on the Sabbath. Jesus asks him, "You loose your cattle and lead them to water every Sabbath; how much better to loose this woman from Satan's eighteen-year hold on her on the Sabbath?" The people rejoiced to see Jesus put his adversaries to shame. Their joyous reaction prompts Jesus to tell two parables assuring them that such small beginnings as his healing this woman indeed herald the advent of God's Kingdom.

General observations. Luke may have drawn the story of the Healing of the Crippled Woman (Lk 13:10-17) from nonMatthean tradition, although there are clear echoes of Mt 12:9-13//Lk 6:6-11. Compare Lk 14:1-6 for yet another story of a Sabbath healing by Jesus that has no parallel in Mt, unless it is Mt 12:9-13. This is probably a case where Luke has other tradition that is similar to Mt 12:9-13 and preferred to use this nonMatthean tradition. However, there are other places in Lk where the same rationale for healing on the Sabbath is used (compare especially Lk 13:15 with Lk 14:5; cf. Lk 6:6-11), so the unit might be a Lukan composition. If Luke was following a source, whatever that might have been, there are also significant Lukan stylistic and compositional elements within this story. For instance, Lk 13:10, "teaching on the Sabbath in a synagogue," is also found in Lk 4:15-16 (cf. Collison 225).

• The two simile parables (Lk 13:18-21) are taken from Mt 13:31-33. Luke used Mt 13:1-23, but omitted Mt 13:16-17, at Lk 8:4-15. Luke then used these previously omitted verses, Mt 13:16-17, at Lk 10:23-24 to introduce the Parable of the Good Samaritan (Lk 10:25-37) and the story of Mary and Martha (Lk 10:38-42). Having chosen to omit both the Parable of the Wheat and the Weeds (Mt 13:24-30) and its interpretation (Mt 13:36-43) from his Gospel altogether, Luke then chose the twin parables of the Mustard Seed and the Leaven that intervene (Mt 13:31-33) for use here and in the same order in which they appear in Mt (Mt 13:31-32//Lk 13:18-19; Mt 13:33//Lk 13:20-21). Luke adopted nothing else from this *third* Matthean discourse (Mt 13:34-53) elsewhere in his Gospel (Lk 13:22-24:52).

Lk 13:15. ὁ κύριος is a favorite Lukan term (cf. Goulder 2:570, 805). Ironically, in spite of the "negative press" given to the Pharisees in Luke's Gospel, the reasoning adopted by Jesus here in Lk 13:15 (and elsewhere at Lk 6:6-11 and 14:5) is precisely a Pharisaic, that is, a Hillelite, argument to support the position that "good" should be done on the Sabbath.

Lk 13:16-17. The healing of the woman "on the Sabbath" is an epiphany of sorts, conveying overtones of being an eschatological event. Satan's kingdom was being broken.

Lk 13:17. The phrase "all the people rejoiced at all the glorious things done by him" also carries overtones of the idea, "today, the Kingdom of God has come near." As such, it provides the basis for the οὖν at Lk 13:18 ἔλεγεν οὖν "*therefore* Jesus used to say" or "*this is why* Jesus would say" (the verb is Imperfect = iterative). For this reason, we regard these two parts as one unit, especially as there is no change of scene.

Lk 13:18-21. These vignettes introduce the theme of the "Kingdom of God" (cf. Lk 13:28-29). They have a common point of reference: the small, non-grandiose nature of the beginnings of the Kingdom of Heaven. Unpretentious people, like small things around the house (a tiny seed, leaven quietly permeating a large mound of dough), are what the chosen of God are like. Note also Luke's reference to "little flock" (Lk 12:32). These two parables also anticipate the question that inaugurates the next pericope in Lk 13:23, "Lord, will those who are saved be few?" Jesus will answer in the affirmative (Lk 13:24).

¶ 83. Will those saved be few?

(Mt 25:1-13; 7:13-14, 21-23; 8:11-12; 19:30//20:16) **Lk 13:22-30**

Having taught the crowds about various kinds of judgment, Jesus moves on "through towns and villages" continuing to teach them. In light of the coming judgment, someone asks, "Will those who are saved be few?" Jesus' answer becomes a dark warning to all of the power structure of Israel that its vaunted self-esteem is misplaced, that many "from east and west and north and south will sit at table in the Kingdom of God" while the arrogant sons of Abraham will be cast out.

***General observations*.** Lk 13:22 continues the theme of traveling and preaching through cities and villages on the "way toward Jerusalem." This vignette is a speech of Jesus composed of elements from Mt 7:13-14, 21-23//Lk 13:24-27; Mt 8:11-12//Lk 13:28-29 and Mt 19:30//Mt 20:16//Lk 13:30.

Lk 13:22-23a is Lukan composition based upon Mt 7:13-14.

Lk 13:23-27. At Lk 13:23-27, Luke returned to Mt 25:1-13 (cf. Lk 12:35-50), this time conflating these verses in Mt with similar teachings to be found in Mt 7:13-14, 21-23. For instance, "through the <u>narrow</u> gate" in Mt 7:13 and "the closed <u>door</u>" in Mt 25:10 became "through the <u>narrow door</u>" in Lk 13:24, even though "the closed door" was also retained from Mt 25:10 in Lk 13:25. Mt 7:13-14, 21-23 and Mt 25:1-13 are related by common wording and several common themes, e.g., "the kingdom of the heavens" (Mt 25:1//Mt 7:21), the cry of "Lord, Lord" from those who would enter (Mt 7:21; cf. Mt 25:11), the denial of entrance with words "I don't know you" (Mt 25:12; cf. Mt 7:23), the separation of two groups of people who are allowed to enter from those who are not (Mt 7 "many" and "few"; Mt 25, "wise" and "foolish"), and the importance of actions rather than intentions

Lk 13:26. The reference to teaching in streets in Lk 13:26b was set up by the Lukan introduction (Lk 13:22; cf. Lk 12:3). The phrase in Lk 13:26 contains the first half of an implied polar comparison: we *descendants of Abraham* "ate and drank with you and you taught in our streets"—and now you turn *us* away? To which Jesus replies: "Yes, and in the Age to Come you will see the great prophets of old at the Banquet of the Messiah and people from other nations will be in your places!" (Lk 13:28-29//Mt 8:11-12; cf. Lk 16:19-31).

Lk 13:28. The phraseology ἐκεῖ ἔσται ὁ κλαυθμὸς καὶ ὁ βρυγμὸς τῶν ὀδόντων, is characteristic of the text of Matthew (cf. Tevis, Display 206). This is the only appearance of this Matthean phrase in Luke. Its occurrence in a parallel literary context with Matthew is strong evidence that Luke used the canonical Gospel of Matthew, not a source such as "Q."

Lk 13:29. Luke's missionary concern is revealed by his addition of "north and south" (Lk 13:29) to "east and west" in Mt. 8:11. Note Luke's other change of Mt's "east and west" at Mt 16:2-3 to "south and west" at Lk 12:54-56, perhaps in preparation for these changes at Lk 13:29.

Lk 13:30. This is another "ending" saying pointing to the great eschatological reversal and hence appropriate here (cf. Mt 19:30 and Mt 20:16). The repeated logion of Mt 19:30 = Mt 20:16 could have been a bit of wisdom to which Luke had independent access. It conforms to Luke's theory of "eschatological reversal." However, within the context of Mt this doubly attested logion frames the Parable of the Vineyard, which Luke will omit later (cf. Lk 18:30-31). Given the repeated language of Mt 19:30 and Mt 20:16, Luke's omission of the parable at Lk 18:30-31 might have been a scribal error, but we doubt it. There is some tension between the teaching of Mt 20:1-15 which Luke omitted and that of Mt 7:24-29 which Luke utilized (Lk 6:46-7:1). Luke probably omitted Mt 20:1-15 in favor of the parable material he took from nonMatthean tradition. Luke seems to have had access to a number of nonMatthean parables.

¶ 84. An interweaving transitional pericope

(Mt 23:37-39) **Lk 13:31-35**

Suddenly Jesus is warned by some Pharisees that agents of Herod are seeking to kill him. Jesus exits, exclaiming that he must continue his course to Jerusalem; that is where prophets should die, not in Galilee.

General observations. Following a scene change (Lk 13:31a), word comes that Jesus' life is threatened (Lk 13:31-32). Jesus affirms the necessity for prophets to die in Jerusalem (Lk 13:33). This introduces Jesus' lament over Jerusalem (Lk 13:34-35) which Luke has drawn from Mt 23:37-39. The use of Mt 23:37-39 concludes Luke's orderly use of Mt 23. Luke already used the content of Mt 23:1-36 in composing Lk 11:37-53 (Mt 23:1//Lk 11:37 and Lk 11:53; Mt 23:36//Lk 11:51).

• The inevitability of Jesus' violent death stemming from his prophetic ministry is a major theme that is incorporated into the Lukan Travel Narrative. The journey to Jerusalem stands under divine guidance and necessity and will culminate in Jesus' death, burial, and vindication (cf. Lk 9:21-27, 43b-45, 51-56; 13:33-35; 17:24-25 and 18:31-33).[4] This understanding of the final journey is part of the larger theme in Luke-Acts that sees the whole event of the appearance of Jesus and the founding of the Church as the fulfilment of the divine will, being the fulfillment of the hope of the prophets.[5]

Lk 13:31-33. Luke continued with a reference to a death-threat from Herod. The purpose of this tangential interruption may have been to provide an introduction to the powerful "Lament over Jerusalem," with its reference to "killing the prophets...sent to you," which was anticipated in Lk 13:28 "all the prophets." In any case, Lk 13:31-33 has no parallel to anything in Mt. These verses cast the Pharisees in a somewhat favorable light, in that they warn Jesus to flee before Herod catches him.

Lk 13:34-35. The "Lament over Jerusalem" echoes other references to Jerusalem (Lk 13:4 and esp. Lk 13:33). The passage itself comes from Mt's description of Jesus' entry into Jerusalem (Mt 23:37-39), which Luke will not use in his later parallel context (cf. Lk 20:47-21:1). Luke has rather moved this prophecy to this earlier point in the Lukan story (Lk 13:35//Mt 23:39), so that the prophecy will be fulfilled within the Lukan narrative (Lk 19:38). If this prophecy is fulfilled at all, it must be fulfilled beyond the narrative in Mt. We remember here that Luke has already used Mt 23:1-36 within Lk 11:37-52. So Luke was maintaining Mt's order here (Lk 13:34-35//Mt 23:37-39) with his use of the balance of Mt 23.

Section Eight. To a Dinner Audience: The Messiah's Banquet Instructions. Lk 14:1–35

After the warning that Herod Antipas was seeking to kill him, Jesus unexpectedly finds himself invited to the home of a ruler of the Pharisees. The occasion immediately turns into a classic Hellenistic question-and-answer dinner discussion about the Messianic banquet. Jesus goes on to teach about true discipleship.

---

[4] See John T. Squires, *The Plan of God in Luke-Acts,* SNTSMS #76 (Cambridge: Cambridge University Press, 1993) 168-170.

[5] Cf. Paul Schubert, "The Final Cycle of Speeches in the Book of Acts," *JBL* 87 (1968) 2-3.

Source-critical observations. Except for Luke's continuing verse by verse use of Mt 10 at Lk 14:26-27//Mt 10:37-38, and the addition of the saying on Salt from Mt 5:13 to conclude Section Eight at Lk 14:34-35, the entirety of Section Eight of Luke's Travel Narrative was skillfully composed from material drawn from nonMatthean tradition. See detailed notes below. We have already explained above Luke's use of the entirety of Mt 9:35-11:1 throughout his Gospel. Of Luke's use of Mt 5:13, we note here that it is the one verse within Mt 5:3-16 that Luke had not yet used (for Mt 5:3-12 cf. Lk 6:20-26, for Mt 5:14-16 cf. Lk 8:16-18 and Lk 11:33-36). Luke's use of the Matthean verses that surround Mt 5:13 has been discussed at the appropriate Lukan contexts above.

¶ 85. Which is more important, mercy or ritual correctness? Lk 14:1-6

In a context of suspicion, a ruler of the Pharisees invites Jesus to dine with him on the Sabbath. The Pharisee has also invited a man who is very sick. Luke says, "And they watched to see what he would do." Jesus promptly healed the man and then posed this question to his hostile audience: "You do not hesitate to take care of your own emergencies, Sabbath or not. Why shouldn't God take care of those who need Him, whether it happens on the Sabbath or not?" The Pharisees could not think of anything to say in reply because their minds were set on obeying a legal demand (no work on the Sabbath) rather than extending God's mercy to those who needed it, when they needed it. Compare "You shall be merciful as your Father is merciful" (Lk 6:36).

General observations. Luke moved from a largely narrative to a more didactic segment of his story with an opening dramatic example of God's mercy overriding a legal demand. This story looks back to the story in Lk 13:10-17, the Healing of the Crippled Woman on the Sabbath, and forward to the several "dining" scenes yet to come. It is a perfect example of Luke's skill in interweaving segments of his narrative. Lk 13:10-17 and Lk 14:1-6 are both healings (ἐθεράπευσεν ὁ Ἰησοῦς, Lk 13:14; ἰάσατο αὐτὸν, Lk 14:4) on Sabbaths (Lk 13:14; 14:1). Both stories involve men in positions of high authority (ἀρχισυνάγωγος, Lk 13:14; τις ἀρχων [τῶν] Φαρισαίων, Lk 14:1). In both stories Jesus encounters opposition (the ἀρχισυνάγωγος in Lk 13:14; the νομικοὶ καὶ Φαρισαίοι in Lk 14:3). Lk 13:15 contains a reference to an "ox or . . . ass" and Lk 14:5 refers to a "son or an ox" falling into a well. The somewhat odd juxtaposition of "son" with "ox" apparently caused copyists problems as the history of the text reveals. The reading adopted by UBS^4 is supported, among others, by $\mathfrak{P}^{45}$ $\mathfrak{P}^{75}$ A B W and $sy^{(p)}$ sa. The alternative reading "ass or ox" is an assimilation to Lk 13:15, with some mss giving all three; see Metzger 1994:138f. The former story contains the phrase, καὶ ἰδοὺ γυνή (Lk 13:11), while this one has καὶ ἰδοὺ ἄνθρωπός τις (Lk 14:2).

Finally, the periphrastic imperfect is used at the beginning of both stories (Lk 13:10; 14:2). These similarities are noteworthy and suggest that Luke either utilized nonMatthean source material where these parallels were already present, or edited and/or composed one (or both) stories to include these similarities.

Lk 14:1-6. The material brought together in this banquet scene (Lk 14:1-24) is gracefully and forcefully deployed in typical Hellenistic fashion with the guest subjected to numerous questions and challenges, all of which he skillfully rebuts. The opening healing story (Lk 14:1-6) contains Lukan characteristics indicating that Luke touched up this account to prepare for the major dialogue with its focus on appropriate responses to the mercy of God. For example, Luke has added νομικός; used the stock phrase Καὶ ἐγένετο ἐν τῷ ἐλθεῖν αὐτὸν, Lk 14:1 (Collison 229; Goulder 2:587); καὶ αὐτοί, Lk 14:1 (Goulder 2:801); νομικός, Lk 14:3 (Collison 174-175; Goulder 2:807), and ἐπιλαμβάνομαι, Lk 14:4 (Collison 49; Goulder 2:587).

¶ 86. The arrogant exclusiveness of lawyers and Pharisees

(Mt 23:6, 12) **Lk 14:7-14**

Having firmly placed acts of mercy as of primary importance, Luke next portrays Jesus giving two further teachings, first to his fellow guests and then to his host. The subtext of both is humility and deference, or rather, their opposites: arrogance and exclusiveness. "You who think you are the elite in the community, why do you choose the most prestigious seats when invited to someone's party? Choose rather the lowest seat so that you will be truly honored when asked to move up to a higher one!" Turning to his host, Jesus goes on, "And you, why do you always invite only your friends, brothers, relatives, or rich neighbors who can reciprocate? You should be sharing your bounty with the poor, the homeless, the lame and the blind! If you do, you will be amply blessed with reciprocation at the resurrection of the righteous!"

General observations. Lk 14:7-14 is from nonMatthean material, although there are echoes of Mt 23:6, 12.

• The references to the πτωχούς, ἀναπήρους, χωλούς, and τυφλούς, echo key categories in Jesus' inaugural sermon (Lk 4:18, poor, blind, and captives; cf. also Lk 7:22, blind, lame, lepers, deaf, dead, poor; cf. Mt 15:29-31). Although Luke called these two didactic sayings a "parable," there is nothing metaphorical or parabolic in them, being prudential admonitions similar to what can be found in Proverbs or Sirach. Be that as it may, this detail does throw light on Luke's understanding of "parable": it taught a moral lesson.

Lk 14:7-14. The reference to the "poor, maimed, etc." in Lk 14:13 with its mention of the "resurrection of the just" is a Lukan transition to pave the way for the impressive story of the Eschatological Banquet (Lk 14:15-33).

• The two sayings about attending feasts (Lk 14:8-11) and giving feasts (Lk 14:12-14)—in the Christian community, to be sure!—have been artistically crafted to act as the preface to a third "feast" story (Lk 14:15-33). As the following synopsis indicates, the two passages are very similar.

Synopsis of Lk 14:7-11//14:12-14

Illustrating their structural and verbal similarities.

Lk 14:7-11	Lk 14:12-14
7 Ἔλεγεν δὲ	12 Ἔλεγεν δὲ καὶ
πρὸς τοὺς κεκλημένους	τῷ κεκληκότι
παραβολήν,	αὐτόν,
ἐπέχων πῶς	
τὰς πρωτοκλισίας ἐξελέγοντο,	
λέγων πρὸς αὐτούς,	
8 Οταν κληθῇς	Ὅταν ποιῇς
ὑπό τινος	
εἰς γάμους,	ἄριστον ἢ δεῖπνον,
μὴ κατακλιθῇς	μὴ φώνει
εἰς τὴν πρωτοκλισίαν,	τοὺς φίλους σου
	μηδὲ τοὺς ἀδελφούς σου
	μηδὲ τοὺς συγγενεῖς σου
	μηδὲ γείτονας πλουσίους,
μήποτε ἐντιμότερός σου	μήποτε
ᾖ κεκλημένος ὑπ' αὐτοῦ,	
9 καὶ ἐλθὼν	καὶ
ὁ σὲ καὶ αὐτὸν καλέσας	αὐτοὶ
ἐρεῖ σοι,	ἀντικαλέσωσίν σε
Δὸς τούτῳ τόπον,	
καὶ τότε ἄρξῃ	καὶ γένηται
μετὰ αἰσχύνης	
τὸν ἔσχατον τόπον κατέχειν.	ἀνταπόδομά σοι.
10 ἀλλ' ὅταν	13 ἀλλ' ὅταν
	δοχὴν
κληθῇς	ποιῇς,
ἀνάπεσε	κάλει
εἰς τὸν ἔσχατον τόπον,	πτωχούς,
ἵνα ὅταν ἔλθῃ	ἀναπείρους,
ὁ κεκληκώς σε	χωλούς,
ἐρεῖ σοι,	τυφλούς·
Φίλε,	
προσανάβηθι ἀνώτερον·	
τότε ἔσται σοι δόξα	14 καὶ μακάριος ἔσῃ,
ἐνώπιον πάντων	ὅτι οὐκ ἔχουσιν
τῶν συνανακειμένων σοι.	ἀνταποδοῦναί σοι,
11 ὅτι	
πᾶς ὁ ὑψῶν ἑαυτὸν	
ταπεινωθήσεται,	ἀνταποδοθήσεται γάρ σοι
καὶ ὁ ταπεινῶν ἑαυτὸν	ἐν τῇ ἀναστάσει τῶν δικαίων.
ὑψωθήσεται.	

• If we subtract Lk 14:11 from the context on the grounds that it is a free-floating logion that Luke will use again to conclude the Parable of the Pharisee and the Publican (Lk 18:14; cf. Mt 23:12; also Mt 18:4 and 20:26-27), we reach the conclusion that these two teachings, together with the Eschatological Banquet, were already a unit, prior to Luke's use of them, in his nonMatthean tradition. Luke appears to have picked up this whole complex literary unit and inserted it at this point in the Lukan narrative. Evidence of some characteristic Lukan terminology is found, however, in the introductions of the two units: Ἔλεγεν δέ + perfect participle (Lk 14:7 and Lk 14:12; cf. Collison 56; Goulder 2:587). See also καὶ αὐτοί, Lk 14:12 (cf. Collison 195).

¶ 87. The eschatological banquet

(Mt 22:1-10) **Lk 14:15-24**

Suddenly, a guest exclaims, "Blessed is the man—undoubtedly someone like us!—who will eat bread in the Kingdom of God!" Jesus answers by telling a seemingly peculiar story of a man who gave a great banquet but all of his rich and busy guests refused to come on one pretext or another. Furious, the man ordered his servant to fill his house with other people, the "poor, maimed, blind and lame." Jesus' parabolic response to the dinner guests implies that God has invited people like these Pharisees to his table, but they are always too busy to come to it; not so, the poor and outcast!

General observations. The structure of the three units in this Section: two shorter parallel units (Lk 14:7-11 and Lk 14:12-14) followed by a single longer one (Lk 14:15-24) is identical to the structure of Lk 15 (Lk 15:3-7, Lk 15:8-10, and Lk 15:11-32). This similarity in structure may provide some evidence of a nonMatthean parable source. It has long been asked what relationship might obtain between this story and the similar Parable of the Marriage Feast in Mt 22:1-10. There is no evidence of Matthean linguistic characteristics present in this (parallel?) Lukan account, which one would expect if Luke were relying upon Mt at this point. Our conclusion is that Luke did not obtain his feast-story from the similar one in Mt 22, but used another source, where it was already combined with the two previous units. Finally, it is worthy of note that the Gospel of Thomas (64) contains a similar parable. The similarity of this Lukan parable with the one in the Gospel of Thomas may suggest that the author of the Gospel of Thomas was familiar with the same story to which Luke had access, or that the author of the Gospel of Thomas was literarily dependent on Lk for this story. We find no merit in the claim made by some that the direction of literary dependence between Lk and Thomas might run in the opposite direction.

Lk 14:15-24. The theme of eating a meal links this Parable of the Great Banquet (Lk 14:15-24) with the preceding and transitional healing narrative (Lk 14:1-6) and the two previous "parables" of this section (Lk 14:7-11 and Lk 14:12-14). The use of a beatitude links the Great Banquet with the preceding parable (Lk 14:14, 15).

• This story concludes the first division (Lk 14:1-24) of this Section (Lk 14:1-35). It contains four admonitions for the Christian lifestyle in response to God's great demonstrations of mercy: first, one should always seek to be merciful even if it must take precedence over the legal demand (Lk 14:1-6). Second, one should not become haughty, but be humble and unassuming in one's actions (Lk 14:7-11). Third, the wealthy should not always associate with their social peers but be inclusive in their fellowship, being hospitable especially to the poor, the maimed, the lame, and the blind (Lk 14:12-14). Finally, God blesses those who respond instantly and wholeheartedly to his offer of salvation (Lk 14:15-24).

• There are a few signs of Lukan characteristic phraseology within this unit: ἕτερος, Lk 14:19, 20 (Collison 38; Goulder 2:593-594); ἀπαγγέλλω, Lk 14:21 (Collison 184); ἀνήρ, Lk 14:24 (Collison 167; Goulder 2:594); and possibly ἡ βασιλεία τοῦ θεοῦ, Lk 14:15 (Collison 170). This indicates that Luke has glossed his nonMatthean source.

¶ 88. Renounce everything and follow me!

(Mt 10:37-38; 5:13) **Lk 14:25-35**

Abruptly changing audiences, Luke pursues similar themes to those which Jesus had just been teaching his Pharisaic interlocutors. Now it is to the "great multitudes" who were following him, no doubt hoping that they too would be included in the Kingdom of God. Jesus warns them: do not allow any distractions to hinder you from responding to God's call! A true disciple will "hate" his own family—even his own life—in order to be with Jesus. He will be called to "bear his own cross" (cf. Lk 9:23-27) like Jesus did. The decision to be a disciple of Jesus is no light matter; it requires as much careful forethought as someone planning to build a building or wage a war. Any less resolute a commitment is like salt that has lost the quality by which its whole value is determined.

General observations. Following a Lukan introduction (Lk 14:25), Luke returned to Mt 10:37-38 for the initial teachings on divisions within the family. It is no surprise that this theme, last seen at Lk 12:49-53, reappears here. A consecutive, even overlapping, series of verses in Mt 10 has been utilized to compose these different Lukan passages (see Lk 12:52-53//Mt 10:34-37 and Lk 14:25-33//Mt 10:37-38). In fact, Luke utilized Mt 10:26-39 verse for verse throughout his Travel Narrative in four successive Lukan literary contexts.

Mt 10:26-33	=	Lk 11:53-12:3
Mt 10:34-37	=	Lk 12:49-53
Mt 10:37-38	=	Lk 14:25-27
Mt 10:39	=	Lk 17:33

See further the related General Observations for Lk 11:53-12:3 and especially for Lk 12:49-53.

• When Luke made use of the Beatitudes in Mt 5:3-12 to compose his parallel Beatitudes and Woes at Lk 6:20-26, he did not attach the saying on salt (Mt 5:13) to them. But Luke had by now utilized the sayings on light from Mt 5:14-16 twice (cf. Lk 8:16-18 and Lk 11:33-36). See the related General Observations for Lk 8:16-18 and Lk 11:33-36. At this point, Luke picked up the single verse he had not yet used (Mt 5:13) between Mt's Beatitudes (Mt 5:3-12) and the sayings on Light (Mt 5:14-16) and used it at Lk 14:34-35 as a conclusion for his Section on The Messiah's Banquet Instructions (Lk 14:1-34). A dinner condiment that has lost its savor is only worthy to be thrown away.

• This is also possibly the first link between the order of Luke's Travel Narrative and Mt 18 since Lk 9:46-48//Mt 18:1-2, 4-5. The appearance of the Parable of the Lost Sheep that follows immediately at Lk 15:3-7 is parallel to Mt 18:10-14. Between Mt 18:4 and Mt 18:10, there are sayings concerned with community regulation and discipleship. Mt 18:8 includes the term "lame" (χωλός) with reference to entering the Kingdom of Heaven, and the lame is one of the four outcast groups (Lk 14:21 and 14:13) to be included among those who will attend the Great Banquet (Lk 14:15-24). Lk 14:34-35 mentions the salt that has become worthless and will be "cast out" ἔξω βάλλουσιν αὐτό. The verses in Mt 18:8-9 say that it is better to cut off the hand or pluck out the eye and "cast it from you" καὶ βάλε ἀπὸ σοῦ, entering the Kingdom of Heaven "lame" or maimed than to be "cast" into the hell of fire βληθῆναι εἰς τὴν γέενναν τοῦ πυρός, Mt 18:9 (note the variant phrase in Mt 18:8, εἰς τὸ πῦρ αἰώνιον). Thus, Luke's material in 14:26-35 contains several echoes of the intervening verses in Mt 18:6-9. Indeed, unless Mt 18:8-9 is echoed here, Luke has not made any use of those verses from Mt 18 nor of the doublet to Mt 18:8-9 at Mt 5:29-30. Be that as it may, all of the material in this part of Lk pertains to true discipleship, a major theme in Mt's chapter on Community Regulations.

Lk 14:25-27. The introduction to this Section (Lk 14:25) is Lukan. But the recurrent theme οὐ δύναται εἶναί μου μαθητής in 14:26, 27 and 33 relates the structure of Lk 14:25-35 to the structure of Mt 10:37-38 (οὐκ ἔστιν μου ἄξιος, Mt 10:37bis and 10:38; cf. also ἄξιος/α in Mt 10:11, 13bis and cf. Mt 10:24-25 for related concerns).

• There are indeed clear parallels between Lk 14:26-27 and Mt 10:37-38, but the differences (Mt's "worthy of me" has become Luke's "be my disciple," and Mt's "love. . . more than me" has become Luke's "hate") are Lukan clarifications of Mt.

Lk 14:28-32. As the synopsis on the next page indicates, these two similes in Lk 14:28-32 have a rigid parallel structure.

Synopsis of Lk 14:28–30//14:31-32

Illustrating their rigid parallel structure.

Lk 14:28-30	Lk 14:31-32
	31 ἢ
28 τίς γὰρ ἐξ ὑμῶν	τίς βασιλεὺς
θέλων πύργον	πορευόμενος ἑτέρῳ βασιλεῖ
οἰκοδομῆσαι	συμβαλεῖν εἰς πόλεμον
οὐχὶ πρῶτον καθίσας	οὐχὶ καθίσας πρῶτον
ψηφίζει τὴν δαπάνην,	βουλεύσεται
εἰ ἔχει	εἰ δυνατός ἐστιν
	ἐν δέκα χιλιάσιν
	ὑπαντῆσαι τῷ
	μετὰ εἴκοσι χιλιάδων
εἰς ἀπαρτισμόν;	ἐρχομένῳ ἐπ' αὐτόν;
29 ἵνα μήποτε	**32** εἰ δὲ μή γε,
θέντος αὐτοῦ θεμέλιον	ἔτι αὐτοῦ πόρρω ὄντος
καὶ μὴ ἰσχύοντος ἐκτελέσαι	
πάντες οἱ θεωροῦντες	πρεσβείαν ἀποστείλας
ἄρξωνται αὐτῷ ἐμπαίζειν	
30 λέγοντες ὅτι	
Οὗτος ὁ ἄνθρωπος	
ἤρξατο οἰκοδομεῖν	
καὶ οὐκ ἴσχυσεν ἐκτελέσαι.	ἐρωτᾷ τὰ πρὸς εἰρήνην.

Common structural features of Lk 14:28-30 and Lk 14:31-32 include the following: τίς; present participle (θέλων/πορευόμενος); aorist active infinitive (οἰκοδομῆσαι/συμβαλεῖν); οὐχί; πρῶτον; καθίσας; third singular indicative (ψηφίζει/βουλεύσεται); εἰ; third singular present active indicative (ἔχει/ἐστιν); preposition plus accusative object ending a question (εἰς ἀπαρτισμόν;/ἐπ' αὐτόν;); μήποτε/μή; genitive absolute construction that combines a masculine singular active participle with αὐτός (θέντος αὐτοῦ/αὐτοῦ...ὄντος); and participle (λέγοντες/ἀποστείλας).

Lk 14:34-35. These verses are similar to Mt 5:13; but the meaning is brought out more explicitly by the phrase "men throw it away" (Lk 14:35a). Luke's addition here shows the influence of Mt 18:8-9, even as the reference to "fire" in Luke's modification of Mt 10:34 did at Lk 12:49.

• The reason for the inclusion of the logion on salt in this context is to provide a transition to Lk 15:2a. Israel's leadership—who were supposedly the "salt" of the nation—had become worthless.

• The saying about hearing (Lk 14:35b) which closes the section links this scene with the opening words in Lk 15:1 where ἀκούειν appears again: the tax collectors and sinners were "all" eagerly drawing near to "hear" Jesus.

• Further linguistic evidence of Luke's redactional activity in this pericope includes θέντος αὐτοῦ, Lk 14:29 (Collison 77-78); ἕτερος, Lk 14:31 (Collison

184; Goulder 2:602); εἰ δὲ μή γε, Lk 14:32 (Collison 102; Goulder 2:602); and δὲ καί, Lk 14:34 (Collison 103; Goulder 2:602).

Section Nine. To Scribes and Pharisees: God Seeks and Saves the Lost. Lk 15:1–32

In response to the grumbling of scribes and Pharisees that Jesus was eating with tax collectors and sinners, Jesus now tells three parables, each of which affirms that God seeks and saves the lost and that the appropriate response to God's salvation of the lost is one of rejoicing, not grumbling.

Source-critical observations. This section of Luke's Gospel is composed of three parables, all about seeking and saving the lost. With the possible exception of Luke's use of the Parable of the Lost Sheep from Mt 18:10-14, the entirety of Section Nine is artfully constructed from nonMatthean tradition.

¶ 89. Israel's lost souls

(Mt 9:10-13) **Lk 15:1-3** (cf. Lk 5:29-32)

In a dramatic change of scene, Luke introduces "all of the tax collectors and sinners" who were eagerly "drawing near to hear" Jesus. Are the "Pharisees and scribes" pleased? On the contrary; they "grumble" that Jesus is defiling himself by associating with such people.

General observations. Lk 15:1-3 echoes Mt 9:10-11. Luke has composed this introduction either reusing Mt 9:10-13 or nonMatthean tradition where Jesus welcomes sinners over the protestations of the religious establishment. Luke previously used Mt 9:1-17 at Lk 5:17-39 in composing the first half of his unit of four controversy stories surrounding the call of Levi (Lk 5:17-6:11//Mt 9:1-17 and Mt 12:1-14; cf. the General Observations for Lk 5:17-26, 27-39; 6:1-5 and 6:6-11). Lk 15:1-3//Mt 9:10-13 sets the theme for a series of three teachings to and against the Pharisees. Their "grumbling" presents the literary occasion for three parables of Jesus illustrating joy—not grumbling!—at the recovery of what has been lost (Lk 15:1-32).

Lk 15:1-3. The Lukan additions in both Lk 5:30 and Lk 15:1-3 include: a form of γογγύζω (cf. Lk 19:7; Collison 46) and a reference to scribes. There is some evidence of Lukan terminology in Lk 15:1-3: Ἦσαν...ἐγγίζοντες (Collison 46, 103-104; Goulder 2:609); the periphrastic imperfect (Collison 73-74); προσδέχεσθαι (Goulder 2:609).

¶ 90. The lost sheep

(Mt 18:10-14) **Lk 15:4-7**

Noticing the Pharisees' harsh attitude toward the "tax collectors and sinners" who were eagerly coming to hear Jesus for the word of salvation, Jesus holds three mirrors up, so they can see how mean spirited they are. The first of the three is the story of a man who is overjoyed when he finds a lost sheep (clearly a symbolic animal).

General observations. Luke may have obtained this parable from Mt 18:10-14 or from nonMatthean tradition. To this parable (Lk 15:4-7, Lost Sheep), a twin is appended (Lk 15:8-10, Lost Coin). The following synopsis will illustrate the close parallel structures between these two examples.

Synopsis of Lk 15:4-7//15:8-10

Illustrating their close parallel structures.

Lk 15:4-7 Lost Sheep	**Lk 15:8-10 Lost Coin**
	8 Ἢ
4 Τίς ἄνθρωπος ἐξ ὑμῶν	τίς γυνὴ
ἔχων ἑκατὸν πρόβατα	δραχμὰς ἔχουσα δέκα
καὶ ἀπολέσας ἐξ αὐτῶν ἓν	ἐὰν ἀπολέσῃ δραχμὴν μίαν,
οὐ καταλείπει	οὐχὶ ἅπτει
τὰ ἐνενήκοντα ἐννέα	λύχνον
ἐν τῇ ἐρήμῳ	καὶ σαροῖ τὴν οἰκίαν
καὶ πορεύεται ἐπὶ τὸ ἀπολωλὸς	καὶ ζητεῖ ἐπιμελῶς
ἕως εὕρῃ αὐτό;	ἕως οὗ εὕρῃ;
5 καὶ εὑρὼν	**9** καὶ εὑροῦσα
ἐπιτίθησιν ἐπὶ τοὺς ὤμους αὐτοῦ	
χαίρων	
6 καὶ ἐλθὼν εἰς τὸν οἶκον	
συγκαλεῖ τοὺς φίλους	συγκαλεῖ τὰς φίλας
καὶ τοὺς γείτονας	καὶ γείτονας
λέγων αὐτοῖς,	λέγουσα,
Συγχάρητέ μοι,	Συγχάρητέ μοι,
ὅτι εὗρον τὸ πρόβατόν μου	ὅτι εὗρον τὴν δραχμὴν
τὸ ἀπολωλός.	ἣν ἀπώλεσα.
7 λέγω ὑμῖν ὅτι οὕτως	**10** οὕτως, λέγω ὑμῖν,
χαρὰ	γίνεται χαρὰ
ἐν τῷ οὐρανῷ ἔσται	ἐνώπιον τῶν ἀγγέλων τοῦ θεοῦ
ἐπὶ ἑνὶ ἁμαρτωλῷ μετανοοῦντι	ἐπὶ ἑνὶ ἁμαρτωλῷ μετανοοῦντι.
ἢ ἐπὶ ἐνενήκοντα ἐννέα δικαίοις	
οἵτινες οὐ χρείαν ἔχουσιν	
μετανοίας.	

Lk 15:4-7 and Lk 15:8-10 together provide an excellent example of what appears to be a typical compositional technique of Luke: presenting didactic material by means of thematic pairs about a man and about a woman.

• A capstone parable follows this initial pair of examples about things that got lost, namely, the story of the Lost Son (Lk 15:11-32).

• There are also interesting structural similarities between the example of the Tower Builder and General Going to War (Lk 14:28-32) and the Lost Sheep/ Lost Coin (Lk 15:4-10). The following synopsis exhibits them.

Synopsis of Lk 14:28-32//15:4-10

Illustrating the close structural and verbal parallels between four examples from Luke's nonMatthean tradition.

Lk 14:28-32	**Lk 15:4-10**
28 τίς γὰρ	**4** Τίς ἄνθρωπος
ἐξ ὑμῶν	ἐξ ὑμῶν
θέλων πύργον	ἔχων ἑκατὸν πρόβατα
οἰκοδομῆσαι	καὶ ἀπολέσας ἐξ αὐτῶν ἓν
οὐχὶ πρῶτον καθίσας	οὐ
ψηφίζει	καταλείπει
τὴν δαπάνην,	τὰ ἐνενήκοντα ἐννέα
	ἐν τῇ ἐρήμῳ
	καὶ πορεύεται
	ἐπὶ τὸ ἀπολωλὸς
εἰ ἔχει εἰς ἀπαρτισμόν;	ἕως εὕρῃ αὐτό;
29 ἵνα μήποτε	**5** καὶ εὑρὼν
	ἐπιτίθησιν ἐπὶ τοὺς ὤμους
	αὐτοῦ χαίρων
θέντος αὐτοῦ θεμέλιον	**6** καὶ ἐλθὼν εἰς τὸν οἶκον
καὶ μὴ ἰσχύοντος ἐκτελέσαι	
πάντες οἱ θεωροῦντες	
ἄρξωνται αὐτῷ ἐμπαίζειν	συγκαλεῖ
	τοὺς φίλους
	καὶ τοὺς γείτονας
30 λέγοντες	λέγων αὐτοῖς,
	Συγχάρητέ μοι,
	ὅτι εὗρον τὸ πρόβατόν μου
	τὸ ἀπολωλός.
ὅτι Οὗτος ὁ ἄνθρωπος	**7** λέγω ὑμῖν ὅτι οὕτως
ἤρξατο οἰκοδομεῖν	χαρὰ ἐν τῷ οὐρανῷ ἔσται
	ἐπὶ ἑνὶ ἁμαρτωλῷ
	μετανοοῦντι
	ἢ ἐπὶ ἐνενήκοντα ἐννέα
καὶ	δικαίοις
οὐκ ἴσχυσεν ἐκτελέσαι.	οἵτινες οὐ χρείαν ἔχουσιν
	μετανοίας.
31 ἢ	**8** Ἢ
τίς βασιλεὺς	τίς γυνὴ
πορευόμενος ἑτέρῳ βασιλεῖ	δραχμὰς ἔχουσα δέκα
συμβαλεῖν εἰς πόλεμον	ἐὰν ἀπολέσῃ δραχμὴν μίαν,
οὐχὶ καθίσας πρῶτον	οὐχὶ
βουλεύσεται	ἅπτει λύχνον
	καὶ σαροῖ τὴν οἰκίαν
	καὶ ζητεῖ ἐπιμελῶς
εἰ δυνατός ἐστιν	ἕως οὗ εὕρῃ;

Parallels between Tower Builder/General and Lost Sheep/Coin (cont.)

Lk 14:31 ἐν δέκα χιλιάσιν	**LK 15:8**
ὑπαντῆσαι τῷ	
μετὰ εἴκοσι χιλιάδων	
ἐρχομένῳ ἐπ' αὐτόν;	
32 εἰ δὲ μή γε,	
ἔτι αὐτοῦ πόρρω ὄντος	**9** καὶ εὑροῦσα
	συγκαλεῖ
πρεσβείαν	τὰς φίλας
	καὶ γείτονας
ἀποστείλας	λέγουσα,
	Συγχάρητέ μοι,
	ὅτι εὗρον τὴν δραχμὴν
	10 οὕτως, λέγω ὑμῖν,
ἐρωτᾷ τὰ πρὸς εἰρήνην.	γίνεται χαρὰ
	ἐνώπιον τῶν ἀγγέλων τοῦ θεοῦ
	ἐπὶ ἑνὶ ἁμαρτωλῷ μετανοοῦντι.

This literary evidence may lead to two possible conclusions:

(1) Luke used Mt 18:10-14 for his version of the Lost Sheep (Lk 15:4-7) and then appended another parable from his nonMatthean tradition and composed the second parable himself;

(2) Luke found the Parable of the Lost Sheep in his nonMatthean tradition together with its twin, the Lost Coin.

• The references to parties with *friends* in all three parables in Lk 15:1-32 (Lk 15:6, 9, 22-30) link the whole of Lk 15 closely with Lk 14:7-24, esp. Lk 14:12-24.

¶ 91. The lost coin
Lk 15:8-10

Jesus' speech to the Pharisees continues with another illustration, serving to reveal how out-of-place their grudging attitude is in the presence of sinners and tax collectors who eagerly long for God's mercy.

General observations. See the notes to Lk 15:4-7 for source-critical comments also relevant to this parable.

Lk 15:8-10. Note that the woman in this parable "lights a lamp" and "does" something to find her lost (hidden?) coin (cf. Mt 5:14-16//Lk 8:16-18/Lk 11:33-36; Mt 10:26-27/Lk 8:16-18/Lk 11:53-12:3; Mt 12:46-50/Lk 8:19-21/Lk 11:27-28). This is a further example of the major Lukan theme of "seeing" ("hearing") and "doing."

¶ 92. The lost son
Lk 15:11-32

Continuing smoothly without a break, Jesus caps the two previous stories with a third which profoundly nuances the message he is conveying to the Pharisaic grumblers. Jesus tells the story of a younger son who turns astray and wastes himself in debauched living until one day, when he suddenly comes to his senses and decides to return home and tell his father that he is not worthy to be called his son. He should rather be one of his father's servants. The father, when he sees the younger son coming home, is overjoyed and orders a feast for his welcome. To this point, the parable accents some of the themes of the parables of the lost sheep and coin. Then, the elder brother appears on the scene. He grumbles about the joyful welcoming feast being prepared for his errant younger brother. The elder brother has faithfully served his father for years, never straying from any commandment of his father, and did his father ever reward him with a feast to which he might invite all of his friends during all that time? Hardly. So he will not participate in any feast for his undeserving younger brother who, the older brother accuses, has been associating with social outcasts. The father's beautifully phrased reply both gently reassures the elder son of his undying love and affection toward him, while pointing out how a father's love may at the same time extend bounteous mercy toward an errant son who wants to mend his ways.

General observations. This beautiful parable comes from Luke's non-Matthean tradition. Luke began this unit with the Pharisees objecting to Jesus extending God's mercy to sinners. Jesus first responds to them by defending the appropriateness of God's mercy and the appropriate response is joy. However, in this third story, a powerful nuance supplements the message of the two immediately preceding parables: the righteousness of the "elder brothers" in Israel has made them too haughty to rejoice when someone *unworthy* is blessed by God (Mt 10:34-39; "unworthy" is a repeated literary feature of the text of Mt). In the next Section, Jesus goes on to speak to his disciples about the Pharisees (Lk 16:1ff.). They look like they are serving God but they really are not. They are actually serving themselves (= wealth/Mammon; see further below).

Lk 15:11-32. Lukan linguistic characteristics are understandably sparse. They consist of the use of two genitive absolutes in Lk 15:14 and 20 respectively (Collison 77-78); ἦν ἀπολωλώς, Lk 15:24 (Collison 73); Ἦν δέ, Lk 15:25 (Collison 70-71); τί ἄν εἴη, Lk 15:26 (Collison 209; Goulder 2:617); and δὲ καί, Lk 15:28, 32 (Collison 103; Goulder 2:617).

Section Ten. To the Disciples and Pharisees: You Cannot Serve God and Money. Lk 16:1–31

Turning to his disciples again, Jesus tells them a parable about a household steward who was fired by his employer for mismanagement. Taking radical action in the light of imminent disaster, the steward calls together his master's debtors and tells each to write a new debt on the ledger books that reduced each debt by an amount equal to the interest charges sometimes levied for goods supplied on credit. Since it was illegal for Jews of the time to charge interest, at least to their fellow Jews, the bookkeeper could make himself righteous by removing these Torah-forbidden interest charges from the debtors' accounts. In doing this, the steward pleased his master's debtors and made his master look like a generous man in the debtors' eyes, all at the same time. In the end, the master commended his steward for his prudence, and he presumably stayed on in his position.

In Luke's account of this parable, Jesus adds a number of further clarifications on the subject of money, ending with: "you cannot serve both God and Mammon."

The Pharisees, now described by Luke as "lovers of money," hear all of this and begin to scoff at Jesus, perhaps because they still misunderstood the parable in spite of all the "morals" Jesus added to it. Jesus responds to this scoffing by accusing the Pharisees of justifying themselves before other people, perhaps by making invidious comparisons between themselves and the "dishonest" steward. "But God," says Jesus to the Pharisees, "knows your innermost thoughts and feelings."

Human measures of value, such as the accumulation of money, become, for God, abominable measures of value. God measures value not by accumulated wealth, but by the Word of God contained in the Torah and the Prophets, as all of God's prophets up through John the Baptist have affirmed. The proclamation of God's Kingdom, which recently has led people eagerly to seek it, does nothing to change the value of God's Word in the Torah and Prophets. Marriage, for instance, as discussed in the Torah, is still highly valued; divorce is not, and remarriage of divorced persons should be forbidden.

Jesus next tells a parable about a rich man and his poor servant, Lazarus, who have both been separated from life by death and from each other by their eternal rewards. The rich man finds himself suffering in Hades for all his sins while his poor servant, Lazarus, whom the rich man had tormented in life, now rests comfortably in the bosom of Father Abraham. A great gulf separates these two, now that their fortunes have been reversed. But the rich man still has an abominable sense of value. Even from Hades, the rich man asks that his former servant come to serve him. But Father Abraham tells him that this is impossible because of the great gulf that separates them. The rich man asks that Lazarus be sent to his living family members as a warning to repent. But Father Abraham says, "If they do not hear Moses and the prophets, neither will they be convinced if someone should rise from the dead."

Source-critical observations. The preceding narrative summary demonstrates that Luke's text, as arranged in this section, is not a disjointed series of unrelated sayings of Jesus, but a series of sayings that can be read in sequence and which can be seen in meaningful relationships to one another.

Lk 16:1-8a. Section Ten of the Lukan Travel Narrative begins with a parable drawn from nonMatthean tradition about a Dishonest Manager who was threatened with loss of his job. He takes radical action and, in the end, merits the praise of his master.

Lk 16:8b-12. Attached to this parable are a series of aitiae also drawn from nonMatthean tradition. Therefore, they may have been attached by earlier redactional activity to the parable as Luke received it.

Lk 16:13//Mt 6:24. As the concluding *aitia* in this long list, however, Luke added the sayings he found at Mt 6:24 about a servant's inability to serve two masters and "You cannot serve God and Mammon." This is only one of the three verses from Mt's Sermon on the Mount that Luke will use within the balance of his Gospel. There is little of the Sermon remaining that Luke also found appropriate for his narrative. Luke gathered all three of these remaining verses from Mt's Sermon on the Mount into the relatively small context of Lk 16:13-18 (Mt 6:24//Lk 16:13, on serving two masters; Mt 5:17-20//Lk 16:17, on the validity of the Law; and Mt 5:31-32//Lk 16:18, on divorce).

Lk 16:14-17//Mt 11:12-13//Mt 5:17-18. Luke composed a transition at Lk 16:14 that included the Lukan editorial aside that the Pharisees were "lovers of money." This aside makes Lk 16:14-18 both relate back to the Parable of the Unjust Steward and its attendant *aitiae* with which this Section begins (Lk 16:1-13) and forward to the Parable of the Rich Man and Lazarus, with which the Section ends (Lk 16:19-31). Sandwiched between these two parables, Luke included traditions about the history and continuing validity of the Law and the Prophets drawn from Mt 5:17-20 and Mt 11:11-12, two Matthean contexts that emphasize these matters. Mt 11:11-12 are two verses that Luke previously omitted from his use of Mt 11:2-19 at Lk 7:18-35. Mt 5:17-20 is one of the last two excerpts from Mt's Sermon on the Mount that Luke used within his Gospel.

Lk 16:18//Mt 5:31-32. Luke's final use of verses from Mt's Sermon on the Mount follows immediately. It is the Teaching on Divorce (Mt 5:31-32), which Luke conflated with material from the more extended Matthean debate about divorce at Mt 19:3-12. The longer discussion of matters relating to the family in Mt 19:3-12 includes some notes about separation of family members (Mt 19:5), a demonstrable Lukan interest (Lk 12:49-53//Mt 10:34-37; Lk 14:25-26//Mt 10:37-38; Lk 18:28-30//Mt 19:27-30). More importantly, this segment of Mt also includes a reference to the authority of Moses (Mt 19:7-8), which relates precisely to the topic Luke was discussing in Lk 16:14-17//Mt 11:12-13//Mt 5:17:18. Luke utilized Mt 5:31-32//Mt 19:2-12 to provide an example of the continuing authority of the Law (cf. Lk 16:17).

Lk 16:19-31. Luke concluded Section Ten with another parable drawn from nonMatthean tradition about a rich man who is suffering in Hades while his servant is lying in the bosom of Abraham. The rich man wants his family to know about the consequences of "love of money" and lack of concern for the poor. He wants someone to visit them from the world of the dead, so they might change their ways. But Father Abraham responds, they have "Moses and the Prophets" to help them change their ways. If the members of the rich man's family won't read these authorities, these family members wouldn't change even if someone should rise from the dead.

¶ 93. The Pharisees are like a dishonest manager

(Mt 6:24) **Lk 16:1-13**

Luke has finished Jesus' polemic against the Pharisees. He portrays Jesus as turning to his disciples to speak. Presumably they have been listening attentively to the foregoing speech to the Pharisees. Now he will talk to his disciples about the Pharisees, who, of course, will be listening to everything he says about them. He tells his disciples a story about the corrupt manager of someone's estate. The manager is called to account and found wanting. But the lesson for the disciples is found in the manager's response. He now acts with admirable stewardship. Likewise, Jesus moralizes to his disciples to exercise appropriate stewardship with their money.

General observations. As with the previous unit, this parable comes from Luke's nonMatthean tradition. Only in the last verse (Lk 16:13) is there a clear use of Mt (Mt 6:24//Lk 16:13). Here Luke copied the text of Mt exactly except for the Lukan addition of the word, οἰκέτης, which makes this logion better fit its new Lukan context. Luke utilized Mt 6:24//Lk 16:13 as the last in a series of somewhat loosely connected *aitiae* to the Parable of the Unjust Steward (Lk 16:1-12).

• While Mt 6:24 is the only clear use of Mt in Lk 16:1-13, it may be noted that Luke did have a contextual parallel for the Lost Sheep, Mt 18:10-14, at Lk 15:4-10, and, within the opening verses of Section Eleven below, Luke will make clear use of Mt 18:6-7//Lk 17:1-2; Mt 18:15-17//Lk 17:3; and Mt 18:21-22//Lk 17:4. Luke never made explicit use of the Parable of the Unforgiving Debtor that concludes Mt's Discourse on Community Regulations (Mt 18:23-35) unless it influenced the text of Lk 12:57-59 (see the General Observations there) and/or perhaps the text of Lk 16:1-12 here.

Possible links between the Parable of the Dishonest Steward in Lk 16:1-12 and the Parable of the Unforgiving Servant in Mt 18:23-35 might include:

(1) the powerful figure of the king/rich man who has a weaker, at times unethical, servant/steward;

(2) the theme of settling large debts;

(3) the apparently lenient settling of some accounts;

(4) the one-on-one negotiations between servant/steward and debtors;

(5) commands issued by the servant/steward to the debtor(s); and

(6) the serious consequences of the servant/steward's actions (prison, punishment, threat of losing a job).

Finally, we take note of the fact that the comments made about the division of the family in Mt 18:25 relate the content of Mt 18:23-35 to the content of Mt 10:37-39 that Luke utilized previously at Lk 12:49-53 and 14:24-27. See the General Observations for those two earlier Lukan contexts.

We do not mean to suggest by this that the text of Mt 18:23-35 necessarily influenced the text *per se* of Lk 16:1-12, but rather to suggest another context in Lk where the sequence and content of pericopes in Mt may have influenced Lk even when he was using nonMatthean tradition.

• Despite the widely-used interpretation of this parable by Jeremias, according to which the original ending occurs in Lk 16:8, it is clear from the context that, as far as Luke was concerned, this story, as modified and shaped by the additional verses (Lk 16:10-13), was understood to be a warning against greed. Echoing the content of Lk 16:1-13, Luke specifically added the comment that the Pharisees were "lovers of money" in the opening verse of the *next* pericope (Lk 16:14) to make Lk 16:14-18 more appropriate to the Lukan context in which Luke placed that collection of verses drawn from Mt.

Lk 16:1-13. The awkward ending in Lk 16:9b, "so that when it fails they may receive you into the eternal habitations," may not be Lukan stylistically, but it does serve to prepare for the eternal judgment motif in the story of the Rich Man and Lazarus (Lk 16:19-31). For these reasons, we are inclined to think that Luke himself combined the materials in Lk 16:9b-13 to serve as a transition to the dominant theme in the pericopes that follow immediately: Jesus' gracious followers, and not the "money-grubbing" Pharisees, are those who have truly listened to and obeyed the teachings of the Law and the Prophets. The *aitiae* to this parable, Lk 16:9b-13, have been edited together using catchwords such as "wisdom" (Lk 16:8a and 16:8b), "unrighteousness" (Lk 16:8a, 9-11), "reception into dwellings" (Lk 16:4, 27), "mammon" (Lk 16:9, 11, 13), "faithful" (Lk 16:10-12), "serving the Lord" (Lk 16:13//Mt 6:24; cf. Lk 16:1-12). Lukan literary characteristics have been noted. They include Ἔλεγεν δέ (Collison 56); καὶ οὗτος (Collison 117; Goulder 2:626); οὐκ ἰσχύω (Collison 53; Goulder 2:626); ἕτερος, Lk 16:7 and twice in Lk 16:13 (Collison 184; Goulder 2:627); and ὑπάρχοντες (Collison 67).

¶ 94. God's Law remains forever

(Mt 11:12-13; 5:17-18//24:34-35; 5:31-32//19:1-9) **Lk 16:14-18**

Stung by his words, the Pharisees, "who were lovers of money and who overheard all this," could not stand it any longer and cried out against Jesus, scoffing at his words. But Jesus, not backing down one whit, now says plainly what he has been saying in word pictures and hints up until now: "You are those who justify yourselves rather than asking God to make you right with Him! But God can see your arrogance, and you will face Him at the Judgment! To be sure, the Law and the Prophets have been in effect even up to the time of John the Baptist, and since then, the Gospel of the Kingdom of God has been preached, so that people have been eagerly forcing their way into it. But no person should think for a moment that God's Law has now been abrogated! Far from it! People constantly break both its spirit and its letter, such as allowing easy divorces! Such as disregarding the poor and sick (=Lazarus), the maimed and blind! Such as expressing opposition to God's forgiveness! No. 'Moses and the prophets' are still in effect and people who disregard them will be called to the bar of judgment."

General observations. Luke's transition from the last pericope to this one included an outburst from the Pharisees which allowed Luke to introduce two themes of fundamental importance for the third and concluding story within this Section, the story about the Rich Man and Lazarus (Lk 16:19-31). These themes are also important for the Parable of the Pharisee and the Tax Collector (Lk 18:9-14) that immediately precedes that point in Lk where Luke begins to follow the basic sequential order of pericopes in Mt once more (Mt 18:15ff.). These two themes are

(1) the abiding significance of God's law and

(2) receiving one's righteousness before God as a gift from God, not as something one has painstakingly earned.

The sayings in Lk 16:14-18 are preparatory for the central point of the classic judgment scene in the story of the Rich Man and Lazarus: "But Abraham said, 'They (the rich man's brothers) have Moses and the prophets; let them hear them.'"

Luke prepared for this striking saying by introducing sayings from Mt 11:13, 11:12 (*sic*), and Mt 5:17-18, that all relate to the history, authority and permanence of the Torah. (See "law and the prophets" in Mt 5:17//Mt 11:12-13//Lk 16:16, the reference to "the Law" in Mt 5:18//Lk 16:17; cf. the reference to the authority of Moses in Mt 19:7//Lk 16:31.)

As an illustration of the kind of committed discipleship now demanded of God's people, Luke next turned to Mt's account of Jesus' dispute with the Pharisees over divorce (Mt 19:1-12; cf. Mt 5:31-32), where he echoed Jesus' critique in Mt 19:1-12: "(Jesus) said to them, 'Because of your hardness of heart (sinfulness) Moses allowed you to divorce your wives, but from the beginning (i.e., with Adam and Eve) it was not so!'" (Mt 19:8). Luke conflated Mt 19:9 with the Matthean doublet at Mt 5:31-32 to produce Lk 16:18. In contrast to the lawlessness of some, Jesus' disciples are to "hear the Word of God and keep it" (Lk 11:28; cf. Lk 8:21).

• The "separation of son from father and mother" expressed in Mt 19:5 may also have attracted Luke to the context of Mt 19:3-9, since the related ideas expressed in Mt 10:37-39 attracted him earlier (see General Observations at Lk 12:49-53 and 14:24-27).

The sayings from Mt 5:17-20//Lk 16:17, Mt 5:31-32//Lk 16:18, combined with that from Mt 6:24 at Lk 16:13 are all sayings of Jesus from the Sermon on the Mount that Luke had not previously utilized. They are also the last few such sayings that Luke used in his narrative.

Among Luke's omissions from the Sermon on the Mount are three of the antitheses in Mt 5 (Mt 5:21-26 "on blood vengeance" but cf. Mt 5:25-26//Lk 12:57-59; Mt 5:27-30 "on adultery" and Mt 5:33-37 "on oaths"). The three antitheses that Luke did not omit he rewrote to eliminate the "antithetical structure" (Mt 5:31-32//Mt 19:3-9//Lk 16:18 "on divorce"; Mt 5:38-42//Lk 6:27-31 "on retaliation"; and Mt 5:43-48//Lk 6:32-36 "on love of enemies"). The inclusion by Luke of the other antitheses, or at least the content of them, in this antithetical form would have contradicted Luke's view of the authority of the Law that is expressed here in Lk 16:14-18.

Luke also omitted any references to almsgiving, prayer and fasting "in secret" (Mt 6:1-18) from his Gospel. Luke would have found secrecy in doing one's religious duties contradictory to his own view that public confession and discipleship were required of Jesus' followers.

He did use the Lord's Prayer from this Matthean context at Lk 11:1-4. Apart from of the potentially offensive "Do not cast what is holy to dogs and don't cast your pearls before swine...(Mt 7:6), *Luke used at least parts of every other pericope within Mt's Sermon on the Mount somewhere in his Gospel*. The Matthean doublet on Divorce at Mt 5:31-32 and Mt 19:3-9 obviously relate those two Matthean literary contexts to one another, and we see them joined in Lk 16:14-16. And the common references to the history, authority and permanence of "the Law (and the Prophets)" in Mt 5:17-20; 11:12-13; and 19:3-9 would have contributed to Luke's bringing together these verses from different literary contexts in Mt at Lk 16:14-18.

Lk 16:16. Luke's version of Mt 11:12-13 exhibits a number of striking modifications. In the Matthean version, Jesus says "the law and the prophets prophesied until John". Since then (namely, John's death), all sorts of violence has broken out and the Kingdom of God (= the faithful) has suffered increasing violence as men have tried to "take it by force"; a possible allusion to Judah the Galilean and the Zealots, and others who wanted to force God to bring in the Day of National Liberation. Luke has changed this to "The period of the Law and the Prophets extended through (the death of) John the Baptist. And since then, the Gospel of the Kingdom of God is preached"—beginning at Nazareth— "and everyone enters it urgently." The difficult word βιάζεται does carry connotations of force and violence. But it is noteworthy that Luke has omitted Mt's reference to "robbers" βιασταί who "seize it" ἁρπάζουσιν αὐτήν (Mt 11:12b). Thus we agree with those who interpret βιάζεται in a positive sense.

Lk 16:17. The flow of logic in these verses, thus interpreted, is as follows: True, the period of the Law and the Prophets extended until John the Baptist, and true again, since then the Kingdom of God is preached (so that everyone wants to press into it), but do not think that the preaching of the Kingdom means God's law is done with! It would be easier for heaven and earth to pass away than for one tiny dot of the Law to be abrogated! So don't think you can use this time of the new era to disregard God's demand — like some who say it is permissible to have divorce for any reason!

Lk 16:18. The law still abides. "Every man who divorces his wife and marries another woman commits adultery (etc.)!" Jesus goes on in the very next story and points out how the rich man and all his brothers are also disobeying Moses and the prophets (see further below).

• We suggest that something of the Apostle Paul's struggle with Torah-observance among his Gentile congregations lies behind these verses in the Gospel of Luke.

• There is some evidence of Lukan stylistic characteristics in this composite group of sayings, indicating his activity: ἡ βασιλεία τοῦ θεοῦ, Lk 16:16 (Collison 170; Goulder 2:633); εὐαγγελίζομαι, Lk 16:16 (Collison 51; Goulder 2:633); ἕτερος, Lk 16:18 (Collison 184; Goulder 2:634); and ἀνήρ, Lk 16:18 (Collison 167; Goulder 2:634).

¶ 95. The Pharisees are like a wicked rich man
Lk 16:19-31

Without pausing, Jesus launches into a curious story about a wicked rich man who died and went to Hades. There he looked up and, to his astonishment, saw the filthy, sick beggar who had always sat in misery at his doorway now resting comfortably in Abraham's bosom. "Father Abraham, help me!" cried the rich man in torment. "Send that beggar to me with a little sip of water!" Father Abraham replied, "Son, you had a life full of easeand comfort while this poor fellow had nothing but misery and sickness. Now he is in comfort and you in anguish. He cannot aid you, nor should he. Besides, there is a great gulf fixed between Heaven and Hades and no one can cross from one to the other!" In despair, the rich man cried, "Father, at least send that beggar to warn my brothers, lest they also come to this place of fiery torment when they die!" Again Abraham said, "Why should I send this beggar when your brothers have Moses and the prophets? Let them hear them!" To which the rich man said, "No, I know my brothers! They don't care about the Law and the Prophets! But if they see some great miracle, like a beggar coming back from the dead, then they will repent of their ways and become obedient to Moses!" But Abraham said, "No they won't. If they refuse to obey Moses now, they won't change even if someone should rise from the dead to warn them!"

General observations. Again, this story is unique to Luke and was probably gotten by him from his nonMatthean tradition. Luke is clearly incorporating significant amounts of nonMatthean tradition as he moved toward the completion of the Travel Narrative.

Lk 16:19-31. There is an illuminating parallel to the central point of this story in the Gospel to the Hebrews. In his *Commentary on Matthew,* Origen quotes a variant of the story of the encounter between Jesus and the rich man to the effect that, when Jesus told the rich man to sell all he had and distribute it to the poor, the rich man refused to do so. Then Jesus upbraided him, saying, "'How can you say 'I have fulfilled the law and the prophets' when it is written in the law: 'You shall love your neighbor as yourself;' and behold, many of your brothers, sons of Abraham, are clothed in filth, dying of hunger (Lazarus!), while your house is full of many good things, none of which goes out to them?'"[6] Here we can see precisely the bearing of the admonition in Lk 16:29, "They have Moses and the prophets. Let them hear them!"

Section Eleven. To the Disciples: On Faith and Works. Lk 17:1–19

Following the Parable of the Rich Man and Lazarus, Jesus continues to teach his disciples about life within the community: not causing brothers and sisters to stumble, correcting errant members of the community, granting forgiveness to those who ask for it (*if* they have truly repented); followers, like servants, should do their duties, without expecting a word of thanks; etc.

Source-critical observations.

Lk 17:1-4//Mt 18:6-7, 15-17, 21-22. With the opening unit of Section Eleven of the Travel Narrative, "On Faith and Works," Luke brought to a close his use of material from Mt's chapter on Community Regulations which, as we have noted often, is the macrostructural parallel in Mt's narrative order to the Lukan Travel Narrative as a whole (see our discussion above, p. 152; also Introduction, p. 19).

Luke made his first use of material from Mt 18 at Lk 9:46-50//Mt 18:1-2, 4-5. He made subsequent use of the Parable of the Lost Sheep at Lk 15:1-7//Mt 18:10, 12-14. Luke may also have alluded to the Parable of the Unforgiving Servant (Mt 18:23-35) that concludes Mt's chapter on Community Regulations both at Lk 12:57-59 and at Lk 16:1-13. The Parable of the Unjust Steward and its attendant *aitiae* (Lk 16:1-13) began the immediately preceding Section Ten of the Travel Narrative.

Having clearly made use of Mt 18:1-2, 4-5, 10, 12-14 and possibly of Mt 18:23-35, Luke now used sayings within Mt 18 that he had not yet used; Mt 18:6-7, on scandals; Mt 18:15-17 and 21-22 on forgiving the sinful brother. The remaining verses within Mt's Community Regulations, with

---

[6] Cited from B. Throckmorton, *Gospel Parallels,* §189 notes.

the important exception of Mt 18:3, find no place in Luke's Gospel. On Mt 18:3, see the introduction to Section Fourteen below, as well as the discussion of Mt 19:13-15//Lk 18:15-17.

Luke omitted not only Mt 18:8-9 ("if your eye offends you, pluck it out") but also its doublet at Mt 5:27-30 when he took materials from Mt's Sermon on the Mount. Mt 18:11 was not in the text of Mt known to Luke (cf. Metzger 1994:36: "there can be little doubt that [this verse is] spurious"). Mt 18:18 on "binding and loosing" and its doublet at Mt 16:19 were never utilized by Luke, as well as the similar Mt 18:19-20: "if two of you on earth agree on anything...for where two or three are gathered together in my name, etc." These sayings in Mt's context were specific legal guidelines for the operation of community *halakoth* (there are a number of rabbinic parallels) and, as such, possibly not well suited to the wider ecumenical context, in Luke's judgment.

Lk 17:5-6//Mt 17:19-20//Mt 21:21. After having included teaching on scandals and forgiving the erring brother if he repents (Lk 17:1-4), Luke moved on to the need for faith to support such a spirit of forgiveness. For this teaching, Luke reached back to Mt 17:19-20, the two verses that conclude the story of the Healing of the Epileptic Boy in Mt 17:14-21, but which Luke omitted from his parallel at Lk 9:37-43a. Luke conflated Mt 17:19-20 with its Matthean doublet at Mt 21:21-22 to compose Lk 17:5-6.

Lk 17:7-10. Luke drew the teachings on obedient service from non-Matthean tradition to attach to the teachings on scandals, forgiveness and faith which he drew from Mt.

Lk 17:11-19. The story of the grateful Samaritan leper who was healed by Jesus was also drawn from nonMatthean tradition. Contrast the reference to a Samaritan village that rejected Jesus at the very beginning of the Travel Narrative (Lk 9:51-56), and the Parable of the Good Samaritan (Lk 10:25-37) in Section One of the Travel Narrative. All three stories in Lk seem to stem from nonMatthean tradition.

¶ 96. Coping with sin inside the community

Mt 18:6-7, 15-17, 21-22 ====> **Lk 17:1-6**

(cf. Mt 17:19-20 with Mt 21:21-22)

Luke portrays Jesus continuing to teach the disciples. However, it is clear that a new subject is being addressed: how true leaders should behave. They have heard many words about laxness; now it is time for positive advice. In this set of teachings, Jesus' words contain three short, inter-related messages. First, woe to the leader who, by some wicked action, sins against his trusting followers, thus causing despair and lack of trust in God to arise among them! He will be most severely punished on the Day of Judgment! Second, switching perspectives, Jesus addresses the topic of what to do if a *follower* sins against the leader. What should the leader do then? He should be merciful. If the brother sincerely repents, he must always be forgiven, even if it happens seven times a day. At this, his disciples break in: "But surely such unruly followers will crush our hearts, causing us to lose *our* faith! How can we possibly forgive our sinful followers so much? We beg you, *increase our faith* so we can forgive them that often!" Jesus replies, "All you need is a tiny amount of faith! Not a great amount! You may feel discouraged and uncertain and frustrated by your errant and wayward followers, but if there is one tiny spark of faith in you, one small burning flame of hope—that's enough to keep going and forgive them!"

General observations. With Lk 17:1-2, Luke again returned to Mt 18. Lk used Mt 18:1-2, 4-5 at Lk 9:46-48. We have also seen some evidence of Luke's knowledge of Mt 18:8-9 at both Lk 12:49 and Lk 14:34-35 and perhaps some knowledge of Mt 18:23-35, the Parable of the Unforgiving Servant, at Lk 12:57-59 and again at Lk 16:1-12. But the last time that Luke certainly made contact with material from Mt 18 was at Lk 15:3-7 (Parable of the Lost Sheep, Mt 18:10-14). Between Lk 15:3-7//Mt 18:10-14 and Lk 17:1//Mt 18:7, Luke has been using material drawn from non-Matthean tradition, with the exception of the collection of traditions from Mt in Lk 16:13-18 (see the General Observations to Lk 16:14-18).

At this point, as Luke prepared to begin a new unit, it is understandable that he would return to the context of Mt 18 for more material. We have evidence here of Luke's use of Mt 18:6-7//Lk 17:1-2, Mt 18:15-17//Lk 17:3, and Mt 18:21-22//Lk 17:4. Note that Luke's use of these verses from Mt 18 was, once again, orderly. In this pericope, Luke selected and adapted the substance of Mt's Community Regulations on how to deal with sinful behavior within the Elect Community.

Lk 17:1. Luke relocated the statement about the inevitability of sinful behavior (Mt 18:7) from its position after the warning against sinning against one of "these little ones" (Mt 18:6) to the beginning of this pericope (Lk 17:1). At the same time, he improved the sense: Mt's ἀνάγκη γὰρ ἐλθεῖν "it is necessary," is not as precise as ἀνένδεκτόν ἐστιν. . . μὴ ἐλθεῖν, "it is not permitted for scandals not to come." This statement sets the stage for the dual instructions for leaders which follow.

Lk 17:2-4. The appearance of the term σκάνδαλον in Lk 17:1 represents the appearance of a literary term characteristic of the text of Mt appearing only in parallel literary contexts in Lk. It is only one of many "one way indicators" of Luke's literary dependence upon the text of Mt (on this term, see Introduction, p. 24).[7]

• In the saying dealing with sins of the followers against the leaders, Luke's "if he repents" (Lk 17:3b-4) is more explicit than Mt's "if he hears you" (Mt 18:15b). The Lukan theme of repentance was introduced into the Matthean source since, as it stands, Mt's wording of Jesus' admonition

7 For a more complete discussion, see *SBL 1991 Seminar Papers* 677, and *SBL 1993 Seminar Papers* 329.

appears to open the door to unlimited forgiveness regardless of repentance on the part of the sinner.

• Luke used ἀφίημι in Lk 17:3b (ἄφες αὐτῷ) as a link to Mt's saying on forgiveness in Mt 18:21f. καὶ ἀφήσω αὐτῷ. But Luke has, once again, avoided the ambiguity in Mt's saying (which counsels unlimited forgiveness with no mention of repentance) by inserting the need for explicit confession, "if he should return to you, saying, 'I repent'" (Lk 17:4b; cf. the parallel, "if he should repent," at Lk 17:3).

Lk 17:5-6. The reference to "the apostles" in Lk 17:5 (parallel to "the disciples" in Lk 17:1) is a well-known Lukan term.

• If we may assume that Luke understood the instruction to forgive the sinning "brother" any number of times, provided he repents each time, as being one requiring a strong faith in God's power to change such a person's life, then we have the rationale for Luke turning to Mt 17:19-20 for the saying about "faith like a grain of mustard seed." Luke had used the rest of the story in Mt 17:14-21 earlier (Mt 17:14-18//Lk 9:37-43a) in the series of stories depicting the disciples' incompetence, blindness, etc. Now he returned to that context and took precisely what he had not yet used, namely, Mt 17:19-20.

However, Luke changed Mt's "mountain, move to yonder place" (Mt 17:20, cf. Mt 21:21, "say to this mountain") to "sycamine tree, be rooted up and planted in the sea" (Lk 17:6). Could "sycamine" (συκάμινος) be a later scribal corruption from a more original "sycamore" (συκομαρέα)? If so, it would have provided an anticipation of the tree mentioned in the Zacchaeus story, unique to Lk (cf. Lk 19:4, συκομορέα), something Luke would have done.

• Note that Mt 21:21 also mentions a mountain being cast into the sea, as well as "what was done to this fig tree (συκῇ)." When Lk reached Mt 21:18-19, the story of the cursing of the fig tree, he omitted it. There is, however, an echo of that account here at Lk 17:5-6. Furthermore, the closing affirmation in Mt 21:22, "All things whatsoever you should ask *in prayer*, believing, you will receive," may have provided Luke with the suggestion that he present here another unit on prayer (Lk 18:1-14; cf. Lk 11:1-13) before the end of the Travel Narrative.

• Luke changed Mt's "And nothing will be impossible to you" (Mt 17:20d) to "it will obey you" (Lk 17:6), referring to the sycamine tree.

• Lukan linguistic characteristics are found throughout the pericope and include πλήν, Lk 17:1 (Collison 121; Goulder 2:643); οἱ ἀπόστολοι, Lk 17:5 (Collison 168; Goulder 2:643); προστίθημι, Lk 17:5 (Collison 64); and ἐλέγετε, Lk 17:6 (Collison 55). Luke has substantially edited his Matthean source.

¶ 97. Don't forget who you are
Lk 17:7-10

Jesus continues his answer in response to the disciples' plea to increase their faith. Having told them that all they will need is the tiniest spark of trust in God to work wonders, he goes on to warn them to remember who they are. They do not know God's timetable with respect to any follower. It is theirs to do their duty and, when they are done, like a good servant, they should not even expect thanks.

General observations. This pericope ends Luke's instructions to the disciples (who are paradigmatic for Luke's audience in the wider, ecumenical Christian communities) regarding the inevitable sins which crop up in everyone's life, and how to deal with them. As such, the whole Section is very reminiscent of Paul's injunctions in Gal 6:1-10 on the same subject. Luke has nonMatthean tradition as his source here.

Lk 17:7-10. There are only a few Lukan linguistic characteristics in this unit: ὅς followed by a participle, Lk 17:7 (Collison 206) and μετὰ ταῦτα, Lk 17:8 (Collison 139). Luke has followed his source closely.

¶ 98. Ten lepers healed
Lk 17:11-19

Resuming his narrative thread, Luke once again mentions Jesus "on the way to Jerusalem," when he is met by some lepers. They beg him to heal them, which he does. However, out of the ten, only one—a Samaritan "foreigner"—comes back to give Jesus heartfelt thanks. Luke's implication seems to be that the other nine who did not thank him were from Judea.

General observations. This account also comes from Luke's non-Matthean tradition. We take the geographical reference to be a narrative marker, indicating that Luke is about to introduce a new theme. Thus this story acts as a transitional pericope to introduce the rest of the material in Section Twelve, "To Pharisees and Disciples: Where is the Kingdom?" (Lk 17:20-37).

The curious phrase "passing along between Samaria and Galilee" has occasioned considerable scholarly discussion. However, it may simply mean that Luke tried to portray Jesus traveling *east* to get to the Jordan River, where he could take the road south along the river until he came to Jericho (the next story). The Jordan River route was not an uncommon way to travel when going south or north.

The occurrence of the word "foreigner" in Lk 17:18 hearkens back to the rejection of Jesus by the Samaritan villagers (Lk 9:51-55; cf. Lk 10:25-37) and forward to the Samaritan mission in Acts 8. In any case, a clear hint is given that "foreigners" know how to thank the Lord Jesus properly. The function of this story, as we have said, is to provide a transition to a whole series of pericopes dealing with the nearness of the Kingdom of God. Hence there is, in the response of the Samaritan leper, one person at least who recognizes the fact that the Kingdom of God came to him that day in the person of Jesus. For Luke, it was clear that Jesus' healings were meant to be understood as epiphanies of God's Kingdom (cf. "If it is by the finger of God that I cast out demons, then the Kingdom of God has come [past tense] upon you!" (Lk 11:20//Mt 12:28). In any case, some such understanding is required in the context because the very next story depicts the Pharisees coming up to Jesus and asking when the Kingdom of God was coming.

Lk 17:11-19. This pericope is replete with Lukan characteristic expressions and terms. To begin with, Jerusalem is given a Lukan spelling (Goulder 2:647). Its occurrence here points back to Lk 9:51-56 and forward to Lk 19:11-28. Καὶ ἐγένετο + the infinitive (Lk 17:11, 14) is typically Lukan (Collison 198-199, 214; Goulder 2:647). Lk 17:12 makes use of the genitive absolute (typically Lukan; Collison 77-78). ἀνήρ is characteristic of Luke's style (Collison 167; Goulder 2:647). Other favorite terms include: ὑποστρέφω (Lk 17:15; see Collison 67; Goulder 2:647), φωνὴ μεγάλη (Collison 187), and δοξάζων τὸν θεόν (Collison 46). The reference to the healed Samaritan "falling at Jesus' feet" is a favorite Lukan expression for the ideal response of the believer (cf. Lk 7:38; 8:28, 35; Goulder 2:647). Finally, the reference to faith "saving you" is a well-known Lukan theme (cf. Lk 7:50; 8:48; 17:19; 18:42).

Section Twelve. To Pharisees and Disciples: Where Is the Kingdom? Lk 17:20–37

Following the unit on Faith and Works, Luke turns to the theme of the Kingdom of God's arrival. Jesus first gives an enigmatic answer which deflects the issue of "when the Kingdom of God is coming" by stating enigmatically, "The Kingdom of God is among you." Jesus follows this statment with a collection of teachings about the day of its coming. In response to a final question about where one might find the Kingdom, Jesus offers another mysterious teaching: "wherever the corpse is, there the vultures will be gathered!"

Source-critical observations. At the beginning of Section Twelve, Luke once again returned to the context of Mt 23:1-26:1, the last long collection of teachings of Jesus in Mt, and made selective use of material drawn from Mt 24:17-41. Luke had made use of Mt 23 in Lk 11:37-52//Mt 23:1-36 and Lk 13:34-35//Mt 23:37-39. Luke had used Mt 24:42-25:1-13 at Lk 12:35-48 and (re?)used Mt 25:1-13 at Lk 13:22-27. For this section of his Travel Narrative, Luke chose to use the section of Mt 24 that immediately precedes the portion of Mt he had previously utilized, namely, Mt 24:17-41 (cf. Mt 24:42-25:13//Lk 12:35-48//Lk 13:22-27). Details about Luke's use of Mt 24:17-41 to compose Lk 17:20-33 are included in the notes below.

Lk 17:20//Mt 16:1. Luke began Section Twelve of the Travel Narrative with a question from the Pharisees, "When is the Kingdom of God coming?" The scene is similar to that set in Mt 16:1. Luke already had conflated Mt 16:1-6 with the Matthean doublet at Mt 12:38-39 to compose Lk 11:29 and used Mt 16:2-3 to compose Lk 12:54-56. So, even though the relationship between Lk 17:20 and Mt 16:1 may seem a distant one when seen in isolation, the connection is there to be seen when one views the whole complex.

Lk 17:33//Mt 10:39. With this use of Mt 10:39, Luke completed his systematic use of Mt 10:26-10:39 that began at Lk 12:2.

¶ 99. Blindness of the Pharisees to the presence of the Kingdom of God
Lk 17:20

Abruptly "the Pharisees" are reintroduced into the narrative. It is as if while hovering in the background, they see the healing of the leper and come to ask Jesus, "When is the Kingdom of God going to come?" The very fact that they have to ask the question, in view of all Jesus has done, proves their blindness. His answer underlines this fact. "You want signs? There will not be any because, for those who can see it, the Kingdom is already here in your midst!"

General observations. This verse is a Lukan composition, but compare the content of Mt 16:1, 4, which Luke utilized at Lk 11:29. Again we are in the presence of a Lukan construction that serves as a transition to the very important speech regarding "signs" in Lk 17:21-37.

Lk 17:20. There is a slight similarity with Mt 24:23. But, as noted above, the basic concept is purely Lukan. The phrase, ἡ βασιλεία τοῦ θεοῦ, is Lukan (Collison 170) and occurs three times in these two verses.

¶ 100. Have faith in the day of the Son of Man!
(Mt 24:17-18, 23-28, 37-41; 10:39) **Lk 17:21-37**

Once again, Luke follows one answer to the blind and unbelieving "Pharisees" with another to "the disciples." However, to them he says: "Don't give up! Don't be misled by false leaders who claim to have seen signs! Trust in God and wait." It is clear from the opening statement that Luke is thinking of the situation of his Gentile audience: "The days are coming when you will desire to see one of the days of the Son of Man and you will not see it." It is clear from Paul's correspondence with the Christians in Thessalonica that some Christians were losing hope in Jesus' return in glory. It is to such despair that Luke's Jesus says, "Do not listen to those who come to you and say, 'There he is!' Such people are deluding you! But be prepared, no matter what the circumstances may be! One day you will see it, just as surely 'where the corpse is lying, there the vultures have gathered!'"

General observations. Luke connected this pericope with the preceding one (Lk 17:20-21) by the repetition of ἰδοὺ ὧδε...ἐκεῖ ἰδοῦ (Lk 17:21), ἰδοὺ ἐκεῖ, ἰδοὺ ὧδε (Lk 17:23). Luke had previously utilized Mt 24:42-25:13 in composing Lk 12:35-48, and Luke seems to have conflated Mt 25:1-13 with Mt 7:13-14, 21-23 at Lk 13:22-27. Now Luke returned to the context of Mt 24 and used it selectively in composing Lk 17:21-37 (Mt 24:23-27//Lk 17:21-25; Mt 24:37-39//Lk 17:26-27; Mt 24:17-18//Lk 17:31-32; Mt 10:39//Lk 17:33; Mt 24:40-41//Lk 17:34-37c and Mt 24:28//Lk 17:37d). Luke initially followed Mt 24:23-27 (par Lk 17:21-24) at the conclusion of which he made the identification of Jesus with the Son of Man (Lk 17:25; cf. the discussion of Lk 7:11-35 above and Acts 7:55-56). He then drew material from Mt 24:37-41 following the Matthean *Stichwort*, παρουσία. By omitting Mt 24:39a, he removed the emphasis on "not knowing" and added the parallel statements about the time of Noah, Lot, and the Son of Man. The paraenetic exhortation (Lk 17:32-33) echoes Mt's Missionary Discourse at Mt 10:39. This is the last verse from Mt 10:26-39 which Luke used, *in Matthew's order,* beginning at Lk 12:2 and culminating here at Lk 17:32-33.[8]

Lk 17:21-37. Evidences of Luke's characteristic terminology are: ἐροῦσιν, Lk 17:23 (Collison 77-78); τῆς γενεᾶς ταύτης, Lk 17:25 (Collison 204); καθώς ἐγένετο ἐν ταῖς ἡμέραις, Lk 17:26 (Collison 133; Goulder 2:656); καθῶς, Lk 17:26, 28 (Collison 155-156); ἧς, Lk 17:27 (Collison 205-206); καθὼς ἐγένετο ἐν ταῖς ἡμέραις, Lk 17:28 (Collison 133; Goulder 2:656); ᾗ, Lk 17:29 (Collison 205); and ἕτερος/α, Lk 17:34-35 (Collison 184; Goulder 2:657).

Section Thirteen. To the Faithful and the Self-Righteous: On Prayer. Lk 18:1–14

Early in his journey to Jerusalem, Jesus taught his disciples about prayer. Now Jesus turns not only to the faithful, but also to the self-righteous for further teachings on prayer. Jesus first tells a story about a widow's persistent prayer and a second about humble praying.

Source-critical observations. This section of the Gospel concludes the portion where Luke departed from following the order of pericopes in Mt in successive divisions of Luke's narrative and, instead, simultaneously followed the order of verses within several distinct Matthean literary units (especially the long speeches of Jesus in Mt). Both of these units come from nonMatthean tradition. See the detailed notes on Lukan composition below.

¶ 101. Pray and don't lose heart! Lk 18:1-8

Jesus now tells a story about a widow who refused to be put off by a judge who would not listen to her. Luke prefaced this story by saying, "Jesus told this story to the

[8] For a detailed discussion of this unit see Dungan, ed., *The Interrelations of the Gospels*, esp. 168-173.

effect that we should always pray and never lose heart—the Son of Man will return as he promised!"

General observations. This story was found by Luke in nonMatthean tradition and placed here to illustrate his theme of untiring prayer to God (cf. Lk 11:1-13, to which this story hearkens back) to send the Son of Man.

Lk 18:1-8. The story is surrounded by signs of Lukan compositional activity. The reference to "the Son of Man" in Lk 18:8 hearkens back to the preceding pericope (Lk 17:20-37), while the use of cognates of δικαῖος point ahead to the story of the Pharisee and the Tax Collector, which follows immediately (Lk 18:9-14). Other Lukan additions are Ἔλεγεν δέ (Collison 56; Goulder 2:662) and προσεύχεσθαι (Collison 63).

¶ 102. Don't pray in a self-righteous manner!

(Mt 18:4; 23:12) **Lk 18:9-14** (cf. Lk 14:11)

Jesus continues teaching his "disciples" on the attitude to have in the interim, through the medium of the story of the Pharisee and the tax collector. Earlier, the Pharisees were portrayed as those who "justified themselves." Here the tax collector humbly begs God to bestow righteousness upon him out of His mercy.

General observations. Luke also drew this parable from nonMatthean tradition. It is linked with the preceding parable on the Wicked Judge by the themes of praying (προσεύχεσθαι, Lk 18:1, 9), and by cognates of δίκαιος (ἐκδικησόν in Lk 18:3; δίκαιοι-ἄδικοι-δεδικαιομένος in Lk 18:9, 11, 14). Luke has connected Lk 18:14 to the parable. The saying here is a precise doublet to Lk 14:11. Lk 18:14 recapitulates the message of the parable and also, in being a close echo of Mt 18:4 (cf. Mt 23:12), prepares for the transition to the next saying about accepting the Kingdom like children (Lk 18:15-17).

Lk 18:9-14. Evidence of Lukan editorial activity includes the uses of δὲ καί, Lk 18:9 (Collison 103); τὴν παραβολὴν ταύτην, Lk 18:9 (Collison 204; cf. Goulder 2:669); προσεύχομαι, Lk 18:10, 11 (Collison 63); ἕτερος, Lk 18:10 (Collison 184; Goulder 2:669); and οὐκ...οὐδέ (Collison 164-165).

Section Fourteen. To the Disciples, a Ruler, and Hearers: On the Kingdom of God. Lk 18:15–30

When some brought children to Jesus, he blessed them and said that the Kingdom of Heaven belongs to them. And whoever would receive the Kingdom of God must become like a child.

As the lawyer at the beginning of Jesus' journey to Jerusalem, so now a ruler asks Jesus, "Good Teacher, what must I do to inherit eternal life?" Jesus protests that only God is truly good and bids the ruler to keep the commandments in the Torah. The ruler says he has kept them all. Jesus tells him he still lacks one thing; he must sell all of his possessions and give the money to the poor. This made the ruler sad; he was very rich.

Jesus goes on to say that it is difficult for the rich to enter the Kingdom of God. Some ask him, "Who can be saved?" Jesus says to trust God, who can do the impossible.

This leads Peter to comment, "Lord, *we* have left everything to follow you..." Jesus assures Peter that everything they had left behind will be restored, and they will have an abundance in this life and Eternal Life as well.

Source-critical observations. At this point (Lk 18:15-17//Mt 19:13-15 plus Mt 18:3!), Luke again began to follow the sequential order of pericopes in Mt, doing so to the end of his Gospel.

Lk 18:15-17//Mt 19:13-15 plus Mt 18:3. For Section Fourteen, Luke followed Mt 19:13-15//Lk 18:15-16 for the story about Jesus blessing the babies. The statement that those who would receive the Kingdom must become like children derived from Mt 18:3. It was the single verse that Luke had not used at Lk 9:46-48//Mt 18:1-5. Such detailed and painstaking utilization would seem to indicate that Luke deliberately circumscribed the entire Travel Narrative (Lk 9:49-18:17) by means of the material in Mt 18:1-5.

Lk 18:18-27//Mt 19:16-26. For the story that begins with the ruler's question, Luke made use of Mt 19:16-26//Lk 18:18-27. Luke had used and edited the inaugural question in Mt 19:16-21 when he conflated Mt 22:34-40 with parts of Mt 19:16-21 at Lk 10:25-28, at the start of the Travel Narrative.

Lk 18:28-30//Mt 19:27-29. Luke closely copied the story of Peter's question and Jesus' answer in Mt 19:27-30//Lk 18:27-30.

Lk 18:30//Mt 19:30//Mt 20:16. We noted above Luke's use of a logion similar to Mt 19:30//Mt 20:16 already at Lk 13:30. A single story intrudes between these comparable logia in Mt, the Parable of the Laborers in the Vineyard. Luke omits that parable from his narrative here at Lk 18:30-31, but includes the logion even if it is slightly out of context here.

¶ 103. Accept the Kingdom like children

Mt 18:3; 19:13-15 ====> **Lk 18:15-17**

Luke continues with the theme of humility, giving a story where Jesus points to infants as the true type of those who receive the Kingdom.

General observations. At the end of the preceding pericope, Luke prepared us to resume following the basic sequential order of pericopes in Mt. Luke created the conclusion to the Parable of the Pharisee and the Tax Collector with a hint from Mt 18:4; being humble as a child and entering the Kingdom like a child. Luke last made use of Mt 18 at Lk 17:4//Mt 18:22. We have suggested above that Luke may reflect some knowledge of Mt 18:23-35, the Parable of the Unforgiving Servant, at both Lk 12:57-59 and Lk 16:10-12. Such reflection would have concluded Luke's work with Mt's chapter on Community Regulations (Mt 18:1-19:1) and brought Luke to the Matthean version of Jesus' teachings on divorce in Mt 19:2-12. Luke had also already used what he wanted from the divorce material in Mt (Lk 16:18//Mt 19:3-12; cf. Mt 5:31-32), so he went on to the next unit: the blessing of the children (Mt 19:13-15).

• Beginning at Lk 18:15, Luke followed the sequential order of pericopes in Mt for the balance of the Travel Narrative (Mt 19:13-20:34//Lk 18:15-43). Note that Lk 19:1-27 is nonMatthean tradition. Jesus' journey to Jerusalem is about to end.

Lk 18:15. Luke has altered Mt's παιδία (Mt 19:13) to βρέφη (Lk 18:15) to stress their greater helplessness. Likewise, in Luke's version, Jesus "touches" the children rather than "laying hands on and blessing them" (Mt), an expression which might not be easily understood.

Lk 18:17. Luke concluded the pericope by attaching Mt 18:3 (cf. Mt 18:1-2, 4-5//Lk 9:46-48), which contains the words "entering the Kingdom of Heaven/God." This served as a transition to the next story, where the issue is "entering the Kingdom" (cf. Lk 18:24, 25). We noted already in the Overview of Part Five how source-critically significant Luke's introduction of Mt 18:3 at just this point in his narrative may be, particularly when combined with other observations about this literary context.

¶ 104. Give your possessions to the poor!

Mt 19:16-30 ====> **Lk 18:18-30**

As if in reply to Jesus' words, a rich ruler of the people asks Jesus how he too may inherit eternal life. Jesus suggests that he try keeping the Commandments. The rich ruler says that he has. But apparently he hasn't, because Jesus interprets them to him further. "One thing you lack: sell your possessions and give the money to the poor and come and follow me." At this, the rich ruler became sad, evidently hearing something he could not do. Looking at him, Jesus comments, "How hard it is for those who are rich to enter the Kingdom of God!" This statement prompts a shocked reaction from the crowd. "Who can do what you ask?" they shout. Jesus answers, "With God, all things are possible." At this, Peter steps forward and proudly announces: "We have left our homes and followed you!" To which Jesus replies, "Yes, and you will be richly rewarded both in this life and the next!"

General observations. Luke continued to follow the sequential order of pericopes in Mt (Lk 18:18-30//Mt 19:16-30) to get this account. He included most of Mt 19:16-30, before skipping the Parable of the Laborers in the Vineyard (Mt 20:1-15), and continued to follow the sequence of pericopes in Mt 20:17-34//Lk 18:31-43. The balance of the Travel Narrative is composed of nonMatthean tradition (Lk 19:1-27).

• This story is linked thematically to the context of the previous story by the idea of "entering the Kingdom of God" (cf. Lk 18:17; Lk 18:29). For Luke, "to enter the Kingdom" is "to find eternal life."

Lk 18:18-19. Luke altered Mt's "what good thing must I do?" (Mt 19:16) to

"Good Teacher, how may I inherit eternal life?" (Lk 18:18) consistent with the ending of his story, "and, in the age to come, inherit eternal life" (Lk 18:30b). We have seen above that Luke made a similar modification at Lk 10:25 near the beginning of the Travel Narrative. For further discussion consult the Excursus following our notes on Lk 11:9-13.

• Luke also altered Mt's address, "Teacher" (Mt 19:16a), to "Good Teacher" (Lk 18:18a) in order to set up the next question back to the rich ruler: "Why do you call me good? No one is good but God alone" (Lk 18:19).

Lk 18:20. In the recitation of the Decalogue that follows, Mt's version follows the order of the LXX whereas Luke is similar to the order in Hellenistic Judaism. Luke omits the reference to Lev. 19:18 in Mt 19:19b.

Lk 18:22. Luke omitted Mt's "If you would be perfect..." (Mt 19:21) as he did at Lk 6:36 (cf. Mt 5:48); it was a Jewish expression easily misunderstood among the Gentile audience for which the Gospel of Luke was intended.

Lk 18:29. Luke temporarily sidestepped Mt's note about "sitting on thrones with the Son of Man judging the Twelve Tribes of Israel" (Mt 19:28); he used it later at Lk 22:28-30 in his own special framework.

• Luke focused Jesus' answer instead on "leaving houses and brothers, etc." (Mt 19:29), to which Luke adds "wife" (Lk 18:29b), a typically Lukan touch (see below at Lk 20:27-40).

• Luke changed Mt's "for my name's sake" (Mt 19:29) to "for the sake of the Kingdom of God" (Lk 18:29b) as more consistent with the basic theme of the story ("entering the Kingdom of God").

Section Fifteen. To the Twelve and a Man: True Blindness. Lk 18:31–43

Jesus takes the Twelve aside and again predicts his future suffering, death and resurrection in Jerusalem in fulfillment of ancient prophecies. They remain "blind" to his meaning. As Jesus draws near to Jericho, an actual blind man hears Jesus coming and shouts out to him, addressing him as "Son of David." "What do you want?" asks Jesus. The blind man begs Jesus to give him sight. Jesus heals him and he becomes one of Jesus' followers, glorifying God before many people, who also give praise to God.

Source-critical observations. Within this section of the Travel Narrative, Luke followed the sequence of pericopes in Mt (Mt 20:17-19//Lk 18:31-34; Mt 20:29-34//Lk 18:35-43).

Lk 18:30-31. Here Luke encountered the Parable of the Laborers in the Vineyard (Mt 20:1-15) and omitted it. See the note to Mt 19:30//Mt 20:16 at the end of the Source-Critical Observations for Section Fourteen above.

Lk 18:31-34. Then Luke resumed following the sequential order of pericopes for the next Passion Prediction Passage (Lk 18:31-34//Mt 20:17-19).

Lk 18:35-43. Luke also continued to follow Mt for the next story of the healing of a blind man (Mt 20:29-34//Lk 18:35-43). Luke conflated this story of two blind men with its doublet at Mt 9:26-31. Mt 9:26-31 was the only literary unit from Mt 8-9 that Luke had not previously utilized. The typically Lukan reference to "salvation by faith" in Lk 18:42 relates to similar wording in Mt 9:29. There is no parallel to the idea of salvation by faith in Mt 20:34, so this connection between Mt 9:29 and Lk 18:42 provides good linguistic evidence that Luke had both stories in Mt in mind when he composed Lk 18:35-43.

¶ 105. Blindness of the disciples

Mt 20:17-19 ====> **Lk 18:31-34**

Immediately, Jesus adds a warning he has given before, namely, that once they reach Jerusalem, "the Son of Man...will be mocked and shamefully treated and spit upon. Gentiles will...kill him and on the third day he will rise" (Lk 18:33). However, the disciples are blind and without understanding.

General observations. Luke skipped over the Parable of the Laborers in the Vineyard in Mt 20:1-16 (Lk 15:11-32 better conveys the point of Mt 20:1-16) in order to append the immediately following prediction in Matthew about the suffering, death and vindication of the Son of Man (Mt 20:17-19//Lk 18:31-34; cf. Lk 9:21-24, 43b-45; 17:22-25; 22:21-23; 24:19-27) to the preceding material about giving up everything to follow Jesus. Another reason for the omission may be that Luke intended to use another vineyard parable later, at Lk 20:9-19//Mt 21:33-46. We have noted above Luke's use, in Lk 13:30, of the repeated logion that frames the omitted parable (Mt 19:30//Mt 20:16).

Lk 18:31-34. There are many Lukan linguistic characteristics throughout, such as τοὺς δώδεκα, used absolutely (Lk 18:31; cf. Collison 168), though here it is also in his source: καὶ αὐτοί, Lk 18:34 (Collison 196; Goulder 2:674); ἦν...κεκρυμμένον, Lk 18:34 (Collison 74; Goulder 2:674); and τὸ ῥῆμα τοῦτο, Lk 18:34 (Collison 204; Goulder 2:674). Luke's editorial activity is consistent with his use of this source.

¶ 106. The blind man who sees Jesus

(Mt 9:26-31) Mt 20:29-34 ====> **Lk 18:35-43**

As if to drive home the point, Luke immediately describes how, as they were entering Jericho, a blind man, hearing that Jesus was passing by, cried out to him, "Jesus, Son of David, have mercy on me!"—evidently expecting that Jesus could cure his blindness. The crowds tried to quiet him, but he shouted all the more insistently, "Son of David, have mercy on me!" Jesus heard him and stopped, inquiring of him what he wanted. He begged Jesus to restore his sight. "Receive your sight," replies Jesus. "Your faith has made you well."

General observations. Luke continued to follow the sequential order of pericopes in Mt (Mt 20:29-34//Lk 18:35-43) to get this story. After the Passion Prediction, Luke came to the story of the sons of Zebedee who have their mother ask Jesus to grant them places of honor at his left and right hand in the Kingdom. Luke had already touched on this squabble as to who was the greatest in Lk 9:46-48 and will make use of part of this story again in Lk 22:24-27. Thus, Luke passed over Mt 20:20-28 for now and came to the story of the healing of two blind men as Jesus was leaving Jericho (Mt 20:29-34). As the synopsis below indicates, Luke modified this story by conflating it with the earlier Matthean doublet at Mt 9:27-31, so that it became a healing of one blind man as Jesus was entering Jericho. Luke attached this story to the next story about Zacchaeus (who lived in Jericho), which he took from his nonMatthean tradition.

Synopsis of Lk 18:35-43

Illustrating the way Luke conflated two healing stories
to produce the story about the healing of the Blind man at Jericho.

Mt 9:26-31	**Mt 20:29-34**	**Lk 18:35-43**
26 καὶ ἐξῆλθεν		**35** Ἐγένετο δὲ
ἡ φήμη αὕτη		
εἰς ὅλην τὴν γῆν ἐκείνην.		
27 Καὶ παράγοντι ἐκεῖθεν τῷ Ἰησοῦ	**29** Καὶ ἐκπορευομένων	ἐν τῷ ἐγγίζειν
	αὐτῶν ἀπὸ Ἰεριχὼ	αὐτὸν εἰς Ἰεριχὼ
ἠκολούθησαν [αὐτῷ]	ἠκολούθησεν αὐτῷ	
	ὄχλος πολύς.	(cf. Lk 18:36)
δύο τυφλοὶ	**30** καὶ ἰδοὺ δύο τυφλοὶ	τυφλός τις
	καθήμενοι παρὰ τὴν ὁδόν	ἐκάθητο παρὰ τὴν ὁδὸν
		ἐπαιτῶν.
	ἀκούσαντες	**36** ἀκούσας δὲ
	(cf. Mt 20:29)	ὄχλου διαπορευομένου
		ἐπυνθάνετο τί εἴη τοῦτο.
	ὅτι	**37** ἀπήγγειλαν δὲ αὐτῷ ὅτι
	Ἰησοῦς παράγει,	Ἰησοῦς ὁ Ναζωραῖος
		παρέρχεται.
κράζοντες καὶ λέγοντες,	ἔκραξαν λέγοντες,	**38** καὶ ἐβόησεν λέγων,
Ἐλέησον ἡμᾶς,	Ἐλέησον ἡμᾶς,	
υἱὸς Δαυίδ.	[κύριε], υἱὸς Δαυίδ.	Ἰησοῦ υἱὲ Δαυίδ,
		ἐλέησόν με.
	31 ὁ δὲ ὄχλος	**39** καὶ οἱ προάγοντες
	ἐπετίμησεν αὐτοῖς	ἐπετίμων αὐτῷ
	ἵνα σιωπήσωσιν·	ἵνα σιγήσῃ,
(cf. Mt 9:31)	οἱ δὲ μεῖζον ἔκραξαν	αὐτὸς δὲ πολλῷ μᾶλλον
	λέγοντες,	ἔκραζεν,
		Υἱὲ Δαυίδ,
	Ἐλέησον ἡμᾶς, κύριε,	ἐλέησόν με.

Healing of the blind man near Jericho (cont.)

Mt 9:28	Mt 20:31	Lk 18:40
	υἱὸς Δαυίδ.	
28 ἐλθόντι δὲ εἰς τὴν οἰκίαν	32 καὶ στὰς	40 σταθεὶς δὲ
προσῆλθον αὐτῷ οἱ τυφλοί,		
καὶ λέγει αὐτοῖς ὁ Ἰησοῦς,	ὁ Ἰησοῦς ἐφώνησεν αὐτοὺς	ὁ Ἰησοῦς ἐκέλευσεν αὐτὸν
		ἀχθῆναι πρὸς αὐτόν.
		ἐγγίσαντος δὲ αὐτοῦ
	καὶ εἶπεν,	ἐπηρώτησεν αὐτόν,
Πιστεύετε ὅτι	Τί θέλετε	41 Τί σοι θέλεις
δύναμαι τοῦτο ποιῆσαι;	ποιήσω ὑμῖν;	ποιήσω;
λέγουσιν αὐτῷ,	33 λέγουσιν αὐτῷ,	ὁ δὲ εἶπεν,
Ναί κύριε.	Κύριε,	Κύριε,
(cf. Mt 9:30)	ἵνα ἀνοιγῶσιν οἱ ὀφθαλμοὶ	ἵνα ἀναβλέψω.
	ἡμῶν.	
29 τότε	34 σπλαγχνισθεὶς δὲ	
	ὁ Ἰησοῦς	42 καὶ ὁ Ἰησοῦς
ἥψατο τῶν ὀφθαλμῶν αὐτῶν	ἥψατο τῶν ὀμμάτων αὐτῶν,	
λέγων,		εἶπεν αὐτῷ,
		Ἀνάβλεψον·
Κατὰ τὴν πίστιν ὑμῶν		ἡ πίστις σου
γενηθήτω ὑμῖν.		σέσωκέν σε.
30 καὶ	καὶ εὐθέως	43 καὶ παραχρῆμα
ἠνεῴχθησαν αὐτῶν	ἀνέβλεψαν	ἀνέβλεψεν
οἱ ὀφθαλμοί.	(cf. Mt 20:33)	
	καὶ ἠκολούθησαν αὐτῷ.	καὶ ἠκολούθει αὐτῷ
καὶ ἐνεβριμήθη αὐτοῖς ὁ		
Ἰησοῦς		
λέγων, Ὁρᾶτε μηδεὶς		
γινωσκέτω.		
31 οἱ δὲ ἐξελθόντες	(cf. Mt 20:31)	δοξάζων τὸν θεόν.
διεφήμισαν αὐτὸν		καὶ πᾶς ὁ λαὸς ἰδὼν
ἐν ὅλῃ τῇ γῇ ἐκείνῃ.		ἔδωκεν αἶνον τῷ θεῷ.

• The typically Lukan conclusion to this miracle story, "Your faith has saved you," (Lk 18:42) probably reflects, "According to your faith, let it happen to you," in Mt 9:29, for which Mt 20:29-34 provides no equivalent. This distinctive parallel with Mt 9:26-31 provides evidence that Luke was conflating Mt 20:29-34 with the Matthean doublet at Mt 9:26-31. Mt 9:26-31 is the only pericope from chapters 8-9 of Mt that Luke had not yet utilized. The phrase "your faith has saved you" (Lk 18:42) is a favorite Lukanism (cf. Lk 7:50; 8:48; 17:19 and 18:42).

• The story of the blind man who "sees" Jesus in faith, and is healed by him, sets the stage for the story of Zacchaeus, who climbs a tree in order to "see" Jesus (Lk 19:3f.).

• Lukan themes dominate the narrative: e.g., the blind, discipleship, the people. Lukan stylistic characteristics within the story include: ἐγένετο δέ, Lk 18:35 (Collison 43; Goulder 2:674); ὄχλου διαπορευομένου, Lk 18:36 (Collison 60); τί εἴη τοῦτο (τίς + the optative), Lk 18:35 (Collison 209; Goulder 2:674); αὐτὸς δέ, Lk 19:39 (Collison 196); ἐγγίσαντος δὲ αὐτοῦ, Lk 18:40 (Collison 77-78); παραχρῆμα, Lk 18:43 (Collison 154; Goulder 2:674); and πᾶς ὁ λαός, Lk 18:43 (Collison 174; Goulder 2:674). Luke has freely rewritten Mt.

Interweaving Transitional Section (First Half).
Preparation for the King to Come into his City. Lk 19:1–27

This Transitional Section consists of two stories, that of Zacchaeus and the Parable of the King coming to claim his city. For narratological overviews and detailed analysis consult the pericope discussions below.

Source-critical observations.

Lk 19:1-10. The story of Zacchaeus comes from nonMatthean tradition.

Lk 19:11-27. The Parable of the Pounds shows similarities with the Parable of the Talents in Mt 25:14-30. We note here that Luke seems to have made allusions to Mt 25:1-13, the preceding literary unit in Mt, already at Lk 12:35-40 and definitely made use of parts of the Parable of the Wise and Foolish Virgins in Lk 13:22-27. If Luke utilized the Parable of the Talents at Lk 19:11-27, even if only for a "contextual parallel" into which Luke inserted comparable nonMatthean tradition, Luke would have completed his use of the first two of the three parables in Mt 25 (The Wise and Foolish Virgins, Mt 25:1-13//Lk 13:22-27, cf. Lk 12:35-40; and Talents, Mt 25:14-30, cf. Lk 19:11-27). The last "parable" in Mt 25, the Judgment of the Nations (Mt 25:31-46), has no parallel in the Gospel of Luke, who might not have wanted to bring its apocalyptic perspective into his narrative, although some of its elements must have been attractive. Luke began to use the next unit in Mt, i.e., Mt 26:1ff., at Lk 22:1ff.

¶ 107. Zacchaeus—portrait of the ideal follower
Lk 19:1-10

On the verge of Jesus' entry into Jerusalem, Luke tells the story of a chief tax collector who so eagerly wishes to see Jesus that he awkwardly climbs a sycamore tree. Immediately understanding the whole situation, Jesus invites him to come down and tells him he would like to come to his house to dine with him. Hearing this, people in the crowd "grumble" at Jesus, complaining that he was "going to be the guest of a sinner." During the meal, Zacchaeus tells Jesus that he had repented of all his evil gain, giving half of everything he had to the poor, and, to anyone whom he had extorted too much tax money, a four-fold restoration. Jesus praises Zacchaeus, saying, "Today salvation has come to this house!"

General observations. This story has been taken from Luke's non-Matthean tradition. As noted above, this story is closely linked with the previous account of the healing of the blind man. Both the blind man and Zacchaeus wish to "see" Jesus. Both become models of discipleship. The story is unusually dense with favorite Lukan themes: repentant tax collectors eagerly seeking to see Jesus, the good rich who give their goods to the poor, opposition to Jesus' associating with sinners (cf. Lk 15:2), and "the Son of Man coming to seek and to save the lost" (Lk 19:10). As such, this story recapitulates nearly all of the main themes emphasized in the entire Travel Narrative, thus serving well as its conclusion.

Lk 19:1-10. Goulder 2:675-678 considers this story a creation of Luke. However, judging from the small number of Lukan linguistic characteristics Goulder found within the story, Luke was more likely editing non-Matthean tradition.

¶ 108. Parable of the king preparing to come to his city

(Mt 25:14-30) **Lk 19:11-27**

In a very important clarification of the direction of his narrative, Luke comments, "Jesus proceeded to tell them a parable because he was near to Jerusalem and because they supposed that the Kingdom of God was to appear immediately" (Lk 19:11). With this introduction, Luke portrays Jesus telling a complex allegorical story about a nobleman who went "into a far country to receive kingly powers," and, while there, gave enormous sums of money to ten servants to manage until he returned. After he had left, however, some dissidents sent an embassy after him saying, "We don't want you to be our king!" Some time later, the nobleman arrived back, having been made king, and asked each of his servants what they had done with what had been entrusted to them. Some had increased the amount, but one had done nothing. The nobleman praised the former, but chastised the latter severely. And then he ordered the citizens who had not wanted him to be their king brought before him and killed immediately. After telling them this story, Luke notes, "Jesus went on ahead, going up to Jerusalem" (Lk 19:28).

General observations. Luke may have found this allegory in his non-Matthean tradition, for it is quite different from the Parable of the Talents in Mt 25:14-30. On the other hand, the story exhibits numerous indications of Lukan compositional activity, so that it may instead be a Lukan revision of such a story, inserted into this Lukan context to serve as an allegory of the fate of Jerusalem and the Church. As such, the story functions for Luke as the prelude to the Triumphal Entry of Jesus into Jerusalem (Mt 21:1-9//Lk 19:28-44), followed by Jesus' grim statement about the imminent destruction approaching Jerusalem. If the story of Zacchaeus looks backward, drawing together many of the themes of the teaching of Jesus during his Journey to Jerusalem, the Parable of the King

Preparing to Come to his City looks forward to the rest of the Gospel and Acts, focusing on the themes of the judgment of Israel and the vindication of the Church (cf. Acts). Looked at in this way, this story and the Interweaving Transitional Section of which it is a part are Luke's composition.

Lk 19:11-27. Evidence of Luke's editorial work within this story would include the following linguistic characteristics: 'Ακούοντων δὲ αὐτῶν, Lk 19:11 (Collison 77-78); παραχρῆμα, Lk 19:11 (Collison 154: Goulder 2:683); ἡ βασιλεία τοῦ θεοῦ, Lk 19:11 (Collison 170); ὑποστρέψαι, Lk 19:12 (Collison 67; Goulder 2:683); ἐξουσίαν, (Collison 173); δὲ καί, Lk 19:19 (Collison 103); ἕτερος, Lk 19:20 (Collison 184; Goulder 2:684); the participle + relative pronoun (five times in Lk 19:21, 22, 26; cf. Collison 78-79); αἵρω, Lk 19:21, 22 (Collison 36); ἔθηκας, Lk 19:21, 22 (Collison 66); πλήν, (Collison 121; Goulder 2:685); and ἀγάγετε, (Collison 35).

PART SIX LK 19:28 – 21:38

THE ARRIVAL OF THE PROPHET-KING IN JERUSALEM

Overview

Part Six of Luke's narrative is composed of two regular Sections preceded by the second half of an Interweaving Transitional Section: the king comes to claim his city (Lk 19:28-44). In the first regular Section the king meets opposition and is rejected by the city's leaders (19:45-20:47). In the second regular Section the king predicts the destruction of the city (21:5-38). A brief interweaving pericope (Lk 21:1-4) connects these two regular Sections.

The second half of the Interweaving Transitional Section portrays Jesus the King (Lk 19:38) coming to claim the city which housed his father's sanctuary (cf. Lk 2:49). Luke had concluded Part Five with the first half of this Interweaving Transitional Section by having Jesus tell of a certain man who had received a kingship and then returned home (Lk 19:11-27). In the second half, Luke makes it clear that Jesus is that very man who has come to his father's home to receive his kingship. But just as the parable said (Lk 19:27), certain ones in the city will not welcome the return of the royal one (Lk 19:39-40).

In the first regular Section, Jesus enters the temple and conducts a series of debates with the leaders of the Jerusalem community (Lk 19:45-20:47). The debates end with a bitter indictment of the scribes (Lk 20:45-47) followed in the interweaving Section by a contrasting example of a poor widow who gives all she has, unlike the hypocrisy of wealthy donors (Lk 21:1-4).

The second regular Section (Lk 21:5-38) begins with a comment by some bystanders on the wealth and opulence of the Temple and its votive offerings. Jesus announces that the Temple will soon be destroyed (Lk 21:5-6). People ask when this will happen (Lk 21:7), and Jesus launches into a grim description of the calamities soon to come all over the world, in the course of which the Temple and even Jerusalem itself will be completely destroyed (Lk 21:8-38).

In the Lukan account, all of the action, after Jesus enters the temple, is bounded by the phrase: "Every day he was teaching in the temple" (Lk 19:47 // 21:37). Thus the words in Lk 20:1: "one day as he was teaching the people in the temple area..." are an attempt to give Luke's audience the impression of actually being there and hearing what the Lord Jesus had to say to the crowds and disciples in the momentous days just before his arrest and execution.

Interweaving Transitional Unit (Second Half).
The King Comes to Claim His City. Lk 19:28-44

¶ 109. Procession down the Mount of Olives
Mt 20:17; 21:1-9 (21:15-16) ====> **Lk 19:28-44**

Jesus is now at the outskirts of Jerusalem (cf. Lk 19:11). Upon his orders, two disciples get a colt and bring it to him. He rides the colt down the slope of the mountain, and a crowd of disciples praise God and cry, "Peace in Heaven" (Lk 19:38). But as Jesus draws near the city, his response is to weep (Lk 19:41). He announces that the city is about to suffer a siege and be destroyed. There may be peace in heaven, but there will soon be death and destruction in Jerusalem.

General observations. The unit opens in Lk 19:28-29 with Luke conflating Mt 20:17 (καὶ ἀναβαίνων ὁ Ἰησοῦς εἰς Ἰερόσυλυμα) and Mt 21:1 (καὶ ὅτε ἤγγισαν εἰς Ἰερόσυλυμα καὶ ἦλθον εἰς βηθφαγὴ εἰς τὸ Ὄρος τῶν Ἐλαιῶν) to form the setting for the arrival of Jesus at Jerusalem. The first reference to "nearing Jerusalem" at Mt 20:17 introduced Jesus' third prediction of the Passion in Mt, which Luke already used at Lk 18:31-34//Mt 20:17-19. Next in Mt's order (Mt 20:20-28) was the story of the Mother of the Sons of Zebedee's request, which Luke may have used much earlier at Lk 9:46-50 (cf. Mt 18:1-6 and Mt 20:20-28). Luke later utilized this same (Mt 18:1-6) or similar (Mt 20:20-28) material when he composed Lk 22:24-27 (cf. the ref. to betrayal at Lk 22:21f. + the argument as to who is greater in Lk 22:24f., followed by the prediction of betrayal and death at Lk 9:43f + argument as to who is greater in Lk 9:46f.).

Next in Mt's order, after the petition by the mother of the sons of Zebedee (Mt 20:20-28//Lk 9:46-48//Lk 22:24-27), comes the healing of two blind men upon leaving Jericho (Mt 20:29-34). Luke had used this unit from Mt already at Lk 18:35-43, but he provided a different setting, namely, when Jesus and his disciples were *entering* Jericho. Next in Mt's order is Mt 21:1: "and when they drew near to Jerusalem...," which Luke blended with Mt 20:17 at Lk 19:28-29. At this point, Luke resumed following Mt's general order of pericopes (Lk 19:29//Mt 21:1).

Lk 19:28-29. These two verses are replete with linguistic characteristics of Luke. Εἰπών (Lk 19:28; cf. 19:30) is used in multiple contexts and appears twice as many times in Luke as in Matthew. It is therefore a typical Lukan compositional characteristic (cf. Goulder 2:687). The use of πορεύομαι in Lk 19:28 (cf. Lk 19:30, 36) is a linguistic usage of Luke (Collison 60). The construction of καὶ ἐγένετο + temporal ὡς is also a Lukan linguistic feature (Goulder 2:687). Finally, the articular participle of καλέω introducing an appositive is designated by Collison 80 as a linguistic characteristic of Luke.

Lk 19:30-31. These verses follow Mt 21:2-3 fairly closely. The use of ὑπαγεῖν is puzzling since Mt 21:2 has πορευέσθε which is a Lukan linguistic preference. Since Luke used πορεύομαι three times in this pericope, including this verse (Lk 19:28, 30, 36), Luke may have used a synonymous expression for variety (cf. Lk 10:3). The collocation of ἐν with the relative pronoun (Lk 19:30) is Lukan (Collison 135).

• According to Bauer, *Lexicon* 739, πῶλος means "horse" when no other animal is named.

• Luke has revised Mt's literal fulfillment of Zechariah's prophetic reference to two animals (Zech 9:9; cf. Mt 21:2//Lk 19:30).

• Luke (19:31) has a very comprehensive theological understanding of prophecy and fulfillment. However, Luke's way of expressing this does not necessarily coincide with Mt's practice of using specific quotations from the Old Testament. Thus, here Luke characteristically omits the wording of the Matthean proof from prophecy (Mt 21:4-5).

Lk 19:32-34. Here Luke develops further the Matthean version of the search for the colt (cf. Mt 21:6). This may well be a characteristic Lukan attempt at verisimilitude because much of the language, grammar and syntax seems to be Lukan. οἱ κύριοι is also found in Lk 16:13; Acts 16:16, 19.

• The clause ὁ κύριος αὐτοῦ χρεῖαν ἔχει forms a small *inclusio* around this unit (Lk 19:31b; 19:34). The use of χρεῖαν ἔχειν is characteristic of Luke (5:31; 9:11; 15:7; 22:71).

Lk 19:35-36. Luke has followed Mt 21:7-8. In 19:35, Luke uses ἐπιβιβάζειν. In the NT only Luke uses this word (Lk 10:34; Acts 23:24).

• Luke omitted Mt's reference to the throwing of the leafy branches in Jesus' path (Mt 21:8; Lk 19:36). Origen considered this feature as well as many others in Mt's narrative of the entry into Jerusalem to be incomprehensible if taken literally. For example, Origen noted that "the branches being cut down from the trees and thrown on the road before him... surely they were a hindrance to his passage rather than a well-devised reception."[1] Luke might have had a similar response to some of the details in this unit of Mt's narrative.

Lk 19:37-38. We noted above that Luke prepared for the arrival of Jesus near Jerusalem with the Parable of the Pounds (Lk 19:11-27). Its chief theme is the return of a man to receive a kingship. Now, as he approaches Jerusalem, Jesus is received in Lk 19:37-38 as a king. The precise term βασιλεύς, a linguistic characteristic of the text of Matthew, does not appear in Mt 21:9. Thus, the appearance of βασιλεύς in Lk 19:38 reveals Luke's intention very clearly.

• As an expansion of Mt 21:9, Luke was careful to point out in Lk 19:37-38 that Jesus was well received by ἅπαν τὸ πλῆθος of his disciples, not some

[1] Cf. *Commentary on John* 10.17; *Ante-Nicene Fathers* 10:396.

unruly rabble as is implied by Mt's narrative. Furthermore they did not shout Mt's politically rebellious slogan "Hosanna (= [O God] please save) the son of David! [O God] please give him help on high!" (for this explanation of the term *hosanna* see now Marvin Pope, *ABD* 3:290f.). Instead Luke's group of disciples uttered the politically innocent exclamation, "Peace in Heaven and glory [to God] in the highest!"

Lk 19:39-40. In contrast to the glowing acceptance of Jesus by his disciples, Lk 19:39-40 announces his rejection by the Pharisees. Thus, Jesus' prophecy in Lk 13:35 is fulfilled. In addition, since Jesus' prediction in Mt 23:39 (cf. Lk 13:35) *follows* Jesus' entry into Jerusalem (Mt 21:8-9//Lk 19:37-38), Luke has altered the order of Mt in such a way that Jesus' prophecy in Lk 13:35 (cf. Mt 23:39) is fulfilled within the Lukan narrative (Lk 19:37-38), rather than beyond the narrative, if it is fulfilled at all, as Mt's text (Mt 23:39) would require. That is, Mt 23:39 cannot possibly predict what is to happen in Mt 21:8-9 since Mt 23:39 obviously follows Mt 21:8-9. Luke's reversal of the order of these verses in Matthew is in accord with a demonstrable Lukan motif of Jesus' prophecy, followed by its fulfillment within the Lukan narrative.

• The connection of events happening in fulfillment of a pre-determined plan is characteristic of Luke (cf. Lk 24:7-8). Despite the hopes of many, this visit will not bring peace (Lk 19:38; cf. 12:51). The Jerusalem leadership begins to line up against Jesus. Rejection is a feature of the beginning of all the major sections of Jesus' ministry in Luke (Lk 4:14-9:50 [4:16-30 at Nazareth by his own people]; 9:51-19:27 [9:51-56 by the Samaritans]; 19:28-21:38 [19:39-40 by the Pharisees]; 22:1-24:53 [22:1-6 by Judas]).[2]

• In Mt 21:15 (cf. Mt 21:9) the children at the temple *cry* Hosanna to the Son of David. In Luke 19:40 Jesus announces that the stones will *cry* out the truth about him (cf. Hab 2:11; Goulder 2:688-689). Does this use of κραζεῖν by Luke reveal Luke's awareness of a neighboring passage in Mt?

Lk 19:41-44. Luke completed the narrative account of the Way to Jerusalem by describing what happened on the descent down the Mount of Olives to the city. Lk 19:41 and 42 do not have parallels elsewhere in the other Synoptic Gospels. Lk 19:41 is an introduction to the account composed by Luke. The use of ὡς is Lukan (about 48 times in Luke-Acts). ἐγγίζειν is also a linguistic usage of Luke (Collison 46) as is κλαίειν (13 times in Luke-Acts as opposed to two times in Matthew; cf. Goulder 2:690).

Lk 19:42-44. These verses complete the transitional unit. Here Jesus pronounces two oracles against Jerusalem (Lk 19:42 and Lk 19:43-44). They are framed by the clauses εἰ ἔγνως (Lk 19:42) and ἀνθ' ὧν οὐκ ἔγνως (Lk 19:44) to indicate something of the pathos of the failure to acknowledge the messianic mission of Jesus: divine punishment will be inevitable.

---

[2] Cf. G. Sterling, *Historiography and Self-Definition: Josephos, Luke-Acts and Apologetic Historiography* SupNT64 (Leiden: E. J. Brill, 1992) 347.

• The oracles are connected by the repetition of ὅτι recitative. The first oracle says that the leaders of Jerusalem should have accepted Jesus' arrival in Jerusalem as a visitation of peace (cf. the Benedictus account in Lk. 1:79). Indeed worthy of note are the large number of echoes between Lk 19:41-44 and the Benedictus materials in Lk 1:71, 74, 78-79). But the understanding of Jesus as the king of peace has been hidden from the eyes of Jerusalem's leaders. The second oracle brings together a catena of passages from the LXX to describe the siege and fall of Jerusalem in 70 CE as a divine visitation of Judgment (cf. Goulder 2:690, who makes a strong case that the two oracles are Lukan *vaticinia ex eventu* in the aftermath of Titus' siege and destruction of Jerusalem). There is Lukan vocabulary here, e.g., the phrase τὸν καιρὸν τῆς ἐπισκοπῆς is characteristic of Luke (cf. Lk 1:68, 78; Acts 1:20). Thus we are inclined to agree with those who argue that these predictions in Luke have been shaped and made more specific in light of the actual events of the destruction of Jerusalem in 70 CE, and, as such, provide a *terminus a quo* for the writing of Luke-Acts (*pace* J.A.T. Robinson). The theme of Jesus as prophet is very strong in Luke; this entire unit, which echoes and imitates the LXX, is therefore a Lukan composition to prepare the way for the dominant theme of the next unit: the destruction of Jerusalem, to which Luke turns very explicitly in Section Two.]

Section One: The King Meets Opposition and Is Rejected by the City's Leaders. Lk 19:45-21:4

¶ 110. Jesus symbolically destroys the Temple

Mt 21:12-13====> **Lk 19:45-48**

No sooner has he made these dire predictions than Jesus goes straight into the Temple and begins to enact God's judgment. He goes up to those who were selling sacrificial animals and casts them out of the Temple, alluding to the words of the prophets Jeremiah and Isaiah. The words of the former in their original context are very strong: "Do you think you can turn the house which bears my name (into)... a den of thieves and I won't see the evil all of you are doing? I can see it plainly enough! And because of your wickedness, I will cast you away from me as I cast away all of your brothers, all (ten tribes of) the offspring of Ephraim!" (Jer 7:11-15).

The chief priests and scribes and city leaders are enraged at Jesus' words and want to kill him, but there is nothing they can do since the crowds hang on his every word. So they must stand by and watch, day after day, as Jesus repeats this message to the people gathered in the Temple precincts.

General observations. The major feature of Luke's account *vis-à-vis* Matthew (Lk 19:45-46//Mt 21:12-17) is its relative brevity. He emphasized "casting out"—a term he gets from Mt but Lk also echoes the wider context in Jer 7, quoted above. This means that, in Luke's perspective, this was no "cleansing" of the Temple; Jesus did not come to Jerusalem as a *reformer*. Like the original sanctuary at Shiloh, Jerusalem's Temple is doomed! Its only remaining function in Luke-Acts is to provide the location for Jesus' and the Apostles' final speeches. By his allusions to Isa 56:7 and Jer 7:11 we are reminded that in Luke's prophecy-fulfillment scheme, the Prophet-Messiah reiterates the earlier announcement of Jerusalem's doom (Lk 13:34-45), which will be the true fulfillment of Jeremiah's prophecy.

Lk 19:45-46. Although Luke was following Mt at this point, he made a number of changes. For example, Luke changed Mt's ἐξέβαλεν in Mt 21:12 to ἤρξατο ἐκβάλλειν (Lk 19:45). This pleonastic/inceptive use of ἄρχομαι + the infinitive is a linguistic characteristic of Luke (Collison 39-40).

Lk 19:47-48. This appears to be a Lukan composition intended to end the scene and provide a transition to the next series of vignettes. All of these vignettes are meant by Luke to characterize a typical day of Jesus' teaching. The periphrastic imperfect (ἦν διδάσκων) at the beginning or close of a section is characteristic of Luke (Collison 73-74).

• Καθ' ἡμέραν is characteristic of Lukan composition (Lk 11:3; 16:19; 19:47; 22:53). Collison views καθ' ἡμέραν as a "probable linguistic usage of Luke" (Collison 137).

• The phraseology ἀρχιερεῖς καὶ γραμματεῖς is found also in Lk 20:1, 19; 22:2, 66; and 23:10. It also appears to be of Lukan composition.

• The occurrences of ὁ λαός (19:48) and ἅπας (19:47) are characteristic Lukan linguistic usages (Goulder 2:691). These cases of recurrent linguistic terminology provide evidence of Lukan composition in Lk 19:47-48.

¶ 111. The Jerusalem leadership questions Jesus' authority

Mt 21:23-27 ====> **Lk 20:1-8**

Unable to stand idly by, the Jerusalem leadership decides to confront Jesus. "Who gave you the authority to do and say these things?" "Answer me this first," replies Jesus. "Was John the Baptist sent by God or acting on mere human authority?" Suddenly realizing they could not say what they actually thought about John (cf. Lk. 7:29-30) for fear of the people, they decline to answer. "Neither will I answer your question," counters Jesus.

General observations. Luke was following the order of Mt's pericopes at this point. He omitted the Matthean account of the cursing of the fig tree (Mt 21:18-22), perhaps because of the earlier parable about a fig tree which symbolically predicted the fate of Jerusalem (Lk 13:6-9), which he had taken from his nonMatthean tradition. Luke then adopted, in the Matthean order, the next four controversy stories (Mt 21:23–22:46; cf. Lk. 20:1-34). He artfully fashioned a classic Hellenistic philosophical tableau in which the Visiting Sage is publicly challenged by his opponents on a range of typical issues: the source of his spiritual authority, his loyalty to the tyrant, ridiculing a point of doctrine, what is the way of salvation, and so forth.[3] Luke makes few changes to Mt 21:23-27.

Lk 20:1. The opening verse is Luke's own composition. The use of καὶ ἐγένετο occurs 24 times in Luke. According to Collison 43, in ten of these instances (Lk 5:12, 17; 7:11; 8:1; 9:18; 11:1, 27; 14:1; 17:11; and 20:1), the phrase opens a new "act" in Luke's drama and is a linguistic usage of Luke. The collocation of ἐν with ἡμέρα (Lk 20:1) preceded by ἐγένετο occurs 9 times in Luke. According to Collison 133, it is a linguistic usage of Luke. The use of διδάσκειν (Lk 20:1) is usually a sign of Lukan composition (Collison 45), although διδάσκειν is also found in Mt 21:23.

Lk 20:2-5. These verses follow Mt 21:23-25 closely.

Lk 20:6. This verse has a major change from Mt 21:26 with the occurrence of ὁ λαὸς ἅπας καταλιθάσει ἡμᾶς. The use of ἅπας is Lukan (Collison 183); it occurs 12 times in Luke and only three times in Matthew. Of course λαός is a favorite Lukan term (Goulder 2: 692). Although καταλιθάζειν is a hapax legomenon, it may echo καταλιθοβολεῖν in Ex 17:4 and Num 14:10 and thus be a Lukan Septuagintism.

• Note also that the *inclusio* of stressing the authority of Jesus in Mt 21:23 and Mt 21:27 was retained by Luke in Lk 20:2 and Lk 20:8, another possible indication of Luke's direct literary dependence upon Mt.

¶ 112. Jesus tells a story about some wicked tenants

Mt 21:33-46 ====> **Lk 20:9-19**

Having countered this oblique attack successfully, Jesus goes on the offensive with an equally veiled accusation of his own. Turning to the people standing around, he tells them a story about certain merciless vineyard tenants who repeatedly beat and drive away the vineyard owner's servants, sent to see how the vineyard is being kept. Finally, the vineyard owner sends his "beloved son," but the tenants murder him in hopes of getting the vineyard for themselves. "What do you think the owner of that vineyard will do to those tenants?" asks Jesus. "He will destroy them and give the vineyard to others!" Clearly sensing Jesus' meaning, the people cry, "God forbid this should happen to Israel!" But Jesus replies with a quote from a Psalm implying that the doom of Israel's leaders is certain. Furious, the scribes and chief priests wish to kill Jesus there and then, but they hold themselves back because they are afraid of what the people would do to them.

General observations. Following the account in which the Jerusalem leaders challenge Jesus' authority (Mt 21:23-27), Mt has two parables

---

[3] Arnold Toynbee has collected a large number of such classic "tableaux"—parallels to Gospel vignettes; cf. the unabridged version of Arnold Toynbee's *A Study of History* (Oxford University Press, 1939) 6:376-539, esp. 377-406.

about vineyards (Mt 21:28-32 and 21:33-46). Luke omitted the first, probably because he had just talked about John the Baptist (cf. Mt 21:32) and because he already had used a parable of two sons (Lk 15:11-32). Nevertheless, the appearance of ἴδοντες...αὐτόν (viz., τὸν υἱόν) in Lk 20:14, also found in the Parable of the Two Sons in Mt 21:32, could be an indication that Luke made passing use of the first parable even as he chose the second for his narrative (Lk 20:14//Mt 21:32).[4]

Lk 20:9. Luke's version of the Parable of the Vineyard contains numerous Lukan changes, particularly at the beginning and end (Lk 20:9, 19). Lk 20:9a contains a pleonastic/inceptive use of ἄρχομαι + the infinitive (λέγειν) which is a linguistic characteristic of Luke (Collison 39-40). Also, the addition of χρόνους ἱκανούς to Mt at Lk 20:9 is Lukan (cf. Lk 23:8 and 28:8).

Lk 20:17-18. In Mt 21:42-44, the parable ends with a verse taken from Ps 118:22 (Ps 117 LXX) to which Jesus adds a warning (Mt 21:44) which is quoted by Luke (Lk 20:18). We note that Mt 21:44: "And he who falls on this stone will be broken to pieces; but when it falls on anyone, it will crush him" has brackets around it and is given a probable authenticity rank of 'C' by the UBS^4 editorial committee. Gundry has answered the UBS arguments (cf. Metzger 1994:47), showing on compositional grounds that it is highly unlikely that Mt 21:44 is a harmonizing addition brought in from Lk 20:18.[5] We agree with Gundry. In our judgment, the UBS^4 editorial committee was misled by its reliance upon the Two Source Hypothesis at this point. This is no "harmonization." Mt 21:44 is what Luke saw in his text of Matthew, as the almost unanimous text critical evidence indicates (include ℵ B C L W Z Δ Θ numerous papyri, numerous versions, and Chrysostom, Cyril, Jerome, Augustine | | omit D 33 it$^{a.b.d.}$ et al. sy^{s} Irenaeus^{lat}, Origen, Eusebius^{syr}). Note that the acceptance of Mt 21:44 creates a sizable "minor agreement" between Mt and Lk against Mk. In our view, Luke simply copied Mt 21:44 in Lk 20:18.

Lk 20:19. In this verse we see a tendency of Luke to prefer the expression οἱ γραμματεῖς καὶ οἱ ἀρχιερεῖς (Lk 19:47; 20:1; 22:2, 66; 23:10). Collison 203 considers it a "probable linguistic characteristic" of Luke.

¶ 113. Will you pay Caesar's tax?

Mt 22:15-22 ====> **Lk 20:20-26**

Unable to kill him themselves, the Jerusalem leaders resolve to use more devious methods to get Jesus put away once and for all. Hoping to be able to turn him over to the Roman authorities on suspicion of treason, they position a few spies in the crowd posing as avid and sincere listeners, who innocently ask Jesus: "Master, we know you speak nothing but the truth; tell us whether we should pay taxes to the Romans?" If Jesus said "no" then the Roman authorities would be instantly notified; if he said "yes"

[4] See Robert Gundry, *Evidence that Luke used Matthew* 1485.

[5] Gundry, ibid., 1487.

then he would lose credibility with the people, who hated the Roman tax. Sensing the trap, Jesus asks for a Roman denarius. "See Caesar's image on it?" asks Jesus. "Give to Caesar what is in his image; but all the more give to God what is in his image!" The spies are astonished at the shrewdness of Jesus' answer and fall silent.

General observations. After adapting Mt's second vineyard parable to his purposes, Luke encountered Mt 22:1-14, which he had already used in Lk 14:16-24. Next comes Mt 22:15-22, the question of paying Caesar's tax. Luke followed Mt's version fairly closely, making modifications mainly at the beginning and end so that it fit better into the dramatic action he was building through this series of vignettes.

Lk 20:20. Luke modified Mt's references to "Pharisees" and "Herodians" (Mt 22:15-16) to "so they (i.e., "the scribes and the chief priests," in Lk 20:19) sent spies." In his retelling of Mt chs. 21-27, Luke has shifted Mt's negative references to the Pharisees (esp. Mt 23) to earlier parts of his narrative and focused exclusively on Jerusalem's chief priests and scribes as being responsible for the death of Jesus. They are the ones who hand Jesus over to the Roman authorities for sentencing (Lk 23:1-3; cf. Lk 22:66). In fact, after Lk 19:39, the Pharisees never appear in Luke's Gospel again.[6]

• The rest of the pericope follows Mt more closely.

• The word ἐπιλάβεσθαι (Lk 20:20, 26) occurs five times in Luke as opposed to once in Mt (Mt 14:31; cf. Lk 9:47; 14:4; 20:20, 26; 23:26). It also occurs seven times in Acts (Acts 9:27; 16:19; 17:19; 18:17; 21:30, 33; 23:19). Collison lists it as a "probable" Lukan linguistic usage (Collison 49-50).

Lk 20:21. In Lk 20:21, we note the collocation of "3rd singular aorist active indicative of ἐπερωτάω + αὐτόν + present active nominative participle of λέγω + διδάσκαλε." This same structure is found in five places in the NT: four times in Lk and once in a parallel in Mt (Lk 18:18; Lk 20:21; Lk 20:27-28//Mt22:23-24; Lk 21:7), suggesting that it is a characteristic Lukan clause (cf. Collison 216).

¶ 114. The Sadducees mock Jesus' teaching on resurrection

Mt 22:23-33,46 ====> **Lk 20:27-40**

Luke next introduces "the Sadducees," a new group of opponents in the audience. They appear to want his opinion on an obscure point of Jewish law concerning the effect of multiple marriages on the marital status of a woman in heaven. Their real purpose, however, is not to learn anything about that but simply to ridicule Jesus' teaching on resurrection, a doctrine they considered unscriptural and ridiculous. Jesus replies to both parts of their question: the impact of multiple marriages on life in the

---

[6] For a fuller discussion see Joseph B. Tyson, *The Death of Jesus in Luke-Acts* (Columbia: University of South Carolina Press, 1986) 148-153 et passim.

resurrection (Lk 20:34-36), and their implicit attack on the doctrine of resurrection as such (Lk 20:37-38). His interlocutors are so amazed at his learning "they no longer dared to ask him any question."

General observations. Luke followed the Matthean order directly for the body of this pericope. However, there are significant compositional alterations in the middle and at the end which reveal Luke's theological and moral agenda.

Lk 20:27-28. The construction "3rd singular aorist active indicative of ἐπερωτάω + αὐτόν + present active nominative participle of λέγω + διδάσκαλε" is also found here, as it was in Lk 20:21, where we identified it as a linguistic characteristic of Luke (see also Lk 18:18 and 21:7). It also appears in the parable in Mt 22:23-24. Collison 216 says, "The collocation καί/δέ + ἐπερωτάω + the third personal pronoun + a participle of λέγω + vocative of διδάσκαλος occurs in 3 instances." He then lists Lk 18:18; 20:21; and 21:7. To these he asks his readers to compare Lk 20:27; 3:10; 3:14; and 20:18.

Lk 20:34-36. These verses differ strikingly from the parallel in Mt 22:29-30. Mt's version depicts Jesus simply denying the premise of the Sadducees: that there will be marriage in the Age to Come. In Mt's version, Jesus' answer means: she will be no one's wife since there is no marriage in heaven, since they will be like angels (i.e., all male? sexless?). However, Luke's version of Jesus' answer strikes off in a very different direction. First of all, he introduced a contrast between οἱ υἱοὶ τοῦ αἰώνος τούτου, "the sons of this age," and οἱ δὲ καταξιωθέντες τοῦ αἰῶνος ἐκεινοῦ τυχεῖν, "those considered worthy (by God) to attain to that age." The first group "marry (male) and are given in marriage (female)." But the second group (cf. Lk 17:27) "neither marry nor are given in marriage." Why not? "Because they are no longer able to die since they now are (εἴσιν – present tense) equal to the (immortal) angels (ἰσάγγελοι) and already now are sons of God (υἱοὶ εἴσιν θεοῦ; the medial location of the verb is emphatic) because they already are sons of the resurrection (τῆς ἀναστάσεως υἱοὶ ὄντες; present participle of result). The repeated "sons of–" language is a Lukan addition (cf. a similar pair in Lk 16:8 καὶ ἐπήνεσεν ὁ κύριος τὸν οἰκονόμον τῆς ἀδικίας ὅτι φρονίμως ἐποίησεν· ὅτι οἱ <u>υἱοὶ τοῦ αἰῶνος τούτου</u> φρονιμώτεροι ὑπὲρ τοὺς <u>υἱοὺς τοῦ φωτὸς</u>). Thus Luke has underwritten a basis for ascetic practices in the church. The believers who refrain from marrying do so as a symbol of their conviction that they have already entered into the immortal life of angels.

Lk 20:40. This verse was inserted here from the conclusion of the next pericope in Mt 22:46 to round off the series of challenges to Jesus.

¶ 115. Is the Messiah no more than David's son?
Mt 22:41-45 ====> **Lk 20:41-44**

Now that his adversaries have fallen silent, Luke goes on to portray Jesus asking them a question of his own. "Do you think that the Promised Messiah is just David's Son? Does not Scripture say that David himself addressed him as 'my Lord'? If David did that, why do you think the Messiah is just the son of David?" Waiting patiently for an answer, Jesus receives none. His foes are baffled by the question.

General observations. Although Luke was following the order of Mt, he omitted the story that came immediately after the Sadducees' mocking question about the resurrection in Mt; i.e., the question about the Great Commandment (Mt 22:34-40). Luke had already utilized it earlier (Lk 10:25-28). After that, in Mt's order, comes the question about David's son (Mt 22:41-45), which Luke adopted as the fitting climax to this tableau: having successfully parried all of their trick questions, the Visiting Sage confounds his learned adversaries with an impenetrable riddle of his own.

Lk 20:41-44. Luke omitted the Matthean description of this question as coming from the Pharisees (Mt 22:41) because, after Lk 19:39, Luke does not have the Pharisees appear again within the Lukan narrative.

• At the beginning of the pericope, εἶπεν δέ + πρός in Luke 20:41 is a Lukan linguistic usage. It occurs at the beginning of a sentence 56 times in Luke and only once in Matthew (Collison 47; cf. Collison 9-10 and 143). Here Jesus is responding to the scribes (Lk 20:39).

• The question is based on a quotation from Ps 110:1 (Ps 109 LXX) which, according to contemporary convention, was ascribed to King David. Luke altered Mt's phrase "David, inspired by the Spirit" to say: "David himself says in the Book of Psalms" (Mt 22:43//Lk 20:42), interpreting the Psalms as prophetic (cf. Lk 24:44; Acts 1:20).

As a clue to Luke's own understanding of the answer to Jesus' question "Is the Messiah more than the son *of David*?" we should remember earlier "son" passages in Luke's Gospel, such as the angel's promise to Mary: "he will be called *son of the Most High*" (ὕψιστος Lk1:32) and the glorious ending of Luke's genealogy: "the son of Adam, the *son of God*" (Lk 3:38).

The Psalm quote was used again by Luke in Acts 2:34-36 and, there, it is clarified further: "Therefore let the whole house of Israel know that God has made (Jesus) both Lord and Messiah." As the resurrected Messiah, since David had called him Lord, indeed he is greater than David.

• By this quote, Luke returned to the theme of Jesus' identity and authority, originally raised in Lk 20:1-8, and here answered—albeit with a riddle—by Jesus himself. All that remains is for the Jerusalem leaders to acknowledge that identity. They refuse to do so!

¶ 116. Scribes who steal from widows
Mt 23:1, 6, 14 ====> **Lk 20:45-47**

Then, without pausing, Jesus turns to his disciples and, in front of all of the people, warns them: "Don't put your trust in scribes! They parade around in their expensive robes so as to be honored by all, and they like to make long, flowery prayers. But they are the kind who will do anything; they even steal from widows! God will soon pay them back with a doubly harsh punishment!"

General observations. Luke continued to follow Mt's order and arrived at Mt 23, the great attack on "scribes and Pharisees." For this story, he abridged Mt 23:1-7, turning Mt's material into a concluding warning about "scribes" (cf. Lk 20:39) to "his disciples" to end his debate tableau. Note Lk 11:49-52 for a similar Lukan summary judgment made to Jesus' "disciples" (i.e., Luke's audience).

• Luke had already used much of Mt 23 at an earlier point in condemning the "lawyers and Pharisees" (Lk 11:37-52).

• As noted above, the Pharisees have been moved off the stage; i.e., at the outskirts of the city (Lk 19:39), in order to focus on "the chief priests, leaders of the people and the scribes" as Jesus' enemies (cf. Lk 20:1, 19, 39). However, as before, the way in which Luke portrayed Jesus first condemning these persons and then giving specific instructions to "his disciples" (= Luke's audience) reveals the important symbolic role these groups of adversaries play in Luke's drama.

Lk 20:45. In Lk 20:45, the genitive absolute with the substantive λαός followed by εἶπεν is a typical Lukan construction serving to paraphrase Mt 23:1 (cf. Collison 77-78, 173-174).

Lk 20:46. In Lk 11:43-44//Mt 23:27-28, Jesus described the *Pharisees* as "loving the best seat in the synagogue, etc." Here, in Lk 20:46, Luke created a doublet of Mt 23:27-28 by portraying Jesus giving a similar warning about the *scribes*.[7]

Lk 20:47. This verse has almost the same wording as the doubtful reading Mt 23:14. Since Mt 23:14 is missing in the best early manuscripts (ℵ B D L Θ several versions and Origen, Cyril and Jerome), and since, when this verse does appear in the MSS, it sometimes comes before and sometimes after Mt 23:13, UBS[4] omits this verse as a harmonization, in our judgment correctly.

• The concluding and seemingly out-of-place reference to those "who devour widows' houses, etc." in Lk 20:47 (missing entirely from Mt 23) is a

---

[7] On the import of Luke's changes to Mt 23 in Lk 20:45-47 for the development of the Synoptic Tradition on the Two Gospel Hypothesis, see William R. Farmer, *The Synoptic Problem* (New York: Macmillan, 1964) 265-266. Compare his more recent statements on this same subject in *Jesus and the Gospel* (Philadelphia: Fortress, 1982) 7-8, and *The Gospel of Jesus* (Louisville: Westminster/John Knox, 1994) 31-33.

Lukan insertion following his typical compositional technique where he introduces a character about to play a role in the drama. In this case the "widow" will appear in the very next vignette—the widow's offering. Compare 4 Ezra 15:49 for a connection between widowhood and the devastation of houses.

• Having had Jesus give an abstract rule of behavior to his "disciples," Luke now moved to introduce unique material to provide a concrete example of it. Luke did the same thing earlier when he connected the abstract admonition to love God and neighbor in The One Who Sees and Does (Lk 10:25-28//Mt 22:34-40) to the (unique) story of the Good Samaritan by means of the question "Who is my neighbor?" (Lk 10:29).

¶ 117. The sacrificial giving of a widow
Lk 21:1-4

As if to emphasize his point, Jesus suddenly notices the rich putting a little of their money into the Temple chest. Then he sees a poor old woman, clearly without a husband to take care of her, drop in two little copper coins. "She is the one who has put in the most!" he says. "Despite her dire poverty she put in all she had to live on, while those others gave a pittance out of all they have to live on!"

General observations. Drawing upon his nonMatthean tradition, Luke inserted a concrete example which underscores the hypocrisy against which Jesus inveighs throughout the Gospel of Luke. The negative attitude toward the rich is typical of Luke (cf. Lk 6:24; 12:16; 14:12; 16:1, 19; 18:22).

Lk 21:1-4. The Temple "treasury" may refer to a large chest or wooden box similar to those found in temples the world over. This unique account is brought in not only to summarize the evaluation of Jesus' opponents, but to facilitate a transition to the next story in Mt's order, namely, the comment on the Temple structures, which Luke converted into a comment on the magnificence of the same (Lk 21:5-7).

• The use of τις with a noun, not followed by a genitive (Lk 21:2), is a linguistic characteristic of Luke (Collison 211).

Section Two: The King Predicts the Destruction of the Temple and the City. Lk 21:5-38

The entire speech of Lk 21:8-36 is a response to the request for a sign as to when the destruction of Jerusalem will take place (Lk 21:7). That is the subject under discussion—nothing less and nothing more.

Jesus solemnly says that the end of the Temple and Jerusalem will soon occur as part of a sequence of momentous events (Lk 21:8-28). In Lk 21:8-11 Jesus describes a period of increasing deterioration of the human and natural world. Then, after a parenthesis in which Jesus provides guidance to his "disciples" on how they are to conduct themselves during this period of persecution (Lk 21:12-19), Jesus goes on to predict that Jerusalem itself will come under direct attack and be devastated by foreign powers (Lk 21:20-24). While this happens, says Jesus, great cosmic omens (σημεῖα) will appear (Lk 21:25). Parenthetically, we note that the Jewish historian Josephus also told of terrifying natural omens and signs which appeared at the Fall of Jerusalem (cf. Jewish War 6:286-315). And then, Jesus continues, after the destruction of Jerusalem, the Son of Man will appear in a great cloud, in great glory. "When they begin to see these things happen," says Jesus to those who inquired of him for a sign (Lk 21:29), "then, lift up your heads for your redemption is near" (Lk 21:28). Jesus concludes his speech with the impressive assurance that "this generation will not pass away till all this has taken place" (Lk 21:32). "So take heed to yourselves and be watchful!" (Lk 21:34). It is evident from Luke's version of this great speech as compared with Matthew, that the recent destruction of Jerusalem by Titus is viewed by Luke as the decisive sign between the time of the historical Jesus and the imminent appearance of the Son of Man and Final Judgment (cf. Lk 21:27, 36).

¶ 118. The Temple is doomed

Mt 24:1-3 ====> **Lk 21:5-7**

Hearing certain individuals in the Temple area oohing and aahing over the magnificence of the buildings and the great amounts of money constantly being dropped into the donations chest, Jesus warns, "Don't think that this huge building will be here much longer! It will soon be completely destroyed—not one stone left on top of another!" Horrified, they ask him when it will happen.

General observations. Luke passed over the parts of Mt 23 that he had already used and resumed following Mt's order at Mt 24:1-3.

Lk 21:5-7. Luke changed Mt's disciples as the persons asking Jesus about the Temple to an anonymous "some," possibly because Luke did not want Jesus' "disciples" (a major term for Luke which at times carries a double meaning referring to his audience, viz., Christians living in the wider *oikoumene*) to ask about the future of the Jewish Temple.

• The use of τινων λεγόντων in Lk 21:5 is a typical Lukan stylistic alteration. Lk has introduced the indefinite pronoun τις more than twenty times into parallel passages of Matthew (cf. Collison 210).

• In Lk 21:7 the collocation καί δέ + ἐπερωτοῦν + 3rd personal pronoun + participle of λέγω + the vocative διδάκαλε also occurs twice elsewhere in Luke at Lk 18:18 and Lk 20:21. It appears to be a Lukan phrase. It never occurs in Mt (Collison 216).

• Luke typically omitted the repetitious apocalyptic Matthean language (see, for instance, the Lukan omissions of Mt's παρουσία at Mt 24:3, 27, 37, 39). Luke's version of the question in Lk 21:7 stressed the end of the

Temple/Jerusalem, not the "end of the age" (cf. Mt 24:3), since Jerusalem had been destroyed by the Romans during the insurrection of 66–70.

¶ 119. False impersonators will appear; wars, earthquakes, and celestial portents

Mt 24:4-7 ====> **Lk 21:8-11**

"First of all," says Jesus, "strangers will appear who will claim to be me. Don't be misled by them. And when you hear of wars and riots, do not be terrified. They too must come to pass before the end. There will be terrifying earthquakes and famine; strange portents in the heavens."

General observations. The basic order of Luke's version of Jesus' speech follows Mt's version (Mt 24:4-36). The alterations, additions and omissions stand out and will be discussed as they appear.

• The opening unit (Lk 21:8-11) is closely modeled on Mt 24:4-8, with only a few stylistic alterations.

Lk 21:8. The verb πλανᾶν occurs only at Lk 21:8a in the Gospel of Luke where it is paralleled by a usage in Mt 24:4. It appears more often in Mt (8 times): four times in this context in Mt 24 to refer to false messiahs (Mt 24:4, 5, 11, 24). The cognate noun is used twice later—referring to the charge that Jesus himself was a false messiah (Mt 27:63, 64). The evidence suggests that Luke took over this non-Lukan technical term from Mt 24:4.

• On the other hand, the term καιρός (Lk 21:8b) occurs in a phrase lacking in the parallel at Mt 24:5, and it is characteristic of Luke (cf. Lk 19:44; 21:36; Acts 1:7; 3:19). Moreover, Collison 46 considers ἐγγίζειν to be a linguistic usage of Luke.

Lk 21:9. In this verse Luke added πρῶτον to balance his revision of Mt 24:6b ἀλλ' οὐκ εὐθέως τὸ τέλος.

Lk 21:11. Lk 21:11b is a Lukan addition replacing Mt 24:8. Luke introduced a list of terrifying terrestrial and cosmic cataclysms to form the backdrop for his amplification on the suffering of believers, mentioned next in Mt 24:9a. That verse would provide Luke with the opportunity to bring in similar material from Mt 10:17f.; see next Section.

¶ 120. You will be persecuted because of me

Mt 24:9; 10:17-22; 24:14 ====> **Lk 21:12-19**

"And you will be persecuted because you bear my name," Jesus adds. "You will be dragged into synagogues and before kings and governors. But don't be anxious. I will help you defend yourself. Even members of your own family will turn you in to the authorities! Everyone will hate you because you bear the name "Christian." But try to endure it; no one can harm your soul—even if they kill your body."

General observations. Luke inserted material taken from Mt 10 into the Matthean context at this point. Using Mt 24:9a as a bridge, Luke amplified and modified the next Matthean section on persecution (Mt 24:9-14) in order to make Jesus' speech apply more aptly to the persecution of Christians in the Mediterranean *oikoumene* after the destruction of Jerusalem by the Roman legions in 70 CE.

• Luke's utilization of the material in Mt's Mission Discourse reveals careful utilization of all of the material there. Luke had already used Mt 9:35-10:16 as the source for his two parallel accounts of the Mission of the Twelve (Lk 9:1-6) and the Mission of the Seventy-two (Lk 10:1-16). Luke then used Mt 10:26-33, 19-20 as the basis for Lk 12:1b-12; Mt 10:34-37 as the basis for Lk 12:49-53; and Mt 10:37-39 as the basis of Lk 14:25-33. Mt 10:24-25 is echoed in Lk 6:37-42. Thus, with the exception of Mt 10:23, which finds its echo in the Lukan Travel Narrative as a whole, the only material in the Matthean Mission Discourse Luke did not explicitly use previously is precisely the two pericopes which appear here in Lk 21, i.e., Mt 10:17-18 and Mt 10:21-22. The following synopsis will indicate how Luke conflated these materials for use here.[8]

Synopsis of Lk 21:12–19

Illustrating Luke's use of Mt 10:17ff. at Lk 12:11f., and subsequent conflation of Mt 10:17-22 and Mt 24:8-14 at Lk 21:12-19.

Mt 10:17-22	Mt 24:8-14	Lk 21:12-19	Lk 12:11-12
17 προσέχετε δὲ ἀπὸ τῶν ἀνθρώπων·	**8** πάντα δὲ ταῦτα ἀρχὴ ὠδίνων.	**12** πρὸ δὲ τούτων πάντων ἐπιβαλοῦσιν ἐφ' ὑμᾶς τὰς χεῖρας αὐτῶν καὶ διώξουσιν,	**11** ὅταν δὲ
	9 τότε		
παραδώσουσιν γὰρ	παραδώσουσιν	παραδιδόντες	εἰσφέρωσιν
ὑμᾶς εἰς συνέδρια	ὑμᾶς εἰς θλῖψιν	εἰς	ὑμᾶς ἐπὶ
καὶ ἐν			
ταῖς συναγωγαῖς		τὰς συναγωγὰς	τὰς συναγωγὰς
αὐτῶν			
		καὶ φυλακάς,	
		ἀπαγομένους	
μαστιγώσουσιν ὑμᾶς·			
18 καὶ ἐπὶ		ἐπὶ	
ἡγεμόνας			
δὲ καὶ βασιλεῖς		βασιλεῖς	καὶ τὰς ἀρχὰς
		καὶ ἡγεμόνας	καὶ τὰς ἐξουσίας,
ἀχθήσεσθε			
ἕνεκεν		ἕνεκεν τοῦ ὀνόματός	

---

[8] For a detailed discussion of the complex compositional features in Lk 21:12-19, see Allan J. McNicol, *Jesus' Directions for the Future: A Source and Redaction-Historical Study of the Use of Eschatological Traditions in Paul and the Synoptic Accounts of Jesus' Last Eschatological Discourse,* New Gospel Studies # 9 (Macon: Mercer University Press, 1996) 132-135.

Luke's Repeated Use of Matthew's Mission Discourse

Mt 10:18 ἐμοῦ	Mt 24:9	Lk 21: 12 μου·	Lk 12:11
		13 ἀποβήσεται	
		ὑμῖν	
εἰς μαρτύριον αὐτοῖς		εἰς μαρτύριον.	
καὶ τοῖς ἔθνεσιν.	cf. Mt 24:14		
		14 θέτε οὖν	
		ἐν ταῖς καρδίαις	
		ὑμῶν	
19 ὅταν δὲ			cf. Lk 12:1a
παραδῶσιν ὑμᾶς,			
μὴ μεριμνήσητε		μὴ προμελετᾶν	μὴ μεριμνήσητε
πῶς ἢ τί			πῶς ἢ τί
		ἀπολογηθῆναι·	ἀπολογήσησθε
λαλήσητε			ἢ τί εἴπητε·
			12 τὸ γὰρ
			ἅγιον πνεῦμα
δοθήσεται γὰρ		15 ἐγὼ γὰρ δώσω	διδάξει
ὑμῖν		ὑμῖν	ὑμᾶς
ἐν ἐκείνῃ τῇ ὥρα			ἐν αὐτῇ τῇ ὥρᾳ
τί λαλήσητε		στόμα καὶ σοφίαν	ἃ δεῖ εἰπεῖν.
20 οὐ γὰρ ὑμεῖς			
ἐστε οἱ λαλοῦντες			
ἀλλὰ τὸ πνεῦμα			
τοῦ πατρὸς ὑμῶν			
τὸ λαλοῦν ἐν ὑμῖν.			
		ᾗ οὐ δυνήσονται	
		ἀντιστῆναι	
		ἢ ἀντειπεῖν ἅπαντες	
		οἱ ἀντικείμενοι ὑμῖν.	
21 παραδώσει		16 παραδοθήσεσθε	
δὲ		δὲ καὶ ὑπὸ γονέων	
ἀδελφὸς ἀδελφὸν		καὶ ἀδελφῶν	
εἰς θάνατον			
καὶ πατὴρ τέκνον,		καὶ συγγενῶν	
καὶ ἐπαναστήσονται			
τέκνα ἐπὶ γονεῖς			
		καὶ φίλων,	
καὶ θανατώσουσιν	καὶ ἀποκτενοῦσιν	καὶ θανατώσουσιν	
αὐτούς.	ὑμᾶς,	ἐξ ὑμῶν,	
22 καὶ ἔσεσθε	καὶ ἔσεσθε	17 καὶ ἔσεσθε	
μισούμενοι ὑπὸ	μισούμενοι ὑπὸ	μισούμενοι ὑπὸ	
πάντων	πάντων τῶν ἐθνῶν	πάντων	
διὰ τὸ ὄνομά μου·	διὰ τὸ ὄνομά μου.	διὰ τὸ ὄνομά μου.	
	10 καὶ τότε	18 καὶ θρὶξ	
	σκανδαλισθήσονται	ἐκ τῆς κεφαλῆς ὑμῶν	
	πολλοὶ	οὐ μὴ ἀπόληται.	
	καὶ ἀλλήλους		
cf. Mt 10:17	παραδώσουσιν		
	καὶ μισήσουσιν		

Luke's Repeated Use of Matthew's Mission Discourse

Mt 10:22	**Mt 24:10** ἀλλήλους·	**Lk 21:18**
	11 καὶ πολλοὶ	
	ψευδοπροφῆται	
	ἐγερθήσονται	
	καὶ πλανήσουσιν	
	πολλούς·	
	12 καὶ	
	διὰ τὸ πληθυνθῆναι	
	τὴν ἀνομίαν	
	ψυγήσεται	
	ἡ ἀγάπη τῶν πολλῶν.	
ὁ δὲ	**13** ὁ δὲ	**19** ἐν τῇ
ὑπομείνας	ὑπομείνας	ὑπομονῇ ὑμῶν
εἰς τέλος	εἰς τέλος	
		κτήσασθε
οὗτος σωθήσεται.	οὗτος σωθήσεται.	τὰς ψυχὰς ὑμῶν.
	14 καὶ	
	κηρυχθήσεται	
	τοῦτο τὸ εὐαγγέλιον	
	τῆς βασιλείας	
	ἐν ὅλῃ τῇ οἰκουμένῃ	
	εἰς μαρτύριον	
cf. Mt 10:18	πᾶσιν τοῖς ἔθνεσιν,	
	καὶ τότε	
	ἥξει τὸ τέλος.	

¶ 121. Jerusalem will be destroyed and the Son of Man will appear

Mt 24:15-21, 29-31 ====> **Lk 21:20-28**

"When you see a great army camped outside the walls of Jerusalem," Jesus continues, "flee for your lives, for it will surely be destroyed according to God's vengeance. Woe unto those who live in Judaea in those days, for they will be killed, driven into exile and enslaved. There will be terrifying signs in the heavens; the ocean waves will beat furiously on the shores. But then the Son of Man will appear in the heavens with great power and glory to save his own! So take heart! When you see these things begin to happen, know that your Rescuer is almost here!"

General observations. For this momentous speech, Luke *historicized* Mt's account of the eschatological Desolating Sacrilege in Jerusalem, supplementing it with references to sieges of the holy city in scripture (Mt 24:15-22//Lk 21:20-26). After this, Luke followed Mt 24:29-31 to create his account of events at the end (Lk 21:27-28). Although there are some omissions (see below), Luke resumed the order of Jesus' speech in Mt 24:15, except that Luke again historicized the reference to Dan 9:27 in Mt 24:15 to make it recall the recent (to Luke and his audience) destruction of

Jerusalem by the Romans under Titus in 70 CE, a theme to which Luke will return later. The following synopsis reveals these details. The parallels presented out of their original order are located in boxes to alert the reader to this fact.

Synopsis of Lk 21:20–36

Illustrating Luke's repeated use of Mt 24 in Lk 17 and again in Lk 21

Lk 17:20-37	**Mt 24:15-42**	**Lk 21:20-36**
20 Ἐπερωτηθεὶς δὲ ὑπὸ τῶν Φαρισαίων πότε ἔρχεται ἡ βασιλεία τοῦ θεοῦ ἀπεκρίθη αὐτοῖς καὶ εἶπεν, Οὐκ ἔρχεται ἡ βασιλεία τοῦ θεοῦ μετὰ παρατηρήσεως,	**15** Ὅταν οὖν ἴδητε τὸ βδέλυγμα τῆς ἐρημώσεως	**20** Ὅταν δὲ ἴδητε κυκλουμένην ὑπὸ στρατοπέδων Ἰερουσαλήμ,
	τὸ ῥηθὲν διὰ Δανιὴλ τοῦ προφήτου ἑστὸς ἐν τόπῳ ἁγίῳ, ὁ ἀναγινώσκων νοείτω,	τότε γνῶτε ὅτι ἤγγικεν ἡ ἐρήμωσις αὐτῆς.
	16 τότε οἱ ἐν τῇ Ἰουδαίᾳ φευγέτωσαν εἰς τὰ ὄρη,	**21** τότε οἱ ἐν τῇ Ἰουδαίᾳ φευγέτωσαν εἰς τὰ ὄρη
cf. Luke 17:31 **31** ἐν ἐκείνῃ τῇ ἡμέρᾳ ὃς ἔσται ἐπὶ τοῦ δώματος καὶ τὰ σκεύη αὐτοῦ ἐν τῇ οἰκίᾳ, μὴ καταβάτω ἆραι αὐτά,	**17** ὁ ἐπὶ τοῦ δώματος μὴ καταβάτω ἆραι τὰ ἐκ τῆς οἰκίας αὐτοῦ,	καὶ οἱ ἐν μέσῳ αὐτῆς ἐκχωρείτωσαν
καὶ ὁ ἐν ἀγρῷ ὁμοίως μὴ ἐπιστρεψάτω εἰς τὰ ὀπίσω.	**18** καὶ ὁ ἐν τῷ ἀγρῷ μὴ ἐπιστρεψάτω ὀπίσω ἆραι τὸ ἱμάτιον αὐτοῦ.	καὶ οἱ ἐν ταῖς χώραις μὴ εἰσερχέσθωσαν εἰς αὐτήν, **22** ὅτι ἡμέραι ἐκδικήσεως αὗταί εἰσιν τοῦ πλησθῆναι πάντα τὰ γεγραμμένα.
	19 οὐαὶ δὲ ταῖς ἐν γαστρὶ ἐχούσαις καὶ ταῖς θηλαζούσαις ἐν ἐκείναις ταῖς ἡμέραις.	**23** οὐαὶ ταῖς ἐν γαστρὶ ἐχούσαις καὶ ταῖς θηλαζούσαις ἐν ἐκείναις ταῖς ἡμέραις·

Luke's Repeated Utilization of Mt 24 in Lk 17 and Lk 21

Lk 17:20	**Mt 24:20** προσεύχεσθε δὲ	**Lk 21:23**
	ἵνα μὴ γένηται ἡ φυγὴ ὑμῶν	
	χειμῶνος μηδὲ σαββάτῳ.	
	21 ἔσται γὰρ τότε	ἔσται γὰρ
	θλῖψις μεγάλη	ἀνάγκη μεγάλη
	οἵα οὐ γέγονεν	
	ἀπ' ἀρχῆς κόσμου	ἐπὶ τῆς γῆς
	ἕως τοῦ νῦν	
	οὐδ' οὐ μὴ γένηται.	
	22 καὶ εἰ μὴ	καὶ
	ἐκολοβώθησαν	
	αἱ ἡμέραι ἐκεῖναι,	
	οὐκ ἂν ἐσώθη πᾶσα σάρξ·	ὀργὴ τῷ λαῷ τούτῳ,
	διὰ δὲ τοὺς ἐκλεκτοὺς	
	κολοβωθήσονται	
	αἱ ἡμέραι ἐκεῖναι.	
		24 καὶ πεσοῦνται
		στόματι μαχαίρης
		καὶ αἰχμαλωτισθήσονται
		εἰς τὰ ἔθνη πάντα,
		καὶ Ἰερουσαλὴμ
		ἔσται πατουμένη
		ὑπὸ ἐθνῶν,
		ἄχρι οὗ πληρωθῶσιν
		καιροὶ ἐθνῶν.
21 οὐδὲ	**23** τότε ἐάν τις ὑμῖν	
ἐροῦσιν, Ἰδοὺ ὧδε	εἴπῃ, Ἰδοὺ ὧδε ὁ Χριστός,	
ἤ, Ἐκεῖ,	ἤ, Ὧδε,	
	μὴ πιστεύσητε·	
	24 ἐγερθήσονται γὰρ	
	ψευδόχριστοι	
	καὶ ψευδοπροφῆται	
	καὶ δώσουσιν	**25** Καὶ ἔσονται
	σημεῖα μεγάλα	σημεῖα
	καὶ τέρατα	
	ὥστε πλανῆσαι,	
	εἰ δυνατόν,	
	καὶ τοὺς ἐκλεκτούς	
ἰδοὺ	**25** ἰδοὺ προείρηκα ὑμῖν.	
γὰρ ἡ βασιλεία τοῦ θεοῦ		
ἐντὸς ὑμῶν ἐστιν.		
22 Εἶπεν δὲ		
πρὸς τοὺς μαθητάς,		
Ἐλεύσονται ἡμέραι		
ὅτε ἐπιθυμήσετε		
μίαν τῶν ἡμερῶν		
τοῦ υἱοῦ τοῦ ἀνθρώπου		
ἰδεῖν καὶ οὐκ ὄψεσθε.		
23 καὶ ἐροῦσιν ὑμῖν,	**26** ἐὰν οὖν εἴπωσιν ὑμῖν,	

Luke's Repeated Utilization of Mt 24 in Lk 17 and Lk 21

Lk 17:23	**Mt 24:26**	**Lk 21:25**
Ἰδοὺ ἐκεῖ,	Ἰδοὺ	
[ἤ,] Ἰδοὺ ὧδε·	ἐν τῇ ἐρήμῳ ἐστίν,	
μὴ ἀπέλθητε	μὴ ἐξέλθητε·	
	Ἰδοὺ ἐν τοῖς ταμείοις,	
μηδὲ διώξητε.	μὴ πιστεύσητε·	
24 ὥσπερ γὰρ	**27** ὥσπερ γὰρ	
ἡ ἀστραπὴ ἀστράπτουσα	ἡ ἀστραπὴ	
ἐκ τῆς ὑπὸ τὸν οὐρανὸν	ἐξέρχεται ἀπὸ ἀνατολῶν	
εἰς τὴν ὑπ' οὐρανὸν		
λάμπει,	καὶ φαίνεται	
	ἕως δυσμῶν,	
οὕτως ἔσται	οὕτως ἔσται ἡ παρουσία	
ὁ υἱὸς τοῦ ἀνθρώπου	τοῦ υἱοῦ τοῦ ἀνθρώπου·	
[ἐν τῇ ἡμέρᾳ αὐτοῦ].		
cf. Lk 17:37		
Ὅπου τὸ σῶμα,	**28** ὅπου ἐὰν ᾖ τὸ πτῶμα,	
ἐκεῖ καὶ οἱ ἀετοὶ	ἐκεῖ συναχθήσονται	
ἐπισυναχθήσονται.	οἱ ἀετοί.	
	29 Εὐθέως δὲ	
	μετὰ τὴν θλῖψιν	
	τῶν ἡμερῶν ἐκείνων	
	ὁ ἥλιος σκοτισθήσεται,	ἐν ἡλίῳ
	καὶ ἡ σελήνη	καὶ σελήνη
	οὐ δώσει τὸ φέγγος αὐτῆς,	
	καὶ οἱ ἀστέρες πεσοῦνται	καὶ ἄστροις,
	ἀπὸ τοῦ οὐρανοῦ,	
		καὶ ἐπὶ τῆς γῆς
		συνοχὴ ἐθνῶν ἐν ἀπορίᾳ
		ἤχους θαλάσσης καὶ σάλου,
		26 ἀποψυχόντων ἀνθρώπων
		ἀπὸ φόβου
		καὶ προσδοκίας
		τῶν ἐπερχομένων
		τῇ οἰκουμένῃ,
	καὶ αἱ δυνάμεις τῶν οὐρανῶν	αἱ γὰρ δυνάμεις τῶν
		οὐρανῶν
	σαλευθήσονται.	σαλευθήσονται.
	30 καὶ τότε	**27** καὶ τότε
	φανήσεται τὸ σημεῖον	
	τοῦ υἱοῦ τοῦ ἀνθρώπου	
	ἐν οὐρανῷ,	
	καὶ τότε κόψονται	
	πᾶσαι αἱ φυλαὶ τῆς γῆς	
	καὶ ὄψονται	ὄψονται
	τὸν υἱὸν τοῦ ἀνθρώπου	τὸν υἱὸν τοῦ ἀνθρώπου
	ἐρχόμενον ἐπὶ τῶν νεφελῶν	ἐρχόμενον ἐν νεφέλῃ
	τοῦ οὐρανοῦ	
	μετὰ δυνάμεως	μετὰ δυνάμεως
	καὶ δόξης πολλῆς·	καὶ δόξης πολλῆς.

Luke's Repeated Utilization of Mt 24 in Lk 17 and Lk 21

Lk 17:24	Mt 24:31 καὶ ἀποστελεῖ	Lk 21:27
	τοὺς ἀγγέλους αὐτοῦ	
	μετὰ σάλπιγγος μεγάλης,	
	καὶ ἐπισυνάξουσιν	
	τοὺς ἐκλεκτοὺς αὐτοῦ	
	ἐκ τῶν τεσσάρων ἀνέμων	
	ἀπ' ἄκρων οὐρανῶν	
	ἕως [τῶν] ἄκρων αὐτῶν.	
		28 ἀρχομένων δὲ τούτων
		γίνεσθαι
		ἀνακύψατε καὶ ἐπάρατε
		τὰς κεφαλὰς ὑμῶν,
		διότι ἐγγίζει
		ἡ ἀπολύτρωσις ὑμῶν.
		29 Καὶ εἶπεν
	32 Ἀπὸ δὲ τῆς συκῆς	
	μάθετε τὴν παραβολήν·	παραβολὴν αὐτοῖς·
		Ἴδετε τὴν συκῆν
		καὶ πάντα τὰ δένδρα·
	ὅταν ἤδη	**30** ὅταν προβάλωσιν ἤδη,
		βλέποντες ἀφ' ἑαυτῶν
	ὁ κλάδος αὐτῆς	
	γένηται ἁπαλὸς	
	καὶ τὰ φύλλα ἐκφύῃ,	
	γινώσκετε ὅτι	γινώσκετε ὅτι ἤδη
	ἐγγὺς τὸ θέρος·	ἐγγὺς τὸ θέρος ἐστίν·
	33 οὕτως καὶ ὑμεῖς,	**31** οὕτως καὶ ὑμεῖς,
	ὅταν ἴδητε πάντα ταῦτα	ὅταν ἴδητε ταῦτα γινόμενα,
	γινώσκετε ὅτι ἐγγύς ἐστιν	γινώσκετε ὅτι ἐγγύς ἐστιν
	ἐπὶ θύραις.	ἡ βασιλεία τοῦ θεοῦ.
cf. Mt 5:18a		
ἀμὴν γὰρ λέγω ὑμῖν	**34** ἀμὴν λέγω ὑμῖν	**32** ἀμὴν λέγω ὑμῖν
ἕως ἂν παρέλθῃ	ὅτι οὐ μὴ παρέλθῃ	ὅτι οὐ μὴ παρέλθῃ
	ἡ γενεὰ αὕτη	ἡ γενεὰ αὕτη
	ἕως ἂν πάντα ταῦτα γένηται.	ἕως ἂν πάντα γένηται.
ὁ οὐρανὸς	**35** ὁ οὐρανὸς	**33** ὁ οὐρανὸς
καὶ ἡ γῆ,	καὶ ἡ γῆ παρελεύσεται,	καὶ ἡ γῆ παρελεύσονται,
ἰῶτα ἓν ἢ μία κεραία	οἱ δὲ λόγοι μου	οἱ δὲ λόγοι μου
οὐ μὴ παρέλθῃ ἀπὸ τοῦ	οὐ μὴ παρέλθωσιν.	οὐ μὴ παρελεύσονται.
νόμου		
ἕως ἂν πάντα γένηται.		
	36 Περὶ δὲ	
	τῆς ἡμέρας ἐκείνης καὶ ὥρας	
	οὐδεὶς οἶδεν,	
	οὐδὲ οἱ ἄγγελοι τῶν οὐρανῶν	
	οὐδὲ ὁ υἱός,	
	εἰ μὴ ὁ πατὴρ μόνος.	
25 πρῶτον δὲ		
δεῖ αὐτὸν πολλὰ παθεῖν		

Luke's Repeated Utilization of Mt 24 in Lk 17 and Lk 21

Lk 17:25	Mt 24:36	Lk 21:33
καὶ ἀποδοκιμασθῆναι		
ἀπὸ τῆς γενεᾶς ταύτης.		
26 καὶ καθὼς ἐγένετο	37 ὥσπερ γὰρ	
ἐν ταῖς ἡμέραις Νῶε,	αἱ ἡμέραι τοῦ Νῶε,	
οὕτως ἔσται καὶ	οὕτως ἔσται ἡ παρουσία	
ἐν ταῖς ἡμέραις		
τοῦ υἱοῦ τοῦ ἀνθρώπου·	τοῦ υἱοῦ τοῦ ἀνθρώπου.	
	38 ὡς γὰρ ἦσαν	
	ἐν ταῖς ἡμέραις [ἐκείναις]	
	ταῖς πρὸ τοῦ κατακλυσμοῦ	
27 ἤσθιον, ἔπινον,	τρώγοντες καὶ πίνοντες,	
ἐγάμουν, ἐγαμίζοντο,	γαμοῦντες καὶ γαμίζοντες,	
ἄχρι ἧς ἡμέρας	ἄχρι ἧς ἡμέρας	
εἰσῆλθεν Νῶε	εἰσῆλθεν Νῶε	
εἰς τὴν κιβωτόν	εἰς τὴν κιβωτόν,	
	39 καὶ οὐκ ἔγνωσαν	
καὶ ἦλθεν ὁ κατακλυσμὸς	ἕως ἦλθεν ὁ κατακλυσμὸς	
καὶ ἀπώλεσεν πάντας.	καὶ ἦρεν ἅπαντας,	
28 ὁμοίως καθὼς ἐγένετο		
ἐν ταῖς ἡμέραις Λώτ·		
ἤσθιον, ἔπινον,		
ἠγόραζον, ἐπώλουν,		
ἐφύτευον, ᾠκοδόμουν·		
29 ᾗ δὲ ἡμέρᾳ		
ἐξῆλθεν Λὼτ ἀπὸ Σοδόμων,		
ἔβρεξεν πῦρ καὶ θεῖον		
ἀπ' οὐρανοῦ		
καὶ ἀπώλεσεν πάντας.		
30 κατὰ τὰ αὐτὰ		
ἔσται ᾗ ἡμέρᾳ	οὕτως ἔσται [καὶ] ἡ παρουσία	
ὁ υἱὸς τοῦ ἀνθρώπου	τοῦ υἱοῦ τοῦ ἀνθρώπου.	
ἀποκαλύπτεται.		
31 ἐν ἐκείνῃ τῇ ἡμέρᾳ	**cf. Mt 24:17-18**	
ὃς ἔσται	**24:17** ὁ	
ἐπὶ τοῦ δώματος	ἐπὶ τοῦ δώματος	
καὶ τὰ σκεύη αὐτοῦ		
ἐν τῇ οἰκίᾳ,		
μὴ καταβάτω ἆραι αὐτά,	μὴ καταβάτω ἆραι	
	τὰ ἐκ τῆς οἰκίας αὐτοῦ,	
καὶ ὁ ἐν ἀγρῷ ὁμοίως	**18** καὶ ὁ ἐν τῷ ἀγρῷ	
μὴ ἐπιστρεψάτω	μὴ ἐπιστρεψάτω	
εἰς τὰ ὀπίσω.	ὀπίσω ἆραι τὸ ἱμάτιον αὐτοῦ.	
32 μνημονεύετε		

Luke's Repeated Utilization of Mt 24 in Lk 17 and Lk 21

Lk 17:32		**Lk 21:33**
τῆς γυναικὸς Λώτ.	**cf. Mt 10:39**	
33 ὃς ἐὰν ζητήσῃ	**10:39** ὁ εὑρὼν	
τὴν ψυχὴν αὐτοῦ	τὴν ψυχὴν αὐτοῦ	
περιποιήσασθαι		
ἀπολέσει αὐτήν,	ἀπολέσει αὐτὴν	
ὃς δ' ἂν ἀπολέσῃ	καὶ ὁ ἀπολέσας	
	τὴν ψυχὴν αὐτοῦ	
	ἕνεκεν ἐμοῦ	
ζῳογονήσει αὐτήν.	εὑρήσει αὐτήν.	
34 λέγω ὑμῖν, ταύτῃ τῇ	**Mt 24:40** τότε	
νυκτὶ ἔσονται δύο	δύο ἔσονται	
ἐπὶ κλίνης μιᾶς,	ἐν τῷ ἀγρῷ,	
ὁ εἷς παραλημφθήσεται	εἷς παραλαμβάνεται	
καὶ ὁ ἕτερος ἀφεθήσεται·	καὶ εἷς ἀφίεται·	
35 ἔσονται δύο ἀλήθουσαι	**41** δύο ἀλήθουσαι	
ἐπὶ τὸ αὐτό,	ἐν τῷ μύλῳ,	
ἡ μία παραλημφθήσεται,	μία παραλαμβάνεται	
ἡ δὲ ἑτέρα ἀφεθήσεται.	καὶ μία ἀφίεται.	
[**36** δύο ἔσονται ἐν τῷ ἀγρῷ,		
εἷς παραληφθήσεται,		
καὶ ὁ ἕτερος ἀφεθήσεται.]		
37 καὶ ἀποκριθέντες		
λέγουσιν αὐτῷ, Ποῦ, κύριε;		
ὁ δὲ εἶπεν αὐτοῖς,		
	cf. Mt 24:28	
Ὅπου τὸ σῶμα,	**24:28** ὅπου ἐὰν ᾖ τὸ πτῶμα,	
ἐκεῖ καὶ οἱ ἀετοὶ	ἐκεῖ συναχθήσονται	
ἐπισυναχθήσονται.	οἱ ἀετοί.	
		34 Προσέχετε δὲ ἑαυτοῖς
		μήποτε βαρηθῶσιν ὑμῶν
		αἱ καρδίαι
		ἐν κραιπάλῃ καὶ μέθῃ
		καὶ μερίμναις βιωτικαῖς
		καὶ ἐπιστῇ ἐφ' ὑμᾶς αἰφνίδιος
		ἡ ἡμέρα ἐκείνη **35** ὡς παγίς·
		ἐπεισελεύσεται γὰρ
		ἐπὶ πάντας τοὺς καθημένους
		ἐπὶ πρόσωπον πάσης τῆς γῆς
	Mt 24:42 γρηγορεῖτε οὖν,	**36** ἀγρυπνεῖτε δὲ
	ὅτι οὐκ οἴδατε ποίᾳ ἡμέρᾳ	ἐν παντὶ καιρῷ
	ὁ κύριος ὑμῶν ἔρχεται.	δεόμενοι ἵνα κατισχύσητε
		ἐκφυγεῖν ταῦτα πάντα
		τὰ μέλλοντα γίνεσθαι
		καὶ σταθῆναι ἔμπροσθεν
		τοῦ υἱοῦ τοῦ ἀνθρώπου.

[Luke had already made use of Mt 24:42-51 in Lk 12:35-48.]

Lk 21:21-22. This is a rough approximation of Mt 24:16f., to which Luke, in Lk 21:22, added an echo of Deut 32:35. The repeated use of ἐν + a prepositional phrase as a substantive in Lk 21:21 is a Lukan characteristic (cf. Collison 227), as is the use of the word πίμπλημι in Lk 22:22.

Lk 21:23. The phrase ἐν γαστρί plus ἔχειν in Lk 21:23 (from Mt 24:19) occurs only here in Lk. It occurs in the parallel in Mt here and twice elsewhere in Mt (1:18, 23). As such, it is an example of a recurrent phrase in one Gospel that appears only once in a parallel context in another Gospel. We consider such evidence a one-way indicator that Luke made direct use of the canonical Gospel of Matthew. For an explanation of the meaning of the term "one-way indicator," see Introduction, pp. 21-24.

Lk 21:24-26. These verses, couched in scriptural language, amplify reminiscences of the actual destruction of Jerusalem in 70. The cosmic omens that appeared during the terrible carnage accompanying that event were also mentioned by Josephus, *Bell. Iud.* 6:286-315.

• Since Luke had already used material drawn from Mt 24:23-28 (Lk 17:23-24, 37), he was able to pass straight from Mt 24:22 to Mt 24:29f.//Lk 21:25-26. The above synopsis reveals Luke's double utilization of Mt 24:15-42.

Lk 21:28. Luke modified the ending of Mt's prediction regarding the gathering in of the elect (Mt 24:30-31) to a more personal and direct "your redemption is at hand." The ἀπολύτρωσις originally promised at the birth of Jesus will finally become a reality for all who believe in him (cf. Lk 1:68; 2:38; cf. 24:21; Goulder 2:714).

¶ 122. The final exhortation to vigilance

Mt 24:32-36 ====> **Lk 21:29-36**

Jesus is describing a terrifying future, but he insists that those true to God will have nothing to fear. "When you see these fearful events begin to happen, don't let your hearts fail you. They are signs that God is preparing the way for the Kingdom! You can be certain what I say is true! So watch and be vigilant, praying that God will give you the strength to endure the trials and tribulations that are sure to be everyone's lot. And may you be able to stand with confidence before the Son of Man on the Day of Judgment, and may you know that you have been faithful to him, come what may."

General observations. Luke continued to follow Mt's order and content fairly closely. The main alterations are easily explainable according to known aspects of Luke's theology and compositional techniques.

Lk 21:29. The construction εἶπεν δέ + παραβολή is an obvious Lukan addition (Collison 47-48), as is the addition of ἡ βασιλεία τοῦ θεοῦ in Lk 21:31 to the parallel Mt 24:33 (Collison 169-170).

Lk 21:32. An example of a "one-way indicator" of literary dependence of Luke upon Mt occurs at Lk 21:32//Mt 24:34. The formulation ἀμὴν λέγω ὑμῖν + οὐ μὴ + Aorist subjunctive verb + ἕως ἄν + Aorist subjunctive verb is a recurrent linguistic feature of the text of Matthew (see Mt 5:18, 26; 10:23; 16:28; 23:39; 24:34; 26:29.[9] The same formulation occurs at Lk 21:32 in a passage parallel to Mt's order of pericopes (Mt 24:34). In fact, if Lk 22:18 is a Lukan construction based upon the similar formula at Lk 22:16//Mt 26:29, then every occurrence of this formula in Luke's Gospel can be explained on the basis of Luke's having fragmentarily copied the formula from Mt (Lk 12:59//Mt 5:26; Lk 9:27//Mt 16:28; Lk 13:35//Mt 23:39; Lk 21:32//Mt 24:34; and Lk 22:16//Lk 22:18//Mt 26:29). However, the reverse is not true, because Matthew can utilize this formula not only in contexts parallel to Luke (Mt 5:26//Lk 12:59; Mt 16:28//Lk 9:27; Mt 23:39//Lk 13:35; Mt 24:34//Lk 21:32; Mt 26:29//Lk 22:16//Lk 22:18), but also in literary contexts independent of Lk (Mt 5:18 and 10:23). Thus not all of the occurrences of this formula in Mt can be explained on the basis of Matthew copying Lk. This complex structure of data is regarded by us as another "one-way indicator" of Luke's direct dependence upon canonical Mt. For an explanation of the meaning of the term "one-way indicator," see Introduction, pp. 21-24. For other examples, see our discussions at Lk 7:23; 8:40-56; 9:10f.; and 21:32.

Lk 21:34-36. These verses did not come directly from Matthew. There are similarities to Paul's wording in 1 Thess 5:3. Perhaps Luke knew of that letter, or had access to the same source material Paul drew upon and utilized it to complete Jesus' speech here. In any case, Lukan linguistic characteristics, such as the use of προσέχετε ἑαυτοῖς (Lk 21:34) and the use of δέομαι give evidence of Lukan editorial activity.

¶ 123. Jesus teaches in the Temple

(Mt 21:17-18) **Lk 21:37-38**

Luke concludes this Section by saying that Jesus taught in this manner "every day in the Temple." At night he lodges on the Mount of Olives. In contrast to the hostile reception of the Jerusalem authorities, the people come early every morning to listen to Jesus.

General observations. This brief unit was composed by Luke. It has many parallels with Lk 19:47-48. As in Lk 19:47, Lk 21:37 has the periphrastic imperfect with the participial form of διδάσκειν used in conjunction with a reference to Jesus being in the temple by day. Lk 19:45-48 forms an *inclusio* with Lk 21:37-38, rounding out and concluding Luke's dramatic scene of Jesus teaching in the Temple. Note that at the beginning and end of both the Birth and Passion Narratives, Luke has action in the Temple (Lk 1:5; 2:41-51; 21:37f.; 24:53).

---

9 See David Peabody, "A Pre-Markan Prophetic Sayings-Tradition and the Synoptic Problem," *JBL* 97 (1978) 391-409, esp. 398.

Lk 21:37. The statement τὰς δὲ νύκτας ἐξερχόμενος ηὐλίζετο εἰς τὸ ὄρος τὸ καλούμενον ᾽Ελκαιῶν echoes the text of Mt 21:17 καὶ καταλιπὼν αὐτοὺς ἐξῆλθεν ἔξω τῆς πόλεως εἰς Βηθανίαν καὶ ηὐλίσθη ἐκεῖ.

Lk 21:38. The reference to rising early in the morning (ὀρθρίζειν, Lk 21:38) perhaps echoes Mt's use of πρωΐ (Lk 21:38//Mt 21:18, cf. Goulder 2:717).

PART SEVEN LK 22:1–24:53

THE ARREST, DEATH, AND RESURRECTION OF JESUS THE KING

Overview

Luke's narrative of the final, climactic events of Jesus' *bios* (Book One) can be divided into four general Sections:

The first Section (Lk 22:1-46) centers on Jesus' last chance to be with all of his disciples before his arrest: the Passover Meal.

The second Section (Lk 22:47-23:25) includes Jesus' arrest, the three trials, the public humiliation and betrayal by his disciples.

The third Section (Lk 23:26-56b) describes Jesus' crucifixion, death, and burial.

The fourth Section (Lk 23:56c-24:53) is the conclusion of Book One and contains the accounts of the first glorious day of appearances of the risen Jesus to his disciples and eleven apostles.

Section One: Jesus' Last Passover Meal. Lk 22:1-46

¶ 124. The plot against Jesus

Mt 26:2-5 ====> **Lk 22:1-2**

Luke carefully sets the scene for the critical events that are about to happen. It is the time of the Feast of Unleavened Bread, called Passover, and Jerusalem is bustling with pilgrims, many of whom are visiting the Temple daily to hear Jesus. The chief priests and scribes have resolved to kill Jesus, but it must be done in such a way that they will not be blamed; too many of the people are on his side.

General observations. At Lk 21:37-38, Luke had finished his account of Jesus' final judgment upon Jerusalem. He then narrated the response of the leaders of Jerusalem to Jesus' challenge.

For his introduction, Luke used Mt 26:1-5. He had already used the intervening material, Mt 24:37-25:46, or echoed it, elsewhere:

Mt 24:37-39//Lk 17:26-30
Mt 24:40-41//Lk 17:34-35
Mt 24:42-51//Lk 12:39-46
Mt 25:1-13//Lk 13:22-27
Mt 25:14-30//Lk 19:11-28

Luke omitted the next account, Mt's Last Judgment scene (Mt 25:31-46). Luke seems to have substituted the Parable of the Pounds (Lk 19:12-27) for

Mt's Parable of the Talents (Mt 25:14-30). Luke had utilized Mt 25:1-13, Mt's Parable of the Wise and Foolish Virgins, in at least one and perhaps two earlier contexts (Lk 12:35-40 [?] and Lk 13:22-27). So there is other evidence that Luke can substitute a parable from his own parable material for one utilized by Matthew. In this case, the Parable of the Rich Man and Lazarus (Lk 16:19-31) may well have functioned as Luke's parabolic statement about the future judgment. If this is characteristic of Luke, then Luke could omit Mt 25:31-46 as redundant, because he had at least alluded to it in one or two previous contexts.

Skipping over Mt 25:31-46, Luke moved ahead to the next point in Mt's narrative, the plot against Jesus. This brought Luke to Mt 26:1, with its characteristic Matthean summary phrase, "When he had finished all these sayings—" (cf. Mt 7:28; 11:1; 13:53; 19:1), which is an indication that Mt is about to embark upon a new Part in the Matthean narrative. Luke did the same, now following fairly closely the general order of Mt.

Lk 22:1. Luke began with an inceptive use of ἐγγίζειν, which is a linguistic characteristic of Luke (Collison 46). Moreover, Luke, following the precedent of the LXX, identified the feast as "the Feast of Unleavened Bread" (Lk 22:17; Acts 12:3; 20:6; cf. Marshall *Luke* 786), adding "which is called Passover," cf. Mt 26:2.

Lk 22:2. Earlier, in Lk 20:19, the chief priests and scribes sought to "place their hands" on Jesus. They could not do so because "they feared the people" (Lk 20:19; cf. Acts 5:26). Almost the same terminology was used here by Luke in Lk 22:2. The phrase appears to be something of a repeated linguistic usage of Luke (Goulder 2:804).

• Marshall *Luke* 787 argues that πῶς (Lk 22:2, again at 22:4) is characteristic of Luke. Moreover, ἀναίρεσθαι occurs nineteen times in Acts as well as at Lk 23:32. All of these linguistic data suggest that Luke composed Lk 22:1-2 using Mt 26:1-5 as his only source.

¶ 125. Judas' betrayal

Mt 26:14-16 ====> **Lk 22:3-6**

Suddenly, the Chief Priests and scribes are aided in their scheme by none other than the ruler of the powers of evil, Satan, who enters into one of Jesus' chosen Twelve disciples, Judas Iscariot, and makes him go out and confer with them to plan a way to betray Jesus into their hands when the crowds are not present. Delighted at this turn of events, they pay Judas money.

General observations. Luke was following the order of Mt, but he omitted Mt 26:6-13 because he had included a similar story of a sinful woman at Lk 7:36-50. He thus moved directly to the next unit in Mt (Mt 26:14-16) and simultaneously tightened up the narrative flow. Even so, he did add a few items to the Matthean account.

Lk 22:3. The use of Σατανᾶς to refer to the Evil One is not unusual for Luke (Lk 10:18; 11:18; 13:16; 22:3, 31 and Acts 5:3; 26:18). It also occurs three times in Mt (4:10; 12:26; 16:23). We conclude that this is a familiar term for Luke. Luke attributed the betrayal to the direct intervention of Satan who "entered into Judas" (Lk 22:3; cf. a similar motif in the story of Ananias and Sapphira [Acts 5:3]). The addition ὁ καλούμενος is a typical Lukan phrase occurring 23 times in Luke-Acts (and not once in Matthew or Mark; cf. Collison 179).

Lk 22:4. Luke added a reference to στρατήγοι. This term would be added again to Mt's account of the arrest (cf. Mt 26:55) in Lk 22:52 and amplified: στρατηγοὺς τοῦ ἱεροῦ and means the Jewish "temple police." This is also probably the meaning here in Lk 22:4. Although the word στρατηγός usually means Roman law enforcement officials in Acts, the use of the term "temple police" seems to be congruent with Luke's tendency to downplay the role of the Roman soldiers in Jesus' crucifixion.

Lk 22:5. Mt's account specifies that Judas was paid "thirty pieces of silver," a detail for which Luke substituted the general word "money" (Lk 22:5). The idea is an allusion to an Old Testament text in Mt (Zech. 11:12f.) and Luke may not have noticed this.

¶ 126. Preparation for the Passover Meal

Mt 26:17-19 ====> **Lk 22:7-13**

The first day of the Feast of Passover arrives. Jesus and his disciples have spent the night on the Mount of Olives (cf. Lk 21:37). He sends Peter and John into Jerusalem where they will be met by a man carrying a jar of water who will lead them to the room where they will celebrate the Passover Meal with Jesus.

General observations. Luke continued to follow Matthew (26:17-19) in perfect order. However, his version of the account containing Jesus' instructions to Peter and John on where to find the room in which they will keep the Passover amplified precisely those points at which Mt's account is vague or non-existent. Hence, all of these additions are to be attributed to Luke.

Lk 22:7. Luke adds the phrase "on which the Passover lamb had to be sacrificed," a clarification for Luke's Gentile readers.

Lk 22:8. Luke changed Mt's "the disciples came to Jesus, saying, 'Where...'" to give the initiative to Jesus, who chooses the two chief disciples, Peter and John, to go and find the designated room. Luke consistently revised Mt's account to make it clear that Jesus has a complete understanding of God's purposes, down to the smallest details, and is completely in control of what is taking place.

• The reference to Peter and John as the pair chosen to find the room anticipates their significant activities as a pair later in the narratives of

Acts (Acts 1:13; 3:1-11; 4:13, 19; 8:14; cf. the reference to James and John in Lk 9:54 and Peter, James and John in Lk 5:1-11). This tradition, if we may call it such, may be related to the striking series of negative comparisons between John and Peter in the Gospel of John.[1] Thus Lk 22:8 is yet another case where Luke specified, by means of a brief reference, figures who will play an important role later in his narrative.

• All of Lk 22:8 is Luke's own composition. Such terms as εἰπών, πορεύεσθαι, and ἑτοιμάζειν (cf. Lk 22:12, 13) are all linguistic characteristics of Luke (Goulder 2:721).

Lk 22:10a. With the mention of a man carrying a jar of water, Luke improved the exceedingly vague πρὸς τὸν δεῖνα in Mt 26:18a. The reference to βαστάζειν in Lk 22:10 also appears to be a Lukan linguistic characteristic. It occurs nine times in Luke-Acts as opposed to only once in Mark and three times in Matthew.

Lk 22:11. Luke omitted Mt's reference to "My time is at hand," perhaps as inappropriate in this context (see Lk 21:8; cf. Mt 24:5). Otherwise, all of Lk 22:11 is based upon Mt 26:18b.

Lk 22:12. This is Luke's addition to round out the narrative he has constructed.

Lk 22:13. This verse is essentially the same as Mt 26:19.

EXCURSUS: LUKE'S REVISION OF MATTHEW'S ACCOUNT OF THE LAST SUPPER

In good Hellenistic fashion, Luke portrayed Jesus as giving a lengthy final speech to his disciples, covering a number of important topics. Since the concept of describing the thoughts of a character was not invented until many centuries later in Western literature, it was the custom in Hellenistic biography for the protagonist, such as a general, statesman, or philosopher, to make a speech on the eve of some momentous event to let the audience know what his thoughts and intentions were. One might recall the famous speeches of the dying Socrates in Plato's *Phaedo* or Paul's final oration to the Milesian elders depicted in Acts 20:17-38. From this perspective, Mt's very brief Last Supper scene (Mt 26:20-29) would not have been adequate to fulfill the expectations of Luke's audience. This is our explanation as to why Luke brought in material from Mt 20:25-28 and 19:28, as well as adding considerable other nonMatthean tradition of his own, to make the Last Supper much more significant. What were some of his specific reasons for his revisions?

Most important, Luke rearranged and augmented the contents of Mt 26:20-35 because Mt's account may have seemed dramatically deficient to Luke. As we can see from other alterations Luke made in the material he got from Mt, in his view Jesus must appear to be fully in control of everything that transpired during the climactic

---

[1] On this little understood subject, see especially A. J. Droge, "The Status of Peter in the Fourth Gospel: A Note on John 18:10-11," *JBL* 109 (1990) 307-311.

final hours of his ministry. Nothing must appear to have happened unintentionally to Jesus, God's Prophet and King. Therefore, according to Luke's conception of this last meal, which was the occasion of Jesus' final interaction with his chosen Twelve Apostles before his arrest, Jesus must appear to conduct the meal as if in full awareness of everything about to happen and prepare for it. In sharp contrast to Mt, Luke took great pains to portray Jesus as preparing all of the key actors for their final roles. Viewed in this way, numerous features of Mt's narrative needed revision, rearrangement and augmentation.

For example, Mt's version of the dinner had no distinct beginning point; everyone just sort of gathers and starts eating. Then, in the middle of the meal, with no warning or preamble, Jesus abruptly drops a bombshell announcement that one of them is going to betray him. Mt describes each disciple reacting in shock. "Is it I?" they ask, as if they didn't know whether they would betray him or not—a curious idea. When the real traitor, Judas, asks the same question, Mt has Jesus answer: "You have said so!"—which might have seemed to be a rather weak response on Jesus' part, since Luke's audience could not be expected to understand this idiomatic Hebrew expression.

At this point, Mt's narrative seems to break and start all over again as if nothing had happened: "Now as they were eating..." Jesus breaks bread and passes it around with wine, saying something to the effect that this is the blood of the new covenant and that he will never drink wine with them again until they are in the Father's Kingdom. The disciples make no response to these momentous statements. Instead, Mt's account abruptly says they all sang a hymn (Luke's audience might have wondered how they could *sing a hymn* after all that's happened) and got up and left.

Outside in the dark night, walking along the road to the Mount of Olives, Mt's Jesus tells his disciples that they will all fall away and deny him, at which point Peter protests that he certainly would not. Jesus reaffirms his prediction, Peter protests again, and then Jesus says nothing, either to Peter or to the rest. Finally, they arrive at Gethsemane.

Mt's account could be viewed, from the perspective of Hellenistic historiography, as disjointed, clumsy, and incomplete. For an example of the Hellenistic standard we assume as the basis of these observations, see the discussion in the Introduction, "Luke's Compositional Techniques," pp. 29-35.

If we assume that Luke's main source is the Gospel of Matthew, what did he do with this narrative? As usual, he preserved but rearranged most of these elements, adding new material where necessary. First of all, unlike Mt, Luke began the whole scene with a dramatic pronouncement from Jesus: "This is my last meal with you!" Against the background of this stark pronouncement, Luke's Last Supper develops by stages and contrasts until it reaches a grim ending, a tension-filled conclusion in view of the terrifying events that will come next. Second, instead of the events being scattered over two locations (inside and outside), Luke grouped all of them into a single setting. It was Jesus' last meal with his disciples, his last opportunity to interact with and instruct the Twelve (a group which Luke immediately reconstructs following Judas' betrayal and death, in Acts 1).

Where Matthew didn't try to describe the *whole* Passover Meal, going instead to the middle: "while they were eating..." Luke describes a meal from start to finish. He began with Jesus' announcement that this was the last time he would eat and drink with his disciples, presenting a suitably dramatic entry into the evening's activities. Here we have the "earnestly earnest" saying and the "eat of it" saying to serve as a pair with the next verse, "will not drink it again" (Lk 22:18//Mt 26:29)—another Lukan eating/drinking reference. Neither of these is to be confused with the words of institution which come next; Lk 22:15-18 is a prior and separate stage, namely, Jesus the prophet announcing that this is their last eating/drinking together (a theme he returns to at the end in Lk 22:30 to round out the scene).

For the next stage, which opens at Lk 22:19, Jesus passes the broken bread around using words which are a conflation of Mt 26:26 and either 1 Cor 11:24 or a tradition similar to that utilized by Paul. After the supper is over, Jesus passes the second cup (Lk 22:20), this time conflating Mt 26:27 and words similar to those utilized by Paul at 1 Cor 11:25, whence Luke got the detail of "the cup after supper."

After the supper is finished, it is time for Jesus' "final announcements" to the Twelve. First he states that one of them who *is betraying* him (present participle) is at that very moment also eating with him, pretending that everything is all right. This alteration of the Matthean version greatly increases the ironic tension in the scene, but it also means that Luke omitted much of Mt's version at this point. Luke changed Mt's description of the disciples asking Jesus, "Is it I?" into the rhetorical question: Who among us would do such a terrible thing? (Mt 26:22 καὶ αὐτοὶ ἤρξαντο συζητεῖν πρὸς ἑαυτούς becomes Lk 22:23 τίς ἄρα εἴη ἐξ αὐτῶν ὁ τοῦτο μέλλων πράσσειν). Note that Luke added to this scene a slightly modified version of Mt 18:1-5, that the Twelve immediately began to wrangle over who should take control after Jesus was dead and gone (Lk 22:24 , 26, 27 reading μέγας/μείζων as a *terminus technicus* meaning "leader"; cf. the Gospel of Thomas #12 which contains the same cluster of themes of Jesus' "departure" and who would be "great" = leader afterwards; see also Mt 20:26-28; 23:11). The effect this Lukan addition causes is to heighten the shame of the Twelve: right after Jesus announced that he was going to be betrayed and killed, they begin to quarrel over who should be the new leader. Luke has ventured far from Mt's version to increase the negative picture of the Twelve Apostles (cf. Lk 9:37-62).

Why would Luke have added this material from Mt 18:1-5 (//Lk 22:24-29) near the end of his Last Supper account? There must have been a very powerful motivation. That is, *Luke's portrayal of Jesus' reaction to the squabbling of the disciples* must be regarded as evidence of primary importance for our understanding of Luke's own ecclesiastical situation. First, Lk 22:27 created a thematic unity of Jesus' teachings on power between Mt 20:20-28 (skipping the "ransom" saying; on this see below) and Mt 19:28 (cf. Mt 19:30 and Mt 20:26-27). In the process, Luke brought back the theme of "table" (Mt 20:28) which will be a key element in Jesus' next prophetic pronouncement (Lk 22:30). But first, he portrays Jesus insisting that they—the early Church's "pillar apostles"—must be willing to serve, not rule over the Church like foreign kings (Lk 22:25//Mt 20:25). Having said this, Luke portrays Jesus going on to make a positive reaffirmation of the Twelve (Lk 22:28-30, an echo of Mt 19:28): they will all be rehabilitated and given fitting rewards—12 thrones in Christ's Kingdom where they will again sit at table with him and eat and drink, going back to the opening theme (Lk 22:16, 18, 30).

Next, in Lk 22:31-34, Luke replaced the dialogue between Peter and Jesus in Mt 26:33-35 with a different exchange in which the prophecy of Peter's denial is preceded by an assurance that he will "turn again and strengthen his brothers" (Lk 22:32). This reassurance was clearly important for Luke, who plans to have Peter be the leader of the reconstituted Twelve in the first half of Acts. Thus it is precisely here, in Jesus' last words to Peter, that Luke echoed Mt 16:17-19 (Peter's confession; cf. Lk 22:32) and Mt 16:22-23 (the reference to Satan; cf. Lk 22:31), which Luke had not used earlier.

With all these matters taken care of, Luke was ready to conclude the Last Supper scene with an ending entirely of his own making. He portrays Jesus asking the disciples if they had need of anything when he sent them out on their (first) mission (Lk 22:35-38; cf. Lk 9:1-6). They say "no." Jesus now says, "This time, you will need to be prepared to take care of yourselves." In contrast to the earlier mission they will need swords. Then, with a reference to Isa 53:12, Luke has Jesus prophesy that he will be "numbered with the transgressors." This will be fulfilled when Jesus is arrested as a robber (Lk 22:52) and crucified between criminals (Lk 23:32). There is no singing of a hymn. The group exits and heads for the Mount of Olives, concluding Luke's version of the Last Supper. The shadow of the Crucifixion looms.

¶ 127. Eating the meal

Mt 26:20-21a, 26-29 ====> **Lk 22:14-20** (cf. 1 Cor 11:23-26)

"When the hour came," Luke wrote, "Jesus sat at table with the Twelve Apostles." Jesus announces that he has earnestly desired to eat this Passover Meal with them before he suffers, that he will not eat it again until it is fulfilled in the Kingdom of God. Then, taking a cup of wine, he bids the disciples share it together, saying that he will never drink it again until the Kingdom of God comes. Jesus breaks bread and passes it around, saying, "This bread is my body broken for you; when you eat bread together in the future, do so in memory of me." After the meal, according to ancient custom, Jesus passes around another cup of wine, saying, "This cup of wine is God's new covenant in my blood poured out for you."

General observations. Luke was following Mt's basic order for the Last Supper, but he made significant internal alterations to create a unified banquet scene. We present Lk 22:14-24 in three synopses: the first synopsis focuses on the beginning of the meal (Lk 22:14-15) and the announcement of betrayal (Lk 22:21-23, placed here according to Mt's sequence but discussed below at ¶ 128). The second synopsis (Lk 22:16-20) focuses on the meal itself as an anticipation of eating in the Kingdom of God. The third focuses on the words of institution (Lk 22:19-20).

Synopsis of Lk 22:14-15, 21-24

Illustrating Luke's use of Mt 26:20-25 to create the opening statement (Lk 22:14-15) and the announcement of the Betrayer (Lk 22:21-24).

Mt 26:20-25	Lk 22:14-15	Lk 22:21-24
20 Ὀψίας δὲ	**14** Καὶ ὅτε	
γενομένης	ἐγένετο ἡ ὥρα,	
ἀνέκειτο	ἀνέπεσεν	
μετὰ τῶν δώδεκα.	καὶ οἱ ἀπόστολοι	
	σὺν αὐτῷ.	
21 καὶ	**15** καὶ	
ἐσθιόντων αὐτῶν		
εἶπεν,	εἶπεν	
	πρὸς αὐτούς,	
Ἀμὴν λέγω ὑμῖν ὅτι	Ἐπιθυμίᾳ ἐπεθύμησα	
εἷς ἐξ ὑμῶν	τοῦτο τὸ πάσχα	**21** πλὴν ἰδοὺ
	φαγεῖν μεθ' ὑμῶν	ἡ χεὶρ
παραδώσει με.	πρὸ τοῦ με παθεῖν·	τοῦ παραδιδόντος με
22 καὶ		cf. Lk 22:23
λυπούμενοι σφόδρα		
ἤρξαντο λέγειν αὐτῷ		
εἷς ἕκαστος,		
Μήτι ἐγώ εἰμι, κύριε;		
23 ὁ δὲ ἀποκριθεὶς		
εἶπεν,		
Ὁ ἐμβάψας μετ' ἐμοῦ		μετ' ἐμοῦ
τὴν χεῖρα		
ἐν τῷ τρυβλίῳ		ἐπὶ τῆς τραπέζης·
οὗτός με παραδώσει.		
24 ὁ μὲν υἱὸς		**22** ὅτι ὁ υἱὸς μὲν
τοῦ ἀνθρώπου		τοῦ ἀνθρώπου
		κατὰ τὸ ὡρισμένον
ὑπάγει		πορεύεται
καθὼς γέγραπται		
περὶ αὐτοῦ,		
οὐαὶ δὲ		πλὴν οὐαὶ
τῷ ἀνθρώπῳ ἐκείνῳ		τῷ ἀνθρώπῳ ἐκείνῳ
δι' οὗ		δι' οὗ
ὁ υἱὸς τοῦ ἀνθρώπου		
παραδίδοται·		παραδίδοται.
cf. Mt 26:22		**23** καὶ αὐτοὶ
		ἤρξαντο συζητεῖν
καλὸν ἦν αὐτῷ		
εἰ οὐκ ἐγεννήθη		πρὸς ἑαυτοὺς
ὁ ἄνθρωπος ἐκεῖνος.		τὸ τίς ἄρα εἴη
25 ἀποκριθεὶς δὲ		ἐξ αὐτῶν
Ἰούδας		ὁ τοῦτο μέλλων
ὁ παραδιδοὺς αὐτὸν		πράσσειν.
εἶπεν,		**24** Ἐγένετο δὲ καὶ
Μήτι ἐγώ εἰμι, ῥαββί;		φιλονεικία ἐν αὐτοῖς,
λέγει αὐτῷ,		τὸ τίς αὐτῶν
Σὺ εἶπας.		δοκεῖ εἶναι μείζων.

Lk 22:14. Luke changed Mt's "evening" to ἡ ὥρα. This phrase occurs in Luke-Acts over thirty times. In the Passion narrative, Luke used it to highlight the gravity of the event as well as to indicate a specific time (see, e.g., Lk 22:53, 59; 23:44; 24:33). Moreover, in contrast to Mt, Luke used ἀναπίπτειν to describe the posture of the guests at the meal, a word he used earlier (Lk 11:37; 14:10; 17:7). Luke also changed Mt's "twelve disciples" to "apostles" in order to distinguish between many "disciples" and the Twelve "Apostles" (cf. Lk 6:13). This distinction will be critical later (cf., e.g., Lk 24:33).

Lk 22:15 appears to be Luke's construction based on Mt 26:21 or a similar tradition. Luke added the words Ἐπιθυμίᾳ ἐπεθύμησα in Lk 22:15. This construction (the repetition of a verb = Hebrew intensive idiom) has been identified as a Septuagintism (cf. Gen 31:30; Ps 105:4) and is characteristic of Luke's usage (cf. Acts 5:28; 23:14).

Synopsis of Lk 22:16-18

Illustrating Luke's utilization of Mt 26:27-29 to describe the "first cup" as a symbolic anticipation of the Messianic Banquet in the Kingdom of God.

Mt 26:27-29	Lk 22:16-18	1 Cor 11:24-26
	16 λέγω γὰρ ὑμῖν ὅτι	
	οὐ μὴ φάγω αὐτὸ	
	ἕως ὅτου πληρωθῇ	
	ἐν τῇ βασιλείᾳ τοῦ θεοῦ.	
27 καὶ λαβὼν	**17** καὶ	
ποτήριον	δεξάμενος ποτήριον	
καὶ εὐχαριστήσας	εὐχαριστήσας	
λέγων,	εἶπεν,	
Πίετε ἐξ αὐτοῦ πάντες,		
	Λάβετε	
28 τοῦτο γάρ ἐστιν	τοῦτο	
τὸ αἷμά μου	καὶ διαμερίσατε	
τῆς διαθήκης	εἰς ἑαυτούς·	
τὸ περὶ πολλῶν		
ἐκχυννόμενον		
εἰς ἄφεσιν ἁμαρτιῶν.		
29 λέγω δὲ ὑμῖν,	**18** λέγω γὰρ ὑμῖν, [ὅτι]	
οὐ μὴ πίω	οὐ μὴ πίω	
ἀπ' ἄρτι	ἀπὸ τοῦ νῦν	
ἐκ τούτου τοῦ	ἀπὸ τοῦ γενήματος	
γενήματος		
τῆς ἀμπέλου	τῆς ἀμπέλου	
ἕως τῆς ἡμέρας ἐκείνης	ἕως οὗ	cf. 1 Cor 11:26
ὅταν αὐτὸ πίνω		
μεθ' ὑμῶν καινὸν		
ἐν τῇ βασιλείᾳ	ἡ βασιλεία	
τοῦ πατρός μου.	τοῦ θεοῦ ἔλθῃ.	

Lk 22:16. The statement in Lk 22:16: "I will not eat the Passover again until my suffering is completed/accomplished (τὸ με παθεῖν πληρωθῇ) in the

Kingdom of God (ἐν τῇ βασιλείᾳ τοῦ θεοῦ) means, in our opinion, "I will not eat until all events take place according to God's Plan" (cf. the repeated references to this concept after the resurrection: Lk 24:26-27, 44 δεῖ πληρωθῆναι). In other words, this is not a direct reference to some far distant event, but quite specifically to the "eating and drinking" with his disciples following the "fulfillment"—that is, the crucifixion and resurrection which for Luke inaugurates the era of the Kingdom. As such, this might point toward the repeated "eating" references later at the conclusion in Lk 24:30-35, 41-43. Luke is also thinking of the meals joyfully celebrated by Christians in the early Church (cf. Acts 2:46-47). It is to be remembered that the Lord's Supper was always part of a regular meal.

Lk 22:17-18. These verses complete the first stage of the meal. They are based on Mt 26:27-29. However, Luke divided the Matthean passage in half (i.e., created a doublet), placing the statement "I shall not drink again of this fruit of the vine until I drink it new with you in my Father's kingdom" (Mt 26:29) directly after Lk 22:15-16, so that it forms a parallel to the opening statement's reference to "eating" in the Kingdom of God—even though Luke was utilizing Mt's cup terminology from the words of institution at the Last Supper (Mt 26:27f.). Although the words of Lk 22:18 are similar to Mt 26:29: "I will never drink wine again until the Kingdom of God comes," the meaning is very different. This is another example of Luke deeschatologizing a saying of Jesus. In Luke's context, this "prophecy" will be literally fulfilled on Sunday. Thus, Lk 22:15-18 forms an initial unit whose central point appears to be: this is the last Passover I will eat with you until all Scriptures are fulfilled in me (= the crucifixion) and then I will eat with you again (literally, after the resurrection, next Sunday).

• The phrase ἀπὸ τοῦ νῦν (Lk 22:18) is a significant Lukan term. It occurs five times in Lk (1:48; 5:10; 12:52; here; 22:69), once in Acts (18:6), once in 2 Cor 5:16, and nowhere else. It means "from now on," as we can see from Jesus' warning to the High Priest (see discussion below at Lk 22:69).

Lk 22:19-20. These verses are Luke's "institution of the Eucharist" proper. He put it here, following Mt's order (thereby creating a second passing of the cup), but conflated Mt 26:26-28 with a tradition also known to Paul (cf. 1 Cor 11:23-26). Paul accentuates the fact that the meal is to be re-enacted among the faithful: "Do this in my memory!" (1 Cor 11:24). The following synopsis presents evidence suggesting that Luke used both Mt 26:26-28 and a tradition now found in 1 Cor 11:24-25 to create Lk 22:19-20.

Synopsis of Lk 22:19-20

Illustrating Luke's use of Mt 26:26-28 and 1 Cor 11:24f.
to form the Words of Institution.

Mt 26:26	Lk 22:19-20	1 Cor 11:24-25
26 Ἐσθιόντων δὲ αὐτῶν		
λαβὼν ὁ Ἰησοῦς ἄρτον	19 καὶ λαβὼν ἄρτον	ἔλαβεν ἄρτον
καὶ εὐλογήσας	εὐχαριστήσας	24 καὶ εὐχαριστήσας
ἔκλασεν	ἔκλασεν	ἔκλασεν
καὶ δοὺς τοῖς μαθηταῖς	καὶ ἔδωκεν αὐτοῖς	καὶ
εἶπεν,	λέγων,	εἶπεν,
Λάβετε φάγετε,	cf. Lk 22:17	
τοῦτό ἐστιν	Τοῦτό ἐστιν	Τοῦτό μού ἐστιν
τὸ σῶμά μου.	τὸ σῶμά μου	τὸ σῶμα
	τὸ ὑπὲρ ὑμῶν διδόμενον	τὸ ὑπὲρ ὑμῶν·
	τοῦτο ποιεῖτε	τοῦτο ποιεῖτε
	εἰς τὴν ἐμὴν ἀνάμνησιν.	εἰς τὴν ἐμὴν ἀνάμνησιν.
27 καὶ λαβὼν	20 καὶ	25 ὡσαύτως καὶ
ποτήριον	τὸ ποτήριον	τὸ ποτήριον
	ὡσαύτως	
καὶ εὐχαριστήσας	cf. Lk 22:17	
ἔδωκεν αὐτοῖς		
	μετὰ τὸ δειπνῆσαι,	μετὰ τὸ δειπνῆσαι
λέγων,	λέγων,	λέγων,
Πίετε ἐξ αὐτοῦ πάντες,		
28 τοῦτο γάρ	Τοῦτο τὸ ποτήριον	Τοῦτο τὸ ποτήριον
ἐστιν		
τὸ αἷμά μου		
τῆς διαθήκης	ἡ καινὴ διαθήκη	ἡ καινὴ διαθήκη
		ἐστὶν
	ἐν τῷ αἵματί μου	ἐν τῷ ἐμῷ αἵματι·
τὸ περὶ πολλῶν	τὸ ὑπὲρ ὑμῶν	
ἐκχυννόμενον	ἐκχυννόμενον.	
εἰς ἄφεσιν ἁμαρτιῶν.		
		τὸν θάνατον τοῦ κυρίου
		καταγγέλλετε
	cf. Lk 22:18	ἄχρις οὗ ἔλθῃ.

The "cup after supper" is mentioned here in Lk 22:20 and in 1 Cor 11:25a and nowhere else in the NT. Indeed, the wording is strikingly similar in both cases:

Lk 22:20 καὶ τὸ ποτήριον ὡσαύτως μετὰ τὸ δειπνῆσαι λέγων...

1 Cor 11:25a ὡσαύτως και τὸ ποτήριον μετὰ τὸ δειπνῆσαι λέγων...

As noted above, by this process, Luke referred to *two* cups at the Last Supper—leading to centuries of attempts to emend the text to bring Luke's account into greater harmony with the other Synoptics. To this end, half of Lk 22:19 and all of Lk 22:20 have been deleted in the past (e.g., the recommendation of the minority group of the UBS4 editorial committee; see Metzger 1994, 148-150). The textual base for omitting Lk 22:19b-20 consists of D and some versions of the Itala. The textual support for the longer reading includes 𝔓75 ℵ A B C L W Δ Θ Ψ numerous versions and patristic quotations. UBS4 includes it with a "confidence grade" of {B}. One argument usually advanced against the genuineness of the longer reading says that it is a harmonization with the Eucharistic usage of the Pauline churches in 1 Cor 11. For the Two Gospel Hypothesis, this close echo of a Pauline letter is viewed by us as a sign of genuineness; we have found other examples of a close bond between phrases in Lk and passages in the genuine letters of Paul. Nor is the customary argument that Luke avoids substitutionary atonement language valid, particularly when it relies on an emended text of Lk 22:19b-20 as part of its evidence. Finally, the alleged appearance of non-Lukan vocabulary in these two verses can be accounted for by his importation of Pauline liturgical expressions. We agree with the UBS4 majority position, therefore, in concluding that Luke's version of the words of Jesus associated with the bread and wine (Lk 22:19b-20) are a conflation of Mt 26:26-28 and 1 Cor 11:24-25.

¶ 128. He who is betraying me is here at the table

Mt 26:23-25 ====> **Lk 22:21-23**

Without pausing, Jesus then announces, "But, note well! The hand of the man who is betraying me is with mine on the table! The Son of Man must indeed suffer what has been determined by God, but woe to the man who brings it about!" The disciples are stunned by Jesus' words and ask each other who would do such a thing?

General observations. Luke now incorporated Mt's account of the exchange between Jesus and Judas in Mt 26:21-25. However, he greatly abbreviated Mt's version in order to bring into the Last Supper an earlier vignette where the Twelve quarrel among themselves over who should be the leader after Jesus' death (Lk 22:24-27). Luke's purpose for bringing together Jesus' announcement of his betrayer (Lk 22:21-23) and this struggle for dominance (Lk 22:24-27) may have been that he saw that struggle among the eleven in continuity with Judas' betrayal of Jesus. At least that would appear to be the effect of placing it where he does. Although this makes it a strikingly severe judgment upon the Twelve, it is not unlike what we have seen from Luke's hand earlier (Lk 9:28-62). More on this in the next pericope.

Lk 22:21-23. These verses show numerous signs of Lukan editing. Πλήν is a frequently used word in Luke (15 times in the Gospel, 4 times in Acts; cf. Collison 120-121). Πλὴν οὐαί occurs three times (Lk 6:24 [no parallel with Mt]; Lk 17:1//Mt 18:7 and here in Lk 22:22; cf. Mt 18:7).

• Luke skillfully inserted τραπέζῆς at Lk 22:21 so there would be an echo later when Jesus looks forward to the τραπέζης μου ἐν τῇ βασιλείᾳ μου at Lk 22:30. This additional detail suggests that Luke's portrayal of Jesus' last earthly banquet with his disciples—to be repeated by them in memory of him—was intentionally described by Luke a proleptic taste of the Messianic banquet in his Kingdom.

• The construction τίς + optative (Lk 22:23) occurs eleven times in Luke-Acts and never in Mt (or Mk; cf. Collison 209). Goulder notes that τίς with the partitive genitive occurs five times in Lk as opposed to once in Mt (Goulder 2:809; cf. Collison 210).

¶ 129. Leaders must serve—I will reward you in my kingdom!

(Mt 18:1-5; 20:25-28; 19:28) Mt 26:31-35 ====> **Lk 22:24-38**

No sooner does Jesus announce that his betrayer is present and the Twelve react in shock, than they suddenly begin quarreling over who should take over Jesus' position as the leader, as if he were dead already. Jesus scolds them for their arrogance, warning that their attitude makes them no different than Gentile tyrants whom God will certainly destroy. "Whoever would be a leader like me must follow my example and serve," warns Jesus. He goes on to temper his harsh rebuke by promising them, who alone have been with him through everything, twelve positions of highest honor in his Kingdom. Turning to Peter, Jesus tells him that, although he will turn against him, Satan will not be able to keep him. He will become the leader. Finally, Jesus makes sure the disciples have swords; they will soon use them in fulfillment of scripture.

General observations. As noted above in the Excursus, Luke made general use of Mt 26:31-32, but he also brought together two other Matthean texts (Mt 20:25-28; 19:28) and echoed Mt 18:1-5, to make a new complex that became a definitive statement by Jesus at the Last Supper on the disciples' use of their power (after the Resurrection). The major break with the Matthean order signals the importance of this statement for Luke's ecclesiology. Echoes of conflict between the apostles can be clearly detected in Paul's letters and the Gospel of John.

Lk 22:24. This verse contains considerable evidence of Lukan compositional activity. ἐγένετο δέ is a Lukan linguistic characteristic (Collison 43). We also note that δὲ καί occurs in Luke-Acts 48 times as opposed to only 6 times in Matthew and twice in Mark (cf. Goulder 2:802 whose figures are incorrect).

• The use of τό in a construction that raises an indirect question is also characteristic of Luke (Goulder 2:806).

• The term φιλονεικία is a NT *hapax legomenon* at Lk 22:24. Could it be an echo of 1 Cor 11:16? The clause in 1 Cor 11:16 δοκεῖ φιλόνεικος εἶναι also appears in Lk 22:24 δοκεῖ εἶναι. Furthermore, this reference to φιλόνεικος can also point forward to the squabbling at Corinthian Eucharists described by Paul in 1 Cor 11:17-22. These could be additional indications that Luke is quite familiar with not only the Gospel of Matthew but also the Pauline tradition preserved in 1 Cor 11, not only with the received terminology on the supper but also the rebuke against squabbling which Luke also seems to have combined with Mt 26:26-29.

Lk 22:25. The addition of the reference to benefactors (εὐεργέται) is a nice touch for audiences in the Greco-Roman world.

Lk 22:26. Three of Luke's seven uses of μείζων appear within this literary context (Lk 22:24, 26, 27; see also Lk 7:28bis, 9:46 and 12:18). The Matthean parallel here is not μείζων, but μέγας (Mt 20:26). That Luke should alter μέγας to μείζων is understandable because the comparative degree of the adjective is proper Greek while the positive degree is more typical of Hebrew style or the LXX. Our conclusion is that this cluster is an echo of what is otherwise a fairly wide-spread Matthean phrase that includes μείζων (cf. Mt 11:11; 18:1, 4; cf. Mt 5:19). The echoes with Mt 18:1-5 are especially noticeable.

Lk 22:27-30. The words ἐν μέσῳ (Lk 22:27) occur frequently in Lk-Acts (Lk 2:46; 8:7; 10:3/Mt 10:16; 21:21; 22:55; 24:36; Acts 1:15; 2:22; 4:7; 17:22 and 27:21), and may be considered a characteristic expression of Luke which is almost always missing from the Matthean parallel context.

• Luke omitted the specific reference to Jesus' death as a ransom in Mt 20:28. Compare the related Lukan omission of "ransom" at Mt 20:28; cf. Lk 18:27. However, Isa 53 hovers in the background throughout the Last Supper scene in Lk. Jesus announces the new covenant of Jer 31:31. Now Luke has Jesus the King bestow upon the Twelve the covenantal blessings of the Kingdom (Lk 22:29). When the Kingdom comes they will again *eat and drink* with him (Lk 22:30), a wide-spread Lukan motif (17 times in Luke-Acts). In the unique passage about the swords, there is an explicit quotation of Isa 53:12 "he was numbered with the transgressors," (see further below).

Lk 22:31-32. This is Lukan composition. It prepares for the dominant role Peter will play in Acts 2-12. The occurrence of δεῖσθαι (Lk 22:32) is one of fifteen usages of this expression in Lk. It occurs only once in Mt and is characteristic of Luke's theme of prayer. Lk 22:31-32 is an anticipation both of Peter's betrayal and his restoration. Jesus prays (δέομαι, Lk 22:32) and later invites Peter and the other disciples to pray (προσεύχομαι, Lk 22:40, 46). Instead they fall asleep and Peter betrays Jesus. Ultimately, however, Jesus' prayer is answered when Peter is rehabilitated.

Lk 22:33. This verse may reveal Luke's knowledge of Peter's martyrdom, which suggests the possibility that Luke knew of Paul's martyrdom as well. Both apostles were probably executed in Rome during the reign of Nero, just prior to the outbreak of rebellion in Judea in 66.

Lk 22:35. Lk 22:35 curiously echoes the instructions of Jesus to the "72 others" "not to take purse, bags, or sandals" (Lk 10:4) rather than the instructions to the Twelve to take "no staff, nor bag, nor bread, nor money" (Lk 9:3).

Lk 22:36-38. With all these matters taken care of, Luke was ready to conclude the Last Supper scene with an ending entirely of his own making. He portrays Jesus asking the disciples if they had need of anything when he sent them out on their (first) mission. They say "no." Jesus now says, "This time, you will need to be prepared to take care of yourselves." In contrast to the earlier mission, now they will need swords because, Jesus prophesies, he will be "numbered with the transgressors" (a reference to Isa 53:12). This prophecy will be immediately and literally fulfilled (another Lukan trademark) when Jesus is arrested as a criminal (Lk 22:52) and crucified between two criminals (Lk 23:32).

• Now, at the end of Jesus' ministry, the hour of crisis has arrived. The expression ἀλλὰ νῦν ...τοῦτο τὸ γεγραμμένον δεῖ τελεσθῆναι ἐν ἐμοί (Lk 22:36) is a distinct echo of what Jesus said at the beginning of his ministry and a similar quotation from Isaiah σήμερον πεπλήρωται ἡ γραφὴ αὕτη ἐν τοῖς ὠσὶν ὑμῶν (Lk 4:21; cf. Lk 4:18-19//Isa 61:1-2; 58:6, another text from Isa). Thus, from beginning to end, the ministry of Jesus according to Lk unfolds according to the scriptures.

¶ 130. Jesus piously submits to God's will

Mt 26:30, 36-46 ====> **Lk 22:39-46**

Jesus and the disciples return to the Mount of Olives for the night, as is their custom. Beseeching his disciples to pray for God to protect them from temptation, he goes off by himself and devoutly submits his will to God, come what may. Coming back, he finds that his disciples have fallen asleep "out of sorrow." Jesus wakes them, warning them once more to be on guard against temptation—well knowing what is about to happen.

General observations. Luke continued to follow the order of Mt's pericopes (Mt 26:36-46) for this account. However, he made considerable editorial changes in Mt's account of Jesus' prayer in Gethsemane. The complex Matthean structure is greatly reduced. The three-fold request that the disciples keep watch, while Jesus prays in the supine posture (signifying total submission) for the cup to be removed, and then returns to find the disciples sleeping, was altered by Luke. Instead, Luke softened Jesus' agony (we take Lk 22:43-44 to be a later addition, see below) so that Jesus appears to be in more control of events. Luke thereby speeded up the action by removing unnecessary repetition and made the disciples' seemingly uncaring behavior milder.

Lk 22:39. Instead of Mt's vague phrase: "they went out to the Mount of Olives" (Mt 26:30), Luke described Jesus purposefully leading the disciples: "he came out and went...to the Mount of Olives and the disciples followed him." The use of πορεύεσθε with εἰς (Lk 22:39) is a Lukan linguistic characteristic (Collison 129). Earlier, Luke had established the fact that Jesus spent time at the Mount of Olives (Lk 21:37). Now, in Lk 22:39, Luke announced that Jesus went to the Mount of Olives to pray, in keeping with his custom.

Lk 22:40. Luke placed the instruction to pray against temptation in Mt 26:41 at the beginning of the scene (Lk 22:40) and then repeated it again at the end (Lk 22:46), creating a doublet which forms a nice *inclusio*. Prayer is an essential factor in meeting the challenges of Satan, who seeks to test the disciples (Lk 11:4; 22:31-32). Unlike Jesus, the disciples fail to pray, and the later narration in Lk depicts the sad consequences.

Lk 22:41. Luke avoided Mt's depiction of Jesus lying face down before God, the position of abject submission (*proskynesis*) commonly expected of subjects when asking royalty for anything. Instead, Luke depicts Jesus as kneeling, possibly a more noble posture.

Lk 22:43-44. These verses are considered to be an interpolation by UBS^4. The ms. evidence against their genuineness is very strong: $\mathfrak{P}^{75}$ ℵ^{1} A B N T W and a few early versions. In favor are the original hand plus the second corrector of ℵ, as well as D L Δ Θ Ψ, numerous versions and virtually all of the patristic citations. The UBS committee therefore regards it as an ancient and honorable early reading, but not original. B. Ehrmann has made a strong case for the view that these verses are both literarily and theologically intrusive in Luke's account.[2] However, David Crump has made a strong case for the genuineness of these verses, noting the presence of several literary characteristics of Luke.[3] On the other hand, ἀγωνία, ἱδρώς, and θρόμβος are *hapax legomena*. On balance we incline to omit, mainly because of the ms. evidence.

Lk 22:46. In place of the Matthean γρηγορεῖτε καὶ προσεύχεσθε (Mt 26:41), Luke has ἀναστάντες προσεύχεσθε. The use of ἀνιστάναι as a participle is characteristic of Luke (cf. Lk 22:45; Goulder 2:743, 800).

---

[2] See B. Ehrmann, *The Orthodox Corruption of Scripture; The Effect of Early Christological Controversies on the Text of the New Testament* (New York: Oxford University Press, 1993) 187-194.

[3] See D. Crump, *Jesus the Intercessor* WUNT 2/49 (Tübingen: J.C.B. Mohr, 1992) 116-121.

Section Two: Jesus' Arrest, Trials, and Public Humiliation. Lk 22:47-23:25

¶ 131. The authorities seize Jesus in the middle of the night
Mt 26:47-56 ====> **Lk 22:47-53**

As Jesus was speaking, suddenly a crowd including Temple police appears, led by none other than Judas. He obviously knew where to find Jesus in the middle of the night. Judas tries to kiss Jesus in greeting, but Jesus pulls back. The other disciples ask Jesus if they should fight, and, before he can answer, one of them strikes at the head of the slave of the High Priest, cutting off his right ear. Instantly Jesus forbids any more fighting, and heals the slave's wound. "Why did you come out with such a force tonight?" Jesus asks the chief priests and elders: "Were you too afraid of me when I was there with you in the Temple day after day? Afraid what the people would do to you? Never mind; this is Satan's brief moment. Let's go!"

General observations. Luke continued to follow Mt's order for this account. The significant Lukan additions and omissions can easily be explained according to Luke's compositional agenda.

Lk 22:47. Luke followed Matthew fairly closely here, modifying the account only to emphasize that "Judas was leading" everybody (cf. Acts 1:16b), unlike Mt, where Judas is simply in the crowd. Repeated terminology and a similarity of theme with Lk 22:1-3 (the beginning of this chapter in Lk) seem to us to indicate that this is the beginning of a Section in Lk. However, the general themes of testing and trial featuring Judas are common to both units. Compare also ἐκ τοῦ ἀριθμοῦ τῶν δώδεκα (Lk 22:3) and εἷς τῶν δώδεκα (Lk 22:47). The use of ὁ λεγόμενος (Lk 22:47) echoes a similar Lukan usage at Lk 22:1. In Lk 22:47b ἐγγίζειν (cf. Lk 22:1 again) is a linguistic usage of Luke (Collison 46).

Lk 22:48. Luke inserted the title "Son of Man" into the Matthean context (Mt 26:49-50) to bring this fateful moment into line with what Jesus had said about Judas at the Last Supper (Lk 22:21).

Lk 22:49. In contrast to Mt, where the disciples begin to resist without first asking Jesus' permission, Luke portrayed them as asking Jesus what to do. However, they take action before receiving an answer.

Lk 22:50. In contrast to Mt's "ear," Luke specified *right* ear," which appears to be a secondary addition to the original account.

• Luke skipped cleanly over Jesus' words recorded in Mt 26:52-53. Luke wanted to give no hint that Jesus was even potentially prepared to resist arrest, or could use overwhelming, divine force if he had wanted to. Such ideas were absolutely outside the Lukan portrayal of Jesus as the non-resisting, non-retaliating Savior of the poor, disenfranchised and outcast.

Lk 22:53b. Luke added the reference to "your hour and the power of darkness" (cf. Mt 26:55) to underline the metaphysical clash going on behind the scenes. The reference to darkness anticipates the eclipse which occurs the next day precisely at noon, the moment of Jesus' death (Lk 23:44-45).

¶ 132. Jesus is taken to the High Priest's house; Peter follows him.

Mt 26:57-75 ====> **Lk 22:54-65**

The Temple authorities seize Jesus and take him away, bringing him into the house of the High Priest for safe-keeping. Peter follows, attempting to mingle with the crowd sitting around a fire in the courtyard. But a serving maid spots him and says, "You were with him!" Peter vehemently denies it. Again someone else insists that he was one of Jesus' group, but again Peter denies any knowledge of Jesus. A third person calls attention to his Galilean accent, but again Peter denies knowing Jesus. Suddenly a rooster crows, and Peter sees Jesus turn and look at him, as if to say, "Remember what I told you?" Suddenly Peter realizes what he's done, and he rushes out, weeping in bitter shame. Meanwhile, those holding Jesus began to beat him and spit on him. They blindfold him and hit him repeatedly, saying, "Come on you prophet! Tell us who is hitting you!"

General observations. Although Luke is following the general order of events in Mt 26:57-75, as with his account of the Last Supper, he considerably rearranged Mt's narrative order to produce a much more powerful account of Jesus' initial appearance before the Jerusalem authorities.

Synopsis of Lk 22:54–65

Illustrating Luke's revision of Mt 26:57-75 to create a midnight detention at the High Priest's house (Lk 22:54-65), followed by a morning hearing before the Jerusalem authorities (Lk 22:66-71).

Mt 26:57-75	**Lk 22:54-65**	**Lk 22:66-71**
57 Οἱ δὲ κρατήσαντες	**54** Συλλαβόντες δὲ	**66** Καὶ ὡς ἐγένετο ἡμέρα,
τὸν Ἰησοῦν ἀπήγαγον	αὐτὸν ἤγαγον καὶ εἰσήγαγον	
πρὸς Καϊάφαν τὸν ἀρχιερέα,	εἰς τὴν οἰκίαν τοῦ ἀρχιερέως·	
		συνήχθη
ὅπου οἱ γραμματεῖς καὶ οἱ πρεσβύτεροι		τὸ πρεσβυτέριον τοῦ λαοῦ,
συνήχθησαν.		
58 ὁ δὲ Πέτρος	ὁ δὲ Πέτρος	

Synopsis of Luke's Account of Jesus' Midnight Detention and Morning Hearing (cont.)

Mt 26:58 ἠκολούθει αὐτῷ	Lk 22:54-56	Lk 22:66-71
ἀπὸ μακρόθεν	ἠκολούθει μακρόθεν.	
ἕως τῆς αὐλῆς τοῦ		
ἀρχιερέως		
καὶ εἰσελθὼν ἔσω		
ἐκάθητο μετὰ τῶν		
ὑπηρετῶν		
ἰδεῖν τὸ τέλος.		
59 οἱ δὲ ἀρχιερεῖς		ἀρχιερεῖς τε
cf. Mt 26:57		καὶ γραμματεῖς,
		καὶ ἀπήγαγον αὐτὸν
καὶ τὸ συνέδριον ὅλον		εἰς τὸ συνέδριον αὐτῶν
ἐζήτουν ψευδομαρτυρίαν		
κατὰ τοῦ Ἰησοῦ		
ὅπως αὐτὸν		
θανατώσωσιν,		
60 καὶ οὐχ εὗρον		
πολλῶν προσελθόντων		
ψευδομαρτύρων.		
ὕστερον δὲ		
προσελθόντες δύο		
61 εἶπαν,		
Οὗτος ἔφη,		
Δύναμαι καταλῦσαι		
τὸν ναὸν τοῦ θεοῦ		
καὶ διὰ τριῶν ἡμερῶν		
οἰκοδομῆσαι.		
62 καὶ ἀναστὰς		
ὁ ἀρχιερεὺς εἶπεν αὐτῷ,		
Οὐδὲν ἀποκρίνῃ τί		
οὗτοί σου		
καταμαρτυροῦσιν;		
63 ὁ δὲ Ἰησοῦς ἐσιώπα.		
καὶ ὁ ἀρχιερεὺς εἶπεν		**67** λέγοντες,
αὐτῷ,		
Ἐξορκίζω σε		
κατὰ τοῦ θεοῦ τοῦ		
ζῶντος		
ἵνα ἡμῖν εἴπῃς		
εἰ σὺ εἶ ὁ Χριστὸς		Εἰ σὺ εἶ ὁ Χριστός,
ὁ υἱὸς τοῦ θεοῦ.		cf. Lk 22:70
		εἰπὸν ἡμῖν.
64 λέγει αὐτῷ ὁ Ἰησοῦς,		εἶπεν δὲ αὐτοῖς,
Σὺ εἶπας·		
πλὴν λέγω ὑμῖν,		Ἐὰν ὑμῖν εἴπω,
		οὐ μὴ πιστεύσητε·
		68 ἐὰν δὲ ἐρωτήσω,
		οὐ μὴ ἀποκριθῆτε.
ἀπ' ἄρτι		**69** ἀπὸ τοῦ νῦν

Synopsis of Luke's Account of Jesus' Midnight Detention and Morning Hearing (cont.)

Mt 26:64 ὄψεσθε τὸν υἱὸν τοῦ ἀνθρώπου καθήμενον ἐκ δεξιῶν τῆς δυνάμεως καὶ ἐρχόμενον ἐπὶ τῶν νεφελῶν τοῦ οὐρανοῦ.	**Lk 22:54-65**	**Lk 22:69** δὲ ἔσται ὁ υἱὸς τοῦ ἀνθρώπου καθήμενος ἐκ δεξιῶν τῆς δυνάμεως τοῦ θεοῦ.
cf. Mt 26:63-64a **63** ὁ δὲ Ἰησοῦς ἐσιώπα. καὶ ὁ ἀρχιερεὺς εἶπεν αὐτῷ, Ἐξορκίζω σε κατὰ τοῦ θεοῦ τοῦ ζῶντος ἵνα ἡμῖν εἴπῃς εἰ σὺ εἶ ὁ Χριστὸς ὁ υἱὸς τοῦ θεοῦ. **64** λέγει αὐτῷ ὁ Ἰησοῦς, Σὺ εἶπας·		**70** εἶπαν δὲ πάντες, Σὺ οὖν εἶ ὁ υἱὸς τοῦ θεοῦ; ὁ δὲ πρὸς αὐτοὺς ἔφη, Ὑμεῖς λέγετε ὅτι ἐγώ εἰμι.
65 τότε ὁ ἀρχιερεὺς διέρρηξεν τὰ ἱμάτια αὐτοῦ λέγων, Ἐβλασφήμησεν· τί ἔτι χρείαν ἔχομεν μαρτύρων; ἴδε νῦν ἠκούσατε τὴν βλασφημίαν·	cf. Lk 22:65	**71** οἱ δὲ εἶπαν, Τί ἔτι ἔχομεν μαρτυρίας χρείαν; αὐτοὶ γὰρ ἠκούσαμεν ἀπὸ τοῦ στόματος αὐτοῦ.
66 τί ὑμῖν δοκεῖ; οἱ δὲ ἀποκριθέντες εἶπαν, Ἔνοχος θανάτου ἐστίν.	cf. Lk 22:63-65 **63** Καὶ οἱ ἄνδρες οἱ συνέχοντες αὐτὸν ἐνέπαιζον αὐτῷ	
67 Τότε ἐνέπτυσαν εἰς τὸ πρόσωπον αὐτοῦ καὶ ἐκολάφισαν αὐτόν, οἱ δὲ ἐράπισαν	δέροντες, **64** καὶ περικαλύψαντες αὐτὸν ἐπηρώτων	
68 λέγοντες, Προφήτευσον ἡμῖν, Χριστέ, τίς ἐστιν ὁ παίσας σε;	λέγοντες, Προφήτευσον, τίς ἐστιν ὁ παίσας σε;	
cf. Mt 26:65	**65** καὶ ἕτερα πολλὰ βλασφημοῦντες ἔλεγον εἰς αὐτόν.	

Synopsis of Luke's Account of Jesus' Midnight Detention and Morning Hearing (cont.)

Mt 26:68	Lk 22:55	Lk 22:66-71
	περιαψάντων δὲ πῦρ	
	ἐν μέσῳ τῆς αὐλῆς	
	καὶ συγκαθισάντων	
69 Ὁ δὲ Πέτρος	ἐκάθητο ὁ Πέτρος	
ἐκάθητο		
ἔξω	μέσος αὐτῶν.	
ἐν τῇ αὐλῇ·		
καὶ προσῆλθεν αὐτῷ	56 ἰδοῦσα δὲ αὐτὸν	
μία παιδίσκη	παιδίσκη τις	
	καθήμενον πρὸς τὸ φῶς	
λέγουσα,	καὶ ἀτενίσασα αὐτῷ	
	εἶπεν,	
Καὶ σὺ ἦσθα	Καὶ οὗτος	
μετὰ Ἰησοῦ τοῦ	σὺν αὐτῷ ἦν·	
Γαλιλαίου.	(cf. Lk 22:59)	
70 ὁ δὲ ἠρνήσατο	57 ὁ δὲ ἠρνήσατο	
ἔμπροσθεν πάντων	λέγων,	
λέγων,		
Οὐκ οἶδα τί λέγεις.	Οὐκ οἶδα αὐτόν, γύναι.	
71 ἐξελθόντα δὲ	58 καὶ μετὰ βραχὺ	
εἰς τὸν πυλῶνα		
εἶδεν αὐτὸν ἄλλη	ἕτερος ἰδὼν αὐτὸν	
καὶ λέγει τοῖς ἐκεῖ,	ἔφη,	
Οὗτος ἦν	Καὶ σὺ ἐξ αὐτῶν εἶ.	
μετὰ Ἰησοῦ τοῦ		
Ναζωραίου.		
72 καὶ πάλιν ἠρνήσατο	ὁ δὲ Πέτρος ἔφη,	
μετὰ ὅρκου ὅτι		
Οὐκ οἶδα τὸν ἄνθρωπον.	Ἄνθρωπε, οὐκ εἰμί.	
	59 καὶ διαστάσης	
73 μετὰ μικρὸν	ὡσεὶ ὥρας μιᾶς	
δὲ προσελθόντες οἱ	ἄλλος τις διϊσχυρίζετο	
ἑστῶτες		
εἶπον τῷ Πέτρῳ,	λέγων,	
Ἀληθῶς	Ἐπ᾽ ἀληθείας	
καὶ σὺ ἐξ αὐτῶν εἶ,	καὶ οὗτος μετ᾽ αὐτοῦ	
	ἦν,	
καὶ γὰρ ἡ λαλιά σου	καὶ γὰρ	
(cf. Mt 26:69)	Γαλιλαῖός ἐστιν.	
δῆλόν σε ποιεῖ.		
74 τότε ἤρξατο	60 εἶπεν δὲ ὁ Πέτρος,	
καταθεματίζειν		
καὶ ὀμνύειν ὅτι		
Οὐκ οἶδα τὸν ἄνθρωπον.	Ἄνθρωπε, οὐκ οἶδα ὃ	
	λέγεις.	
καὶ εὐθέως	καὶ παραχρῆμα	
	ἔτι λαλοῦντος αὐτοῦ	

Synopsis of Luke's Account of Jesus' Midnight Detention and Morning Hearing (concl.)

Mt 26:74	**Lk 22:60**	**Lk 22: 66-71**
ἀλέκτωρ ἐφώνησεν.	ἐφώνησεν ἀλέκτωρ.	
	61 καὶ στραφεὶς ὁ κύριος ἐνέβλεψεν τῷ Πέτρῳ,	
75 καὶ ἐμνήσθη ὁ Πέτρος	καὶ ὑπεμνήσθη ὁ Πέτρος	
τοῦ ῥήματος Ἰησοῦ εἰρηκότος ὅτι	τοῦ ῥήματος τοῦ κυρίου ὡς εἶπεν αὐτῷ ὅτι	
Πρὶν ἀλέκτορα φωνῆσαι	Πρὶν ἀλέκτορα φωνῆσαι σήμερον	
τρὶς ἀπαρνήσῃ με·	ἀπαρνήσῃ με τρίς.	
καὶ ἐξελθὼν ἔξω ἔκλαυσεν πικρῶς.	**62** καὶ ἐξελθὼν ἔξω ἔκλαυσεν πικρῶς.	
cf. Mt 26:66-68		
66 τί ὑμῖν δοκεῖ;		
	63 Καὶ οἱ ἄνδρες	
οἱ δὲ ἀποκριθέντες	οἱ συνέχοντες αὐτὸν ἐνέπαιζον αὐτῷ	
εἶπαν, Ἔνοχος θανάτου ἐστίν. **67** Τότε ἐνέπτυσαν εἰς τὸ πρόσωπον αὐτοῦ		
καὶ ἐκολάφισαν	δέροντες,	
	64 καὶ περικαλύψαντες	
αὐτόν,	αὐτὸν	
οἱ δὲ ἐράπισαν	ἐπηρώτων	
68 λέγοντες,	λέγοντες,	
Προφήτευσον ἡμῖν, Χριστέ,	Προφήτευσον,	
τίς ἐστιν ὁ παίσας σε;	τίς ἐστιν ὁ παίσας σε;	
	65 καὶ ἕτερα πολλὰ	
cf. Mt 26:65	βλασφημοῦντες ἔλεγον εἰς αὐτόν.	

Lk 22:54. The unit opens with a usage of συλλαμβάνειν from Mt 26:55. Characteristically, Luke then omitted Mt's reference to the fulfillment of scripture (Mt 26:56) and resumed following Mt at Mt 26:57.

Lk 22:54b-62. Luke moved Peter's denial from its current location in Mt's order *after* the trial at the High Priest's house (Mt 26:69-75) forward, so that it occurs precisely at the same moment Jesus is being mocked and mistreated at the High Priest's house, greatly increasing the ironic contrast. Other than this, Luke made few changes in Mt's story, except for the striking addition at the end, after the third denial, when Luke's account says: "Jesus turned and looked at him" (Lk 22:61), as if to say: "I heard what you just said. Remember what I said you would do?" Then Peter remembers and is overcome with shame and guilt. This brilliant touch heightens the dramatic irony and prepares perfectly for the events to follow.

Lk 22:63-65. Luke then moved Mt's account of the slapping and spitting and demanding that Jesus prophesy (Mt 26:67-68) forward so that it follows immediately after the fulfillment of Jesus' prophecy regarding Peter, thus heightening the dramatic irony of *that* detail as well. Note that Luke added the comment that *someone blindfolded Jesus* prior to the demand that he prophesy (Lk 22:64), a detail, which, since it is lacking in Mt's version of the story, makes the question: "Who struck you?" seem pointless because Jesus could see who it was. Luke corrected this. We believe Luke's addition of the blindfold could be evidence of Luke's secondary character compared to the version in Mt.[4]

Lk 22:66. Luke concluded the scene in the High Priest's house by using material from Mt 27:1 to create a transition to a wholly new setting: a formal, *morning* hearing before the council of elders (Lk 22:67-71). In the process, Luke changed the nature of Mt's scene in the High Priest's house, turning it into a kind of midnight detention of Jesus until daybreak, when a full-fledged hearing could be convened before the Jewish council of elders in Jerusalem. It is the disciples who, under the cover of darkness, are the real betrayers of Jesus. Always concerned about procedure, Luke has provided for more formal, explicit charges against Jesus by the leading Jerusalem authorities, to stand over and against the three hearings before the Roman authorities, in each of which Jesus is going to be declared innocent of any wrongdoing.

¶ 133. Jesus is examined by Jerusalem's council of elders

Mt 27:1; 26:59-66 ====> **Lk 22:66-71**

At daybreak, Jesus is brought before Jerusalem's Council of Elders and Priests, who examine him concerning his claim to be the Messiah, the King of the Jews. "Tell us if you really are the Messiah," they demand. Jesus refuses to participate in the proceedings, telling them, "If I said anything, you would not believe it. Nevertheless, know this: the Son of Man will soon be seated in honor at the right hand of God the All-Powerful!" "Well, are you saying you are the Son of God, then?" they sneer. "You are talking, not me" says Jesus. At this, the questioning abruptly breaks off. "He has incriminated himself by his own words," they cry, and prepare to take Jesus to Pilate to get permission to execute him.

---

[4] A fuller discussion of this "major agreement" of Mt and Lk against Mk (Mt 26:67-68//Lk 22:64; cf. Mk 14:65) and the manner in which this tradition may have developed, assuming the Two Gospel Hypothesis, may be found in Farmer, *The Synoptic Problem; A Critical Analysis* (New York: Macmillan, 1964) 148-151 and 284-286; cf. ibid., *The Gospel of Jesus. The Pastoral Relevance of the Synoptic Problem* (Louisville: Westminster/John Knox,1994) 134-136.

General observations. Luke followed the basic narrative order of Mt to get this account. But as usual, there are substantial changes in internal order and content. Mainly, Luke split Mt's version of the midnight scene in the High Priest's house (Mt 26:57-75) into two different events. The hearing before the council of elders as retold by Luke has greater legitimacy and gravity because it takes place in the light of day (Lk 22:66). The motive for Luke's creating a daylight hearing before the Jewish council in place of Mt's middle-of-the-night charade is, as pointed out above, to regularize the official Jerusalem opposition to Jesus, bring it out into the light of day and thereby emphasize it more fully than Matthew does. This seems to be part of Luke's agenda: to remove as much blame as possible from the Romans for Jesus' gruesome execution. The other alterations Luke introduced into this scene have mainly to do with making the hearing more comprehensible to his wider Greco-Roman audience.

Lk 22:66. The unit opens with the phraseology καὶ ὡς ἐγένετο ἡμέρα. The use of κάι ὡς to open a temporal sequence is Lukan (Lk 1:23 with ἐγένετο; 2:39; 19:5, 41). The use of καὶ ἐγένετο is a classic Lukan Septuagintism (cf. Collison 42). The reference to day comes in Mt 27:1. The rest of Lk 22:66 clearly echoes Mt 26:57 (ἀπήγαγον) and Mt 26:59 (συνέδριον).

Lk 22:67a. Luke omitted the early portion of the trial scene before the "Sanhedrin" in Mt (Mt 26:59-63a). The false witnesses and ancillary accusation (destroy the temple) were not important and only muddied the dramatic flow. Instead, Luke zeroed in on Mt 26:63b: "And the High Priest said to him, 'I adjure you by the living God, tell us if you are the Christ, the Son of God.' " Luke split this into two separate questions (Lk 22:67a, 70a). He dealt with "*Christos*" separately, getting this potentially disturbing political title out of the way quickly, focusing attention on the second title: "Son of God," as the more theologically important issue. As a result, Luke had to create Jesus' first answer, "If I told you, you would not believe and, if I should question you, you would not answer" (Lk 22:67-68), which is a parallel to σὺ εἶπας in Mt 26:64. Luke used the latter as an answer to the second question (Lk 22:70b).

Lk 22:69. Luke took this statement from Mt 26:64, but he completely de-eschatologized Mt's quotation of Dan 7:7-13, turning Jesus' prediction of divine judgment into a simple forecast of his own imminent (ἀπὸ τοῦ νῦν = "from this time on" New American Bible, "from now on" RSV, NIV, New Jerusalem) glorification to God's right hand, a theme Luke repeats at the crucifixion (Lk 23:42f.) and again in the martyrdom of Stephen (Acts 7:56). The cognate terms ἀπ' ἄρτι and ἀπὸ τοῦ νῦν appear at exactly the same point in their respective sentences (Lk 22:69//Mt 26:64) and they serve the same grammatical function. Compare the very similar sentence constructions at Mt 23:39//Lk 13:35 where ἀπ' ἄρτι appears in the text of Matthew, but Luke has no parallel to this construction. The expression ἀπ' ἄρτι is found in the Gospels of Matthew and John, but not in Mark or Luke.

Matthew uses the expression ἀπ' ἄρτι three times in his Gospel. All three Matthean usages are in texts paralleled by Luke. Every time the expression appears in the text of Matthew, the parallel text of Luke either lacks the expression (Mt 23:39; cf. Lk 13:35) or the expression ἀπὸ τοῦ νῦν *is* found (Mt 26:29//Lk 22:18; Mt 26:64//Lk 22:69). Luke uses ἀπὸ τοῦ νῦν three other times within his Gospel and once in Acts (Lk 1:48; 5:10; 12:52; Acts 18:6). Collison (158-159) notes that "The expression ἀπ ' ἄρτι, used 3 times in Mt (and at Jn 13:19; 14:7; and Rev 14:13), is condemned by the Atticists"; cf. Collison 163 on Luke's avoidance of ἄρτι. This evidence is wholly consistent with the Two Gospel Hypothesis whereby Luke made direct use of Matthew. If the Atticists condemned ἀπ ' ἄρτι, it would be appropriate for Luke, who is generally regarded as a better Greek stylist to have improved Mt's Greek expression.

Lk 22:70-71. By taking both the second question from Mt 26:63b and the answer in Mt 26:64a, Luke combined these with the reaction of the High Priest in Mt 26:65 to conclude the scene. The reaction of the court in Luke: "What further testimony do we need? We have heard it ourselves from his own lips," is puzzling. Jesus has said nothing incriminating, yet they act as if he has. (Note that Luke has dropped Mt's reference to "blasphemy" in Mt 26:65.) We suggest that either Luke was intentionally making the court appear irrational or had the testimony of Mt 26:59-62 in mind. Luke's version of the trial focuses on a single issue: whether his inquisitors will accept Jesus as the "Son of God." When it becomes apparent to them that Jesus refuses to accept their obvious belief that he is not the "Son of God," they fly into a rage, acting as if he has condemned himself somehow—when he obviously has not. This leaves Luke's audience with one conclusion: the Jerusalem authorities who condemned Jesus were blindly opposed to Jesus actually being the Son of God. This, of course, is precisely the conclusion Luke intended to leave with his audience. The leaders of Israel's religious establishment blindly rejected the Truth standing before them. Indeed, Jesus the Prophet tells them this is precisely what they are now doing: "If I did tell you who I was, you wouldn't believe me!"

¶ 134. Jesus is found innocent in three trials before the Roman authorities

Mt 27:2-26 ====> **Lk 23:1-25**

Because they cannot carry out capital executions themselves, the chief priests and scribes get up and take Jesus to Pilate for sentencing. Once there, they accuse Jesus of two new charges intended to alarm this Roman governor: "This man tells others not to pay the tribute tax to Rome! And he says *he* is our King rather than Caesar!" Pilate asks, "*Are* you the king of the Jews?" "These are other people's words," says Jesus, "not mine." "He hasn't done anything illegal," Pilate tells the Jewish authorities; "I'm going to release him." Furious, they shout, "But this man has been stirring up the people from Galilee to Jerusalem! You must put a stop to it!" "So he is a Galilean?" asks Pilate. "Then I will send him to the governor of Galilee, Herod Antipas. Let him decide what to do with this man." So Jesus is taken to Herod, who also finds Jesus innocent of any wrong-doing. After his guards rough him up a little, Jesus is brought back to Pilate. He is now dressed in mock-royal robes. Once again, Pilate addresses the Jerusalem authorities: "I have examined this man in light of the charges you brought against him. So has Herod. Neither of us finds him guilty of anything. I am going to release him." Enraged, they shout, "Release somebody else! This man should be crucified!" "Why?" asks Pilate. "What has he done? I can find no reason to execute him!" But the Jerusalem elders continue to insist vehemently, "Crucifiy him! Crucifiy him!" Bowing to their demand, Pilate sentences Jesus to be crucified by them.

General observations. Although Luke followed the general order of events in Mt to get this scene, he made numerous alterations. Instead of Mt's somewhat hurried, disjointed portrayal of events, Luke created a dramatic series of sharply etched trial scenes, as Jesus is brought before one Roman authority after another; first Pilate, then Herod, and finally Pilate again. Each trial scene is linked to the previous one by a powerful, recurrent phrase: "I find no cause (for execution) in this man." Luke's uncharacteristic repetitive prolongation of this part of Mt's Passion Narrative was intended to counterpoise the rabid hatred of the Jerusalem authorities, who are portrayed as senselessly screaming for Jesus' blood, over against the perplexity and genuine concern of the Roman and Jewish civil authorities, who repeatedly find him innocent.

Clearly, the basic outlines of the story are there in Mt, to wit, that Pilate thought Jesus was innocent but bowed to the vehement insistence of the Jerusalem authorities, permitting Jesus to be crucified by them. Luke lifted up these two themes to a much more explicit level by means of three trials, each saying more or less the same thing. As such, this is a good example of a basic theme in Luke: Jesus received widespread support among the people of Israel but was adamantly opposed by Jerusalem's religious leaders.

Luke's trial scene is so disjunctive from Mt that the possibility must be left open that Luke utilized another source at this point. Our analysis proceeds on the assumption that, at the least, Luke had Mt 27:2-26 as the basic source, and, since we are focusing upon this aspect of Luke's literary strategy, we choose not to go into the matter of possible use of other sources at this point.

With this general perspective in mind, we would like to make the following detailed observations.

Lk 23:1-3. These verses are a combination of Mt 27:2, 11-14. Luke omitted Mt's mention of the death of Judas (Mt 27:3-10) because he intended to provide his own version of the death of Judas in Acts 1:16-20. The word ἀνιστᾶν (Lk 23:1) is a linguistic characteristic of Luke (28 times in Luke and only twice in Matthew; cf. Collison 37). ἅπας τὸ πλῆθος is also a Lukan construction occurring 7 times in Luke-Acts and never in Matthew or Mark (Goulder 2:807).

Lk 23:2-3. This is based upon Mt 27:11, to which Luke introduced some modifications. The phrase ἤρξαντο δὲ κατηγορεῖν αὐτοῦ λέγοντες is very similar to Paul's trial before Felix: ἤρξατο κατηγορεῖν... λέγων in Acts 24:2 (cf. Goulder 2:757). We suspect that the specific charges mentioned in Lk 23:2 are Lukan composition. In Mt's version, Pilate's question (Mt 27:11a) seems unmotivated (How did Pilate find out Jesus was the king of the Jews?). Luke remedied this lack by having the Jerusalem authorities *accuse* Jesus of this charge, which prompts Pilate to ask Jesus, "Are you indeed the king of the Jews" (Lk 23:3a), which, with Jesus' brief answer, is now based directly on Mt 27:11a.

Lk 23:4-5. These verses appear to be drawn from Mt 27:13-14. For an echo of Luke's language in Lk 23:5, note Acts 10:37. Why did Luke deviate so radically from Mt? It is possible that Mt's version may have seemed dramatically deficient to Luke. For one thing, the false and groundless accusations mentioned in Mt 27:13 are not specified, leaving the audience wondering what they could have been. Luke remedied this lack by stating what they are; i.e., they truly are false and groundless. Moreover, Mt's conclusion "and Pilate wondered greatly" is hardly the reaction Luke is interested in, being too wishy-washy and ambiguous. So Luke has Pilate say decisively: Οὐδὲν εὑρίσκω αἴτιον ἐν τῷ ἀνθρώπῳ τούτῳ, thus sounding the major theme of this pericope for the first time: the Roman authorities repeatedly proclaim Jesus' innocence. We note in passing that Luke does not drop this theme at the end of this series of trials, but in fact continues it to the end of the crucifixion scene: the *Lukan additions* stress Jesus' *innocence*, the judgment of the second thief (Lk 23:41), and finally the centurion's reaction at the Cross (Lk 23:47).

Lk 23:4 ὁ δὲ Πιλᾶτος εἶπεν πρὸς τοὺς ἀρχιερεῖς καὶ τοὺς ὄχλους,
οὐδὲν εὑρίσκω αἴτιον ἐν τῷ ἀνθρώπῳ τούτῳ.
Lk 23:14 εἶπεν πρὸς αὐτούς, ἐγὼ οὐθὲν εὗρον ἐν τῷ ἀνθρώπῳ τούτῳ αἴτιον.
Lk 23:22 ὁ δὲ τρίτον εἶπεν. . . οὐδὲν αἴτιον θανάτου εὗρον ἐν αὐτῷ

That these formulations may be Luke's own creation (of a triplicate, no less!) can be supported from Luke's exclusive use of the neuter substantive of αἴτιος in contrast to the feminine noun ἡ αἰτία which is found everywhere else:

Mt 27:37 ἐπέθηκαν ἐπάνω τῆς κεφαλῆς αὐτοῦ τὴν αἰτίαν αὐτοῦ
Mk 15:26 καὶ ἦν ἡ ἐπιγραφὴ τῆς αἰτίας αὐτοῦ
Jn 18:38 λέγει ὁ Πιλᾶτος... αὐτοῖς, Ἐγὼ οὐδεμίαν εὑρίσκω ἐν αὐτῷ αἰτίαν.
Jn 19:4 Καὶ... ὁ Πιλᾶτος λέγει ὅτι οὐδεμίαν αἰτίαν εὑρίσκω ἐν αὐτῷ.
Jn 19:6 λέγει αὐτοῖς ὁ Πιλᾶτος... ἐγὼ γὰρ οὐχ εὑρίσκω ἐν αὐτῷ αἰτίαν.

Luke *can* use the feminine noun; cf. Lk 8:47 ἰδοῦσα δὲ ἡ γυνὴ ὅτι οὐκ ἔλαθεν τρέμουσα ἦλθεν καὶ προσπεσοῦσα αὐτῷ δι' ἣν αἰτίαν ἥψατο αὐτοῦ ἀπήγγειλεν ἐνώπιον παντὸς τοῦ λαοῦ καὶ ὡς ἰάθη παραχρῆμα. The use of the neuter substantive is typical of Greek philosophical writing (so Liddell-Scott *s.v.* αἴτιος II.2). An echo of this use occurs at Heb 5:8f. καίπερ ὢν υἱός, ἔμαθεν ἀφ' ὧν ἔπαθεν τὴν ὑπακοήν, καὶ τελειωθεὶς ἐγένετο πᾶσιν τοῖς ὑπακούουσιν αὐτῷ αἴτιος σωτηρίας αἰωνίου. Otherwise, the papyri provide no basis for making any distinction between the two forms; both are equally common in legal contexts. We conclude from this evidence that Luke was editing and using his own linguistic preference rather than the term found in the tradition at this point.

Lk 23:6-12. This is probably a Lukan composition whose central purpose is to canvas the entire Roman judiciary present in Jerusalem, to remove all doubt what *all* the civil authorities thought of Jesus of Nazareth. Herod the Tetrarch is portrayed as being eager to see Jesus, an obvious echo of the earlier Lukan references to Herod at Lk 9:7-19; 13:31-32. Here Herod's wish to see Jesus is fulfilled and he finds nothing worthy of punishment in Jesus. So, after letting his guards playfully torture Jesus a little (an echo of Mt 27:27-30, transposed to this Jewish context!), Herod sends Jesus back to Pilate. At the end of the pericope, a subsidiary theme emerges: Herod and Pilate agree on Jesus' innocence; for this reason "they became friends that very day" (Lk 23:12).

Lk 23:13-16. The focal point of the pericope is Pilate's reaffirmation of his earlier (and Herod's intermediate and supporting) judgment: "Nothing deserving death has been done by this man!" The language of this vignette is filled with Lukan linguistic characteristics. The most notable example is πρός with a verb of saying (Lk 23:14) which occurs 151 times in Luke/Acts and never in Matthew (cf. Goulder 2:808). The clause παιδεύσας οὖν αὐτὸν ἀπολύσω in Lk 23:16, repeated in Lk 23:22b, may also be Lukan. παιδεύειν occurs only in Lk among the canonical Gospels.

Lk. 23:17. We concur with UBS[4] that Lk 23:17 is not original (*omit*: 𝔓[75] A B L T and a few early versions | | *include* ℵ W Δ Θ Ψ and most Byz. witnesses).

Lk 23:18-19. Luke abbreviated the Matthean version of the Barabbas incident (see Mt 27:17-26) and the reference to Pilate's wife's dream (Mt 27:19). Mt 27:19 is Mt's main reference to Jesus' innocence; Pilate's wife refers to Jesus as τῷ δικαίῳ ἐκείνῳ "that righteous [= innocent?] man" —wording that could be the source for Luke's version of the centurion's statement at the crucifixion: Ὄντως ὁ ἄνθρωπος οὗτος δίκαιος ἦν (Lk 23:47). In his version of the Barabbas incident, Luke did recount that Barabbas's crime was murder in the city (Lk 23:19). That the Jerusalem leadership was willing to free Barabbas was, in Luke's estimation, another example of that leadership's perfidy.

Lk 23:20-23. Here we have a modification of Mt 27:21-23. Lk 23:20 alters the first two elements of Mt's three-fold question-and-answer structure in Mt 27: 21-23 by the summary: "Pilate, *wishing to release Jesus...*" only to be rebuffed by the local authorities who insist on Jesus' crucifixion. Then Luke 23:22a picks up the third question of Pilate in Mt 27:23a: "Why, what evil has he done?" To this Luke *added Lk 23:22b:* the third, emphatic repetition of οὐδὲν αἴτιον θανάτου εὗρον ἐν αὐτῷ. After this, Luke resumed Mt's version at Mt 27:23b: "But they shouted all the more..." which Luke changed to the more effective "their voices prevailed."

Lk 23:24-25. This is Luke's summary of Mt 27:24-26. Luke may have omitted the reference to Pilate's washing his hands (and the subsequent self-oath of the Jews) in favor of the more direct "So Pilate gave sentence that their demand should be granted." The rest of Lk 23:24-25 follows Mt 27:26.

Section Three: Jesus' Crucifixion, Death, and Burial. Lk 23:26-56b

¶ 135. Jesus speaks a final warning to the women of Jerusalem

Mt 27:31b-32 ====> **Lk 23:26-31**

The Jerusalem leaders finally have Jesus in their power and immediately take him outside the city to crucify him without delay. They seize a passer-by to carry his cross for him. Women who are following behind begin to weep, lamenting Jesus' death. "Don't cry for me!" he tells them. "Weep for yourselves and your own children, for I tell you they will see such days of terror they will wish they had never been born!" Two thieves are also taken out to be killed with Jesus.

General observations. Luke followed the basic order of Mt 27 for this account. However, he deliberately omitted the single most damning passage in Mt's entire narrative regarding Roman involvement in Jesus' death; i. e., the unit where the Roman soldiers viciously torment Jesus (scarlet robe, crown of thorns, mock and beat him; Mt 27:27-31). Instead, Luke has *Herod Antipas'* soldiers mock Jesus (Lk 23:11, see above). We interpret this as another attempt on the part of Luke to shift blame for Jesus' death away from the Roman authorities. Indeed, in the pericopes to come, Jesus will be ringed about by sympathetic voices, creating a sharp contrast to the words of hatred and vengeance of Jerusalem's "high priests and elders." In place of Mt's beating scene, Luke substituted a scene not found in Mt: Jesus' warning to the women of Jerusalem about the impending destruction of the city. Given Luke's historical perspective, this is clear evidence that Luke understood the crucifixion of Jesus to have led directly to the disastrous destruction of Jerusalem under Titus in 70 C.E.

Lk 23:26. This verse repeats Mt 27:31b and then adds to the information in

Mt 27:32 the secondary details that Simon of Cyrene was a man "who was coming in from the country" and the detail "to carry the cross *behind Jesus*." The use of ἀπήγαγον in Lk 23:26 comes from Mt 27:31 (cf. Mt 27:2). καὶ ὡς (Lk 23:26), used temporally, is a 'likely' linguistic characteristic of Luke (Collison 117). ἐπιλάβεσθαι occurs 12 times in Luke-Acts as opposed to only once in Matthew and is a "probable" linguistic usage of Luke (Collison 49-50).

Lk 23:27-31. This is a Lukan composition on the theme of Jesus' prophetic announcement of the future calamity of the Fall of Jerusalem (cf. Lk 19:41-44; 21:20-24). Luke had omitted the Matthean account of the acceptance of responsibility by "all the people" present for the death of Jesus (Mt 27:24-25a). In Lk 23:27-28, Luke brought over from Mt 27:25 the references to λαός and τέκνα and restricted the address of the word against the city to the "daughters of Jerusalem." Whereas in Matthew "all the people" at the scene took direct responsibility for their actions in putting Jesus to death, Luke redirected his readers' attention to the actual destruction of Jerusalem which occurred in their time. Undaunted in the least by his own impending death, Jesus the Prophet of God gives his final warning to the "daughters of Jerusalem" about *their* own impending destruction.

Lk 23:29. This is a deliberate contrast with Lk 11:27-28. There the womb and the breasts that nourished Jesus were honored. Now, in Lk 23:29, the wombs and breasts of these women will be dry and barren. This verse also echoes Lk 21:23 which is also a text on the Fall of Jerusalem. In days to come, barrenness will be reckoned as a blessing.

Lk 23:30. The phraseology of Lk 23:29-30 reflects a number of Septuagintisms—especially terminology drawn from Hosea 9:12-16 and 10:8. Luke has placed this terminology in the mouth of the prophet Jesus who will be the agent to bring these ancient prophetic words to fulfillment.

Lk 23:31. The verse may have been a traditional proverb which Jesus spoke to his own generation. Luke applied it to the fall of Jerusalem.

¶ 136. The crucifixion of Jesus of Nazareth

Mt 27:27-31, 33, 35, 37-38, 41-44 ====> **Lk 23:32-43**

Jesus and two thieves are led outside the city walls to be killed. The procession arrives at a place called The Skull. Jesus and the two robbers (transgressors) are crucified. Jesus prays God to forgive those who are killing him. While the crowds watch in silence, the Jerusalem authorities cannot resist gloating over their victim. "If *this* is the Christ of God, his *Chosen One*, let God prove it by saving him!" The soldiers also mock him, offering him sour vinegar to drink and saying, "If you really are the king of the Jews, save yourself!" —for someone had put a placard over Jesus' head that reads: "This is the King of the Jews." One of the robbers screams at him, "Are *you* the Christ? Then save yourself and us!" The other robber rebukes him, saying, "Do *you* dare call upon *him?* We are being punished for what we did, but he is the righteous one!" Then turning to Jesus the robber says, "Jesus, remember me when you enter into your kingdom!" Jesus replies, "Today you will be with me in Paradise!"

General observations. Luke followed Mt's order for the crucifixion account, although, as before, he omitted some material from Mt, transposed other material, and inserted nonMatthean tradition in order to bring his version into line with his literary and theological agenda. We believe there is a distinct possibility that Luke used another source at this point. However, our focus remains on Luke's use of Matthew. We will discuss each of these alterations of Mt as they come up.

Lk 23:32. Luke framed the crucifixion with an *inclusio* on the fate of the two criminals (Lk 23:32-33 and 39-43). Luke 23:32-33 is based upon Mt 27:33. The net effect is that the emphasis on the fulfillment of Isa 53:12 is deepened. Jesus is numbered with the transgressors (cf. Lk 22:37). Evidence of Lukan terminology would include the use of ἄγειν (Lk 23:32; Collison 35) and ἕτερος (Collison 184-185). The reference to κακοῦργοι (Lk 23:32; cf. Lk 23:33 and 39) is unusual. The only other place this term occurs in the NT is 2 Tim 2:9. ἀναιρεῖν may also be Lukan (21 times in Lk-Acts; Mt 2:16; 2 Thess 2:8; Heb 10:9; and nowhere else in the NT).

Lk 23:33. The wording is quite similar to Mt 27:33, with Luke omitting the unnecessary Hebrew word, Golgotha. The use of καλεῖν (Lk 23:33) in the form of an articular participle introducing an appositive is Lukan (Collison 80; cf. 179).

Lk 23:34. Lk 23:34a contains a major text-critical dilemma. A number of early witnesses omit the verse entirely: $\mathfrak{P}^{75}$ $\aleph^{1}$ B D* W Θ $it^{a.d}$ syr^{s} $cop^{sa\ bo}$. The great majority of witnesses, including other important early ones, include it: $\aleph^{*\ 2}$ A C D^{2} L Δ Ψ and a large number of patristic citations. UBS^{4} places it within ⟦ ⟧ indicating their view that it is not original with a grade of {A}. Nevertheless, they leave it in the text because "it bears self-evident tokens of its dominical origin" (Metzger 1994, 154). What this statement might mean is uncertain. We are inclined to accept this verse as original for two main reasons. The evidence in Sinaiticus suggests an answer to the conflicting text-critical evidence. The original hand included it; the first corrector omitted it, possibly under the influence of anti-Jewish sentiment which permeated the orthodox Church from the mid-second century onwards. Indeed, it was a widely held view among Christians from the late first century onwards that the "Judaioi" had brought death and destruction upon their nation by crucifying the Son of God (cf. Melito's "Easter Homily"; Justin Martyr *Apol*. I:30). From this perspective, it could have seemed inappropriate for Jesus to forgive his persecutors; various attempts were made to drop it from Luke's text.

Our second consideration is that Jesus' act of forgiveness fits perfectly into Luke's moral and theological agenda (cf. Goulder 2:765). For example, his account of the first Christian martyr, Stephen, is a story which echoes the death of Jesus precisely at those three points where Luke's Gospel differs from Mt's version: the two—strikingly different—sayings from the cross (Lk 23:34 and 23:46), and this plea for forgiveness (cf. Acts 7:59-60). Lk 23:34b is dependent upon Mt 27:35.

Lk 23:35. Luke was primarily dependent upon Mt 27:41-43 for this verse, although he shortened it considerably and rephrased the taunt. The words "If he is the *Christ of God,* his *Chosen One*" are a deliberate echo of several momentous earlier usages of these terms: the angels (Lk 2:11), Peter (Lk 9:20), the Voice of God at the Transfiguration (Lk 9:35; cf. Acts 2:36; 3:18). They come back now filled with rage, not honor and reverence, in a bitterly ironic way (similar to Mt's powerful use of Ps 22:8 in Mt 27:42-43). Luke introduced a reference to the people in Lk 23:35a, portraying them impassively standing around, watching all that happened, instead of Mt's violent, taunting, jeering mob (Mt 27:38-40). Luke wanted everyone to be on Jesus' side (or at least not opposed to him) except the Jerusalem authorities. In fact, this half-verse could be based upon Ps 22:7:

Ps 22:7 Πάντες οἱ θεοροῦντες με ἐξεμυκτήρισάν με

Lk 23:35a καὶ εἱστήκει ὁ λαὸς θεωρῶν, ἐξεμυκτήριζον δὲ καὶ οἱ ἄρχοντες...

Note that Luke *has split the action in two.* The *crowd* stands and watches, while the *leaders* mock and deride. This would be consistent with Luke's editorial concern to restrict Jesus' opposition to the Jerusalem leadership.

Lk 23:35-38. Here Luke substantially altered Mt's narrative order. The unit is an interweaving of several events: a conflation of Mt 27:34 and Mt 27:48 (sour wine/wine vinegar); the mocking by the soldiers (Mt 27:27-31) and the chief priests, scribes and elders (Mt 27:41, especially Mt 27:42a); and a reference to the inscription (Mt 27:37). Luke omitted Mt's other mention of the offer of wine mixed with gall (Mt 27:34). It may have seemed superfluous to the narrative. The effect of Luke's revisions is to condense the activity into one drink-insult, one reference to him as "king"—a jeer fittingly coming from soldier's lips—concluding with a reference to the sign over Jesus' head, where it fits in with the soldier's taunting reference to "king."

• Some suggest that the soldiers referred to in Luke's account were not Pilate's Roman soldiers, but Herod Antipas' (presumably Jewish) guard. Granted Luke has done all he could to portray the local religious authorities as the only persons who persecuted Jesus, including ignoring the scene in Mt 27:27-31 where the Roman soldiers beat and mock Jesus, even as he transfers some of its content to Herod's soldiers in Lk 23:11. However, the "soldiers" mentioned at the crucifixion in Lk 23:36 are described as ἐνέπαιξαν δὲ αὐτῷ καὶ οἱ στρατιῶται while the term Luke uses for Herod's soldiers in Lk 23:11 is ὁ Ἡρῴδης σὺν τοῖς στρατεύμασιν αὐτου. A comparative examination reveals that the term στρατιῶται is used exclusively of *Roman* soldiers throughout the Gospels (Mt 8:9; 27:27; 28:12; Mk 15:16; Lk 7:8; Jn 19:2; 19:23, 24, 32, 34). Thus, while Luke does remove most, he does not remove all guilt from the Romans.

Lk 23:39-43. In this unit Luke used Mt 27:44 to conclude the *inclusio* that began at Lk 23:32-33 and to create a dialogue not found in any other crucifixion account. This scene plays three key roles in Luke's agenda:

(a) It introduces into the crucifixion scene a person from the opposite end of the social spectrum from the powerful priests and the passive crowd by letting him instantly recognize Jesus' innocence and majesty. Thus, for Luke, the divine purpose of God is immediately recognizable in Jesus' death—by a down-trodden person!

(b) It reinforces, in the very midst of the worst the religious leaders can do to hurt Jesus, Luke's major theme of Jesus' control over all situations. He portrays Jesus calmly reassuring the thief that the two of them will be in Paradise within the hour. The one who had been derided as impotent (Lk 23:35, 39) actually is able to bring salvation (Lk 23:42-43).

(c) It halts the horrible stream of abuse aimed at Jesus from all of his tormentors and prepares the reader/listener for Jesus' noble final words, leaving them—and certainly not Mt's terrifying, wordless scream in Mt 27:50—in the audience's memory as the Lord's last words: "Father, into your hands I commend my spirit" (Lk 23:46).

¶ 137. The death of Jesus

Mt 27:45, 51, 50, 54-55 ====> **Lk 23:44-49**

Just then, about noon, the sun's light begins to fail and darkness falls over everything. It gets darker until mid-afternoon when the Temple veil protecting the Holy of Holies suddenly tears open by itself. At that moment, Jesus cries out, "Father! Into thy hands I commit my spirit!" and dies. The Roman centurion watching all this praises God and says, "Certainly this man was innocent." The crowds begin to leave, weeping bitterly. Some of the women who were friends of Jesus stand nearby, watching everything.

General observations. Luke continued to emphasize in his own way that the death of Jesus brings salvation. Jesus' death quickly began to have the effect of bringing repentance; first to the centurion (Lk 23:47); and then to the crowd (Lk 23:48). In order to accomplish his theological purposes, Luke had to make major omissions and narrative changes to Mt's more apocalyptic account.

Lk 23:44-45. These verses are based upon Mt 27:45, 51a. We surmise that Luke brought together the two signs of divine anger to reinforce each other dramatically. The temple curtain tears apart just before Jesus' death, an eerie portent of the impending destruction of Jerusalem.

Throughout his revision, Luke had no intention of using Mt's references to the sun's darkening and the earthquake in their original apocalyptic meaning. We understand Mt's account, with its references to the earthquake, the tombs opening, and the dead being resurrected and coming into Jerusalem (Mt 27:51b-53), to indicate his belief that the era of the general resurrection *had begun at Jesus' death*. Jesus' death formed the apogee of the "woes of the Messiah," after which, according to the kind of Jewish apocalyptic prophecy Mt exhibits, came the Final Day of Judgment. In Mt therefore, Jesus' resurrection is not viewed as an isolated resuscitation, but as an *eschatological event*; i.e., the first sign of the *general* resurrection. (We might note that this is precisely the same view as the Apostle Paul in 1 Cor 15:20: "Christ has been raised from the dead, the first fruits of them that sleep"; cf. 1 Cor 15:23.)

But Luke, reacting to the destruction of Jerusalem, as well as the deaths of Peter and Paul, historicized and de-eschatologized the death of Jesus, treating it in Hellenistic fashion as an individual resurrection of a spiritual being from the realm of the dead.[5] As such, it was the preeminent sign, among many, of Jesus' divine status.

The addition of the phrase τοῦ ἡλίου ἐκλιπόντος in Mt 27:45 //Lk 23:45 to explain the darkness at the crucifixion (cf. Lk 22:32) echoes Joel 2:31 (cf. Acts 2:20). The reference to the darkness serves here as a Lukan substitute for the Matthean account of the graves of the dead being opened (cf. Mt 27:51b-53). Note also that Jesus, as the New Adam (cf. Lk 3:38) has just opened the doors of paradise to one of the thieves (Lk 23:43).

Lk 23:46. This critical verse is based upon Mt 27:50. Luke, however, did not echo Ps 22 (=Ps 21 LXX) which is formative for Mt 27:46-50 and the entire Matthean Passion Account. Instead, Luke echoed Ps 31:5 (=Ps 30:5 LXX) as the scriptural basis for Jesus final words.

Ps 30:5 <u>Εἰς χεῖράς σου παραθήσομαι τὸ πνεῦμά μου</u>,
ἐλυτρώσω με Κύριε ὁ Θεὸς τῆς ἀληθείας.

Lk 23:46 Πάτερ, <u>εἰς χεῖράς σου παρατίθεμαι τὸ πνεῦμά μου</u>.

These words from Ps 31:5 (=Ps 30:5 LXX) are intended by Luke to replace both anguished cries in Mt's account (Mt 27:46 and 27:50), but the specific location and choice of wording may have been suggested to Luke by the presence of the term τὸ πνεῦμα in Mt 27:50. In any case, it was Luke's intention to leave the impression that Jesus' last moments were *not* filled with confusion and dreadful agony—as is clearly the situation in Mt—but instead with steadfast courage and confidence in God's deliverance.

Luke's drastic revision at this point fits in with similar alterations made by Luke previously, all of which tend to portray Jesus as being much more in control of the situation. It also provides the model and example of perfect

[5] Compare the re-appearances of Herakles, Achilles, etc., in Hellenistic literature. For examples, see *Documents for the Study of the Gospels,* David R. Cartlidge and David L. Dungan, trans. and ed., 2d revised and enlarged edition (Minneapolis: Fortress, 1994) 185-200, 225, 236-238.

martyrdom, which is then echoed faithfully by the dying Stephen in Acts 7:59-60.

Lk 23:47-48. This material is based upon Mt 27:54-56. Foremost in this passage is Luke's alteration of the pronouncement of the centurion in Mt 27:54:

Mt 27:54 Ὁ δὲ ἑκατόνταρχος... λέγοντες, Ἀληθῶς <u>θεοῦ</u> <u>υἱὸς</u> ἦν οὗτος.

Lk 23:47b ὁ ἑκατοντάρχης...λέγων, Ὄντως ὁ ἄνθρωπος οὗτος <u>δίκαιος</u> ἦν.

This change is consistent with Luke's major purpose indicated throughout the trials and execution scenes. Numerous actors, from many perspectives, all pronounce Jesus *innocent*, making the Jerusalem leadership's insistence on his guilt stand out all the more glaringly as completely groundless and wicked.

However, for Luke, Jesus was much more than just innocent. He was δίκαιος—the Righteous One. The term functions as a Christological confession later in Acts. Likewise, the crowd (Lk 23:48) reflects sorrow and repentance for Jesus' death. Lk 23:49. This verse appears to echo directly Ps 38:12 (= Ps 37:12 LXX). This text is connected with material drawn from Mt 27:55 to bring back into the narrative the women who had been with Jesus from Galilee (Lk 8:1-3). The phraseology ἀπὸ τῆς Γαλιλαίας (Mt 27:55//Lk 23:49) is significant because this phrase seems to be characteristic of the text of Mt (Mt 19:1; cf. Mt 21:11.[6] This is good literary evidence that Luke is dependent upon Mt. The concluding reference to the "women who... stood and saw these things" (Lk 23:49b) is a final dramatic touch: all of Jesus' male supporters have long-since disappeared. Now the women step forward and begin to play their decisive role in the ensuing events following Jesus' death.

Lk 23:49 concludes the responses to the crucifixion. Typically, Luke inserts a detail that causes this scene to dovetail into the next: the reference to the women. This reference to women forms an *inclusio* around the next unit (Lk 23:49 and Lk 23:55-56).

¶ 138. Joseph of Arimathea buries Jesus

Mt 27:57-61 ====> **Lk 23:50-56b**

One man in the Jerusalem Council named Joseph of Arimathea, a good man who looked forward to the Kingdom of God, is deeply opposed to what the other leaders have done to Jesus. He goes to Pilate and asks permission to bury Jesus properly. Pilate willingly agrees, and so Joseph goes back, takes Jesus' corpse off the cross and places it in a brand new tomb hewn out of rock. The women who have come with Jesus from Galilee see where it is put and go home to prepare spices to anoint Jesus. They are prevented from doing it immediately because the Sabbath is just beginning and no "work" is permissible.

---

[6] See Robert Gundry, "Matthean Foreign Bodies," 1490 (full citation above, p. 10).

General observations. Luke followed Mt's order for the account of the burial of Jesus, but expanded it considerably, introducing clarifications for the sake of his non-Jewish audience.

Lk 23:50-51. The phraseology is based upon Mt 27:57-58. Interestingly, Luke omitted Mt's identification of Joseph of Arimathea as "a rich man," who was a "disciple of Jesus," preferring instead to describe him at some length as "a good and righteous man, etc." Clearly, Luke was giving a capsule iconic description of the man who performed this act of devotion at some potential risk to himself. The term ἀνήρ (Lk 23:50) which occurs 127 times in Lk-Acts (8 times in Mt) is a linguistic characteristic of the text of Luke (Goulder 2:800). The Lukan descriptions of Joseph in Lk 23:50 as ἀγαθός and δικαίος would have resonated with a Hellenistic audience (cf. Simeon in Lk 2:25).

Lk 23:50. The use of ὑπάρχειν (Lk 23:50) occurs 40 times in Lk-Acts and is a linguistic characteristic of the text of Luke (Goulder 2:809; cf. Collison 66-67). This word occurs only 3 times in Matthew and is absent from Mark. Collison (66-67) adds that ὑπάρχω, used as a substitute for εἶναι, is a linguistic characteristic of Luke.

Lk 23:50. Luke apparently omitted ὀψίας δὲ γενομένης (Mt 27:57) to describe the time of the burial, but used Mt 28:1 (ἐπιφώσκειν) to say that the burial took place on the Day of Preparation, just as the Sabbath was about to come (Lk 23:54).

Lk 23:51. Here again, Luke used the key term βουλή. This is a technical term in Luke-Acts to describe the plan of God as it is unveiled in the Christ-Event. However, as Squires argues, βουλή is also used by Luke (Lk 23:51 and Acts 27:12, 42) to refer to human plans that are attempts to thwart God's will.[7]

Lk 23:52. This is very similar to Mt 27:58-60. Indeed, every word in Mt 27:58a is found in Lk 23:52.

Mt 27:58a. οὗτος προσελθὼν τῷ Πιλάτῳ ᾐτήσατο τὸ σῶμα τοῦ Ἰησοῦ.
Lk 23:52 οὗτος προσελθὼν τῷ Πιλάτῳ ᾐτήσατο τὸ σῶμα τοῦ Ἰησοῦ.

Goulder (2:772-773) has drawn attention to the considerable number of minor agreements between Matthew and Luke against Mark at this point. Of these, he notes ἐνετύλιξεν αὐτό (Mt 27:59/Lk 23:53) and προσελθών (Mt 27:58/Lk 23:52) as especially significant. Gundry considers resumptive οὗτος a linguistic characteristic of the text of Matthew (Mt 3:3; 5:19; 7:12; 12:23; 13:19; 14:1; 21:10, 11; 26:23; 27:37). Its appearance here in the text of Luke is an indication of direct Matthean influence on Luke (Mt 27:58/Lk 23:52).[8] ἐπιφώσκειν in Mt 28:1 and Lk 23:54 are the only NT usages of this

[7] See John T. Squires, *The Plan of God in Luke-Acts* SNTSMS 76 (Cambridge University Press, 1993) 1.
[8] Robert Gundry, "Matthean Foreign Bodies," 1490-1491.

word. Its appearance in these parallel contexts supports our view of the direct literary relationship between Matthew and Luke.

• This combination of evidence:
   (a) extended verbatim parallel wording between Mt and Lk,
   (b) repeated and extensive agreements between Mt and Lk against the text of Mk, and
   (c) a characteristic syntactical usage of Mt appearing in the text of Lk at this point

represents a concatenation of linguistic agreements between Mt and Lk that are difficult to explain on the Two Source Hypothesis.

Lk 23:54-56a. These verses are based upon Mt 27:61. Luke altered the reference to the women to bring this reference into line with the earlier one to "women who had come with him from Galilee" (Lk 23:49). Luke added the explanatory "It was the Day of Preparation and the Sabbath was beginning" to prepare for the explanation why the women did not immediately anoint Jesus' body in Lk 24:56a-b.

• Luke omitted the specific names of the women in Lk 23:55 who came to the tomb (Mt 27:61; cf. Mt 27:56). However, the reference to women who followed Jesus from Galilee (Lk 23:49) echoes Lk 23:27 and Lk 8:1-3, where these women were first named, and looks forward to Lk 23:55 and to Lk 24:6-10, where the women are named again, and to Lk 24:22-24 which includes an explicit retrospective reference to the women's roles in Luke's narrative.

Lk 23:54-56a. This unit reflects a utilization of material from Mt 28:1 and Mt 27:61. Luke's reference to women here (Lk 23:55) reflects the earlier language of Lk 23:49/Mt 27:55-56 and other Lukan contexts.

Section Four: Conclusion of Book One.

Appearances of the Risen Jesus. Lk 23:56c-24:53

¶ 139. The women do not find Jesus' body in the tomb

Mt 28:1-10 ====> **Lk 23:56c-24:12**

As soon as the Sabbath is over, the women hurry to the tomb to anoint Jesus' body. When they get there, they are greatly disturbed to find the tomb open and his body gone. Suddenly two men in shining robes appear to them and ask, "Why do you seek the living among the dead?" They remind the women that Jesus had told them long before that he would be crucified and, on the third day, rise again from the dead. The women run back and tell the eleven apostles what they have seen, but they don't believe them. Peter runs back to the tomb to see for himself; all he sees are the cloths that had wrapped Jesus' body. He returns, wondering what has happened.

General observations. Luke continued to follow Mt's order for this account, except that he skipped Mt 27:62-66, the story of the attempt to bribe the guards to put out a false rumor regarding the theft of Jesus' body. That account may have been repellent to Luke for a number of reasons. First, it brought Pilate back into the picture in a scene where the Jerusalem authorities basically told him what to do—which was not consistent with the carefully nuanced relationship between them Luke had constructed so far. Second, it re-involved the Roman soldiers in the dramatic action, and Luke had finished with them by means of the centurion's glowing statement. This narrative would only muddy the water. Third, it introduced the concept of a rumor concerning *possible* underhanded dealings by Jesus' disciples that was out of line with Luke's portrayal of them following Jesus' resurrection. So he omitted this story and went straight to Mt 28:1. However, even though he omitted this anecdote, Luke appears to reflect an awareness of Mt 27:62-66 by the conflation of παρασκευή (Mt 27:62) with ἐπιφώσκειν (Mt 28:1) to form Lk 23:54.

Lk 23:56-24:1 contains a μέν...δέ construction which is used in order to highlight Luke's view that the resurrection took place early in the morning on the first day of the week. Indeed, Lk 24 is a series of epiphanies of angels and the resurrected Jesus that all appear to have taken place on this day (cf. Lk 24:1, 13, 28-33). Mt 28:1 says that the women went to the tomb after the Sabbath and then uses ἐπιφώσκειν to describe the "dawning" of the new day (i.e., Saturday evening according to the Jewish reckoning of the day). Thus, Mt leaves the impression that the women discover the tomb as empty on Saturday evening. Luke, however, in Lk 23:54-56, moved this same visit of the women back to the day of Preparation for the Sabbath (Friday afternoon). Luke then has a second visit on Sunday morning, the important "first day of the week" (Lk 24:1). Luke highlights the morning visit by using ὄρθος at Lk 24:1 (cf. Acts 5:21), a derivative of ὀρθρίζειν (Lk 21:38; cf. ὀρθρινός at Lk 24:22). βάθυς appears here (Lk 24:1) and at Acts 20:9 (only other occurrences: Jn 4:11; Rev 2:24). ὄρθρός also appears at Jn 8:2, but nowhere else in the NT.[9]

• Luke omitted the list of names at Mt 28:1 since he was soon going to provide a different list in a much more formal way at Lk 24:10.

Lk 24:2-9. These verses are closely related to Mt 28:2-7. However, as in the account of Jesus' death, Luke omitted the earthquake. He also omitted the descent of the angel, the rolling away of the stone, and the fainting of the guards in Mt 28:2-4, in favor of a more mysterious and subtle scene: the women arrive at the tomb and are horrified to find it opened and the body

[9] On the issue of the time of the women's arrival at the tomb and a discussion of why Luke and Mark may have modified Mt on this point, see W. R. Farmer, "Notes for a Compositional Analysis on the Griesbach Hypothesis of the Empty Tomb Stories in the Synoptic Gospels," in *Occasional Notes on Some Points of Interest in New Testament Studies*, pamphlet (Macon: Mercer University Press, 1980) 7-14.

missing. Suddenly *two* shining men appear next to them—an augmentation of Mt's single angel. The use of "two" here may be to recall the phraseology ἄνδρες δύο in Lk 9:30 (cf. Acts 1:10). Again, at Lk 9:30, the two "men" are Moses and Elijah; could Luke be hinting that they were here as well in further anticipation of Jesus' "exodus" (cf. Lk 9:31)?

• Lk 24:4 contains ἀπορεῖν (ἀπορία in Lk 21:25; cf. Acts 25:20) which, along with καὶ ἐγένετο, is a linguistic usage of Luke (Collison 42).

Lk 24:4-5. The words of the angel in Mt required modification because Luke's narrative plan contained no appearances of Jesus in Galilee (although Lk 24:6b still contains the word). There are numerous echoes between Lk 24:5 and Mt 28:4-5. In Mt 28:4, the appearance of the angel produces fear (φόβος) and shaking (σείειν). Mt 28:4 also says the guards became as dead. Φόβος and its cognates are characteristic of Mt.[10]

• The women are told by the angels to remember that Jesus had already told them in Galilee about the Passion and the Resurrection (Lk 24:6-8). The verb μιμνήσκεσθαι and its cognates are stock terminology in Luke-Acts to heed the divine word (cf. Lk 11:16).[11] These verses are then meant to relate the women retrospectively to what has happened before; i.e., it would appear that the women were disciples in Galilee (Lk 8:1-3; cf. Lk 23:55). Yet according to earlier places in the Gospel of Luke, the Passion predictions were spoken exclusively to the Twelve (cf. Lk 9:18-22; 9:43-44; 18:31-33). Are we to conclude that Luke understood these women to have been present with the Twelve?

Lk 24:12. This verse was barely included in the text on a split vote by UBS[3] with a grade of {D} (see Metzger, *Textual Commentary* 1974, 184). By UBS[4] it was included by the majority of the editorial committee with a grade of {B} (see the explanation in Metzger 1994, 157). We agree with the latter position. The textual evidence for inclusion is very strong. *Include:* 𝔓[75] ℵ A B L W Δ Θ Ψ plus numerous versions and fathers; however, D and *it.* omit. Note also within this verse are several Lukan linguistic characteristics, such as ἀναστάς, θαυμάζειν, and τὸ γεγονός (Goulder 2:800, 805, 802).

¶ 140. Jesus appears to two associates of the apostles in Emmaus Lk 24:13-32

Later in the day, two friends of the eleven apostles go to a nearby village named Emmaus. As they are walking along, Jesus appears and joins them, but they are mysteriously prevented from recognizing him. "What are you men talking about?" he asks. "Have you heard about all that just happened in Jerusalem?" they ask. "No," says Jesus. "Well, three days ago, Jesus of Nazareth, a mighty prophet of God, was condemned and crucified by our chief priests and rulers! We thought he was going to

---

[10] Robert Gundry, "Matthean Foreign Bodies," 1491-1492.

[11] Cf. R. J. Karris, "Women and Discipleship in Luke," *CBQ* 56 (1994) 14-15.

liberate Israel but instead they killed him! This morning some women in our group astonished us with the news that they had discovered his tomb empty. They said they had seen two angels who told them Jesus was alive! Some of our group rushed to the tomb and indeed found that what the women said was true about the tomb being empty." "How can you be so blind?" says Jesus. "Did you not learn that it was necessary for God's Messiah to suffer as the scripture predicted and then enter into his glory?" Then Jesus interprets the scripture from Moses through all the prophets about all the things concerning himself. When they come to Emmaus, the two men invite this seemingly reluctant, apparent stranger to break his journey and stay with them for the night. At dinner, Jesus takes bread, blesses it, breaks and gives it to the two men. God opens their eyes and they realize who he is, but Jesus suddenly vanishes. They immediately rise up and rush back to Jerusalem where they find the eleven apostles pondering the news that Jesus has just appeared to Simon. The two men tell the apostles that Jesus has appeared to them as well when he broke bread with them.

General observations. At this point, Luke departed entirely from the general order of pericopes in Mt, finishing his composition with stories that are unique among the Gospels. Whether this material came from earlier tradition or was created by Luke himself is a question we will not attempt to answer here. Instead, in our concluding remarks we will focus on how the material in Lk 24 functions within the larger narrative of Luke-Acts.

The central feature of the conclusion of the Gospel according to Luke is the return of Jesus from death and the complete rehabilitation of the eleven apostles. Jesus comes to them and, finally, God opens their minds so that they can understand the Scriptures and see that what has happened to Jesus was God's plan from the beginning.

Note that the Holy Spirit is given to the apostles *twice*, first to understand the Scriptures (Lk 24) and second—after Jesus' definitive departure into heaven (Acts 1:9-11)—to enable them to speak and understand all languages, so they can be Christ's witnesses to all nations (in Acts 2; cf. Lk 24:48).

At several points, Luke included minor details which were then picked up in the opening two chapters *of his next book*, the Acts of the Apostles. We have seen this overlapping or interweaving compositional technique used frequently in transitional passages in earlier parts of the Gospel of Luke and will comment on it in the material below.

Other critical compositional elements of Luke's narrative should be mentioned as well. Luke stopped following the order of Mt at Mt 28:11-15, the bribery of the Roman guards. Since he omitted the antecedent to this story (Mt 27:62-66), Mt 28:11-15 could hardly fit. Nor did Luke use any details from it. In view of the continuation in Acts, Luke had entirely different purposes in mind for the conclusion to his biography of Jesus.

Nor did Luke take over Mt's conclusion (Mt 28:16-20), although he preserved significant echoes of it, indicating to us that he was quite aware of the importance of its contents (see further below).

The most important compositional elements of Lk 24:13-32 are five:

1. a *first appearance to two non-apostles* (Jesus appears to the "eleven apostles" later)
2. teaching while on a journey
3. an extensive explanation that the "redemption of Israel" did succeed; Jesus did not fail.
4. emphasis upon the biblical prophecy-fulfillment scheme; and
5. a foundational ritual established in the recognition of the Risen Lord Jesus in the "breaking of the bread," in conjunction with the spoken word of interpretation of Scripture.

We will consider each of these in order.

Lk 24:13. We have seen that one of Luke's most commonly employed narrative devices to organize his narrative and present new material is to construct a travel scene, where Jesus teaches "on the road" (cf. Lk 24:28, 32; see Introduction 33f.). Such is the case here. "Emmaus" has no other significance for this account than that it is a destination for two friends of the apostles, providing a vehicle for the very important teaching Jesus gives in the context of breaking bread with the two men. As soon as it is accomplished, the two rush back to Jerusalem.

Lk 24:17-24. What is the teaching that Luke wanted to include within this brief story he created? It is nothing less than the fundamental explanation of Jesus' death as given by the Risen Jesus; certainly an important message for Luke's audience. Jesus meets two associates of the apostles and one of them named "Cleopas" brings up the most sensitive question of all: Jesus, it looks like you failed. ...παρέδωκαν αὐτὸν οἱ ἀρχιερεῖς καὶ οἱ ἄρχοντες ἡμῶν εις κρίμα θανάτου καὶ ἐσταύρωσαν αὐτόν. ἡμεις δὲ ἠλπίζομεν ὅτι αὐτός ἐστιν ὁ μέλλων λυτροῦσθαι τὸν 'Ισραήλ (Lk 24:20-21a). In other words, no sooner had Luke completed the description of Jesus' death, than the narrative immediately has the risen Jesus encounter two close associates of the Apostles who ask the question on everyone's mind—only they are too afraid to voice it: "Jesus was condemned and crucified by the Jerusalem authorities. And we had hoped he was about to redeem Israel—*but we were sadly mistaken because Jesus didn't do it!*" At this, Jesus demonstrates his impatience with these disciples and says: "O foolish men, slow to believe what the prophets have spoken! *Was it not necessary that the Christ should suffer and enter into his glory?*" There can be little doubt that this question was one of the most frequently encountered objections to the Christian gospel in the wider Gentile mission. Thus, in the closing portion of his Gospel, as well as in Acts, Luke turned to this issue no less than five times (Lk 24:26, 46; Acts 3:18; 17:2-3; 26:22-23).

• The reference to the λύτρωσις τοῦ Ἰσραήλ (Lk 24:21) brings up one of the most important themes of Luke's entire *bios.* Luke introduces the term λύτρωσις at the very beginning in the "prophecy of Zechariah" (Lk 1:67-79; see above). After this magnificent hymn, which beautifully summarizes important themes of the Hebrew prophetic books (especially Isaiah), Luke introduced in quick succession two more "prophets" who repeat the theme of the redemption of Israel: Simeon (Lk 2:25) and Anna (Lk 2:38). In this way, Luke powerfully reinforced the idea that Jesus of Nazareth is God's chosen one to bring redemption to Israel (cf. Lk 24:21); he will bring her "consolation" (παράκλησις τοῦ Ἰσραήλ Lk 2:25). Then at the end of his *bios* of Jesus "the prophet of the Most High," Luke completed the circle and came back to this central concept. Redemption comes through the passion of the Messiah. Luke touched on it once more in Acts 1:6. Luke's understanding of this very sensitive question is given in the story line of Acts: the Kingdom will come through the mission of the apostles and the expansion of the Church. As such, it was not an open threat to the imperial power.

• We note the striking fact that according to the Gospel of Luke, Jesus Christ did not appear first to any of the eleven apostles but rather to *associates* of theirs. Given our assumption that Mt was Luke's main source, this radical departure must have been intentional. How can we account for it? Our major clue is the name Κλεοπᾶς in Lk 24:18. This name could be the Greek form of the Semitic name Κλωπᾶς (קְלוֹפָא), a person mentioned in Jn 19:25.[12] Later tradition identified Cleopas/Klopas as the *brother of Joseph*, making him the *uncle of Jesus* (Eusebius, *H. E.* 3:11, 32:1-4, 6; 4:22,4). His son Simeon, a *cousin of Jesus*, was appointed the second bishop of the Christian community in Jerusalem after the death of Jesus' brother James, after the rebellion of 66–70. *This would have made Simeon a contemporary of Luke*; i.e., since tradition records that Simeon was martyred during the reign of Domitian. For these reasons, we suggest that Luke may here be drawing upon reliable early tradition *from within Jesus' family* (cf. 1 Cor 15:7a, ἔπειτα ὤφθη Ἰακώβῳ = Jesus' "brother").[13]

Lk 24:25-27. No sooner has Cleopas expressed his sad conclusion that Jesus the mighty prophet had failed, than Luke portrayed Jesus' reaction as being one of instant anger: "Oh how foolish you are, and how slow of heart to believe all that the prophets have written! Don't you realize that they all say that the Messiah of God *must suffer and die and then enter into his glory?* And beginning with Moses and all the prophets, he interpreted for them in all the scriptures the things concerning himself" (Lk: 24:25-27). Here Luke returned to the bedrock of his narrative (one clearly related to the basic structure of Mt): the prophecy-fulfillment scheme.

---

[12] Cf. Bauer *Lexicon s.vv.* Κλεοπᾶς + Κλωπᾶς; Moulton-Milligan mention three occurrences of Κλεοπᾶς on 2nd century A.D. ostraka.

[13] See Bauckham, *Jude and the Relatives of Jesus,* 5-133 (full citation above, p. 77).

Luke will repeat this motif almost immediately when Jesus reappears to the eleven apostles in the very next vignette (Lk 24:44f.). It then becomes a central feature of the speeches of Peter and Stephen in Acts. The use of δεῖ (Lk 24:26) to refer to the fulfillment of God's purposes and will (βουλή, cf. Lk 23:51, Acts 2:23, 4:28, 20:27) echoes a central theme of Luke-Acts (see Introduction, p. 39).

Lk 24:30-31 (cf. Lk 24:35b). The meal was another favorite motif of Luke, in this instance serving as a paradigmatic example for the Christian churches: "where two or three are gathered in my name, lo I am in the midst of them" (Mt 18:20).

¶ 141. Jesus appears to the eleven apostles in Jerusalem

(Mt 28:18-20) **Lk 24:33-49**

The two men immediately rise and return to Jerusalem to tell the eleven apostles that they have seen and spoken with the risen Jesus. The apostles tell them Jesus has appeared to Peter, too. Suddenly, Jesus stands before them. They are terrified, thinking he is a ghost. "Touch my hands and feet!" he says to them. "I am no ghost! Here, give me something to eat!" and they give him fish, which he eats before them. The disciples are overjoyed that it really is the bodily Jesus risen from the dead. Then he opens their minds to understand the Scriptures, saying "Everything written about me in the Law and Prophets must be fulfilled; namely, that the Messiah of God must die and rise on the third day, and that repentance and forgiveness of sins should be preached to all nations." Jesus then bids them remain in Jerusalem until they have been given power from heaven to become his witnesses to all nations.

General observations. Instead of an appearance to the Apostles in Galilee as in Mt, Luke has Jesus appear to them exclusively in or near Jerusalem. This prepares the audience/reader for the continuation in Acts, as Peter and the others teach daily in the Temple.

Lk 24:33. The phraseology "Where they found the eleven gathered together" makes it obvious that the persons to whom Jesus appeared in the previous story could not have been members of the eleven apostles. The reference to the eleven is an anticipation of the narrative in Acts 1.

Lk 24:34. Luke now picked up the theme of Peter's special position *vis-à-vis* the rest of the disciples that is hinted at elsewhere in Luke and given decisive emphasis in the Last Supper scene (Lk 22:32). This verse, although apparently a minor detail, is in fact critical for Luke's entire historical picture, since it prepares the way for Peter's hegemony in Acts 2-12. The fact that Jesus is described as appearing first to Peter *and then* to the rest of the disciples, is, in our view, a deliberate allusion to the pre-Pauline tradition recorded in 1 Cor. 15:5: "...and (Jesus) appeared to Cephas, then to the twelve [sic]."

Lk 24:35b is a possible allusion to the saying about "never eating again until all things are fulfilled in the Kingdom of God" (Lk 22:16), prior to the words of institution in Lk 22:19b. In Luke's eyes, Jesus' mission has indeed been at least partially fulfilled "in the Kingdom of God," and the faithful can now enter into his presence through "breaking bread" together (cf. the central importance of eating meals together in Acts).

Lk 24:36-42. This is Luke's attempt to provide a literal fulfillment of Jesus' repeated prophecy that he would be captured by evil men, be killed, and on the third day rise from the dead (cf. Lk 9:22, 44; 18:31-33; cf. Lk 13:32-33; 24:6-7, 19-27; Acts 3:13-15; 10:39-41). Here Jesus proves that it really is he, not some phantom of his former self. The account (especially when Lk 24:40 is included; and we do concur) exhibits close parallels with the appearance to Thomas (Jn 20:24-25) and eating fish with the disciples at the Sea of Tiberias (Jn 21:12).

Lk 24:44-48. This is Luke's decisive rehabilitation of the eleven apostles. Despite all the earlier passages where the apostles are portrayed as being blind, obtuse, incompetent, petty, vengeful and cowardly, in this scene they are finally given a divine opening of their minds (Lk 24:45). At last they understand the scriptures. Now they understand why everything happened the way it did. Now they understand that nothing was accidental, or outside of God's plan. Now Jesus adds the important words: "repentance and forgiveness of sins should be preached in (my) name to all nations" (Lk 24:47; cf. Lk 3:3/Mk 1:4 and Acts 5:31), which we consider to be an intentional echo of Mt 28:19-20. This verse, with its weighty pronouncement: "you are my witnesses" (Lk 24:48) is the "Lukan Great Commission." What this Commission means will be spelled out in detail in Luke's second book, the Acts of the Apostles. Thus, we have a typical Lukan compositional technique, whereby he prepares in one scene for important events to take place later.

Lk 24:49. Here is another example of Luke's anticipatory technique. See especially the mention of "stay in the city (cf. Acts 1:4) until you are clothed with power from on high," an anticipation of the baptism of the Holy Spirit described in Acts 2:1-4.

• In sum, this pericope consists of numerous features intended to overlap with the narrative in Acts, and prepare the way for the events in the sequel.

¶ 142. The eleven remain in Jerusalem

(Mt 28:16-20) **Lk 24:50-53**

The eleven leave Jerusalem and go out to nearby Bethany, across the Kidron valley. There Jesus blesses them and is taken up to heaven. The disciples bow in worship and then return to Jerusalem with great joy, where they pass their days in the Temple, blessing God for all they have witnessed.

General observations. The previous pericope and this one have very close ties to the narrative in Acts 1:2-11, which is a retrospective summary of these events. However, commentators have noticed numerous minute discrepancies between the two accounts, so that paralleling them is not as straightforward as one might expect. Indeed, the history of the text of Lk 24:32-53 and Acts 1:2-11 reveals numerous ancient attempts to bring the two narratives into closer agreement as well.

• This "exodus" scene was anticipated in Lk 9:31 (cf. Lk 9:51 if the reading is ἀναλήμψις). As Elijah was taken up into heaven and his return was anticipated, so now Jesus, *the* prophet *par excellence,* is taken up to heaven and his return is anticipated (Lk 24:51/Acts 1:9).

Lk 24:50. The reference to Bethany may be motivated by its association with "mount of olives" (Lk 19:29); i.e., Jesus parts from the apostles on a mountain (cf. Mt 28:16).

Lk 24:51b. The phraseology καὶ ἀναφέρετο εἰς τὸν οὐρανόν has in the past been questioned as to its originality. However, UBS[4] includes it, as do we, primarily because the ms. evidence is overwhelming, but also because its omission is understandable as an attempt to bring this passage into greater harmony with the next "ascension" described in Acts 1:9-11 (cf. the revealing discussion of the ancient attempts to emend the text in ℵ* D it^{a,b,d,e} in Metzger 1994, 189f.).

Lk 24:52. Καὶ αὐτοὶ προσκυνήσαντες αὐτόν has also been questioned, but in view of the overwhelming ms. evidence, and especially Mt 28:17 καὶ ἰδόντες αὐτὸν προσεκύνησαν.... we are inclined to view this as original in the text of Luke. Granted, this appears to leave Luke with *two ascensions*, since commentators commonly refer to Lk 24:52 as an ascension. However, this is impossible in view of Acts 1:3-4 οἷς καὶ παρέστησεν ἑαυτὸν ζῶντα μετὰ τὸ παθεῖν... δι' ἡμερῶν τεσσεράκοντα ὀπτανόμενος αὐτοῖς καὶ συναλιζόμενος... αὐτοῖς κτλ. One cannot reconcile the notion of "ascension" with "staying with them 40 days." In view of the very definite departure into heaven described in Acts 1:6-11, with the accompanying explanation of the two angels, it is evident that the previous "being lifted into heaven" is no more than a temporary "disappearance," followed by a lengthy stay (40 days). It is possible that what Luke had in mind are the numerous other appearances of the risen Jesus described in 1 Cor 15:3-7.

CONCLUSION

When the work began which has resulted in this volume, the group had set itself a daunting but nonetheless modest goal. Challenged by other scholars, especially at the Jerusalem Symposium on the Interrelation of the Gospels in 1984, advocates of the Two Gospel Hypothesis set out to give a pericope-by-pericope demonstration of (a) how Mark used Matthew and Luke and (b) how Luke used Matthew.

The latter demonstration was especially daunting because it had never been done, not even by the original Griesbachians. As work progressed on this part of the project and pieces began to fit, firm optimism began to emerge that a credible explanation of Luke's use of Matthew was possible. About two years ago, having charted the sequential relationship of Luke to Matthew in Luke 3-9, the mood changed. Hard on the heels of that advance came the painstaking process of tracing Luke's relationship to Matthew in the Travel Narrative, which for one hundred and fifty years has been the graveyard of Synoptic hypotheses. With the development of a similar chart which showed the pattern of Luke's intricate but orderly use of Matthew in the Travel Narrative, our sense of the value of this work underwent a significant transformation. We now believe that we have presented evidence which makes it difficult to hold any other position than that Luke used Matthew directly as his primary source.

That bold assertion is based on three kinds of phenomena which have been presented in this book. The most important is the evidence that Luke followed the sequential order of Matthew in the major narrative sections of his Gospel. In Lk 3-9, Luke followed a pattern of cyclic progression. In Lk 9-19, Luke combined the material from Matthew's great speeches in thematic sections of the Travel Narrative, often following the internal order of those sayings units within their Matthean contexts. And in Lk 20-24, he adopted Matthew's basic sequential order. A second level of evidence for the direct dependence of Luke on Matthew is the number of cases, not at all inconsiderable, where Luke has preserved key phrases that were created by Matthew for redactional summaries or introductions. But what was perhaps the most delightful surprise for us was the third level of evidence of Luke's use of Matthew. We discovered that, time after time, Luke's use of Matthew was best and most easily explained by Luke's widely recognized compositional concerns; e.g., the units on prayer in Lk 11:1-13 and 18:1-14. Throughout our compositional analysis, we observed remarkable ways in which Luke's purposes and characteristics dovetailed precisely with his use of Matthew.

The net result of this study is, then, that we believe that more than a demonstration that Luke *might* have used Matthew as his source has been achieved. We believe that it will be difficult to argue that the data in Luke can be explained *any other way* than that Luke was thoroughly conversant with canonical Matthew and made it the basis of his Gospel.

Certainly further research is needed to pursue many details not covered by our Demonstration, to ferret out and present anomalies to our hypothesis; in short, to test our results. For one thing, future research must include a more refined analysis of Luke's use of nonMatthean tradition.

We now turn our attention to a pericope-by-pericope compositional analysis of Mark's use of both Matthew and Luke. With this effort, we intend to update and refine Owen's and Griesbach's original attempts. Beyond that, we are working toward a redactional analysis of Matthew independent of any assumption of Matthew's dependence on Mark and "Q." That task will ultimately include a tradition-historical separation of the sources of Matthew, including what may go back to the historical Jesus.

If further examination and debate does bear out the main outlines of our contention that *we now have hard evidence that the author of the Gospel of Luke made direct and systematic use of the canonical Gospel of Matthew*, then it follows that the entire currently held understanding of the development of earliest Christianity—especially as it rests on the belief in "Q"—will need a complete overhaul, since a whole series of misconceptions and false conclusions would have to be given up. As is made clear in the Introduction, this overhaul would necessarily extend to the very instruments used by all scholars in Gospel research: the synopsis and the critical text. In this sense, *Luke's Use of Matthew* presages the beginning of an exciting new era in New Testament studies.

APPENDICES

Chart A. The Galilean Ministry (Lk 3:1–10:22 // Mt 3:1–18:5).

Chart B . Graphic Display of Parts Two, Three and Four – the Galilean Ministry.

Chart C. The Travel Narrative (Lk 9:51–19:27).

Chart D. The Passion Narrative (Lk 19:28–24:53 // Mt18:1–28:20).

[These charts are located in a pocket attached to the back cover.]

SELECT BIBLIOGRAPHY

The Research Team published a series of reports in the SBL Seminar Papers (1992 through 1995) containing a redactional analysis of the Gospel of Luke utilizing the Two Gospel Hypothesis. Because of the many helpful suggestions and criticisms we received on those reports, as well as our own on-going research, the current volume supercedes those reports. The following items are a selection of writings by members of the Institute Research Team or other authors that clarify or substantiate aspects of our redactional analysis of of the Gospel of Luke based on the Two Gospel Hypothesis. The references are listed alphabetically, most recent writings first.

J. G. Franklyn Collison

———, "Eschatology in the Gospel of Luke." In *New Synoptic Studies*, edited by William R Farmer (see below), 363-371.

———, "Linguistic Usages in the Gospel of Luke. " In *New Synoptic Studies,* 245-60.

———, "Linguistic Usages in the Gospel of Luke." Unpublished dissertation, Southern Methodist University, 1977. Available from UMI Dissertation Services, 300 N. Zeeb Road, Ann Arbor MI 48106 (1-800-521-0600).

O. Lamar COPE

———, *Matthew, a Scribe Trained for the Kingdom of Heaven.* CBQ Monogr. Ser. 5. Washington: Catholic Biblical Association of America, 1976.

David L. DUNGAN

———, "Two Gospel Hypothesis." In *Anchor Bible Dictionary*, 6 vols. Edited by David Noel Freedman et al. Garden City: Doubleday, 1992; 6:671-679.

———, ed. *The Interrelations of the Gospels. A Symposium Led by M. E. Boismard, W. R. Farmer, F. Neirynck, Jerusalem 1984*. Leuven: University Press, 1990.

———, "Synopses of the Future." *Biblica* 66 (1985) 457-492.

———, "Theory of Synopsis Construction." *Biblica* 61 (1980) 305-329.

William R. FARMER

———, and Henning Graf Reventlow ed. *Biblical Studies and the Shifting of Paradigms 1850-1914.* JSOTSuppl.Ser. 192. Sheffield Academic Press, 1995.

———, *The Gospel of Jesus: The Pastoral Relevance of the Synoptic Problem.* Louisville: Westminster/John Knox, 1994.

———, "Luke's Use of Matthew: A Christological Inquiry." *Pacific School of Theology Journal* 40 (1987) 39-50.

———, ed. *New Synoptic Studies: The Cambridge Gospel Conference and Beyond.* Macon: Mercer University Press, 1983.

———, *Jesus and the Gospel: Tradition, Scripture and Canon.* Philadelphia: Fortress Press, 1982.

———, *Synopticon: The Verbal Agreement Between the Greek Texts of Matthew, Mark and Luke Contextually Exhibited.* Cambridge University Press, 1969.

———, *The Synoptic Problem: A Critical Analysis.* New York: MacMillan, 1964; repr. Macon: Mercer University Press, 1978.

Thomas R. W. LONGSTAFF

———, and Page Thomas ed. *The Synoptic Problem: A Bibliography 1716–1988.* New Gospel Studies #4. Macon: Mercer University Press, Leuven: Peeters, 1988.

———, and J. Bernard Orchard, ed. *J. J. Griesbach: Synoptic and Text-critical Studies 1776-1796.* SNTS Monogr. Ser. 34. Cambridge University Press, 1978.

Allan J. MCNICOL

———, *Jesus' Directions for the Future. A Source and Redaction History Study of the Use of the Eschatological Traditions in Paul and in the Synoptic Accounts of Jesus' Last Eschatological Discourse.* New Gospel Studies 9. Macon: Mercer University Press, Leuven: Peeters, 1996.

David J. NEVILLE

———, *Arguments from Order in Synoptic Source Criticism: A History and Critique,* New Gospel Studies 7. Macon: Mercer University Press, Leuven: Peeters, 1993.

J. Bernard ORCHARD

———, and Harold Riley, *The Order of the Synoptics: Why Three Synoptic Gospels?* Macon: Mercer University Press, 1987.

———, "Are All Gospel Synopses Biassed?" *Theologische Zeitschrift* 34 (1978) 149-162.

———, and Longstaff, T.R.W., ed. *J. J. Griesbach: Synoptic and Text-critical Studies 1776-1796.* SNTS Monogr. Ser. 34. Cambridge University Press, 1978b.

———, *Matthew, Luke and Mark.* Manchester: Koinonia, 1976.

David B. PEABODY

———, "Johann Jacob Griesbach," in *Dictionary of Major Biblical Interpreters.* Edited by Donald K. McKim. Westmont: InterVarsity Press, forthcoming, 1997.

———, "H. J. Holtzmann and His European Colleagues: Aspects of the Nineteenth-

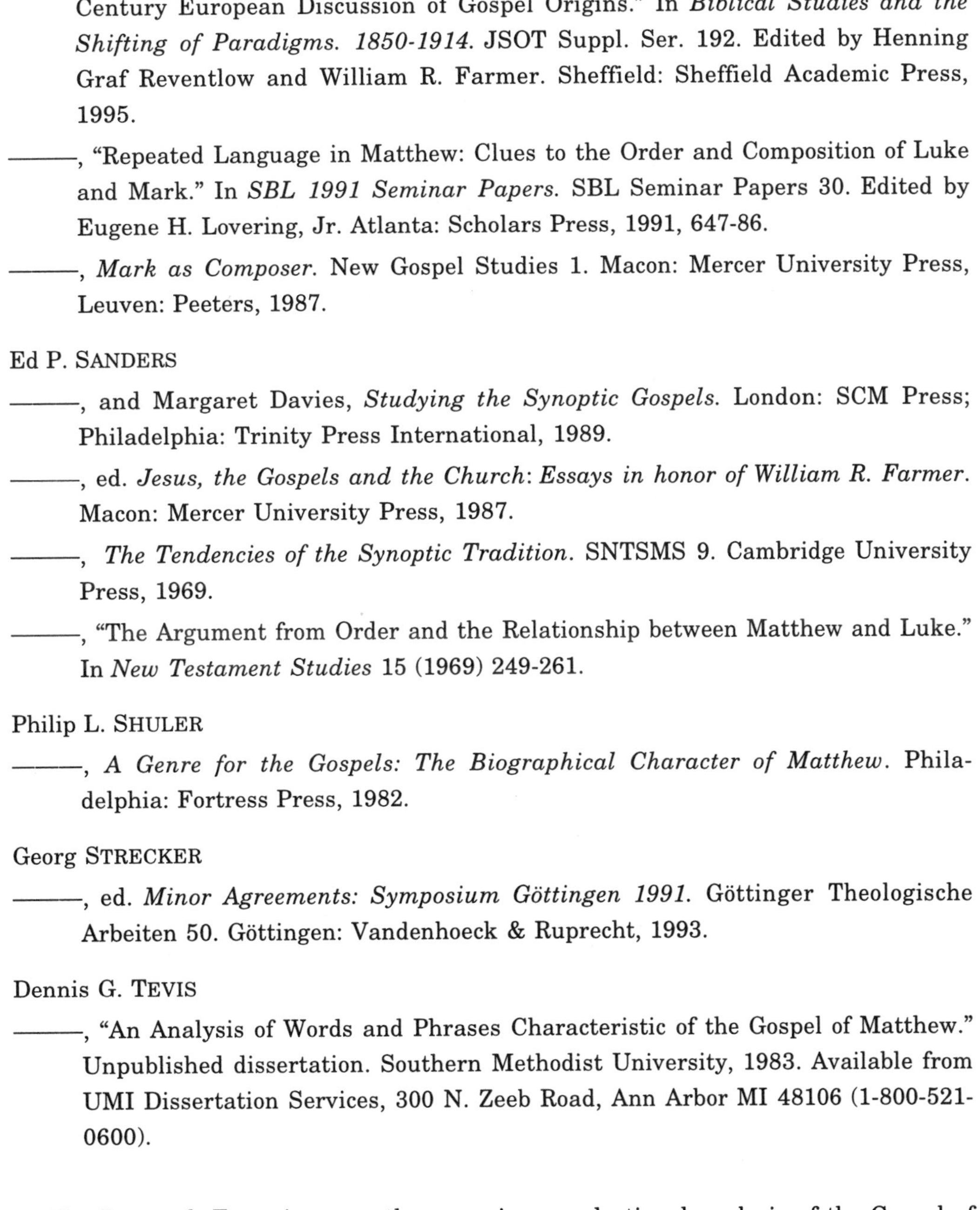

Century European Discussion of Gospel Origins." In *Biblical Studies and the Shifting of Paradigms. 1850-1914.* JSOT Suppl. Ser. 192. Edited by Henning Graf Reventlow and William R. Farmer. Sheffield: Sheffield Academic Press, 1995.

———, "Repeated Language in Matthew: Clues to the Order and Composition of Luke and Mark." In *SBL 1991 Seminar Papers.* SBL Seminar Papers 30. Edited by Eugene H. Lovering, Jr. Atlanta: Scholars Press, 1991, 647-86.

———, *Mark as Composer.* New Gospel Studies 1. Macon: Mercer University Press, Leuven: Peeters, 1987.

Ed P. SANDERS

———, and Margaret Davies, *Studying the Synoptic Gospels.* London: SCM Press; Philadelphia: Trinity Press International, 1989.

———, ed. *Jesus, the Gospels and the Church: Essays in honor of William R. Farmer.* Macon: Mercer University Press, 1987.

———, *The Tendencies of the Synoptic Tradition.* SNTSMS 9. Cambridge University Press, 1969.

———, "The Argument from Order and the Relationship between Matthew and Luke." In *New Testament Studies* 15 (1969) 249-261.

Philip L. SHULER

———, *A Genre for the Gospels: The Biographical Character of Matthew.* Philadelphia: Fortress Press, 1982.

Georg STRECKER

———, ed. *Minor Agreements: Symposium Göttingen 1991.* Göttinger Theologische Arbeiten 50. Göttingen: Vandenhoeck & Ruprecht, 1993.

Dennis G. TEVIS

———, "An Analysis of Words and Phrases Characteristic of the Gospel of Matthew." Unpublished dissertation. Southern Methodist University, 1983. Available from UMI Dissertation Services, 300 N. Zeeb Road, Ann Arbor MI 48106 (1-800-521-0600).

The Research Team is currently preparing a redactional analysis of the Gospel of Mark based on the Two Gospel Hypothesis. For an early draft, see William R. Farmer, et al., "Narrative Outline of the Markan Composition According to the Two Gospel Hypothesis," in *SBL 1990 Seminar Papers,* SBL Seminar Papers 29. David J. Lull, ed. Atlanta: Scholars Press, 1990; 212-39.

INDICES

The Scripture index is not exhaustive. The citations are complete for all of the most important discussions. The format of the Scripture index is as follows: the scripture references are in **bold**, with all page numbers in normal type.

Scripture Index